Imagine Harmony

How to Evolve
From Stress to Gratitude

by
Dale R. Duvall

Dale R. Duvall
Imagine Harmony
603 Seagaze Drive
Oceanside, California 92054

drduvall@yahoo.com
www.imagineharmony.org

Special discounts are available on quantity purchases by corporations, associations, and others. For details, contact the publisher at the address above.

Printed in the United States of America

ISBN 978-1535392181

First Edition

Acknowledgments

We do not treat nor diagnose physical or mental illness and do not attempt to solve personal problems or heal ills. We do, however, teach people how to manage the stress that causes the problems and inhibits their own natural healing systems. Further, we teach the student to reconfigure genes and alter gene expression to shut down those gene functions that are detrimental while activating and energizing those gene functions that are advantageous to perfect health, happiness, vitality, longevity, and harmony.

The material in this book is provided for educational and informational purposes and is not intended to be a substitute for professional counseling, therapy, or medical treatment. Nothing in this book is intended to diagnose or treat any pathology or diseased condition of the mind or body. All the information, techniques, skills and concepts contained within this book are meant to augment, and not to replace, professional medical or psychological diagnosis, treatment or even advice. There are no known contraindications to the practice of Medimaginosis, but the reader is advised to consult a qualified healthcare professional when abnormal conditions persist.

The Imagine Harmony Program has adopted and adapted some of the strategies and teachings of many experts to whom we are eternally grateful. They include, but are not limited to, Dr. Andrew Weil, Dr. Deepak Chopra, Dr. Bruce Lipton, Dr. Richard Carlson, Dr. Jon Kabat-Zinn, Dr. Herbert Benson, Dr. Neil Neimark, Nigel Marsh, Tim Strouse, Dr. Wayne Dyer, Dr. Steven Gurgevitch, Judith Conroy, William Lee Rand, Geshe Kelsang Gyatso, Dr. Rudolph Tanzi, Dr. Martin L. Rossman, Dr. Glenn Schiraldi, Eckhart Tolle, Eknath Easwaran, Michelle and Dr. Joel Levey, Dr. Bruce Hubbard, Shakti Gawain, Dr. Chuck T. Falcon, Dr. Robert A Emmons, Dr. Lissa Rankin, Dr. Albert Einstein, and Dr. Dean Ornish.

Table of Contents

PART I - Introduction

PART II - Control the Breath and the Mind/Body will Follow

PART III - Perception Lights the Way and Meditation Provides the Means

PART IV - Evolving from Stress to Gratitude Meditation 2 & 3

PART V – Medimaginosis

PART VI - Creating Perfect Health, Happiness, Vitality, Longevity, and Harmony

PART VII – Appendix and Glossary

PART I

Introduction

1.1 What's it about?

In the beginning, all was bliss and harmony. And then there was stress. Outside the Garden of Eden was reality: wild animals, hostile tribes, poisonous snakes, insects, inescapable freezing cold, and unbearable heat. Imagine life before refrigerators, clean running water, electricity, or toilet paper, and then imagine life before soap. How stressful is it to wake up hungry and thirsty in a cold dark cave with two children screaming, bugs crawling all over everything, and no idea where to start looking for something to eat? Stress and ill health are not new to the human, but only the human has a mind that can imagine a better environment and then create it. Only the human has a mind that can imagine and create an illness or wellness. Only the human can imagine and create mental and physical evolution. Just as the mind can create a blister when touched by an object that it <u>believes</u> is red-hot, or control heart rate by imagining danger or contentment, it can turn OFF gene functions that cause disease and turn ON latent gene functions that heal. Attitude (or perception) is part of the equation. As we have heard for years, attitude is everything, but few people have ever found a way to create or control this key element.

This book is about Stress Management and Conscious Control of the Mind/Body and Gene Expression. It's about taking control of the body, mind, and spirit, emotional balance, health, happiness, vitality, longevity, and harmony. It's about realizing that we <u>can</u> take control and then learning to operate the controls effectively. We are not victims of heredity or controlled by outside forces and circumstances. If we cannot find the circumstances we need, we can make them. We have the mental capacity to identify, accept, and adapt to the things that are beyond our control, the strength to improve the things we can control, and the wisdom to know when to let it go, let it be, and move on. Our thirty-year quest to find the path and evolve from stress to gratitude and harmony involved hundreds of books, experts, courses and seminars, three trips to the Orient, and thousands of research and study hours. It could have been done in a matter of a few weeks if this book had been available to us. This book brings together recent scientific data and documented ancient wisdom to establish the existence of an innate capacity. The physical body will respond to the human mind, but we need to know how to do it. And this is the manual.

Regardless of earthly treasures, the mind and body are our most precious possessions, and their health is our most valuable asset. Treat them with care. We need to act now like we will need them for a hundred more years, creating a mind and body for longevity, over maximum performance. Since we all own a mind and body, we are just about even with the richest people on Earth, plus or minus the value of health and happiness. Maybe that's what they meant when they said that we are all created equal.

We have condensed and simplified our study of psychoneuroimmunology and epigenetics to a practical path of stress management and harmony that leads to and sustains perfect health, happiness, vitality, longevity, and harmony. Psychoneuroimmunology is a rather cumbersome term used to characterize the investigation (ology) of the interaction between the mind (psycho), the brain and nervous system (neuro), and the body's biochemical resistance to disease and abnormal cell development (immun). Psychoneuroimmunology is simply the study of the mind/body connection, and epigenetics is the study of gene expression and how cells adjust their biology to the environment, emotional as well as physical. Internal cells read the environment through the nervous system and the chemical soup in which they are bathed. Between the sensory evaluation of the world and the signals to the cells, is the MIND: the interpreter. We can live in a healthy environment but have a bad attitude that perceives that environment in unhealthy ways, constricting the blood supply to the cells and building up toxins.

We studied the brain, limbic system, endocrine system, and autonomic nervous system in depth and found that every answer created more

2

questions. The deeper into detail we went, the further we seemed to be straying from finding peace of mind. It is good to expand one's knowledge and views, but it is possible to get caught up in the small stuff and fail to see the obvious. One of our researchers shared an experience he had while shopping in a jewelry store. He asked the jeweler what the difference was between 14K and 18K gold. Fifteen minutes later, the jeweler was still talking about melting points, viscosity, cohesion, and color changes with varying percentages of copper, nickel, silver, and zinc alloys when our researcher caught him taking a breath and said, "I just wanted to know the price."

Knowing what part of the brain produces what hormone or what role one's mother played in causing feelings of inadequacy as a child is of no more value to a seeker of harmony, balance, perfect health, happiness, vitality, and longevity than the knowledge of how a computer chip works is to a grandmother who wants to send an email to her grandson. We just need to know what buttons to push. Our quest can be likened to an explorer trying to find a safe passage through the wilderness, trying countless paths and enduring many failures. *Imagine Harmony* is an aerial view of the entire journey that reveals the best path. Although the chemical makeup of the soil below is not discernible, the reader knows that it has been studied by others and found to be "nice to know but not relevant to the trek." The reader can follow the path of the pioneers who have been there.

Animals have been given sharp appendages to defend themselves, but the human was given a far greater gift. Of all the species on earth, only the human has evolved the gifts of conscious awareness, reason, and imagination: the ability to alter our minds, bodies, and environment with conscious thought. With these gifts, we do not need sharp appendages and do not need to act like animals. We can think ourselves sick or well, create a headache or cure it, create a rash or remove it, create a tumor or remove it. We only need to learn how to use this ability more effectively. Unlike other life forms on our planet, humans have evolved a mind (imagination, consciousness, reason, and awareness of itself) and the knowledge that we can create our perceptions, feelings, reactions, and thus, our environment. The human mind creates its own world with the ability to alter its brain, body, and even gene expression. That is conscious evolution.

The reader will learn, in the time it takes to read this book, what we spent thirty years of study and research to learn. *Imagine Harmony* is an enjoyable stress management program using breath work, chi and health awareness, meditation, the parasympathetic nervous system, and imagery to access the Subconscious controls of the mind/body and gene expression to create perfect health, happiness, vitality, longevity, and harmony. It combines science and spirituality without drugs, dogma, or superstition, and at its core is a fun practice that we call Medimaginosis.

Medimaginosis is an omni-denominational meditation/imagery/wisdom-driven wellness practice that directs the mind, body, and soul to manifest harmony and to evolve as one cohesive, synergistic unit with perfect health, happiness, vitality, longevity, and harmony. *Imagine Harmony* is a series of six lessons (Part I through Part VI) beginning with relaxation and culminating in conscious control of physiological and psychological responses to daily life without the risks associated with pharmaceuticals. The system harmonizes the mind/body/soul structure (whole self) facilitating greater conscious control of autonomic functions, psychophysiology, and gene expression.

The Imagine Harmony Program expands perceptions, develops conscious control, and promotes harmony in thought, feeling, and behavior; emotionally, physically, mentally, and spiritually; in mind, body, and soul.

1.2 Why Imagine Harmony ~ How to Evolve from Stress to Gratitude?

The original title was, *The Psychophysiological Effects of Stress and Psychoneuroimmunology on Epigenetic Gene Expression*, and was the result of years of research and study of stress and conscious control over psychophysiology and autonomic functions. We were told that our students, and those who need it most, would not likely relate to the original title and would benefit more from a practical how-to book. Harmony seems a bit more student friendly, is inclusive of and goes beyond happiness, and is the ultimate objective of all pursuits. Harmony is the pleasing or congruent arrangement of all parts and has been associated with nirvana, paradise, utopia, and Heaven. It is the embodiment of bliss, happiness, love, respect, peace and joy. It is the resolution of discord, conflict, and resistance in all forms. Harmony is sweet freedom to fly in any direction, totally unobstructed by anything, propelled by inspiration and chi. Harmony is the absence of fear.

This is not hocus-pocus; thoughts change body chemistry, and we will show how to consciously direct them. Although simple, easy and logical, the

<u>Imagine Harmony Program</u> is a comprehensive attitude adjustment program that works.

1.2.1 **All things are possible**

Science has confirmed what the sages, prophets, and spiritual leaders have been saying for thousands of years. All things are possible when the soul is willing to believe we can. We no longer need to search the Universe for that which can only be found within. Everything we are looking for is already within us. We just need to learn how to gain access to it and then convince our soul (OM, or connection to the Source of all things) that our objective is a worthy endeavor. We have the ability to translate words and concepts into the sensory language of the mind/body and communicate with it as well as a vast reservoir of wisdom. It requires the skillful use of our uniquely human gifts of conscious awareness, reason, and imagination.

You hold in your hand, the "How to" manual for developing those gifts, managing the harmful effects of stress, and controlling your mind, body, happiness, and life itself.

Albert Einstein described the physical world, which includes our bodies, as a complex, interweaving organization of energy that is in changing states of relationship and transformation. Gene Deitch had the right idea when he created Tom Terrific and his wonder dog Manfred. Tom is a black and white pencil drawing of a boy who wears a funnel upside down for a hat and would always save the day with his talking dog Manfred. Tom is terrific. He can change into anything he wishes, from a speeding train to a bucket of water. He does it all. He is whatever, whenever, and wherever he wishes. Tom knows that all matter is made up of atoms and subatomic particles that are made up of quarks (tiny strings of vibrating energy) and <u>not stable solid matter at all</u>. He knows that matter (or the energy that is its essence) cannot be created or destroyed, only changed. He knows that rearranging these energy fields alters the perception of matter and that the combinations are infinite. Tom Terrific knows how to rearrange these energy fields and although we have not evolved to that level yet, we have evolved the ability to alter our own psychophysiology, our perceptions, and our environment.

Physicists tell us that the apparent solidity of matter is an illusion created by our senses. Seemingly solid matter, including the human body, is almost entirely empty space. If we imagine a baseball as the nucleus of a hydrogen atom, the electron revolving around it would be about 30 miles away and all that space between is a dynamic field of energy and invisible forces. The distances between the atoms compared to their size can be thought of as a microcosmic version of outer space. Even inside every atom, there is mostly empty space, force fields, and vibrational frequencies. We are more like a musical note than solid matter. Existence is a universal symphony, and the essence of all things is an incomprehensible, possibly infinite, dynamic, vibrating energy.

Imagine that we could travel back in time to the post-Civil War era. If we were to announce to the world that within three or four decades, man would be able to fly: and then within the lifespan of an average human, a man will be able to walk around on the moon and return safely; or fly from Los Angeles to New York, have lunch and return to Los Angeles for dinner on the same day, the response would probably include the word impossible. As we now know, it is possible and so is most of what we now believe to be impossible today. Nelson Mandela said, "It always seems impossible until it's done."

Conscious control of the mind/body and breaking the barriers of doubt begins with subconscious acceptance of an imagined concept. In 1954, it was believed that no human being could run the mile (1.6km) any faster than four minutes and that it was beyond the limits of human endurance. They said that it was impossible. Believing otherwise, on May 6, 1954, the English athlete Roger Bannister ran the mile in under four minutes, astonishing the world, altering beliefs and self-images, and redefining POSSIBLE. Then, within 56 days, John Landy broke Bannister's record in Finland and by 1957, 16 other runners had also broken the four-minute mile. By 2012, over 1200 runners had broken this barrier including a forty-year-old man and 17 high school kids. All it took was for someone to believe that it was not impossible by updating limiting beliefs and mental barriers. These are not isolated cases; people break barriers all the time.

Wilma Rudolph was born with polio, and the doctors told her mother that the child would never walk. They were apparently unaware of Dr. Herbert Benson's study of the faith factor and stubbornly refused to venture beyond the Newtonian paradigms. But Wilma was taught to believe otherwise and at age 16, she won a bronze medal at the 1956 Olympics in Australia, and in the 1960 Olympic games in Rome, she won three gold medals. On October 16, 2011, Fauja Singh became the first 100-year-old to finish a marathon (26 miles) and on February 24, 2013 (just five weeks shy of his 102nd birthday) he successfully completed the 10 kilometer run at the Hong Kong Marathon in 1 hour 32 minutes and 28 seconds. It is conscious evolution and is more a matter of choice than chance.

All animals have a brain and a body that operate as one unit but only humans have a creative Conscious mind with the ability to control the expression and interaction of genes within the inherited DNA structure. The body is a manifestation of the mind, and when we learn to manage the mind, the body will follow. The body will reflect and adapt to attitudes, beliefs, and perceptions of the mind. Trying to manage or change the body without changing the mind is a waste of time. The key to perfect health, happiness, vitality, longevity, and harmony is in the human MIND. It can shut down those genes that negatively influence the immune system, and it can activate combinations of genes that can cause the immune system to operate at a level beyond anything previously believed possible.

With the uniquely human gifts of conscious awareness, reason, and imagination, we can learn to translate words into the language of the mind/body and communicate with it. We can learn to shut down or reconfigure those genes that are detrimental to our health or conscious objectives while energizing those gene functions that are advantageous to our conscious visions.

Contrary to what many of us have been taught, our psychophysiology is not fixed by our genes. Identical twin girls born with the same DNA and genes were adopted at birth by two different families, both of similar geographical locations and socioeconomic backgrounds. The girls knew that they were adopted but had no idea that they had a twin until they were in their mid-twenties. The difference between the two families was that one was obese, and the other was normal. As one might guess, the twin raised by the obese family was 80 pounds overweight while the other was normal. Like juggling or riding a bicycle, gene functions can be controlled; we just need to learn how.

The immune system is innate. It is programmed from birth to sustain perfect health, but harmful perceptions alter gene expression and affect the immune system in negative ways causing blockages and malfunctions to occur that can eventually lead to the death of the organism. It can also manifest objectives far beyond the normal maintenance level creating a higher awareness and any objective it believes is worthy. Just like Roger

Bannister, when we believe we can do a thing that others believe is impossible, we find a way to do it.

1.2.2 **Benefits or What's in it for me?**

We have stated that the Medimaginosis wellness practice manifests perfect health, happiness, vitality, longevity, and harmony, but the practitioner reaps a plethora of other related benefits as well. A general feeling of well-being with the ability to remain calm and think clearly conveys assertiveness and self-confidence in social situations. In the midst of the storm, we are able to remain calm where we would have previously gone over the edge. Our thoughts are clear, instead of jumbled and racing, and we feel stronger physically because we are free of the affliction of stress and anxiety. We develop an awareness of the relaxation response, learn to make time for ourselves, strive for a healthy lifestyle, and promote harmony as much as possible in every situation. We make time to love, remain balanced and centered, happy and at peace. We practice healthy ways of managing stress and focus on what matters: what is really important in life.

We learn to breathe. Seriously, our breath (and life itself) is in the present moment, and we learn to be conscious of it and maintain that awareness at least 25% of the time. No more blindly drifting through life on automatic pilot, aimlessly bumping into metaphorical walls. We focus on the Principles of Harmony because the benefits are endless, and a positive life force energy attitude is critical to health, success, and peace of mind. We enjoy having less stress in our lives and more drive to achieve our objectives.

We become more relaxed and in tune with our mind, body, and soul. Where we might have automatically <u>reacted</u> to a negative situation with anger or frustration in the past, the practitioner of Medimaginosis will <u>respond</u> calmly and appropriately to each challenge seeking solutions and feeling more confident. We learn to open up the heart and let the sun shine in; accepting and adapting to the present moment with wisdom and curiosity.

People who wallow in suffering under the guise of "being with" or "experiencing" their pain are simply feeding a self-centered Ego and a "poor me" attitude. Far from denial, we <u>recognize</u> harmful thoughts and memories, but only long enough to <u>neutralize</u> them by putting them in a more relevant context of the current moment: noticing that they are outdated and no longer applicable. They might have been appropriate at one time, but not now. We replace these harmful thoughts and memories with the Principles of Harmony sighting our right to choose the thoughts upon which to focus.

A benefit that may take some time is propagation. When others see what our students have, they will want it too. The Principles of Harmony, with the help of Medimaginosis, can be a great boost to the inevitable but lopsided evolution of mankind. Our ability to create weapons and steal from each other seems to be evolving faster than our mental capacity for unity and cooperation. *Imagine Harmony* will help to even that out.

Dr. Bruce Lipton pointed out the evolutionary similarities between cell cooperation (multicellular creatures cooperating as one creature like the jellyfish) and large, complicated organisms like humans cooperating as a group to improve the chances of survival. The body is a group of about 55 trillion cells that cooperate and work together as a unit. We humans are slowly evolving as organized units in the form of the European Union, the world economy, corporations, conglomerates, and cooperatives but we need to evolve further to include the human race as one harmonious cooperative where everyone works together to benefit the whole unit. Beyond that we need to realize that we are each a single cell in the body of the Universe, working together as one cohesive, synergistic unit. Fighting amongst ourselves is like liver cells attacking stomach cells; it's foolish and harms the whole unit, endangering the survival of the narrow-minded combatants.

1.2.3 Purpose and Intent

The purpose or mission of this book is to facilitate a sincere resolve to promote harmony, beginning with stress management and ending with conscious control of psychophysiology and gene expression; to teach people to Imagine Harmony and understand that life is not an emergency rather it is a fun adventure experienced in the present moment with curiosity and wonder; that existence is a universal symphony of dynamic pulsating energy, and that only change is permanent; to help people learn to use their own natural wisdom to evaluate their world, and not blindly follow the advice of so-called experts; and that man can not only fly and walk around on the moon, but we can take control of our health, happiness, vitality, longevity and lifestyle with the Conscious mind.

The ultimate purpose of this book is to facilitate universal harmony; the realization that we are one with all that exists, right down to the subatomic level, with the individual right to choose the thoughts upon which to focus. We are free to choose our function within the whole as long as it is compatible and in harmony with the whole.

Separatism in the form of narcissistic egotism, religious righteousness, nationalism, sports fanaticism, or even feelings of race, tribal, or family superiority is a foolish primitive disease that fosters violence and thwarts harmony and cooperation. We need to recognize and merge our love for those close to us with the ultimate goal of understanding, cooperation, peace, and harmony with all that is. Love of one's country, sports team, spouse or child, is perfectly normal, but fanatical attachment is unhealthy and cannot be an excuse for violence or separatism from all that is. Violence, even in defense of right, is wrong. We can evolve to find a better way.

The intent of the Imagine Harmony Program is to slow down the perceived need for egotistical pride, separation, and defense; to re-introduce the Principles of Harmony to a gifted but troubled species, culminating in a boost to the evolution of unity, cooperation, and ultimately: Universal Harmony.

"Humanities most important endeavor is the striving for harmony and morality. Our inner balance and even our very existence depend on it." Albert Einstein

1.3 Beyond the Garden of Eden

Spiders and snakes and killer bees…oh my! Beyond the Garden of Eden, there was disease, conflict, anger, fear, and pain that we call stress.

Before time and space, there was peace, harmony, and balance. Scattered bits of cosmic energy began to merge and became galaxies, solar systems, planets, and eventually the very subtle light that we call life. This life was pure energy, and its nature was dynamic change and flow. It grew and evolved into elegant tones of curiosity, wonder, and joy: consciousness and awareness of itself. It developed concepts of me and mine, and the mind of man was born. With the new powers to dwell on the past and imagine a future, worry and guilt added dimension to the primal reactions of fight, flight, and freeze.

Like all other living things, our cells need to eat, breathe, poop, grow, repair, reproduce, and stay healthy, just on a smaller scale. They are either in a "defense mode" or an "evolve, renew, and repair mode" depending on the signals they receive from the brain. When they are in the "evolve, renew, and repair mode" they do what they were programmed to do; absorbing oxygen and vital nutrients from the blood and excreting waste and toxins, having a wonderful time doing what they do best. Some are immune cells, some are kidney cells, and some are brain cells harmoniously cooperating and doing their respective jobs. Then a vicious man-eating tiger jumps out from behind a tree, and everyone goes into "defense mode." They tense up and contract like a clenched fist preparing for battle and possible injury. It is much more important to live through the threat than to eat or poop at this point, so these functions are shut down. If we don't live through the threat, there will be no need for nutrition or digestion, excepting the tiger perhaps. When stress strikes, our Conscious mind is often turned off, and the Subconscious takes over because it is far faster (reacts with preprogrammed impulses instead of responding with the slower but more aware conscious logic, reason, superior judgment, decision-making, and willpower).

With repeated or continuous alarms from perceived threats, the cells brace for danger and, in our modern stressful world, many people get stuck in this chronic state. Everything is perceived as an emergency. Hypertension and continuous stress (over stimulation of the sympathetic nervous system) results in a chronic state of cellular contraction draining the life force energy of the cells. When the cells are contracted and braced for danger, they are unable to absorb enough nutrition or excrete waste, resulting in starvation and a buildup of toxins. If it is not reversed and the cells are constricted too long, they become vulnerable to disease, the waste buildup becomes toxic, aging is accelerated, and they die.

According to the concept of homeostasis, after a stressor is eliminated, the cells seek to return to their equilibrium state, or the normal level of stress resistance. When they are allowed to expand or open, they virtually always self-repair. A cell in a relaxed state is able to efficiently absorb oxygen and nutrients and release toxins. It is in an "evolve, renew, and repair mode" creating greater health for itself and its body of more than 55 trillion other cells.

During the alarm phase, the body mobilizes the sympathetic nervous system to meet the immediate threat. The body reacts by releasing adrenal hormones that produce a boost in energy, tensing muscles, reducing sensitivity to pain, dilating pupils, shutting down digestion, increasing heart and respiration rates, constricting veins, and rising blood pressure. This high level of arousal is often unnecessary to adequately cope with micro-stressors and daily hassles, yet this is the response pattern seen in humans which often leads to health issues. Even after a threat has passed, its emotional memory keeps popping up and contracting the cells in obscure unrelated places. Commonly, the back and neck tense up, contract the cells, restrict blood flow, and result in oxygen deprivations, cell starvation, and toxic buildup. Stress and its effects are known to be causative, cumulative, precipitating, and aggravating factors in most illnesses.

1.3.1 **The Fire Breathing Dragons of Stress**

Stress is any change that requires adaptation. Everyone experience stress and pain, from the most desperate and underprivileged to the most privileged human beings. It's a common bond we all share. Humans experience stress or perceive things as threatening when they do not believe that their resources for coping are enough for what the circumstances demand. When we think the demands being placed on us exceed our ability to cope, we feel strain and pressure. Some stress is beneficial in that it keeps us on our toes and presents challenges and opportunities but to the extent that we are unable to adapt, harmony is lost. Positive stress helps improve athletic performance and is a factor in motivation, adaptation, and reaction to the environment. Excessive stress, however, is toxic and impels us to engage in negative actions that lead to even greater problems. Stress is like salt or vitamins in that we need it in moderate amounts but too much of a good thing becomes toxic and possibly fatal. When stress begins to overwhelm our ability to adapt, it becomes a great evil dragon lowering our level of consciousness and the control we have over our mind/body and daily life.

A stressor is any event, experience, or environmental stimulus that upsets the body's normal equilibrium and requires adaptation. When these events or experiences are perceived as threats, they make us more prone to both physical and psychological problems. The stressful effect of most stressors depends on our perception and ability to adapt. Symptoms may include a sense of being overwhelmed, feelings of anxiety, overall irritability, insecurity, nervousness, social withdrawal, loss of appetite, depression, panic attacks, exhaustion, high or low blood pressure, skin eruptions or rashes, insomnia, lack of sexual desire or sexual dysfunction, migraines, gastrointestinal difficulties, and menstrual aberrations for women. Feeling a lack of control, wanting what we do not have instead of being grateful for what we do have, resistance to the way things are, resistance to change or pain, judging and comparing, learned helplessness and pessimism, and clinging to a separate self, are common.

Stress comes in many forms including an awareness of incompleteness and insufficiency, the fear of losing control, the physical and mental pain associated with growing old, illness and death, the anxiety of trying to hold on to things that are constantly changing, and a sense that things never measure up to our expectations or standards. We fear getting what we do not want, and we fear not getting what we do want. Anger, fear, guilt, worry, sadness, shame, and other harmful thoughts can overwhelm the mind destroying our peace and happiness. The fear and uncertainty of the threat of terrorist attacks, global warming, and toxic chemicals on the news can cause stress especially because we feel like we have no control over those events. Fears can also hit closer to home; such as being worried about failure to finish a project at work or not having enough money to pay the bills this month.

Stress is a product of our own thought process. It is what we think and how often we have certain thoughts, and a vast majority of these thoughts are related to or focused on the past or the future. Any significant life change can be perceived as stressful, even a happy event like a wedding. More unpleasant events, such as a divorce, a major financial setback, or a death in the family can be significant sources of stress. It boils down to individual perceptions or the way one thinks and their ability to cope. One individual might be too happy to have a lot of spare time at work, while the other might complain about the same situation and fret about becoming bored. Some people are stressed because they have too much to do, while others would look at it as an opportunity to show their abilities. A rich man can be miserable living in the lap of luxury while a poor man can be happy living in an igloo.

The two main classifications of stress are acute and chronic. Acute stress is normal in modern life, while chronic stress can be quite dangerous. Short term acute stress will not last longer than the work day, and may actually benefit health. However, if life feels like one continuous emergency every day of the week, it becomes long-term chronic stress and is dangerous to both physical and mental health. Stressors are more likely to affect our health when they are chronic, highly disruptive, or perceived as

13

uncontrollable. Big stressors tend to include financial troubles, job issues, health, relationship conflicts, and major life changes. Smaller stressors such as long daily commutes, rushed morning routines, and personal conflicts with colleagues can add up and be just as bad for one's health as chronic stress.

A crisis stressor is unforeseen and unpredictable and is completely out of the control of the individual. Catastrophic natural disasters, violence, war and accidents are rare but typically cause a great deal of stress. Ambient or environmental stressors like pollution, toxic chemicals and pharmaceuticals, noise, crowding, and traffic can negatively impact us without conscious awareness. Even common events like marriage, going off to college, the death of a loved one, or the birth of a child require adaptation and can be stressful enough to cause illness especially when they come in clusters. The most common stressors are daily annoyances and minor hassles that test our ability to adapt. They include making decisions, meeting deadlines at work or school, traffic jams, encounters with irritating personalities, and conflicts with other people. We can stress ourselves out just by worrying about things.

Both acute and chronic stress can lead to changes in behavior and in physiology. Behavioral changes can be smoking, eating habits, and physical activity. Physiological changes can be overstimulation of the sympathetic nervous system and the shutting down of immunological function leaving the body vulnerable to disease and infection. Daily chronic stressors have a greater negative impact on individuals' health than do more acute, traumatic stressors that generally have a start and an end point. For example, daily stressors like dealing with traffic, finishing homework assignments, etc., cause more harm to one's health in the long run than do stressors such as a death in the family or an earthquake. Other chronic stress can result from stressful events that persist over a relatively long period of time, such as caring for a spouse with dementia, or frequently reliving brief but emotional events that continue to be overwhelming long after they are over, such as experiencing a physical assault. Research suggests chronic stress at a young age can have lifelong impacts on the biological, psychological, and behavioral responses to stress later in life.

When humans are under chronic stress, unhealthy changes in their physiological, emotional, and behavioral responses are most likely to occur. Hyperactivity of neurons begins to physically change the brain and have severe damaging effects on mental health. A decline in neuroplasticity will occur, and the brain will lose the ability to form new connections and process new sensory information. Studies have also shown that perceived chronic stress and the hostility associated with Type-A personalities are often associated with much higher risks of cardiovascular disease and contribute to the initiation, growth, and metastasis of select tumors.

In recent years our knowledge of modern technology has increased considerably, and as a result, we have witnessed remarkable material progress, but there has not been a corresponding increase in human happiness. There is no less stress in the world today, and there are no fewer problems, in fact, there are more problems and greater dangers than ever before. Stressors have simply changed from smallpox to AIDS, and from lion and grizzly bear attacks to cyber-attacks, oil spills, suicide bombers, and environmental pollution. Like the grizzly bear, stress is cute and playful when it is small but becomes a killer when it grows up.

1.3.2 The Root of All Evil - Inflexible Perception

The root of all evil is not money or power; it is the aberrant premises behind them: the great evil dragons of distorted or obsolete beliefs and attitudes; negative thought and expectation; attachment and inflexible desire; and preoccupation with the past or future. The mother of these debilitating forces is Inflexible Perception. The root cause of all suffering is directly or indirectly related to the inability or unwillingness to accept a situation as a part of the whole and adapt one's self accordingly so as to progress toward Harmony: the ultimate objective of all pursuits and the natural state of all creation.

Inflexible Perceptions are directly or indirectly responsible for all stress and illness, but they are not all negative. People can misuse the concept of positive thinking to stubbornly avoid facing unpleasant realities that require recognition before they can be neutralized, dismissed, and replaced with more appropriate thoughts. Our Inflexible Perceptions of the world and their resulting beliefs, attitudes, thoughts, attachments, preoccupations with past (anger, guilt, depression, shame), and preoccupation with the future (fear, worry, anxiety) will determine our stress level.

Stressors are events, experiences, or environmental stimuli that people perceive as threats. A stressor can be external and related to the environment, but the stress is created by internal perceptions that can lead to anxiety, depression and many other negative emotions. If a man's car is stolen, he can either take the attitude that he is a victim and was violated, or that he finally has the opportunity to buy a new car with the insurance money. Overbearing bosses, ill-behaved children, the breakdown of relationships, traumas, and conflicts do not cause stress on their own. It is the perception of how we will be able to cope with these stimuli that causes the stress. Therefore, the manner in which one thinks about, or perceives, events is the cause of all that furrows the brow and determines our moods, energy level, health, lifestyle, and even longevity. A toy shop is an evil place if we believe that toys corrupt the minds of children.

The mother of all the great evil stress dragons is not our circumstances; it is our perception of them and our resistance to adaptation: Inflexible Perception. The greatest of these dragons are 1) distorted or obsolete beliefs and attitudes 2) negative thought and expectation 3) attachment and inflexible desire 4) preoccupation with the past or future. These basic flaws in our perceptions are what give rise to every bit of stress, anxiety, unhappiness, fear and anger we experience in our lives. If we cannot learn to interrupt the tension states that arise in response to these insidious stressors, we can easily find ourselves living in a continual state of physiologic alarm, literally stewing in our own stress hormones.

1) Distorted or obsolete beliefs and attitudes: Whether the stress response is triggered in any situation depends on two things: our perception of how threatening the situation is to us, and our belief in our ability to adapt or cope with it. Perception is the process of attaining awareness, interpreting, or understanding something using our senses that leads to belief when confirmed. Perceptions, beliefs, and attitudes can be both conscious and subconscious, and we create our lives with them by projecting them into the environment around us. Often we perceive an event as being more of a threat than it really is and do not believe in our ability to deal with it effectively. We do not see the world as it is, we see it as we believe which creates our attitudes, self-esteem, relationships, prosperity, health, and everything else. If our beliefs are distorted, wrong or outdated, our attitudes, feelings, and behaviors will be wrong and inappropriate. The inability or unwillingness to bend or adapt those beliefs to the present moment is like trying to steer an ocean liner with a fixed rudder. It has been referred to as psychosclerosis, or hardening of the attitudes and beliefs.

Sometimes firmly fixed negative beliefs color our world without our realizing it. We may simply feel inadequate without consciously thinking about it, but these feelings were originally created by negative thoughts in the first place. Negative feelings indicate we hold the negative beliefs, attitudes, or assumptions and will generate additional negative thoughts which generate more negative feelings that begin a self-generating doom fulfilling cycle.

Dr. Herbert Benson of Harvard University found that if we truly believe in our personal philosophy or religious faith, we may well be capable of achieving remarkable feats of mind and body. This led to our study of religion and what Benson called the "Faith Factor." We found that all religions were man made and usually founded by profoundly insightful, brilliant, and aware people. These great spiritual leaders began with simple truths, but as time slipped by, these truths have been almost destroyed by the dogma, condemnation, judgment, righteous indignation, superstitious rituals, taboos, fancy robes and goofy hats added by mankind. Almost all of the additions and deletions have diluted or destroyed what the original teacher was trying to say. In most cases, these changes were made by the priesthood (self-appointed 'chosen' messengers of God) to gain control over the populace or attract a following. This has produced the fanaticism we witness today; actions that no enlightened teacher would have approved. The basic truths are simple, very straightforward, and are easily followed, but many of our modern preachers try too hard to make their sermons interesting, to hold on to their flock. The original teachings are overlaid with extraneous matter, and their essence is often completely obscured. In many cases, the deeper original meanings are no longer recognizable, and their transformative power lost. We are told what we must believe in and worship, lest we be labeled an infidel and destroyed. Humans have always fought and persecuted those who do not believe underlinedexactlyunderlined as they do. More people have been killed in the name of religion than for any other reason, and it is a classic example of Inflexible Perception.

2) underlinedNegative thought and expectationunderlined: When Inflexible Perceptions create a negative thought, we are less likely to recognize it even if someone points it out. We will defend it as righteous fact even where there is no justification or evidence. We begin to expect the world to conform to us. We look down on others who see things differently and expect them to conform to our views. When they do not, we react in frustration, anger, even derision and

violence. When we refuse to adapt to the world and expect it to conform to us, negative thoughts are reinforced, and stress levels increase.

Negative thoughts are common in bad moods and depression. Experiments show that spending time thinking about sad or angry situations causes these feelings to arise. Participants spent twenty minutes thinking about the worst things people ever said or did to them, the worst times of their lives, and all their faults and mistakes. All experienced greater stress levels. Habitually thinking about negative things creates depression, and angry thoughts make it more difficult to calm down, to see the other person's point of view, and to act in respectful ways. If no negotiation or solution occurs, angry thoughts simply keep us tense, our feelings inflamed, and our mood disturbed. Similarly, upsetting thoughts can cause anxiety, thoughts of needing addictive substances can cause addiction, dwelling on loss can cause grief, etc.

A wise man once said, "It's all in your head. It really is the thought that counts." Thought is a form of energy that creates psychophysiological changes in the mind/body and is broadcast to the outside world affecting our environment and circumstances. When these thoughts are negative, they lead to even greater stress and more negative thoughts. If we say or think we are sick and tired, we probably are, or soon will be. Chronic heightened emotional states create a perfect breeding ground for illness. There is an obvious relationship between one's mental focus on negative thinking, emotions, expectation, and disease. In a study funded by the Wright State University School of Medicine in Ohio, researchers reviewed studies on the effects of negative thinking on pain symptoms. Patients suffering from chronic fatigue syndrome, fibromyalgia, upper respiratory illness, and surgery are all more likely to suffer from increased pain symptoms if they are prone to negative thinking and rumination.

Researchers studying immune response have shown that the immune system and the nervous system are inextricably intertwined. Unhappiness and negativity is a disease. Psychological and emotional stress can suppress immune functioning and encourage the growth or spread of immune-related disorders such as cancer, AIDS, and autoimmune diseases. Upon disruption of either psychological or physical equilibrium, the body responds by stimulating the nervous, endocrine, and immune systems. The reaction of these systems causes an upset in the homeostasis of the body and has both short and long term effects.

Repeatedly banging one's head against a brick wall with the expectation of breaking through is an example of Inflexible expectation without the willingness to accept the present. Some people expect things to go <u>exactly</u> as planned and when it does not, they get upset, have negative thoughts, and often give up. We need to accept what happens, understand that life is unpredictable to a certain extent and that mistakes happen. The key is flexibility, and adapting to the situation means finding a better way. Man <u>can</u> fly, but not without adaptation. If we expect ourselves and others to do everything right all the time or make our happiness dependent upon a particular outcome, we are destined to feel stressed when things do not go as expected. No one is perfect.

Negative thoughts and expectations are caused by ingrained Inflexible Perceptions and result in harmful beliefs about self-esteem, security, money, people, life, and everything else. Negative emotional states have been linked to nearly all physical and psychological illnesses and diseases from eating disorders to cancer. The negative energy lowers the body's defenses, makes it easier to see ourselves as less attractive, and care less for our physical needs. When we are in a negative state, we do not attract those elements that would make our lives advance rather we attract circumstances, events, and emotions that are detrimental. Everything seems to go wrong.

3) <u>Attachment and inflexible desire</u>: Inflexible Perceptions create inflexible attachments and desires. They cause us to hold on to things, people, ideas, places, work, and self-image too tightly. We cannot seem to allow things to just happen, or allow people just to come and go in our lives. Control is what humans do, but when our perceptions are inflexible, attachments and desires produce stress, pain, sadness, unhappiness, bitterness, and anger. Some develop a need to control everything and everyone. When we cannot let go of these attachments, the dragon comes to life. Attachment to anything which is not permanent will ultimately lead to stress because it will eventually change and we will lose it as we know it. Only change is permanent.

Some people misunderstand attachment, desire, and the idea of letting go. Attachment comes from a place of fear. We get attached to a job because we fear that if we lose it, we will no longer have money to support ourselves and our family. When we are attached to a person, we secretly fear they are going to leave us and we will be left all alone. Nothing is ours to keep, not even our mother, father, spouse, children, friends, bank accounts or career. We are grateful for their presence and the time we spend with them, but irrational attachment and desire prevents us from letting them go with dignity, love, and grace.

The difference between love and attachment is Inflexible Perception. We can love our friends, family, job, house, and life, but should not get dependently attached to any of them because we understand that all things are impermanent, dynamic and constantly changing. Love is not a cause of stress in itself but clinging to those we love will inevitably cause us problems because relationships, like everything else, change and are ultimately impermanent. If we depend on others for our happiness, if we need their approval or attention to find our own self-worth and fulfillment, we will feel stress when we do not get it. We need to learn to love in such a way that those we love feel free. If we love for what we get out of it, it's attachment and not real love.

The natives of southern India used to trap monkeys by cutting a small hole in a coconut just large enough for a monkey to put its hand in. The coconut was then tied to a tree and baited with a small piece of fruit. The monkey smells the fruit, squeezes its hand into the coconut, grabs the prize and finds that the fist full of fruit does not fit through the hole. Just as we sometimes allow unbridled desires and attachment to trap us, the monkey is held prisoner because it will not let go.

To explain it simply, stress develops when we are (rigidly) attached to a particular outcome and things do not turn out (exactly) the way we desire: it is our inability to adjust or adapt to any other outcome.

4) Preoccupation with past or future: Inflexible Perception also spawns the dragon of preoccupation with past and future. These preoccupations adulterate our uniquely human ability to reason and imagine by turning our magical imagination into a trap. We can get caught up in seemingly endless bogs of past (anger, guilt, depression), and future (fear, worry, anxiety) leaving little or no opportunity to focus on the present moment. Without even knowing how or why, these disturbing feelings can take over one's entire life, sometimes in less than a minute. While we are in the past or future, our Subconscious is trying to create opportunities for us in the present moment, but if we are not there, we cannot see them and miss out on great opportunities and life itself. If the mind is not in the present moment, we are vulnerable to stress, depression, and anxiety.

When people are preoccupied with their past, they tend to wallow in distressing and recurrent thoughts. This can be considered obsessive and lead to rituals, repetitive action, and thoughts getting caught in loops that constantly repeat. We are products of our past, but we do not have to be prisoners of it. There is a clear difference between learning from our past and becoming immersed in (or caught up in) a problem, issue, or what we perceive as wrong with life.

Obsessive preoccupation with the past can come out in the form of rumination which is the reliving of past experiences again and again in the mind and often leads to depression. It is accompanied by condemning, all-or-none criticism, and the overwhelming belief that if things had been different, then misery could be avoided. When we ruminate, we cannot seem to shake negative thoughts or let things go. The causes, factors, consequences, and results that happened from a negative emotional experience are replayed over and over again. We let ourselves get upset, and hold ourselves back from moving forward.

The word ruminate originates from Latin for chewing cud. A cow chews their food and then re-chews their food after they have swallowed it. People keep rethinking past scenarios in a similar way, which can be damaging to their mental health. It is an unhealthy obsessive way of thinking and is problematic because these negative thoughts occupy our minds and limit our problem-solving abilities. This type of thinking can cause a person to be in a bad mood, make them feel upset unnecessarily, impair thinking, and drive away needed social support. It is experienced as guilt, regret and anger, over perceived mistakes, losses, slights, lost opportunities, and actions taken or not taken with catastrophic results.

Research has consistently proven that people who ruminate have a greater chance of developing depression and anxiety, and these people are more likely to be self-sabotaging. People who ruminate tend to be overly self-focused and replay scenarios they repetitively think about themselves and their world, which could lead to maladaptive and intrusive thoughts. Intrusive thinking is defined by repetitive thoughts that a person is trying to suppress and may be involuntary, difficult to control, and can interfere with current activities. Intrusive thoughts may also be associated with trauma.

And then there are the preoccupations with our future. The ability to plan, solve problems, and anticipate needs is a gift, but when it becomes a preoccupation it is worry, fear, and anxiety. Most people experience brief periods of worry in their lives without incident and find that a moderate amount of worrying is useful when limited to <u>concern</u>. Concern can prompt people to take precautions or avoid risky behaviors while worry is an anxious preoccupation with an anticipated negative event. Over the course of evolution, worry helped us adapt by directing awareness to true problems that once identified can be effectively addressed. In this way, worry is effective in managing challenges of our everyday life as concern. For some people, this process breaks down. Their minds become trapped in an endless process of "figuring it out." They are plagued by thoughts and images of disastrous outcomes that in reality may never come to pass. Worriers are particularly challenged by problems that have no clear solution. Instead of accepting and managing these difficult realities, they are viewed as evidence of the futility of even trying to work things out. Stress is the point where concern turns to worry and fear.

In reality, 92% of our worries are pure fluff with no substance at all. Studies have shown that 40% of the things people worry about are things that will never happen, and 30% have already happened and cannot be changed with all the worry in the world. Another 12% are needless worries about our health, and 10% are petty, miscellaneous worries leaving only 8% of the things we worry about as real, legitimate worries worthy of concern and planning. Ninety-two percent of our worries are not only a waste of time but are generators of negative energy and stress that we just do not need.

Obsessive preoccupations intensify and prolong distressing emotions. For example, worry reinforces anxious feelings and fear which, in turn, leads to more worry. The process can extend into anxious periods lasting hours, days or weeks, at times spiraling into panic attacks and emotional spikes of anger, guilt, and shame. Obsessive thinking limits effective problem-solving, promotes procrastination, avoidance, and withdrawal, only resulting in further problems. Obsessive thinking plays a prominent role in mood disorders, including dysthymia, major depression, bipolar disorder, and is the defining symptom of Generalized Anxiety Disorder (GAD), Obsessive-Compulsive Disorder (OCD), Panic Disorder, and many other psychological conditions.

Without getting caught up in the suffering of man, we needed to do an in-depth study of it to discover its cause. The cause was found to be stress, and the root of all stress was found to be our own rigid perceptions. We found that the cure is not a pill or years of psychoanalysis, it is already within us. It is being aware that the ultimate goal is not a bigger house or revenge, it is peace of mind and harmony for ourselves and those we love. Even the suicide boomer believes that his action will eventually lead to peace for his people and harmony for himself in a better place. The path from stress to gratitude, peace, and harmony appeared as a golden stairway of six levels with a clear view of paradise at the top. We can do this.

1.3.3 **The Cure is Attainable**

If we treat the cause, the effect will go away. As a matter of fact, human suffering exists and stress of one kind or another is responsible for all of it. We learned that the root cause is Inflexible Perception, that is, the inability or unwillingness to accept life as a part of the whole and adapt one's self accordingly so as to restore homeostasis and Harmony: the ultimate objective of all pursuits and the natural state of all creation. Harmony of the mind releases the immune system to do its job and allows our inherent healing systems to operate at full capacity. When the mind is brought into harmony, it will heal the physical body. The cure then is simply to follow a path that leads to relaxing, letting go of (and replacing) rigid inappropriate perceptions, and learning to be aware, flexible, and adaptable. Plasticity of Perception is the key, and it is attainable in six enjoyable treks.

The cure starts with the decision to be present as much as possible in everything we do. When we are in the past or future, we are not in control of what we are doing; the Subconscious mind is running the show. If we spend too much time reliving events that no longer exist except in the memory, be it a guilt trip or a fond memory that we think will make us feel better, we miss out on the present moment and real life. If past emotions and the fear of what may or may not happen dominate our attention, life can pass us by. The past is long gone, the future does not yet exist, and real life happens only in this very moment. We need to take advantage of it, appreciate it, and treasure it. We need to be present, grateful, patient, kind, happy, healthy, a calm mind at peace, and allow ourselves to be loved.

Our search for the cure to life's greatest scourge began with an interest in psychology, integrative medicine, health, and happiness. It led to a study of psychoneuroimmunology, epigenetics, religion, stress management, meditation, therapeutic guided imagery, and the physics of chi. Eventually, they all began to fit together, and a clear path to the cure revealed itself.

Throughout history, the great wise men and teachers, philosophers, and prophets have disagreed with one another on many different things. It is only on this one point that they are in complete and unanimous agreement: we become what we think about. The mind can change the body merely by thinking. Manage the mind and the body will follow because the body is a manifestation of the mind. It will reflect and adapt to our perceptions, beliefs, and attitudes. Trying to manage or change the body without changing the mind is a waste of time.

Allopathic paradigms are finally beginning to change from a focus on illness to a focus on wellness. Psychological paradigms are changing from a focus on mental illness and unhappiness to mental health and happiness; from fear and anger to gratitude; from ego to conscious awareness; and from stress to calm. A focus on diagnosing and analyzing the past is changing to observing and choosing one's thoughts in the present, and from wallowing in a pit of woes to appreciation and gratitude.

The new paradigm is focused on the present and goes far beyond superficial positive thinking. It teaches us to live in the present, how to avoid getting caught up in negative thought, and makes the link between thought, feeling, and behavior clearer. The new paradigm assumes that the Conscious mind is in control and is an observer of the Subconscious as it jumps from one thought or memory (wrapped in the emotion of the time) to the next; that we become attached to a thought only if we choose to. It teaches people to mindfully observe their thoughts in the present like watching TV. We recognize (past induced) Ego based thought and neutralize them by understanding that they might have been appropriate in the past but not now. We dismiss those thoughts that are destructive or inappropriate and replace them with thoughts that are of our choosing and worthy of our time. It is our thinking about our circumstances, not the circumstances themselves, that determines how we feel. It is impossible to feel sad without having sad thoughts or angry without having angry thoughts. In the absence of thoughts about "what's wrong," the ill feelings disappear, even if the circumstance remains.

The events that cause stress all have one thing in common: we have to think about those events. If we do not think about them, we do not experience stress. When we are depressed, our thoughts are usually in the past. When we are anxious, our thoughts are usually in the future. It is the single act of thinking about them and not the present that causes stress. Inflexible

Perceptions lead to chronic thought which creates chronic stress. Now is usually good. The present moment is always available for us to form whatever perspective we choose. Stress is not in the situation or event; it is in the mind.

According to the new paradigm, changing our health may be as simple as accepting flexibility in our perceptions, beliefs, and attitudes. We have the power to heal ourselves, increase our feelings of self-worth and improve our emotional state. <u>Perceptions, or the way we interpret things, control our beliefs, and when we learn to control our perceptions, we can rewrite or replace harmful beliefs, attitudes, and thoughts, and accomplish wonderful things</u>.

1.4 **Combining Science and Spirituality**

Science and spirituality have been at odds for centuries as a result of politics and power consolidating dogma, but we went back to the basics of all religions and found that, without the add-ons, science and spirituality actually complement each other. The modern study of subatomic particles confirms that matter (as we know it) is really different forms of energy and gives credence to the concept of spirit and the interrelationship of all things. Albert Einstein taught us that science without religion is lame, and religion without science is blind.

1.4.1 **Science**

For over three hundred years, Newtonian physics held that the atom was the smallest particle of the Universe. Then, in the early twentieth century, physicists began to discover that the atom was made up of even smaller particles that they called electrons, neutrons, and protons. Going even deeper, these smaller particles were found to be made up of whirling, vibrating vortices of energy with extended force fields that they called bosons, fermions, and quarks: just pure energy.

Quantum physics began to turn Newtonian physics on its ear with the discovery that everything we thought was physical is immaterial force fields that radiate and absorbs energy. The building blocks of our world are extremely powerful invisible energy vortices. Everything, including us, is made up of these tiny particles of energy, and that means that <u>we are not physical matter</u>. We only appear to be solid and separate from one another on the level at which our physical senses normally perceive. On finer atomic and subatomic levels, seemingly solid matter is seen as smaller and smaller particles within particles which eventually turn out to be just pure energy, the nature of which is to move and flow. What appears to be a hand, a tree or a table, is the result of light (photons) repelling off these energy fields. There is no physical substance in the makeup of atoms.

We are energy and everything within and around us is made up of energy that is constantly rearranging and changing form. We are all part of, and connected to, one great energy field. Things that we perceive to be solid and separate are in reality just various forms of our essential energy which is common to all. Matter is an assortment of vibrating energy fields that some have unwittingly dubbed "vibes", and is not separate or a physical solid. All forms of energy are interrelated and can affect one another in mysterious ways. Thus, the concept of spirit re-enters the world of science.

Einstein taught that this energy cannot be created nor destroyed, only changed, and it is our objective to employ techniques that will direct or channel some of these changes. All things are possible when the soul (heart or spirit) is willing to believe we can. It may just require some adaptation.

Another breakthrough that mainstream science has finally begun to recognize is that genes are tools of the mind and facilitate functions but do not decide the fate of the cell. The brain controls the chemistry of the blood and nervous system, which in turn nourishes and regulates the behavior of the cells and their gene expression. The chemistry released by the brain reflects the perceptions, beliefs, and attitudes we hold in the mind. A conscious human being can change these perceptions, and when powered by a profound belief, or Dr. Benson's Faith Factor, we can change the chemical composition of the blood and the nervous system, which in turn regulates our genetics, psychophysiology, and behavior (the way we respond to the world). This is the foundation of the placebo effect.

Most people think that our genes create unchangeable inherited patterns over which we could not possibly have mind/body influence. They often exclaim, "It's just the way I am" or "I can't help it, I have the FAT gene." But such views are misconceptions. In most families with genetic tendencies to disease, some people will develop the disease and some will not. Having "the gene" is one thing but developing the disease is another. We call the manifestation of gene function, "expression" and our current understanding leads us to believe that almost any gene expression and its corresponding physiologic function can be influenced by imagery, belief systems, and emotional changes. It is not the FAT gene that causes obesity; it is the FAT habits, perceptions, and lifestyle that create obesity.

Trying to blame a disease on the presence of a single gene or trying to cure a disease by targeting a single gene can be problematic at best and even dangerous. Physiological change may require the interaction of dozens of genes working together in a specific pattern of expression (on or off) and no drug or allopathic intervention can hope to target even one or two without side effects that can be worse than the original disorder. The brain or rather the Unconscious mind-of-the-body, on the other hand, knows which genes it needs to reconfigure to manifest a specific expression. The idea is to forget about targeting genes and let the mind do the healing. It is an innate function that simply needs an instruction from the Control Room in the Subconscious. We just need to learn to operate the controls with a deep heartfelt belief in the worthiness of the predetermined result.

1.4.2 Spirituality

Our study of spirituality began with an in-depth look at the top five contemporary monotheistic religions and worked back in time to polytheism (worship of more than one god) and still farther to the beginning of animism (attribution of a spirit to objects and phenomena that organizes and animates the Universe). We went back to the roots of religion and found that they all have a common foundation: seven simple principles that were known to exist over 5000 years ago. Before Hinduism, Abraham, Jesus, Muhammad, or Guru Nanak, the seven Principles of Harmony were universal and remain so today. It is not a religion in itself but rather a philosophy or attitude.

Religions tend to collect add-ons and rituals that often symbolize a core truth but just as often obscure it. They are often complicated and conflicting, but with only a few minor semantic exceptions due to translation ambiguity, all major religions agree on the seven Principles of Harmony. For that reason, our study of spirituality, faith, and belief will not focus on any religion or doctrine. We will focus on the seven principles that are common to them all and have survived the stormy manmade political power struggles. Regardless of one's religious preference, our discussions of spirituality should be compatible and even complimentary. Tapping the awesome nature of the human mind is enhanced dramatically with the use of belief. We can do anything if we are willing to give up the belief that we can't. As you believe, so shall it be done.

Before the 20th century, the terms spirituality and religion were pretty much synonymous. But as spirituality gradually became more associated with thought and a journey intimately linked to the pursuit of personal experience and growth, religion remained linked to membership in a formal institution, participation in formal rituals, and adherence to official denominational doctrines. Spirituality does not depend on collective or institutional context rather it is the feelings, thoughts, beliefs, experience, and behaviors that often arise from the search for a divine being, higher power, or ultimate reality, as perceived by the individual.

Spirituality exists when we imagine a meaning or power beyond our visible world. It is an essential component of deep belief, and it is the power of that deep belief that spirituality brings to the Imagine Harmony Program. Imagination powered by spirituality leads to belief and eventually manifests a more substantive expectation, conviction, and growth. Invisible energy fields like those now acknowledged by science at the subatomic level, have been perceived as angels, gods, spirits, telepathy, communication with the dead, psychic, clairvoyance, premonition, intuition, vibes, ESP, sixth sense, gut feeling, premonition, divine or supernatural revelation. They clearly exist; it is only the personal perceptions and the words used to describe them that vary.

It is difficult to place definite limits on the physical and mental powers of those who hold profound beliefs. Those who discover the exciting and powerful forces of the mind do so by eliciting the Relaxation Response in conjunction with belief in order to bypass the Ego. Logic alone will not allow people to shift their habits, let alone their genes. Our health and lifestyle are created by our mental and emotional attitudes, so changing our beliefs and the way we tune into ourselves and the world can have profound physical effects. The magic of belief is the placebo effect on "supercharge."

We do not believe that reconnecting to our soul means that we have to believe any particular religious dogma. If it helps, that's fine, but it isn't necessary. The Imagine Harmony Program explores spirituality and harness the innate power of core belief, creating harmony, and resulting in the attainment of our objectives without the religious constraints. The discussion of belief should be compatible with all religions because we use original fundamentals upon which they were formed. Perceptions just become more flexible.

1.4.3 **Medimaginosis**

Medimaginosis is based on the results of scientific research and the documented physiological responses to over two thousand years of meditative practice. We begin with the typical modern human afflicted with a multitude of ailments and neurosis mostly attributable to (or at least aggravated by) stress, and end with an evolving human being capable of consciously altering both physiological and psychological responses to daily life. Medimaginosis is the practice of the key process by which we manifest perfect health, happiness, vitality, and a life expectancy far in excess of the current concept of POSSIBLE. It is a transition that takes place over a period of weeks and is accomplished in six stages. It begins with the familiar relaxation and attitude awareness that has been promulgated for decades but seldom executed effectively, and gradually evolves into conscious control of gene expression. Imagine having complete control over of the mind/body instead of the other way around. If practiced consistently, Medimaginosis can make that possible by bringing mind, body, and soul to a natural balance.

Medimaginosis is a term made up of three concepts: MEDI refers to meditation, focused attention, and directed concentration. We learn to relax and practice focusing the mind on the breath, mantra, a predetermined object, or body sensation. Letting go of any trying, we feel the flow and allow the Ego to relax its grip. IMAGI refers to imagination, imagery, and visualized intent. We use our gift of imagination to visualize or sense a predetermined objective or goal. We see it on the screen of the mind's eye (sometimes called the third eye) like a movie, already attained and complete in every detail, feeling it using all senses. NOSIS refers to the Greek word meaning, "to know, wisdom, or believe" as used in the words prognosis and diagnosis. We relax deep into a low alpha or high theta state and explore the wisdom of the True Self or OM. We communicate directly with our own soul, determine whether our visualized objective is worthy, and accept the power to manifest the physiological and psychological changes needed to remain in harmony with the vision, from a source beyond our comprehension.

Medimaginosis uses our innate ability to communicate internally. Just as we communicate with other people, the mind, body, and soul are in constant communication, and all 55 trillion cells communicate with each other through an incredibly elaborate network. This communication is a two-way street and goes beyond the limits of the physical body. The Medimaginosis paradigm uses the ancient concept that we are all one and the seven Principles of Harmony as a foundation upon which we can base our choices, and act appropriately. The excuse, "the devil made me do it" is no longer valid because the "me" in this scenario is making a conscious choice based on universal wisdom. We are not victims; we are in control.

1.5 **Mind/Body/Soul Interaction**

We refer to the mind, body, and soul as one unit (Mind/Body/Soul) because it is. They are in constant communication with each other and cannot function separately. It is like trying to separate the left side of the heart from the right side and expecting it to work properly. The Conscious mind is the self-aware thinker with logic, reason, willpower, language, superior judgment, and decision-making ability. It sends decisions and instructions through the ego gate and into the Subconscious Control Room expecting it to make things happen. The Ego filters and censors information in both direction allowing only that which it deems safe and reasonable to pass. The Subconscious mind stores everything and runs our lives automatically when the Conscious mind is busy thinking about something. The Unconscious mind-of-the-body is an incredibly intricate and compelling phenomenon that blindly manifests the instructions it receives from the Subconscious. The OM has been called the Soul or Spirit, and is centered slightly below the physical heart and above the solar plexus at the middle <u>dantian</u>. It is that part of us that is directly connected to the Source of all things and a vast, possibly infinite, repository of wisdom made up of incomprehensible, dynamic, constantly changing forms of vibrating energy making us part of one big harmonious symphony.

1.5.1 **Conscious mind**: The Conscious mind or self-aware mind, as opposed to the Subconscious and Unconscious part of the brain, is the integrator that makes us human. It is like the captain in the wheelhouse of a huge ocean liner that hosts, feeds, and fills the needs of thousands of passengers. The captain is not the source of power for the boat and cannot be involved in the details of every operation but is the one controlling the speed, holding the course, and directing the mission. It has been estimated that the Conscious mind is associated with about 12% of the brain and can only process approximately 40 nerve impulses per second while the Subconscious process over 40 <u>million</u> impulses per second. In comparison, the Conscious mind is slow, has a short attention span, and cannot be everywhere, so it needs the automatic reactions of the Subconscious, especially in emergency situations where quick action is required. The Conscious mind allows Subconscious programs to control most of our life experience but monitors and observes them so it can step in and stop, alter, or replace harmful, inappropriate, defective, or wrong reactions with more appropriate responses. The Conscious mind knows that feelings are not facts, analyzes the past, imagines the future, expresses free will, and is aware of itself and the present. It is the evolved integration of the human Conscious mind that provides us with logic, reason, willpower, language, decision-making, and superior judgment.

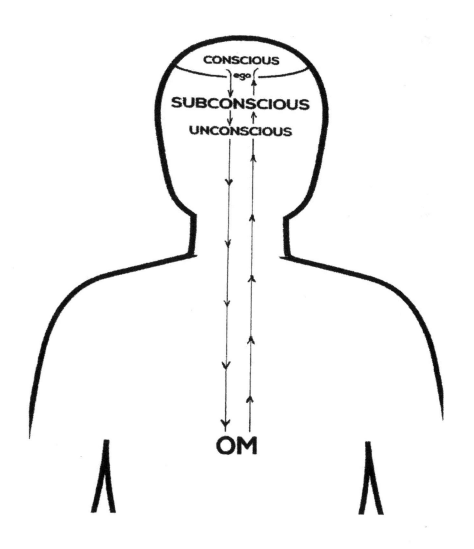

1.5.2 **Ego:** The Ego has one foot in the Conscious mind and one foot in the Subconscious mind and stands at the gate between the two functions filtering and allowing only that information it feels is appropriate to pass. It filters sensory information from the Subconscious going to the Conscious as well as all imagined instructions and goals formed in the Conscious going to the Subconscious. The Ego tries to protect the Subconscious from non-conforming beliefs and thoughts from the Conscious mind and the outside world allowing only those instructions that it deems safe and appropriate to pass through the gate and on to the Subconscious for action in the Control Room. Ego is not evil or even bad, just wrong a lot and although it is a tiny part of whole, Ego thinks that IT alone represents "I" and believes it must fight for itself in the world. Ego is an expression of separateness and is ultimately unaware and unconscious of its own true nature. The Ego is often associated with compulsive thinking in order to be assured of its future existence, automatically reacting from past programming rather than responding from wisdom. Bypassing the Ego is a key part of Medimaginosis.

1.5.3 **Subconscious mind:** The Subconscious mind receives all physical and sensory information and stores it with all past input. It stores everything and can add to or alter memories but (barring physical damage) they will remain until death. Everything we have ever seen, heard, or experienced (including TV shows and scary movies) is sitting somewhere in our Subconscious, affecting our current thoughts, decisions, and actions. Communication through words, thoughts, and images are interpreted on a deeper level than most people realize, both the positive and negative. The Subconscious mind contains the Control Room of the Unconscious mind-of-the-body and operates like a huge impersonal computer. It is our "autopilot", our habits, and all that we do automatically. It acts without conscious thought and runs our lives most of the time. The Subconscious mind, its Control Room, and the Unconscious mind-of-the-body are associated with the neural activity of approximately 82% of the brain, can organize choices and decisions, and are much faster but lack the free will and intentions of the Conscious mind. The Medimaginosis program teaches us to return to conscious awareness as often as possible to take back control.

1.5.4 **Unconscious mind:** The Unconscious mind is the mind-of-the-body and is like a vast computer coordinating and controlling thousands of operations and functions at the same time. This awesome capacity is blind and exists in a dark closet with only the Subconscious to guide it and tell it what the environment is like and what needs to be done. It accepts instructions from the Subconscious Control Room and acts on them without question. Conscious concepts need to pass through the ego gate guarded by the Ego, be accepted by the Subconscious and then, if conditions are right in the Control Room, they pass on to the Unconscious mind where they will manifest as psychophysiological adaptations.

1.5.5 **OM:** OM is that very subtle energy or light at the center of the Soul that was before the body existed and will be after it dies. It radiates in all directions, exists in every living cell, and is the difference between life and death. OM has been called the Soul, Spirit, and the Heart (not to be confused with the organ that pumps blood throughout the body) and is centered slightly below the physical heart and just above the solar plexus at the middle dantian. OM is an extension of the Source of all things and is one's personal connection to a vast, possibly infinite, repository of wisdom made up of incomprehensible, dynamic, constantly changing forms of vibrating energy. OM is that part of us that is infinite, eternal, and directly connected to all that is, making us a part of one big harmonious symphony. It is the stillness underneath the mental noise, the love and joy underneath the emotional pain and stress, and our direct line of communication to what some call God, The Great Spirit, Allah, Yahweh, or Jehovah. Soul is the True Self. Spirit is that part of Soul that is its energy and is directly connected to the Source of all things. Chi is that part of Sprit that is the life <u>force</u> and flows through the body at varying speeds and intensity. OM is the center and essence of them all.

1.6 **Putting it together, what happens, and how it works**

The reader will learn to use the breath, meditation, the parasympathetic nervous system, imagery, and deep wisdom to access the Subconscious controls of the mind/body, manage stress, modulate gene expression, and create any worthy objective.

We develop a worthy concept in the Conscious mind. Then we consciously Recognize, Neutralize, Dismiss, and Replace any harmful subconscious thoughts that conflict with the concept by understanding that the conflicting thought might have been appropriate for past situations but is now obsolete, no longer applicable, and needs to be replaced with compatible, more appropriate thought. We use our gift of imagination to translate the concept into the language of the body, put the Ego to sleep, and enter the gate between the Conscious mind and the Subconscious mind where it is sent to the Control Room of the Unconscious mind-of-the-body.

We use deep meditation to meld our worthy concept with the wisdom of the OM where, with doubt and negative energy removed, we can initiate and stimulate the psychophysiological changes needed to manifest the concept. Self-doubt or lack of faith is considered the greatest obstacle to achievement.

Evolving from stress to gratitude involves several processes but begins with the breath because it can be controlled by the Conscious mind or by the Subconscious autonomic nervous system and effectively connects the two. The breath reacts to psychophysiological functions induced by the environment, and psychophysiological functions react to the breath induced by the Conscious mind. That is, when a frightening event occurs in the environment, psychophysiological functions are stimulated by the sympathetic nervous system and breathing increases, and when we consciously slow our breathing, psychophysiological functions are relaxed by the parasympathetic nervous system. The process is greatly enhanced when imagery or calming thoughts are used and are then supercharged when they are emotionally energized by a deep belief in the predetermined result.

Ego is like concerned parents who mean well but are often misinformed, stubbornly adhere to inappropriate rituals and beliefs, live in the past, and are not always right. They prevent us from doing things that could be harmful or dangerous but in doing so, they sometimes prevent us from venturing into the unknown and discovering great things. We need to listen to them, but when they are wrong or use outdated information, we need to sell them on the new concept or sneak past them when they are not looking. Ego uses only preprogrammed responses and current sensory perceptions while consciousness has access to imagination and superior judgment. When the Conscious mind is able to bypass, or slip by the Ego at the gate to the Subconscious mind, and consult the vast wisdom of OM, it is far more qualified to run the show with a greater purpose in mind and with a uniquely human awareness of what we are doing and where we are going.

Our Ego is there to protect us from the dangerous unknown and just will not allow foolish thoughts to pass through the gate between the Conscious and Subconscious mind until it believes that it is safe and in its best interest. We need to put the Ego to sleep using deep meditation techniques, or it will try to judge and perhaps reject all or part of our worthy concept or intention. When the Ego is asleep or distracted, we can slip the concept through the gate and into the Subconscious. The Subconscious deals in images and emotions, not words, so an affirmation, intention, or concept is translated and conflicting thoughts are neutralized. Then the Subconscious can accept our concept as worthy and will instruct the Unconscious to manifest the psychophysiological adaptations needed.

What the mind can conceive and believe it can create. It has been said many times and in many ways but we need to know how to control or direct this uniquely human ability. The conceiving is not usually the problem. We can come up with all kinds of ideas and plans but the hard part is the believing and creating the energy or motivation to power its manifestation. Using Medimaginosis, we convince the Subconscious that it is possible, that we can do it, that it is a worthy objective, and that we are worthy of it. Inspired by Dr. Herbert Benson's "Faith Factor" and Dr. Bruce Lipton's "Biology of Belief," Medimaginosis goes to the heart of all psychophysiological functions with universal wisdom and energy from the deepest level of self.

The OM is often referred to as Soul, Spirit, Chi or life force energy. It is our incorporeal connection to the Source of all things, connects us to all that is and makes us all one. When we consciously take our worthy concept to the OM, it becomes a part of us and will continue to radiate that concept back to the Unconscious causing the body to adapt or create that image with greater conviction. It can create a rash or remove one, it can create a headache or remove one, and it can create cancer or remove it by altering gene expression. It provides vast amounts of chi energy to reconfigure gene expression by shutting down those gene functions that are detrimental while activating or reactivating, and energizing those gene functions that are advantageous. It is the ultimate placebo effect supported and initiated by the Conscious mind and is powered by belief and great wisdom at the deepest, and possibly infinite, level. The Unconscious mind-of-the-body receives instructions from the Subconscious mind, conceived in the Conscious mind, and energized by the OM.

1.6.1 Meditation

The foundation of all meditation is the ability to focus the mind on a particular stimulus without being distracted by thoughts, feelings or minor physical discomforts. Many brain specialists once thought that meditation just calms the brain down, but subsequent studies have shown that it actually optimizes its function. Brain research has proven that the brain is transformed, and genetic output improves with meditation. We learn to stop fighting with ourselves and to find a place inside that is at peace, a place where we can recharge our batteries. Below all the mind chatter and fight-or-flight anxiety lies a quiet place we call our Personal Place of Peace where we can communicate with our inner wisdom or inner voice. The "inner voice" is what Dr. Walter Cannon of Harvard University called "the wisdom of the body." This quiet place allows us to move beyond our fears, beyond our anxieties and beyond the ego gate into a clearer understanding and knowing of what is. A quiet mind calms our overactive physiology, creating a sequence of physiologic and biochemical changes that improve our mental and physical health.

Medimaginosis initially uses the breath and meditation to elicit the relaxation response and train the mind to focus attention or direct concentration. It slows the repetitive, useless chatter that dominates up to eighty percent of most people's thinking. We use directed concentration to replace the mental static that has no real purpose and seems involuntary, automatic, and incessant. As we advance through the program, those skills are expanded to facilitate even greater benefits. We will use meditation to deepen our focus, neutralize doubt, harmonize chi, and build perceptions that direct behavior and shape biology.

We have all experienced the calm Medimaginosis state in everyday life: daydreaming, watching a movie, driving home on autopilot, practicing meditation or other relaxation techniques. It is simply an altered state of consciousness marked by decreased scope and increased intensity of awareness like a laser beam. It involves a deliberate choice to enter this state of consciousness, to focus our concentration and use our own suggestions to promote growth and healing. Just as someone who is daydreaming can decide to go on or stop at any time, we control the state of deep emersion. Although there are many forms and types of meditation, we have chosen a meditation style that is simple, basic, and perfectly suited to our path. Concentration is subtler and the mind rests lightly, but pleasantly and clearly, upon the point of focus. When it strays, it is gently brought back to this point of focus, without irritation or frustration. We use our breath as a home base because it is always with us and available. We can turn to it not only during our meditation sessions but whenever we wish to calm ourselves, reduce anxiety, tension, nervousness, or out-of-control feelings.

1.6.2 Parasympathetic nervous system

The parasympathetic nervous system (PNS) is that part of the autonomic nervous system (ANS) that controls the relaxation response or "evolve, renew, and repair mode" as opposed to the sympathetic nervous system (SNS) that elicits the fight-or-flight response or "defense mode." The parasympathetic nervous system activates tranquil functions, such as cellular repair, growth, and the immune functions. It tends to act in opposition to the sympathetic nervous system by slowing down the heartbeat and elicits the relaxation response. Negative energy and blockages begin to soften, and the path to the Control Room becomes clearer and easier to navigate. The sympathetic system speeds up functions while the parasympathetic returns us to normal.

We will learn to use the parasympathetic nervous system to counteract the chronic, stress-related overstimulation of the sympathetic nervous system. When the parasympathetic nervous system is dominant, heart rate slows, blood pressure falls, circulation is balanced throughout the body (making hands and skin warm) digestive organs work smoothly, blood vessels dilate, metabolism and immunity are optimal, and the body returns to homeostasis. The emotional experience that accompanies these physiological responses is a sense of well-being that makes empathy and real connection with others more likely. The weeds and debris that block our path begin to dissipate and allow conscious access to the Subconscious Control Room of the Unconscious mind-of-the-body.

1.6.3 Imagery

We use visualization and imagery to take advantage of the connection between the visual brain and the involuntary nervous system. Because the Subconscious cannot distinguish between an actual event and the same event imagined in great detail, we are able to operate the controls of the Unconscious by consciously creating the desired objective in the mind's eye and energizing it. When the visual cortex is activated, even without receiving direct input from the eyes, it can influence physical and emotional states and can help elicit changes in the mind/body.

Some students say they do not visualize well, and that's fine. There are exercises that will help develop the skill, but imagery involves far more than just seeing pictures or visualization and is more about learning to focus. It involves all neurological and sensory stimuli, feelings, and emotions manifesting an internal experience. It is not just the way we <u>see</u> things, but the way we perceive things. Those who do not <u>see</u> pictures should just notice and accept the way they imagine things without wasting a lot of time trying to imagine in a different way. They can listen quietly and with respect, knowing that it's perfectly ok to do it that way.

Imagery affects stress-related health concerns including high blood pressure, pain related to muscle tension, insomnia, depression, anxiety, skin rashes, and irritable bowel syndrome. It has been shown to be effective in alleviating chronic allergies, hives and asthma, rheumatoid arthritis, Crohn's disease and other autoimmune disorders. Over 200 studies offer compelling evidence that imagery can effectively help decrease pain and the need for pain medication, reduce side effects and complications of surgery, lessen stress and anxiety before and after procedures, reduce recovery time, boost self-confidence and self-control, improve sleep, and strengthen the immune system.

1.6.4 Communicating with OM and Tapping its Power

OM communicates directly with the Source of all things, and the Conscious mind communicates with the OM but without Medimaginosis, it seems like a distant inaudible whisper. We all know it is there but perceive it in different ways because we cannot see it. Some imagine a Spirit, Soul, Angel, or a God. Others call it intuition, ESP, or clairvoyance, but it is real and a result of the communication we carry on with the infinite energy of which we are all apart. People describe the process of finding out what is important to them, of tapping into their beliefs, in very different ways; sometimes calling it soul-searching, mulling it over, listening to one's heart, going inside of one's self, praying, or sleeping on it. Some people can act on instincts or common sense immediately while others find that truth or intuition emerges slowly, but most people can feel a kind of internal radar that occasionally calls out to them and know when something "feels right."

Intuition is defined as "power of knowing without recourse to reason" and is perceived by inner seeing, inner listening, and inner feeling. It is the voice of OM. It is our sixth sense. It is like hearing a voice that seems to be coming from a faraway room that we cannot see. Medimaginosis allows us to travel to that room and speak to this great phenomenon directly. It facilitates a two-way conversation with our own personal connection to the Source of all wisdom and regularly gives us many growth opportunities.

OM monitors our every action and thought, and all attempts at contact are received, but the reply is not always accurately perceived and often missed entirely. Preprogrammed Ego based concepts prevent most OM contact from reaching the Conscious mind. The best and clearest communication is when the Ego is bypassed. If we contact our own OM when the heart and mind are in harmony, using silent moments, prayer, or meditation, we can bypass the protective forces of the Ego. OM can then direct our lives as magnetism directs a compass needle. After gaining access to the Subconscious Control Room of the Unconscious mind-of-the-body, we need sufficient power behind our conscious commands. Without power, we can push buttons in the Control Room all day long, and nothing will happen. It is not always easy to believe in ourselves or something we cannot see, so we use the mind's eye to see and elicit the help of our OM. Learning to communicate with our OM will plug our Control Room into a power beyond our comprehension, easily energizing the bodies amazing ability to accomplish things that might have been previously believed to be impossible.

1.7 Introduction to Stress Management

A stressor is any event, experience, or environmental stimulus that upsets the body's normal equilibrium and requires adaptation. How we perceive, interpret, and label our experiences, both real and imagined, will serve either to relax or to stress us. Distress, or negative stress, occurs when we perceive that the challenge facing us is dangerous, difficult, painful, or unfair, and are concerned that we may lack the resources or capacity to respond. Changes in life situations alone are not enough to cause illness and disease, but when these changes are perceived as distressing, they result in emotional and, subsequently, physiological arousal that can become chronic. Other than trauma, nearly all visits to healthcare providers are related to stress.

Stressful situations are not always harmful. The acute stress that results from a fire alarm or almost being hit by a car is not the kind of stress that has damaging effects. This kind of stress mobilizes our emergency responses and capabilities, but chronic stress is a different story. Researchers have found that our well-being actually improves as stress increases to an optimum level and then drops rapidly to illness and death as the perceived stress becomes chronic or overwhelming. Stress can be a catalyst for progress and inspire us to develop our abilities as we attempt to face it. A world without stressful situations would be as insipid as a life without goals. We seek an optimum amount of stress (because it is impossible, and undesirable, to eliminate all stress) and to create the environment we need, preferably with fewer and less dangerous events. As the world continually throws up challenges and obstacles in our path, our objective is to eliminate the harmful effects of stress while enhancing life's quality and vitality.

We evolved over thousands of years as hunter-gatherers where survival meant hunting, gathering food, and protecting ourselves from wild animals. The stress was tangible and produced concrete fight-or-flight responses involving physical exertion. In a relatively short period of time, these ingrained responses have become inappropriate. The struggles for survival were replaced with unfriendly co-workers, fears of losing a job, loss of computer data, or needing to complete a task in a hurry. We cannot attack or run away because of social conventions, instead we internalize the stress where it causes bigger problems. The biochemical process that occurred in the Stone Age still occurs today. Our bodies are programmed to respond to stress physically, and when repressed, cumulative damage results and in our modern society they are more frequent, intense, and severe than they were in times past. As population density increases, so does crime, mental illness, suicide, and a host of other lifestyle related stressors. We seem to be in high gear and on high alert all the time. How many people are stressed to the screaming edge, living in quiet desperation, where they work long, hard hours at jobs they hate, to enable them to buy things they don't need, to impress people they don't like.

Workload and interpersonal conflicts are talking points while absenteeism, lost productivity, and divorce are common manifestations of Inflexible Perceptions. Heart attacks and strokes are leading causes of premature death in spite of better medical technology, drugs, and emergency services to deal with them. It has been said that just relaxing our grip on the past, letting go of worry, and taking a vigorous five-mile walk will do more good for an unhappy but otherwise healthy adult than all the pills and psychology in the world. Anxiety, stress, and insomnia are some of the most troublesome problems to treat with conventional medicine. The drugs used have many side effects, and most are habit-forming. Fortunately, however, natural remedies provide safe alternatives and are becoming the first treatment choice.

We have much greater control over ourselves than we have ever realized. Managing stress is really just exercising that control rather than giving it up to others, or to the environment. No one can <u>make</u> us angry rather we <u>allow</u> ourselves to be angered. Eleanor Roosevelt said. "No one can make you feel inferior without your consent" and Abraham Lincoln said, "Folks are usually about as happy as they make their minds up to be."

How one reacts to disturbing events is mostly a matter of habit. Habits can be changed but it is far easier to replace them, and that is best achieved by learning to elicit the relaxation response and activate the parasympathetic nervous system. We can do this by practicing yoga, meditation, taking biofeedback training, floating in water, petting a dog or cat, and learning conscious breathing techniques. Whatever method is chosen, it needs to be practiced regularly to alter the usual pattern of sympathetic dominance and allow the parasympathetic nervous system to run things more of the time.

Stress management techniques include time management, goal setting, situation management, sleep therapy, nutrition, exercise, assertiveness training, conflict resolution, and social support networking to name a few. While these are all valuable therapies, they deal with the symptoms of stress without tackling the cause. Most drugs used to treat stress are toxic, habit forming and superficial like disconnecting the oil light when it comes on instead of adding oil or finding the cause. Superficial cures trim the weeds, but the roots continue to grow and return with a vengeance. If we wish to control stress, we need to affect the root cause: Inflexible Perceptions. Some people live to the age of a hundred or more and yet they have rarely exercised; some of them have smoked, drank excessively, and have had unhealthy diets. Other people who live seemingly model lifestyles have prematurely died from heart attacks or some other stress-related disease. The roots may not be obvious, but a successful stress management program needs to reach them.

Most people create a great deal of stress by burdening themselves with unnecessary worries that are based on incorrect assumptions and blame their circumstances and other people for their problems. Actual events and other people are perceived in as many ways as there are people aware of them. Everyone has a different perception of everything, no exceptions. To the extent that we learn to take control of our thoughts and perceptions, stress will be reduced. Taking control begins with awareness, which means shifting control from the automatic preprogrammed reactions of the

Subconscious mind to the Conscious mind and creating new, more appropriate responses.

"If you ask what is the single most important key to longevity, I would have to say it is avoiding worry, stress and tension. And if you don't ask me, I'd still have to say it." George Burns

Revenge, anger, sadness, or any other stressful feeling can be immediately diluted by taking a deep breath. <u>Stop, Smile, Breathe, and say Thank You</u>. Focus on that breath and feel it enter the body. Let it out, and imagine it taking all the negativity with it. (Deeper, Slower, Calmer, Regular) Take another breath and say, "Calm Blue Ocean." Imagine being there, taking in the white sand beach, warm sun, blue sky, fluffy clouds, and calming waves. After doing this, it is easier to come back, face the world more rationally and put things in perspective.

The pursuit of excellence is admirable but perfectionism is a compulsive obsession with unrealistically rigid standards. It is another example of Inflexible Perception involving the setting of uncompromising standards while obsessing over details and facts. It is the death of spontaneity, creativity, and good fun. The resulting stress of such rigid perceptions leads to impaired health, poor self-control, troubled personal relationships, low self-esteem, depression, and anxiety. Until these people learn to relax their mind, body, and perceptions, they will fear and anticipate rejection and will react defensively to criticism creating even more stress. Because of their unreasonably high standards, they are inevitably disappointed with the mistakes of others and react with annoyance and resentment. It is far more important to do the right thing than to do things right.

Some of us tend to catastrophize events in our lives; Dr. Jon Kabat-Zinn called it "Full Catastrophe Living." We have to pass this exam! We must get that job! We have to get there on time! If we were only able to substitute the word <u>want</u> or <u>like</u> for <u>must</u> and <u>have</u>, we would experience less stress, and we would perceive situations more realistically. Replacing Inflexible Perceptions with plasticity helps us realize that life is not an emergency. It is a fun adventure of curiosity and wonder.

A sense of humor is invaluable, and a good laugh is one of the best ways to relieve stress and tension. Because these moments are quickly forgotten and often lost forever, it is helpful to make a list of the things that make us laugh. Then adding to it whenever a new joke or situation brings on laughter provides a menu of mood enhancing thoughts to recall in times of distress.

We have determined that the root of all stress is Inflexible Perception and when we learn to control our perceptions and adapt to situations, all other aspects of stress management such as time management, assertiveness, conflicts, and social problems, etc. will all fall in place as an integral part of healthy perceptions. There have been hundreds of books written about stress management and many about time management alone but when our perceptions are managed, time management simply becomes a matter of prioritizing and learning to say "No" politely. Conflict resolution becomes a matter of adaptation, and diet, exercise, and sound sleep are just a part of the person we become. We just feel more like learning about healthy habits.

The very essence of stress management requires confidence in one's self and a decision to control life effectively. A successful stress management program needs to evoke a calm desire for independence, control of one's own destiny, and an openness to new habits and beliefs; plasticity of perception and adaptation. While a boss, job, colleague, or situation, may seem to be the cause of stress, the quickest way to work toward a solution is to recognize that they are only the visible part of the problem. We need to accept responsibility for the solution. We need to perceive events as less stressful and choose responses that are healthier and more life-enhancing. It is futile to tell a stressed-out person to quit working so hard when the bill collectors are calling but when they Stop, Smile, Breathe, and adopt a grateful, open attitude, viable solutions seem to appear out of nowhere.

No one is immune to the crises of life. Crises provoke uncertainty and are characterized by periods of disagreement, internal confrontation, and personal transition. Those who are more effective in dealing with such incidents use the experience to propel themselves forward rather than hold themselves back. They see crisis as an opportunity for growth. Those people who are less successful in dealing with a crisis agonize over the stressful experience, continue to relive it after it is over, feel bitter, and refuse to evaluate their attitudes and behaviors. They are too busy, too tense, lack a sense of humor, and think they do not have time for relaxation. They find it difficult to let it go, like many war victims who let their experience haunt them for the rest of their lives. The cost of being negative and inflexible is high. Rain falls on the good, the bad, and the in-between and is not indicative of divine judgment. The successful accept the present and adapt while focusing on the opportunities, change the trauma from a stumbling block to a building block, and transition from surviving to thriving.

Some people seem to be able to alter the nature of their work and personal lives by changing schedules, rearranging tasks, and offering suggestions for improving things. They do these things naturally because they have learned to accept and adapt to their circumstances. They understand that they cannot change anything unless they first accept it as it is. Adapting often entails letting go of Inflexible Perceptions and replacing them with more appropriate, life-enhancing views and attitudes. When we learn to accept and adapt, we can recognize problems without wallowing in self-pity.

1.7.1 Seven Stages of Adversity

There is no evil greater than anger and no virtue greater than Patience. But Patience takes practice, so we are grateful for every opportunity to practice. When someone harms, frustrates, annoys, rejects, or embarrasses us, we immediately imagine a Big Red Smiling Stop Sign. We Stop, Smile, Breathe, and say, "Thank you, Thank you, Thank you," as a sincere expression of Gratitude for the opportunity to practice Patience, Kindness, and our right to choose the thoughts upon which to focus. We say Thank You silently, or audibly if appropriate, at least once and preferably three times because anything one wants to remember or emphasize should be stated three times. A name, place, concept or idea presented in threes is inherently more interesting, significant, and memorable.

We Recognize, Neutralize, Dismiss, and Replace anger, fear, guilt, worry, sadness, shame, and other harmful thoughts with Gratitude, Patience, and Kindness, knowing that something good will come of this. We are Grateful that it was not worse and feel Compassion for those who are worse off. We begin to understand the powerful connection between thought, feeling, and behavior. We discover that we can choose our feelings, and thus our behavior, by choosing to focus on more appropriate thoughts. Just as emotions trigger thoughts, thoughts trigger emotions. It is impossible to feel sad without spending time with sad thoughts, or angry without dwelling on angry thoughts, so we consciously replace harmful thoughts with Gratitude or some other worthy thought to reverse the cycle. We feel Gratitude and Compassion for our tormentors because they have been valuable teachers and are inflicted with the disease of anger, harming themselves most of all. We accept the situation for what it is and adapt to the present moment with Patient positive thoughts, wisdom, and curiosity. We ask if the problem can be resolved, and look for opportunity. Then, with a calm, peaceful mind, we allow our own natural wisdom to determine the best course of action. We remain balanced and centered, happy and at peace, with a sincere intent to promote harmony and the understanding that everything is and was as it should be. (Some have expressed confusion over the word "should" in the previous sentence. It simply implies that everything might be "as it is and was" to provide us with the opportunity to make it better.) Harmony is the ultimate objective of all pursuits and life is a fun adventure of curiosity and wonder.

The seven stages of adversity are:

1) Situation or event.

2) Stop, Smile, Breathe, and say, "Thank you, Thank you, Thank you," as a sincere expression of Gratitude for the opportunity to practice Patience, Kindness, and our right to choose the thoughts upon which to focus.

3) Recognize, Neutralize, Dismiss, and Replace harmful thoughts with Gratitude, Patience, and Kindness, knowing that something good will come of this. Be Grateful that it was not worse and feel Compassion for those who are worse off.

4) Accept and adapt to the present moment with Patient positive thought, wisdom, and curiosity.

5) Ask if the problem can be resolved, and look for opportunity.

6) With a calm, peaceful mind, we allow our own natural wisdom to determine the best course of action.

7) Remain balanced and centered, happy and at peace, with a sincere intent to promote Harmony.

As one student said, "It is possible to be grateful to everyone and for everything, but it takes practice. It often helps to ask myself what I am most grateful for right now; after I Stop, Smile, Breathe, and say Thank You, of course. I like harmony. It makes me feel better, and anger does not."

People who have acquired the ability to Stop, Smile, Breathe, and say Thank You in the face of a stressor, create the opportunity to rationally select the most appropriate responses rather than reflexively reacting. The pause gives us the opportunity to consciously consider the nature of the threat, weigh the consequences of various possible reactions, and then act appropriately for greatest effect.

Scientific research agrees that smiling relaxes muscles throughout the body and has the same effect on the nervous system as real joy. Every human being emanates an energy field that corresponds to their own inner state, and most people can sense it; animals have an even better sense of that energy. When we smile at a stranger, we become a giver, and there is a noticeable outflow of energy. Besides, smiling people are better looking, less threatening, and a smile encourages others to relax and do the same.

When stress strikes, our first thought should be STOP! We visualize a Big Red Smiling Stop Sign. It is a conscious break between the stimuli and an often inappropriate, obsolete, automatic reaction from the Subconscious mind. When in trouble, or in doubt, it seldom helps to run in circles, scream, or shout. We STOP just for a second to disconnect from mindless reactions and remember what is really important. When conflicts arise with a spouse or family member, it is especially important to remember that love is in the pause. The greater the pause, the greater the love.

Our second thought should be, Smile! That does not mean we should break out in laughter when threatened, but a slight smile projects confidence and control, triggers happy hormones, and is where we really want to be anyway. Smiles are contagious, and if we smile and greet everyone warmly, the world will seem far friendlier. Just as feelings trigger physical responses, physical responses can trigger feelings. A smile will trigger positive hormones and feelings, and positive feelings trigger positive thoughts. Successful people often use the tactic, "Fake it until you make it."

Our third thought should be, Breathe! When stressed, we often forget to breathe, and when we finally do start breathing, it is shallow, rapid, tense, and irregular. We choose to consciously breathe because it stimulates calm, keeps us grounded, and supplies the urgently needed oxygen. When we concentrate on our breath, it generates awareness in the present moment, and we are better able to regain our bearings. We take a deeper, slower breath and silently say or think "ahhhhhh" making it a real letting go kind of breath and then say Thank You to shift our attention from the storm to an attitude of gratitude. Instead of shallow, rapid, tense, and irregular breathing, we consciously think, in-Deeper, out-Slower, in-Calmer, out-Regular (DSCR). That simple breathing technique has been shown to sharply reduce and even eliminate the negative effects of stress including anxiety and panic attacks.

We say, or at least think, the words Thank You as a sincere expression of Gratitude for the opportunity to practice Patience, Kindness, and our right to choose the thoughts upon which to focus. Other people and circumstances do not choose our thoughts; we do. In the face of stress, saying or just thinking Thank You can trigger the response, "For what!?" and the answers lead directly to gratitude and opportunity. In the space of a few seconds, we have gone from a stressed, shocked, and an out of balance victim to an aware, in control, positive problem solver looking for opportunity, confident that something good will come of the situation. We are thankful for what we have and our ability to seek solutions.

Painful situations are a part of life, but our perception of these situations will make all the difference. Holding on to painful memories, fear, and heartache can dramatically affect the mind/body and lead to dysfunctional relationships, depression, stress, and disease. We need to be aware of them and replace them: Recognize, Neutralize, Dismiss, and Replace.

Anxiety has been defined as an unrealistic fear resulting in physiological arousal accompanied by behavioral signs of escape or avoidance. A form of anxiety known as panic disorder is a feeling of terror that strikes suddenly and repeatedly with no warning. It is characterized by a pounding heart, feeling sweaty, weak, faint or dizzy, nausea, chest pain or a smothering sensation. A sense of impending doom and loss of control can lead one to believe they are having a heart attack. Even though most victims know that it is an irrational fear, that it generally peaks within ten minutes, and that no one has ever died from a panic attack, they feel like they are losing their mind or on the verge of death. As with all other forms of stress, these feelings are a direct result of Inflexible Perceptions and are best managed with relaxation techniques and cognitive restructuring. That means replacing harmful thoughts and emotions by visualizing a Big Red Smiling Stop Sign. They Stop, Smile, Breathe, and say Thank You. Instead of panicking over a panic attack, one can recognize it, be mindful of it, replace it with gratitude and look for opportunity. If they focus on the body and relaxation techniques, things will return to normal soon. Deep breaths can counteract the panic since a panicked state is characterized by quick, shallow breaths.

As one student who suffered from panic attacks put it, "I figure, the next time it happens, if I'm going to die, I might as well die with a smile on my face and a Big Red Stop Sign in my head while practicing my (DSCR) Breath." Those who master the "Stop, Smile, Breathe, and say Thank You" technique suddenly seem more confident and assertive even in negative social situations. Eventually, they begin to notice that life no longer has the same power over them that it once did and that they have moments of deep peace and tranquility. It becomes difficult to be stressed if one is thinking only about the present moment. Stress and anxiety come from reliving unpleasant memories, or imagining unpleasant things that have not happened yet and probably never will. When we stay in the present moment, mental relaxation is there for the taking. Now has no room for past or future, guilt or worry.

We are all free to choose what to think and on what to focus, but we often fail to exercise our inherent control over our thoughts and allow them to sail the turbulent seas without a rudder. We have been programmed to be critical rather than supportive and focus on what's wrong rather than what's right. There is no positive without negative, no high without low, and no good without bad. Each must exist to define the other. If focused on the negative, one has less time to notice the positive and a negative bias is the result. If focused on the good, one is less affected by the bad and a positive bias prevails. Negative still exists, in fact, it is essential to maintain balance, but is of little to no concern. When scary things happen on the news, it is helpful to look for the helpers. There are always people who are helping.

When we realize that every situation has good and bad, positive and negative elements, we can redefine a long line at the supermarket from an annoying waste of time to an opportunity to practice patience, awareness, breathing techniques, or study people. Unlike other species, humans have the ability to choose how they perceive situations. Physiologically, we can choose to raise our blood pressure, serum cholesterol, heart rate, and muscle tension, or we can choose to smile, breathe, and be healthier.

1.8 Summary

In Part I, we explained our title, what the book is about, its benefits to the reader, and our purpose or intent in writing the book. We explored the reality of adversity, its cause and cure, and introduced Medimaginosis, how it works, and redefined POSSIBLE. We discussed the relationship between science and spirituality, how they actually support one another, and how both are used to begin our evolution from stress to gratitude, perfect health, happiness, vitality, longevity, and harmony. An introduction to Stress Management provided some insight, perspective, and a simple exercise that works. We end Part I with an Action Assignment and a visual to aid the practice.

In Part II, we will continue our stress management discussion, explore the power of breath control, and learn how it relates to control of the mind/body and eventually gene function. We will learn how simple meditation can focus and enhance that power, and how to practice a basic, no-nonsense meditation session.

1.9 Action Assignment

* Practice the Deeper, Slower, Calmer, Regular breathing technique at every opportunity. Focus on the breath and think: IN – Deeper, OUT – Slower, IN – Calmer, OUT – Regular

* Study the "Seven Stages of Adversity" and eventually commit it to memory:

1) Situation or event.

2) Stop, Smile, Breathe, and say, "Thank you, Thank you, Thank you," as a sincere expression of Gratitude for the opportunity to practice Patience, Kindness, and our right to choose the thoughts upon which to focus.

3) Recognize, Neutralize, Dismiss, and Replace harmful thoughts with Gratitude, Patience, and Kindness, knowing that something good will come of this. Be Grateful that it was not worse and feel Compassion for those who are worse off.

4) Accept and adapt to the present moment with Patient positive thought, wisdom, and curiosity.

5) Ask if the problem can be resolved, and look for opportunity.

6) With a calm, peaceful mind, we allow our own natural wisdom to determine the best course of action.

7) Remain balanced and centered, happy and at peace, with a sincere intent to promote Harmony.

1) Situation or Event

Smile

Breathe

IN-Deeper
OUT-Slower
IN-Calmer
OUT-Regular

Thank you, Thank you, Thank you

3) Recognize, Neutralize, Dismiss, and Replace

4) Accept and Adapt

5) Look for Opportunity

6) Calm, Peaceful, Mind

7) Balanced and Centered, Happy and at Peace

PART II

Control the Breath
and the Mind/Body will Follow

2.1 Taming the Dragons

We have determined that the mother of all the great evil dragons of chronic stress is not our circumstances, it is our perception of them and our resistance to adaptation: Inflexible Perception. In Part II we will explore proven cognitive adaptations and techniques, Dr. Herbert Bensons Relaxation Response, and the incredible facets of breath and meditation.

The journey from an unhealthy, stressed mind and body to gratitude, peace of mind, and control over the mind/body and gene expression is truly a major advance in our evolution. However, taken one step at a time, it is simple, easy, and enjoyable. It is a bit like walking through a beautiful six level garden to get home after being lost in the desert. When we get to the top of the Stairway to Harmony and look back, we wonder why we didn't see it before. It is simply the practice of perception plasticity and the ability to accept and adapt to circumstances. From the bottom of the stairway, however, the ultimate objective cannot be seen or even easily imagined, like not being able to see the beautiful meadow and sweet water brook beyond the great forest. *Imagine Harmony* points the direction so all we need to do is take it one step at a time and as we get closer, the view will become clearer.

As we learned in Part I, the key to happiness does not depend on other people or events, but on how we perceive and respond to them. As the

Buddhists say, suffering is wanting what we do not have and not wanting what we do have, while happiness is precisely the opposite: enjoying what we have and not complaining about or being obsessed with what we do not have. This concept does not mean that we need to give up our values, dreams, and aspirations, only that we need to balance them with the ability to accept things as they are. Then, with a calm, peaceful mind, look for opportunity and allow our own natural wisdom to determine the best course of action. In all situations, we have at least three options. We can change those things that are within our control to reduce the sources of stress, change our attitudes and physiologic responses to those things that are beyond our control, or let them be and move on.

Learning to manage stress, one's own thoughts, body, and gene expression begins with learning to manage the breath. The breath is the only function that can be completely voluntary and conscious or completely involuntary and unconscious. It is the bridge between mind and body, voluntary and involuntary: the connection between the Conscious mind and the Subconscious Control Room of the Unconscious mind-of-the-body. It is the doorway to control of the autonomic nervous system, and can harmonize the influence that the mind has on the body. It is a function we can learn to regulate and develop in order to improve our physical, mental and spiritual well-being.

The breath is controlled by two sets of nerves, one belonging to the voluntary nervous system, and the other to the involuntary (autonomic) nervous system. We can consciously establish rhythms of breathing with our voluntary nerves and muscles that will affect the involuntary nervous system. Learning to breathe, focus, and control our awareness leads to greater calm. Our death grip on the irrelevant will soften, and perceptions become more pliable. Plasticity of Perception allows the wisdom of the OM, creativity, and adaptability into our circumstances and events.

Mastering conscious breath control and a few simple techniques have been found to be the most time-efficient, cost-effective path to increased wellness and optimal health. It increases relaxation and reduces stress by taking advantage of the mind/body connection and affecting both physical and mental health. It offers the possibility of using the Conscious mind and voluntary nerves to modify the Unconscious mind and involuntary nerves, including the balance between sympathetic and parasympathetic activity. The results are long lasting and get better over time, have none of the toxicity associated with pharmaceutical drugs, and do not work in suppressive or counteractive ways.

2.1.1 Slow Down, Simplify, Be Grateful, Patient, and Kind

When we feel ourselves on the verge of being overwhelmed, the "Stop, Smile, Breathe, and say Thank You" response is most important. It is used when we feel a sudden increase in our stress level, but what about the cumulative effects of constant pressure, frustration, annoyances, and embarrassments. Everyday events perceived as hassles have been shown to be cumulative and are even more detrimental to health than a major life change or natural disaster. They are more likely to produce poor mental and physical health, psychological distress and accelerated aging than most major life events because of how frequently they occur. Multitasking and a busy demanding lifestyle can lead to a spinning out of control where too much energy is wasted, and little or nothing gets done well.

When we put the words "Slow down, Simplify, and Be Grateful, Patient, and Kind" at the top of our daily do-list under a one-word reminder of our ultimate objective and current intermediate goal, we tend to put the most important tasks at the top of the list and do them in order. After making the list, we read it again and eliminate the items that don't really need to be there. At the end of the day, if we have not finished the list, at least we know that we have been working on the most important tasks with our full attention and capacity. We waste less time jumping from one unfinished task to another and actually get more done as a result of greater focus and awareness. Quality is vastly improved because we have learned to give our full attention to the task at hand rather than haphazardly pacifying it in order to get on to other tasks that also receive the same superficial attention.

1) SLOW DOWN is the first item on the list because it reminds us to be present. Simply by slowing down, it is possible to orchestrate meaningful moments and to be present in those moments as opposed to completely losing touch with life like finding one's self at work and not remembering the drive. When families slow down, turn off their machines, consume less sugar, and talk to each other, wonderful things happen: children feel more secure, become calmer, more peaceful, and families have more good moments.

It is good to know that we can go fast if we need to but getting stuck in high gear is not only dangerous to our health, it facilitates mistakes and logarithmically increases the likelihood of a catastrophic spin out of control. With more mistakes, quality suffers and often requires a redo that eliminates any time savings gained by speed. In short, haste makes waste. When we allow ourselves to get caught up in the mindless whirlwind that our busy world often becomes, we lose connection with one another and ourselves.

Unless we slow down and consciously pay attention to the present moment, we can find ourselves engaged in multiple tasks without even realizing it. Surfing the web while talking on the phone and eating is a typical example. Whatever we are doing at the moment, we need to consciously perform that task mindfully and with awareness as much as we can. We slow it down enough to notice our breathing from time to time and focus on doing the task at hand well, whether it is thinking, typing on a keyboard, surfing the Internet, completing an errand, eating, or cleaning the house. Korean Zen Master Seung Sahn liked to tell his students, "When reading, only read. When eating, only eat. When thinking, only think."

Those who mindfully slow down, usually get more done and live longer. Who won the real race between the tortoise and the hare? According to Dr. Bob's "The Life Span of Animals" chart, the American Box Turtle can be expected to live 123 years while the Hare gets only ten years at best. It is better to concentrate on one thing at a time and do it well than to do many things haphazardly. Research has shown that when multitasking, each shift from one task to the next requires a reboot time like waking up in the morning. The time it takes to shift and refocus on the new task is minimal but multiplied by the number of shifts, it adds up and all that time is wasted. And before we have time to get into the new task completely, we too often switch again. Multitasking never really allows us to get deeply involved in any task. Even a dull job can be made interesting by focusing on it and trying to do it well. Doing one thing well is more important than doing many things adequately.

The Conscious mind can hold only one thought at a time, and those who are proud of their ability to multitask might be well advised to do the following exercise: Write the numbers one through ten on a piece of paper in reverse order three times as fast as possible and time it. Then simultaneously sing the "Happy Birthday" song out loud while again writing the numbers one through ten in reverse order three times as fast as possible; and again note the time. Neither task is done well. The Conscious mind can rapidly switch from one task to another and make it seem like we are holding more than one thought at a time but with each switch, there is a time lag as each concept needs to boot up again. This fragments attention, reduces quality, facilitates errors, and is seldom enjoyable.

Slowing down means avoiding extremes and seeking the middle way; everything in moderation; temperance in all things; not too much and not too little. When we take that "in the middle" mentality and apply it to other tasks by <u>consciously</u> doing them more slowly and deliberately, we realize that this scurrying around is usually a great mistake. From center court, we have greater control and flexibility. The middle way facilitates harmony and moderation. It leaves room to maneuver right or left, up or down, more or less, without radical changes that enable spin-outs.

Even driving in heavy traffic can be almost stress-free if we move into the center lane on the freeway, go with the flow, and pay more attention to all that is going on around us. There is no more worrying about having to pass cars, and no one is impatiently riding our bumper. Those people just move to the fast lane and arrive at their destination a few seconds sooner. We might ask these people what they plan to do with the two minutes they gained and whether it was worth the increased stress level and risk of an accident. No hurry. No worry. We do what we do to make us happy and when it's not, we don't.

We need to slow down and allow the senses to come alive and smell the roses. Enjoy the softness of a pet's fur, the warmth of a hug, the laughter of a happy grateful child, the delicious aroma of a holiday dinner baking in the oven, the freshness of the air after a rain shower, the pleasing harmony of the songbirds early in the morning, and the elegant beauty of a flower. We should never be so busy that these wonderful moments pass us by unnoticed.

2) <u>SIMPLIFY</u> is the second item on the list and is a reminder to organize and lose the clutter. Most of us have more stuff, obligations, priorities, people and mental clutter than we need to perform optimally. Getting rid of the excess in life makes it easier to focus on the things that are most important. As an addendum to the all-important "Daily Do List," it helps to make a list of minor little annoyances like a squeaky door or a difficult phone call that

needs to be made but never seems to make it to the top of the "Do List." Then vow to resolve at least one each day.

Clutter blocks our view and clogs the mind with <u>material</u>, <u>emotional</u>, and <u>spiritual</u> junk. Much of it has little or nothing to do with our ultimate objective or even our intermediate goals. We just keep taking on more and more responsibility because we fear others will think ill of us if we do not accept greater burdens. It has been said that it is better to let people wonder what our limits are than to take on more than we can handle and show them. We just need to learn to say, "No" politely and delegate. It starts with gratitude and trust, and ends up showing character. "Thank you for thinking of me but I have a previous commitment, and it's important for me to keep my promises." Or, "I would love too, but I'm already booked, perhaps another time."

<u>Material</u> clutter ranges from a messy desk to a closet, office, home or garage full of useless stuff that weighs us down, impedes our progress, and symbolizes obstacles and burdens. Some try to justify living with clutter by contending that they "might need it someday" but that is as foolish as keeping a mechanic in the closet because the car might need to be repaired someday. Heaps and jumbles of stuff that are not making us happy need to be thrown away or donated to charity. Giving makes people feel better, and it is tax deductible. They are just things, but when cleared out, we suddenly feel like taking a deep breath and have a sense of accomplishment. Ideally, everything we own should either be genuinely useful or something that we love. Anything else is just getting in the way. Let the mechanic go, and IF the car breaks down, just be prepared to make a phone call.

<u>Emotional</u> clutter is attachment to people, places, events, and expectation that keep us wallowing around in the past and feeling bad. Just as a driver will occasionally glance back in the rearview mirror to expand awareness, glancing back at our successes can be constructive, but we cannot drive a car with our eyes on the rearview mirror for long periods of time. If it is not making us happy, we let it go. Forgive. Now is good.

<u>Spiritual</u> clutter is one or more beliefs that cause worry, guilt, and suffering. They are burdens that we need to let go. Most religions have a pretty simple, reassuring central theme of gratitude, patience, and kindness upon which one can focus. Alternatively, the Principles of Harmony discussed in Part III will provide a simple, ground roots foundation of spiritual energy

worthy of one's focus. Albert Einstein said, "Out of clutter, find simplicity. From discord, make harmony, In the middle of difficulty, lies opportunity."

Vacation is a scary word for some uptight workaholics because they fear falling behind, being replaced or losing control, but it actually makes people more effective. Unplug and spend a weekend living the way people did a hundred years ago. Turn off all the machines, read books, play games, take a walk, or just sit and visit. Returning from a vacation (even a meditative mini vacation of 30 seconds or a short breathing exercise) often facilitates a fresh new perspective and greater focus. By simply turning off technology and living in the present for a weekend, we can make time for the simple things and recharge our batteries. Research shows that what adults remember with the greatest happiness from their own childhoods are vacations, time outdoors, and family meals.

Another way to simplify and release stress is to write about it. Studies have shown that people who write about their emotions can read it later and see the problem without the clutter. They are calmer and can more easily Recognize, Neutralize, Dismiss, and Replace harmful thoughts without having to go over and over the same disassociated negative thoughts. Then they can put it away, throw it in the trash, or burn it and forget about it.

The words "Be Grateful, Patient, and Kind" could have been simply, "Be Happy" because, when integrated, they are synonymous. All three need to merge and work as one to unlock the state of happiness as symbolized in the Key 2 Happiness, but each virtue is a powerful force in itself. It is also important to remember that happiness is not a place so we cannot go there, but we can BE there, and it is not a condition, it is a choice.

3) GRATITUDE is that part of the Key 2 Happiness that provides the leverage to turn the lock. A growing body of research suggests that giving thanks is good for our health. Maintaining an attitude of gratitude is a powerful antidote to virtually all stress, unhappiness, and frustration and can improve psychological, emotional, and physical well-being. The lack of gratitude is one of the biggest barriers we as a civilization face on our path to happiness and harmony. We need to spend more time being grateful for what we have and less time grasping or pining over the things we do not have. Advertisers constantly remind us of all the things we do not have and absolutely cannot do without while ignoring the fact that it is probably more than an evolutionary accident that mankind has survived for millennia without these things. Peace of mind lies not in our circumstances, but in how we respond to them. Not getting what we want can sometimes be a stroke of luck and if we can find a way to be thankful for our troubles, they can become blessings.

Being grateful also forces people to overcome what psychologists call the "negativity bias" or the innate tendency to dwell on problems, annoyances, and injustices rather than upbeat events. Focusing on blessings can help ward off depression and build resilience in times of stress, grief or disasters. There are grateful people, and there are depressed people, but there are no truly grateful, depressed people.

Both ancient teachings and modern medical researchers agree that one of the quickest, most direct routes to restoring harmony and balance in our lives is to foster gratitude and appreciation. The moment we shift from a mind state of negativity or judgment to one of appreciation, there are immediate effects at many levels of our being: brain function becomes more balanced, harmonized, and supple; heart begins to pump in a much more coherent and harmonious rhythm; and biochemical changes trigger a host of healthy balancing reactions throughout the body.

Humans, especially children, cannot be happy unless they learn to feel gratitude. Young children have a natural affinity to gratitude, but as they get older, the give and take of life can be driven by expectations if we do not reinforce an attitude of gratitude toward life. Kids who feel and act grateful tend to be less materialistic, get better grades, set higher goals, complain of fewer headaches and stomach aches, choose better friends, and feel more secure and satisfied with their family, school, and activities than those who do not. Children, as well as adults, can choose how they feel and how they look at the world. When children are thanked for doing something they should do like cleaning their room, it reinforces and internalizes the idea often causing them to continue to do it on their own (as long as it is sincere and not overdone). To help lay the groundwork for gratefulness in our children, each night just before bed, we can ask them to talk about their favorite thing about the day and what they are looking forward to tomorrow.

Adults who frequently feel grateful have more energy, more optimism, more social connections and more happiness than those who do not. They earn more money, sleep more soundly, are more physically active, and have greater resistance to viral infections. Numerous studies suggest that grateful people have higher levels of subjective well-being, cope better with a life transition, and are more satisfied with their lives and social relationships. They are less stressed, are seldom depressed, and have higher levels of control of their environments, personal growth, and a purpose in life.

When we focus on the good stuff in our lives, we discover a greater capacity for generosity, cheerfulness, and contentment. Experiencing and expressing gratitude opens the heart and activates positive emotion centers in the brain. It can open us to life more deeply and connect us more intimately with each other. Gratitude strengthens the immune system, lowers blood pressure, encourages us to take better care of our health, and reduces aches, pains, and symptoms of illness. It is often helpful to spend a moment or two contemplating the question, "For what am I most grateful now?"

4) PATIENCE is an equal partner with gratitude and kindness in the quest to unlock the gate to happiness, joy, peace, and harmony. Patience is the ability to control one's emotions even when being criticized or attacked and refers to the character trait of being steadfast. It often involves trust, reflects the state of one's mind/body, and is a mental skill that one will never forget. Dr. Jon Kabat-Zinn has said that patience is a form of wisdom because it demonstrates an understanding and acceptance of the fact that

sometimes things need to unfold in their own time. Some things just should not be rushed.

We tend to lose our patience when we are on a tight schedule or trying to multitask. Impatience creeps in insidiously, often manifesting anxiety, worry, or unhappiness without our even realizing it. It is one of those things that we need to Recognize, Neutralize, Dismiss, and Replace. Recognizing (or being aware of) impatience gives us a chance to learn from it and the realization that we have the power to pause, breathe, and replace it. Life is not a race to death, it is a fun adventure experienced in the present moment, the Now, with curiosity and wonder.

The best things in life usually require time and dedication, and if we are impatient, we are more likely to give up on relationships, goals, and other things that are important. Good things may not always come to those who wait, but most good things that do come, do not happen right away. Some of our happiest memories are of times when patience paid off, like a long term goal finally realized, a long-awaited vacation, or a little extra time to spend leisurely with a loved one.

Patience might be easier to maintain if babies didn't cry, dishes didn't break, computers didn't crash, and people didn't make mistakes, but that is never going to happen. We need to expect the unexpected and accept the twists and turns in life with adaptability. This applies not only to events but also the behavior of those around us. Those who get upset over minor things are not in touch with the fact that nobody's perfect. Making a concerted effort to be more patient in relatively inconsequential short-term situations will gradually develop the strength to remain patient in even the most trying and enduring situations. Even if the occasion is not an isolated incident but is instead caused by repeated neglect and carelessness, losing one's patience is not going to make it any better.

Patience often involves the choice of either a small reward in the short term or a more valuable reward in the long term. When given a choice, all animals, humans included, are inclined to favor short-term rewards over long-term rewards. This is despite the often greater benefits associated with long term rewards. In the long run, developing patience requires a change in attitude about life, but one can immediately make progress by learning to relax and engage the Conscious mind when first feeling impatient. Those who practice patience reap great rewards, and Medimaginosis is the perfect venue.

Patience is necessary for an ethical life and one's long-term happiness, even if it is sometimes difficult in the short term. When impatience is triggered by an event beyond our control, we need to learn to let it go and focus on more appropriate thoughts. It may not always be easy to remember to do that, but it is the only healthy thing to do. "The patient man shows much good sense, but the quick-tempered man displays folly at its height" (Torah Proverbs 14:29, NAB)

5) KINDNESS is the last item on the Key 2 Happiness but is by no means least. Of all the laws, rules and regulations of mankind, we only need one: Be Kind. All the others are just elaborations in varying degrees of complexity. Kindness is the foundation of our humanity, and such things as love, respect, and compassion for others are kindness ennobled. Kindness means sharing happiness, respect, and never laughing at another person's dream. Kindness means empathy, encouragement, understanding, concern, sincerity, and trust. It has been said that one can conquer a man who never gives by giving; subdue untruthful men by truthfulness; vanquish an angry man by gentleness; and overcome the evil man by kindness.

Kindness is defined as the practice, quality or act of being good, pleasant, friendly, generous, and warm-hearted in nature; facilitating the comfort of others. Kindness is a universal language that, according to Mark Twain, the deaf can hear, and the blind can see. It is a language that all major religions teach, is understood by all life forms, instills positive feelings, and makes this world a better place to live. Lao Tzu said, "Kindness in words creates confidence, kindness in thinking creates profoundness, and kindness in giving creates love."

Just as uncooperative behavior can spread and persist, kindness is contagious. When we see someone help another it gives us a good feeling, which in turn often causes us to do something altruistic as well. Research has shown that a single act of kindness extended by a human being toward another, results in a significant improvement in the functioning of the immune system and increased production of serotonin in the recipient of the kindness, the person extending the kindness, and persons observing the act of kindness. (Serotonin is a naturally occurring neurotransmitter that works like antidepressants and makes us feel light, happy, and at ease. It serves as a pathway for pleasure in the brain and has a calming, mood-regulating, and anti-anxiety effect.) Research on the viral nature of kindness has shown that an act of kindness toward one person will cause that person to be kind to four other people, those four people will be kind to four more people, and so on. The general consensus among researchers in this arena is that humans are hard-wired to cooperate with one another. Human kindness is inherent, is our fundamental strength, and will determine the fate of our species.

An act of kindness is inherently heartwarming, but there is something even more magical about doing something nice for someone and telling no one about it, not even the dog. It is a boost to our self-esteem when we know, deep inside, that we are nicer than other people think we are and not the other way around. It is better to know we are kinder than we say we are than to say we are kinder than we know we are. We always feel good when we do something nice for someone but telling someone else about it is a secret attempt to gain approval. Telling others how nice we are feeds our ego but dilutes the positive feeling. The warm feeling we get for giving without expecting anything in return has more psychophysiological benefits than most people realize.

Scientific research has found convincing evidence that not only does being kind help make the world a better place, it also offers significant health benefits, reverses feelings of depression and provides a sense of social connection. Social support does not depend on the number of people one is associated with but rather the quality of their relationship. One of the most significant things we can do to become happier and healthier is to improve the quality of our friendships and relationships. Performing kind acts enhances feelings of joyfulness, optimism, emotional resilience, self-worth, and vitality. It is often accompanied by a rush of euphoria, followed by longer and longer periods of calmness and serenity involving physical sensations and the release of endorphins (the body's natural painkillers) sometimes referred to as a warm fuzzy. The health benefits and sense of well-being can last for hours or even days whenever the act is recalled and, if practiced regularly, can produce a more permanent sense of increased well-being. Stress-related health problems subside, attitudes that damage the body (including chronic hostility) are reduced and we feel emotions that strengthen the immune system.

As children, we learned, "Sticks and stones can break my bones, but words can never hurt me." And it's true for those who have learned that they are only words and thoughts like "fat" or "stupid," and that we have the ability to dismiss these thoughts and replace them with better thoughts. But for many others, harsh words that trigger bad thoughts can cause a wound that festers for years and the pain can last a lifetime, while broken bones heal. People might forget the exact words but not how they made them feel. Until everyone learns to Recognize, Neutralize, Dismiss, and Replace unkind words and thoughts, it is good to put all words through three filters before passing over the lips: 1) Is it true? 2) Is it necessary? 3) Is it kind? If one is unable to say something nice, say nothing at all.

Some people have trouble falling asleep because they still feel embarrassed about something that happened that day or are worried about something over which they have no control. We suggest that they start doing something nice for someone every day, tell no one about it, and think about how they feel about that at bed time. Then if sleep is still elusive, plan a good deed for tomorrow and go to bed with that deed in mind. Such thoughts have been linked to sounder sleep and better dreams.

Unexpected kindness is one of the most powerful, least costly, natural and effective agents of social change. Just one act of kindness can turn the tide of another person's life and when practiced regularly, can add years to one's life. We all have the power to make someone feel better and everyone involved benefits. Kindness in the simplest sense is a silent smile and the more we practice it, the easier it becomes. No one needs a smile as much as the person who has none to give. There are hundreds of languages in the world but a warm smile speaks them all. It costs nothing but gives much, enriching those who receive as well as those who give and is the universal language of kindness. Smile at strangers, especially those who are having a bad day, volunteer to help wherever there is a need, write a note to let someone know they are appreciated, give a compliment, write an unexpected thank you note, yield the right-of-way, let someone pass or cut in line. Being kind to one's self and forgiving trivial mistakes is equally important and it's good to remember that it is better to be KIND and happy than to be RIGHT and miserable.

The solution to over stimulation of the sympathetic nervous system or inappropriate activation of our fight-or-flight response is simple: for a sudden increase in stress level we visualize a Big Red Smiling Stop Sign, Stop, Smile, Breathe, and say Thank You; and for heading off the cumulative effects of stress we Slow down, Simplify, and Be Grateful, Patient, and Kind.

2.2 **The Dynamism of Breath**

Breath has a direct connection to emotional states and moods. When anxious, angry, afraid, or upset our breathing is rapid, shallow, tense, and irregular but when we are calm and in control, our breathing is deeper, slower, calmer, and more regular. Breath is one autonomic function that most people already agree we can control with the Conscious mind. We cannot always center ourselves emotionally by an act of will, but when we use our voluntary nerves to make our breathing Deeper, Slower, Calmer, and Regular, everything else will follow. It is easier to consciously regulate our breathing than to will a mood change.

The respiratory system can be either completely voluntary or completely involuntary and is an intermediary between the mind and body. It opens a direct line of communication between the Conscious mind and the subconscious involuntary nervous system. Conscious breath control can be used to accelerate healing, reduce pain, center the mind, control anxiety, and regulate mental states. It is the beginning of conscious control of the autonomic nervous system, and because air intake is essential for life, the brain responds to the respiratory system with urgency. It is a place where we can begin to plug into our nervous system and control its overall function and balance. It is free, easy to use, free of the toxicity normally associated with pharmaceutical drugs, requires no equipment, and is a tool we always have with us. Conscious regulation of breath is the most efficient and effective relaxation technique available.

In many languages, the words for spirit, life energy, and breath are one and the same. The Sanskrit word is *prana*, in Hebrew it is *ruach*, in Greek it is *pneuma*, and in Latin it is *spiritus.* Related words are *respiration* and *inspire* noting that the opposite of inspire is expire or death. It has been said that breathing is the movement of spirit in matter and the key to health and wellness. Historically, spirituality and science seemed to have irreconcilable differences, but recent advances in physics and neuro-science have drawn them closer together and are paving the way to greater compatibility. Harmony and rhythmic movement is the essence of all being from the subatomic level to the outer reaches of the Universe. Our breath is a function we can learn to regulate and develop in order to improve our physical, mental and spiritual well-being. By using breath as a technique of harmonizing the functions of the nervous system, there seems to be no limit to what part of the mind/body we can reach. No disorder is out of bonds.

Wherever we have nerves in the body, which is everywhere, we have the possibility of influencing function.

Before they compete, top athletes breathe. Tuning into their breathing creates immediate physical and mental focus, strengthens will, fuels determination, and renews commitment to an objective. Martial artists, healing artists, performing artists, and top performers of all kinds use conscious breathing to channel and focus their attention and energy. Conscious breathing harmonizes opposing forces and creates balance, trust, and acceptance.

We typically use two breathing patterns: chest or thoracic breathing, and abdominal or diaphragmatic breathing. Chest or thoracic breathing is often associated with anxiety or other emotional distress. It is shallow, tense, and often irregular and rapid. Abdominal or diaphragmatic breathing is the natural breathing of newborn babies and sleeping adults. Newborns come into the world breathing deeply, but as we age, stress and outside influences can alter that pattern, and many of us start to breathe shallower from the upper chest where lung volume is minimal.

Awareness of the in-and-out flow of breath teaches us to let go, open and receive without stopping to judge or criticize. When we make the inhale active and controlled, and let the exhale be relaxed and comfortable, we are training this balance of opposites physically. We balance <u>control</u> with just <u>letting things happen</u> by themselves, work with play, and an intense, active life with rest and relaxation. They become as natural as the balanced flow between day and night, waking and sleeping, high and low tides, or seasonal growth and decay. By increasing our awareness of our breathing patterns and shifting to more abdominal breathing, we can reduce the muscle tension and anxiety present with stress-related symptoms or thoughts. Diaphragmatic breathing has been shown to be effective in reducing generalized anxiety disorders, panic attacks and agoraphobia, cold hands and feet, depression, irritability, muscle tension, headaches, and fatigue.

Hyperventilation syndrome, often associated with anxiety, is also known as "over breathing" and is the result of abnormally rapid breathing. Although it feels like a lack of oxygen, it is over exhalation of, or excessive loss of, carbon dioxide. This loss of carbon dioxide triggers symptoms such as gasping, trembling, choking and the feeling of being smothered. Regrettably, over breathing often perpetuates more over breathing, lowering carbon dioxide levels more, and becomes a nasty downward spiral.

A consciously aware person can recognize the anxiety-provoking situation causing the rapid breathing and immediately visualize a Big Red Smiling Stop Sign. This reminds the person to consciously use the <u>Deeper, Slower, Calmer, Regular Breath</u> and transition to a more preferable "Diaphragmatic Breathing" described later.

A few conscious breaths can re-energize and relax us, bring clarity, restore emotional balance, and help us to recover from stress. Conscious breathing is a natural centering technique that helps us to feel grounded and is the quickest and most effective way to clear one's head, settle the stomach, and calm nerves. The more conscious we are of our breathing, the more conscious we become of everything. When we learn to control our breathing, we will be able to control the level of stress we feel. Slow, deep breathing takes awareness and practice, but a little effort goes a long way. Once we learn to take slow, deep breaths from the belly, we will have an unstoppable weapon against stress. The Vietnamese Buddhist teacher Thich Nhat Hanh wrote, "Feelings come and go like clouds in a windy sky. Conscious breathing is my anchor."

The yoga <u>Bellows Breath</u>, or Stimulating Breath as it is often called, is used to wake up in the morning, warm up, stimulate circulation and awareness when feeling drowsy and disconnected, or when there is a need to be particularly alert. Imagine breathing fast full breaths as if running up a hill while remain completely still and perfectly relaxed. It triggers physical, emotional, psychological, and spiritual healing. And in the process, it naturally produces unusually beautiful and powerful feelings and sensations, thoughts and images. The <u>Bellows Breath</u> provides an energy boost that can be compared to the high one feels after a workout and increases alertness if done for a full minute. This can be a real life saver when driving long distances.

Although the <u>Bellows Breath</u> can be done in the prone position, the exercise usually starts by sitting upright with back straight, eyes closed, and shoulders relaxed. With the mouth closed but relaxed, inhale and exhale quickly and evenly through the nose. Aim for three short in-out cycles per second, but stop after 15 seconds the first time. It produces a quick movement of the diaphragm, suggesting a bellows. Most people use their fingers to keep track by counting three breaths per finger. If one chooses to continue, the duration of each rep can be increased by five seconds: five fingers. Always breathe normally between reps, and doing the exercise for more than one minute is probably counterproductive. Ideally, one will feel the muscular effects of this breathing exercise at the base of the neck (just above the collarbone), the chest, and at the diaphragm.

2.2.1 Relaxation Response

Evolving from stress to gratitude begins with learning to take control of the mind/body with the Conscious mind which requires the ability to focus and access the Subconscious mind. We use the breath as a passport to go through the gate between the Conscious mind and the Subconscious mind, but these skills are far easier to practice if we are in a relaxed state. Therefore, we need to spend some time learning more about the relaxation response and then we will practice focusing our attention and gaining access to the Control Room of the Unconscious mind-of-the-body.

The Relaxation Response is a term popularized by Dr. Herbert Benson, a cardiologist and Professor of Medicine at Harvard Medical School, and counters the fight-or-flight response which is a term coined in the 1920's by another Harvard Medical School professor, psychologist Dr. Walter Cannon. The relaxation response is a facilitated healing state that heals from the inside out and can be defined as our personal ability to make our mind/body release chemicals and brain signals that make our muscles and organs slow down and increase blood flow to the brain: physically relaxed and mentally alert. Drugs can do some of this, but they often have unwanted side effects. We can get our body to relax just as well without drugs while remaining conscious and aware at the same time.

Dr. Benson and his team found that learning to elicit the relaxation response can counter the fight-or-flight response even more effectively than drugs. Just as the fight-or-flight response is hard-wired into our brains, so is the relaxation response. We do not need to believe it will work, any more than we need to believe our leg will jump when the doctor taps our patellar tendon with a little rubber hammer. We just need to give it a little push when the autonomic nervous system is stuck in "defense mode."

The relaxation response is a physiologic response, and there are many ways to elicit it, just as there are many ways to increase our pulse rate (another physiologic response). Advantageous genomic pattern changes have been shown to occur in practitioners of many different relaxation response modalities including dance, singing in the shower, progressive muscle relaxation, visual imagery, breathing techniques, meditation, self-hypnosis, yoga, and biofeedback. The method does not seem to matter as much as one's attitude and willingness to use a particular technique consistently. It is not the modality that produces the common relaxation response state, it is the mental silence that they all use that leads to the ideal environment for the positive effects of plasticity to occur.

When we are overwhelmed with excessive stress, life becomes a series of short-term emergencies. It is like the body is reacting to an external threat that never goes away and the "defense mode" has become the default setting for our nervous systems. There is a cumulative buildup of stress hormones, and we lose the ability to relax and enjoy the moment. If not properly metabolized over time, excessive stress can lead to disorders of the autonomic nervous system, hormonal system, and immune systems creating headache, irritable bowel syndrome, high blood pressure, susceptibility to infection, chronic fatigue, depression, and autoimmune diseases like rheumatoid arthritis, lupus, and allergies.

The autonomic nervous system (ANS or involuntary nervous system) is a control system that acts largely unconsciously and regulates such functions as heart rate, digestion, respiratory rate, pupillary response, urination, and sexual arousal. The two major parts of the ANS are; the sympathetic nervous system (SNS) which is associated with the "defense mode" and the fight-or-flight response; and the parasympathetic nervous system (PSN) which is associated with the "evolve, renew, and repair mode" and the relaxation response. Although they work together, they have opposite actions where one activates a physiological response, the other inhibits it.

The fight-or-flight (or freeze) response is an acute physiological stress response of the sympathetic nervous system that occurs in response to a perceived harmful event, attack, or threat to survival. The main function of the sympathetic nervous system is to activate the "defense mode" and the physiological changes that occur during the fight-or-flight response. The relaxation response enables the parasympathetic nervous system which activates the "evolve, renew, and repair mode" and returns the body to homeostasis or normal function where rest, digestion, and conscious thought resumes after the fight-or-flight response.

The fight-or-flight response is a primitive, automatic, inborn response that is hard-wired into our brains and represents a genetic wisdom designed to protect us from bodily harm. When our fight-or-flight response is activated, the "evolve, renew, and repair mode" is shut down. We go into "defense mode" and a series of very dramatic changes occur. The respiratory rate increases, blood is shunted away from the digestive tract and directed into muscles and limbs, pupils dilate, awareness intensifies, sight sharpens, impulses quicken, perception of pain diminishes, and we become prepared for fight or flight both physically and psychologically. The rational mind is bypassed, fear is exaggerated, thinking is distorted, and we see everything through the filter of possible danger. We narrow our focus to those things that can harm us and short-term survival, not the long-term consequences.

Our fight-or-flight response is designed to protect us and when actual physical survival is threatened it comes in handy. The threats we face in our modern lifestyle, however, are not normally physical, they are psychological in the form of long lines at the grocery store, traffic, disrespectful teenagers, deadlines, financial problems, and arguments. These threats are frequent, persistent, and cumulative causing chronic stress conditions and an elevated flow of toxic stress hormones into the body that can lead to high blood pressure, increased heart rate, muscle tension, and irrational behavior. The stress hormones need to be metabolized through physical activity, or the perceptions that created the hormones in the first place need to be more flexible and adaptable. It is counterproductive to run away or attempt to wrestle the boss into submission, but learning to accept and adapt to changing lifestyles is a characteristic of higher intelligence and is critical to our survival.

We do not have to make it complicated. An enjoyable walk in a park or garden can be all it takes to shake off the tension of a difficult day. Water can work wonders in one or more of its many forms and be far more effective than television when it comes to unwinding. Almost any body of water has a very relaxing quality, and when combined with soothing music, it can be a great stress buster. Just observing and losing one's self in the sights and sounds of the ocean, a pond, brook, river, fountain, or waterfall is very therapeutic. If that is not readily available, visit the same image on the internet with music or spend a few minutes watching the fish in an aquarium.

The immune system works best when relaxed and the breath is deep, slow, calm, and regular. We need to learn techniques that protect us in a world of psychological as well as physical danger and the simplest, most effective way to quiet the mind/body is a deliberate elicitation of the relaxation response. With a little practice, it will counteract the toxic effects of chronic stress by slowing breathing rate, relaxing muscles, and reducing blood pressure. It is easily learned, costs nothing, and has no side effects.

2.2.2 **Breath Awareness**

As stated earlier, learning to take control of the mind/body with the Conscious mind begins with relaxation, developing our ability to focus, and fully engaging the "evolve, renew, and repair mode." We will first learn to stay focused on our breath, breathe more efficiently, and develop natural but seldom used skills. Then we will use these newly developed skills to go deeper into the Subconscious and eventually learn to operate the controls of the Unconscious mind-of-the-body.

One of the five principles of yoga is pranayama which is defined as the "control of life force," and is aimed at increasing vital energy in the body and mind. By bringing awareness to our body and consciously practicing breath control exercises, we can bring many positive changes to our physical, mental, emotional, and spiritual well-being. The first step is to become more conscious of breathing simply by observing it without attempting to alter it in any way. It is useful to know one's natural breathing pattern and where it usually goes. We sense it, feel it, watch it, listen to it, and tune into the details of our breathing without judgment or trying to influence it.

Breathing strongly influences physiology and thought processes, including moods. By simply focusing our attention on our breathing without doing anything to change it, we can move in the direction of relaxation. We develop the habit of shifting our awareness to our breath whenever we find ourselves dwelling on stressful situations. Always return to the breath. It is our ground, our reference point, our anchor, our calm port in the storm. When distracted by harmful activity in the mind, we recognize it but do not engage it, instead, we just notice it and then let it go. Always return to the basics; always return to the breath.

A great racecar driver told us that his first driving lesson as a teenager was to simply sit in the driver's seat of his father's car, learn the location of, and become familiar with the controls. Then, before he was allowed to put the car in gear, he had to spend hours getting the feel of the controls. When he was finally able to operate each control efficiently with his eyes closed (including the lights and windshield wipers), he was allowed to move the car in a large empty parking lot. Before one can take control of the road and become a great world-class driver, one must develop the skills needed to operate the controls. The same applies to taking control of the mind/body and gene expression. We have to develop the skills needed to operate the controls before we can use them efficiently to direct our evolution.

The following three exercises are <u>awareness skills</u> that are needed for optimum health and prerequisites for the <u>Three Imperative Breathing Techniques</u> that we will introduce later. The first skill, the "Observe the Natural Breath" is so simple that anyone can do it but is so difficult that most people cannot do it for more than a few seconds. Our objective here is to develop concentration and get better at staying focused. The second skill, the "Exhalation Focus and Squeeze" teaches us to use more of our lung capacity. And the third skill, the "Diaphragmatic or Abdomen Breath" is the corner-stone of good health and is the way we were meant to breathe, before we developed unhealthy habits and beliefs.

1) <u>Observe the Natural Breath</u>: We lie or sit in a comfortable but dignified manner with the spine straight and turn our attention to our breath. We gently relax or close our eyes to reduce distractions, maintain awareness, and focus on breathing. After taking a few deep breaths, we let the breath come naturally without trying to influence it, and look for details in the breathing with the mind. Ideally, it will be slow and calm, but depth and rhythm may vary. We follow the natural ebb and flow of our breath without trying to direct it: we just observe.

By paying attention to the breath, we will rapidly alter our state of consciousness, begin to relax, and slowly detach from emotions of the past (anger, guilt, depression, and shame), and emotions of the future (fear, worry, and anxiety). We observe the peak between the in-breath and out-breath, notice the temperature change at the end of the nose as it cools on the in-breath and warms on the out-breath. Note that a Natural Breath occurs when the autonomic nervous system triggers the diaphragm to contract. We notice the motion of the diaphragm, the pause at the end of the out-breath, and the depth or volume of each breath. Some can even feel their heart beat and the blood flow during the silence after the out-breath. When one feels sleepy, it is often an indication that consciousness is spreading out and wandering so we refocus on the breath and direct consciousness to a laser-like focus on the breath, observing it in every detail. When distracted, we return to the breath. Always return to the breath. Feeling sleepy is also a common occurrence among those who are not getting enough sleep at night.

Breath is life, and when our attention is focused on our breath, we become aware of and focused on our own body and life as it is in the present moment; not reliving an irrelevant past or worrying about things in the future that will probably never happen anyway.

2) <u>Exhalation Focus and Squeeze</u>: Next, we focus our attention on the exhalation. Most people will use effort to inhale but none to exhale. Their exhalation is usually passive, takes less time than inhalation and does not move nearly as much air in and out of the lungs as it could. The more air we move, the healthier we will be because the functioning of all systems of the body depends on delivery of oxygen and removal of toxins. To get more air into the lungs, we concentrate on getting more air out of them by attending to exhalation. <u>The more air we exhale, the deeper the next inhalation will be</u>.

At the end of a normal breath, we gently squeeze out a little more air, and then a little more. To do this, we relax the diaphragm, contract the abdominal muscles, and use the intercostal muscles between the ribs to compress the rib cage. After a normal inhale, we focus on the exhale and rather than blowing it out all at once, we let it out slowly through pursed lips. At the end, there is always a little left so, as if blowing out a candle, we gently blow out a little more...three times. Notice that the next inhalation is naturally deeper. Five to ten breaths are usually enough to improve awareness, extend normal exhalation, increase natural volume, awaken intercostal muscles, and tone abdominal muscles.

3) <u>Diaphragmatic or Abdomen Breath</u>: After learning to focus on the breath, extend the exhalation, and increase natural volume, we are ready to learn how to breathe naturally again. The way we breathe can make a tremendous difference in how we feel and age, yet it receives little attention. We were born with natural breathing skills, but as we get older, we start sucking in the gut and restricting our breathing to the upper chest because we think we need to have a big chest and a small waist. This gradually makes shallow "chest breathing" feel normal. That is not to say that a big tummy and a small chest is preferable, but those who have created a mind/body for longevity over maximum performance seem to be someplace in the middle. The secret is to return to a more natural pattern of

respiration as observed in very young children. When they inhale, their little tummies blow up like tiny beach balls and contract on the exhale.

This natural breathing is called diaphragmatic breathing, often referred to as abdominal breathing, belly breathing, or deep breathing. It is done by contracting the diaphragm located at the base of the lungs dividing the chest from the abdomen and is the most efficient muscle of breathing. When the diaphragm contracts the middle fibers, which are formed in a dome shape like an upside down bowl, it pulls the lungs downward and presses against a relaxed abdominal area to make room for the lungs to expand, drawing in air. Air coming in through the nose fully fills the lungs, pushes the belly outward and opens the lower rib cage with little movement of the upper chest. As we breathe out, abdominal and intercostal muscles contract to help move the relaxed diaphragm back up expelling carbon dioxide and other toxins from the lungs. The best way to get a sense of diaphragmatic awareness is to hold the breath for a few seconds, after a natural exhale, until the autonomic nervous system wants to take over and trigger a breath. Then let it happen and notice how the upper belly area (diaphragm) responds first, just like little babies before they learn that they are supposed to have a big chest and a small waist.

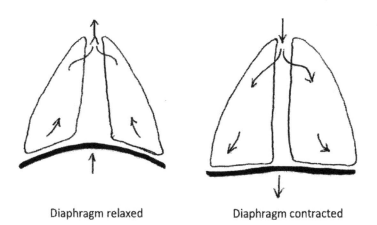

Diaphragm relaxed   Diaphragm contracted

Shallow "chest breathing" restricts the diaphragm's range of motion and the many small blood vessels in the lower portion of the lungs that are instrumental in carrying oxygen to cells never get a full share of oxygenated air. The bottom of the lungs has the greatest capacity but is seldom used in most people. While deep breathing produces relaxation, shallow breathing often feels tense, constricted, and makes us feel short of breath and anxious. The characteristics of optimal breathing (at rest) are that it is diaphragmatic, <u>Deeper, Slower, Calmer, and Regular</u>.

When we first relearn the "Diaphragmatic Breathing" skill, it may be easier to follow the instructions lying down, but as we gain more practice, it can be done almost anywhere. Basically, we contract the diaphragm and relax the abs to breathe in, then relax the diaphragm and contract the abs to breathe out. The initial focus of attention is on the relaxed expansion of the abdomen and then the expansion of the lower rib cage during the inhalation without a rise in the upper chest. The exhalation focus is on gently contracting the ads (or allowing normal elasticity to return) while the diaphragm relaxes. With practice, it will become natural again as it was at birth.

a) With the eyes closed, or relaxed and half closed, we lie or sit in a comfortable but dignified manner with the face, neck, shoulders, and body relaxed and the spine straight. Start by taking a deep breath and then observing the natural inhalation and exhalation of the breath without trying to change it.

b) Until body awareness develops sufficiently, beginners can place one hand on the upper chest and the other just below the navel. Then begin to inhale deep and slow through the nose so that the lower belly expands, like a balloon, out against the hand. Correct "Diaphragmatic Breathing" will produce a noticeable lateral expansion of the rib cage but the hand on the upper chest should remain as still as possible. The abdomen muscles are relaxed so that each inhalation expands the belly.

c) On each exhale, relax the diaphragm and allow the abs to draw the navel back toward the spine to push air out through pursed lips. The hand on the upper chest should remain as still as possible.

d) Repeat ten times.

Some people may notice an increased effort and conscious focus will be needed to use the diaphragm correctly at first, but the "Diaphragmatic Breathing" will become easy, automatic, and natural again like learning to sit up straight or ride a bicycle. According to the University of Texas Counseling and Mental Health Center, "Diaphragmatic Breathing" allows one to take normal breaths while maximizing the amount of oxygen that goes into the bloodstream. It is a way of interrupting the sympathetic nervous systems dominance, triggering the body's normal relaxation response, and promoting the formation of nitric oxide which opens up blood vessels.

The "Diaphragmatic Breathing" skill is inborn but often lies dormant. Reawakening it strengthens the diaphragm, improves circulation, increases oxygen supply, slows the breathing rate, and uses less effort and energy to breathe. It is more efficient, facilitates a slower heartbeat, normalizes blood pressure, and allows us to tap one of the body's strongest self-healing mechanisms.

2.2.3 Three Simple but Imperative Breathing Techniques

The three conscious "Breath Awareness" skills practiced above develop greater awareness, focus, and control. They form the foundation for the Three Imperative Breathing Techniques that we will be using to evolve from stress to gratitude and take conscious control of our mind/body. We have learned to direct our focus and have taken a few small steps toward learning to take control of elementary functions. Now we will learn to apply these skills to the Three Imperative Breathing Techniques that we will use for the rest of our lives. They are as important to one's health as eating well, getting enough quality sleep, and personal hygiene. They will be used in times of stress and are vital tools in our evolution. Without them, life will be shorter and far less comfortable.

These three techniques are wonderfully effective ways to reduce stress, regulate mood, and feel energized. As opposed to emotion-laden thoughts and images, when we have our attention focused on our breath, we are in a safe place. Just as we begin to breathe faster and shallower when stressed, we begin to calm down and feel safe when we consciously breathe slower and deeper. Breath controls psychophysiology just as psychophysiology controls breath. When we change our breath, we change our mind/body.

The first technique, the Three-Part-Breath is used to oxygenate, detoxify, energize, focus, and ground us in the present moment. The second technique, the (DSCR) or Deeper, Slower, Calmer, Regular Breath was introduced in Part I and is used for sudden increases in stress. It is the perfect breath to use in the "Stop, Smile, Breathe, and say Thank You" scenario. The third technique, the (5-7-9) Breath is used to erode the many layers of accumulated stress and is a natural tranquilizer for the nervous system.

1) <u>Three-Part-Breath:</u> Although many people think that a deep breath comes solely from expansion of the chest, it is not the best way to take a deep breath. To get a full deep breath, we need to use the diaphragmatic inhale, expand the air into the mid-rib, and then the upper chest.

Deep breathing calms and grounds the mind, oxygenates and detoxifies the cells of the body, and focuses our attention on the present moment. Researchers have shown that the <u>Three-Part-Breath</u> takes in seven times more oxygen than normal breathing and can dramatically increase energy levels. It is one of the first breathing techniques taught to new yoga practitioners and is used extensively by athletes. The "three parts" are; the abdomen area from the lower part of the belly up to the navel; the rib cage from the navel to the middle of the chest; and the upper chest from the middle of the chest to the collar bones. During the <u>Three-Part-Breath</u>, we first send the air to the bottom of the lungs by contracting the diaphragm (expanding the abdomen); then, fill up the mid rib cage laterally; and finally, fill the upper chest all the way up to the collarbone (raising the shoulders and extending the spine). Then we exhale completely by first, relaxing the shoulders and upper chest, letting out the air naturally; relaxing the rib cage; and finally, contracting the abs.

The <u>Three-Part-Breath</u> can be done standing, sitting, or lying down with the spine straight so that the abdomen is not compressed. Lying down makes it easier to feel the breath moving through the body. We begin with ease and gradually let the breath deepen, never forcing the breath or trying to breathe too deeply. It is important for the lungs to feel comfortably full, but not strained, and to let the breath be easy and smooth. At the top of the inhale, the chest should lift up slightly and at the bottom of the exhale, the abdomen should be all the way in.

a) With the eyes closed, or relaxed and half closed, we lie or sit in a comfortable but dignified manner with the face, neck, shoulders, and body relaxed and the spine straight. Start by taking a deep breath and then observing the natural inhalation and exhalation of the breath without trying to change it.

b) Part one uses the "Diaphragmatic Breath" skill, inhaling deeply through the nose and expanding the abdomen like a balloon.

c) Part two draws in a little more breath to expand the mid rib cage.

d) Then Part three draws in a little more air to expand the upper chest (all the way up to the collarbone) raising the shoulders and extending the spine slightly.

e) On the exhale, expel all the air slowly through pursed lips. Let the breath go first from the upper chest, then from the rib cage, and finally, let the air go from the lower lungs drawing the navel back toward the spine.

f) Repeat as desired. Focus on the breath ONLY. If dizziness is experienced or if the breath becomes strained, stop the exercise and return to the normal breathing pattern.

2) (DSCR) Deeper, Slower, Calmer, Regular Breath: The (DSCR) Breath is both powerful and very easy to perform. When upset, we cannot always just tell ourselves to settle down, but we can always change our breathing to affect our physiology. Voluntary, slow, deep breathing resets the autonomic nervous system, activates the parasympathetic nervous system (evolve, renew, and repair mode), and synchronizes physiological processes that may be functioning too fast or conflicting with the homeostasis of the cells.

In Part I, we learned that when someone harms, frustrates, annoys, rejects, or embarrasses us, we Stop, Smile, Breathe, and say Thank You, and the "Breathe" part is where this technique is needed most. Everybody already knows how to stop, smile, and say thank you, but when sudden stress strikes, we sometimes forget how to breathe. When stressed, our breathing is shallow, rapid, tense, and irregular, so we need to consciously breathe Deeper, Slower, Calmer, and Regular. Periodically squeezing out a little more air on the exhale will naturally make the inhale deeper. This technique uses all three of the skills learned in the Breath Awareness section: 1) Observe the Natural Breath, 2) Exhalation Focus and Squeeze, 3) Diaphragmatic or Abdomen Breath.

We start by practicing this technique consciously, and eventually exhalations will naturally become deeper and longer. This is a simple technique but an effective one, and will become a healthy, natural habit. It will become an automatic "go to" when things get hairy.

a) Breathe IN and think or say the word DEEPER. Inhale slowly through the nose, and feel the air push the abdomen out, not the upper chest. Use the "Diaphragmatic Breath" skill here.

b) Breathe OUT and think or say the word SLOWER. Exhale slowly through pursed lips to keep from blowing it out all at once. Use the "Observe the Natural Breath" skill to observe the pause between the out-breath and the in-breath and notice the transition from one to the other.

c) Breathe IN and think or say the word CALMER. Inhale slowly through the nose, and feel the air fill the abdomen, not the upper chest.

d) Breathe OUT and think or say the word REGULAR. Exhale slowly through pursed lips to keep from blowing it out all at once.

e) At the end of the OUT-breath on every third set, squeeze out a little more air as if blowing out a candle. Use the "Exhalation Focus and Squeeze" skill here.

f) Repeat as needed and as many times a day as practicable: in line at the supermarket, during commercials while watching TV, at a traffic light, and of course, whenever stress strikes. We practice this during periods of potential boredom but mostly because we want it preprogrammed into our stress response. We want to automatically go to it when stress strikes suddenly.

Making the breath Deeper, Slower, Calmer, and more Regular whenever we think about it keeps our attention in the present moment more of the time and our brain sharper. Squeezing more air out of the lungs at the end of every third breath makes the next in-breath naturally deeper, and being conscious of when the third breath will occur sharpens awareness. It is helpful to place removable sticky notes in areas around the house and workplace where it might be appropriate to take a "breather" throughout the day.

Another very helpful strategy is to turn down or mute the sound on the TV during commercials and practice breathing techniques. Grounding ourselves in the present moment is far healthier than listening to a pill pusher trying to convince us that we have a disease and need to buy drugs. Returning to the present moment on a regular basis also prevents us from getting lost in the latest murder mystery or sensationalized news story.

3) (5-7-9) Breath: Chronic stress can create longer and longer periods of higher and higher blood pressure readings while the (5-7-9) Breath slowly reduces the sustained periods of time stuck in "defense mode" and progressively reduces hypertension. This technique is easy to do, takes only about 2 ½ minutes, costs nothing, requires no equipment, and is a natural

tranquilizer for the nervous system. Unlike tranquilizing drugs, which are often effective when first taken, but then lose their power over time, this technique is subtle when first tried but gains in power with repetition and practice. As stated above, the (DSCR) Breath is used with the "Stop, Smile, Breathe, and say Thank You" scenario for sudden increases in stress while the (5-7-9) Breath is used with the "Slow down, Simplify, and Be Grateful, Patient, and Kind" attitude to erode the many layers of accumulated stress.

Briefly, the (5-7-9) Breath entails breathing IN through the nose for a count of five, holding it for a count of seven, and then exhaling through pursed lips to a count of nine. It should be done at least twice a day and cannot be done too frequently. This is, however, a very powerful psychophysiological technique and the beginner should not do more than four breaths at one time for the first few days of practice. As one feels more comfortable with it, the exercise can be extended but to no more than eight breaths at a time. Some beginners feel a little lightheaded at first, but that will pass.

The key to this technique is to remember the numbers 5, 7, and 9. The time spent on each phase (faster or slower count) is not critical, but the ratio of 5-7-9 is very important. The exhalation takes almost twice as long as inhalation. Those who have trouble holding their breath can speed the exercise up by counting faster, but they need to maintain the ratio of 5-7-9. With practice, one can slow it all down and get used to inhaling and exhaling more and more deeply.

We often prepare by closing our eyes and "observing the natural breath" for a few seconds and although it can be done anywhere and in any position, beginners find it easier to sit in a dignified manner with their back straight. Then take a deep breath and exhale with an audible sigh allowing the jaw and shoulders to relax and...begin.

a) Sit up straight and breathe IN silently through the nose to the count of five.

b) Hold to the count of seven.

c) Exhale through pursed lips to the count of nine.

d) Repeat as needed but never with more than eight breaths at a time. Focus on the count 5, 7, or 9, and the number of breaths completed ONLY.

With practice, this can become a very powerful means of eliciting the relaxation response that gets more effective over time. It shifts energy from the sympathetic to the parasympathetic nervous system, with many physiological benefits. Most people are pleasantly surprised by how quickly and easily this technique can calm, center, and relax them; and how soon they begin to achieve high levels of health when they consistently do it twice a day. We suggest that it be done before going to work and before bed, and in addition to the (DSCR) Breath when time permits.

Many students associate it with brushing their teeth because both need to be done at least twice a day and can be done in private without being disturbed. In addition to the sticky notes used to remind us to practice the (DSCR) Breath, some students find it helpful to make two more signs or sticky notes sporting the numbers "5-7-9." One is placed on the bathroom mirror and the other on the door they use to leave the house in the morning. Do not leave the house without at least doing the (5-7-9) Breath. We NEED to check-in with our mind/body and the present moment before thrusting it into battle with the outside world. It takes 2 ½ minutes and even if one is late for work, an additional 2 ½ minutes late will make no difference to the boss. It will, however, produce a calmer, more stable late person with greater physical and mental balance, clarity, and awareness. Most people appreciate the note on the door the most because it reminds those who have not done it to stop and do it before leaving, and those who have done it leave the house feeling like they have it all together. Confucius said. "I hear and I forget. I see and I remember. I do and I understand."

Some have said that they find it difficult to stop thinking about all the things they need to do and practice the (5-7-9) Breath. They fear that they will lose track of their train of thought or even forget something. The solution: Write them down. Put them in order of importance, let them go with the knowledge that they can be retrieved by simply looking at the list, and do the (5-7-9) Breath. Then return to the list with a calmer, re-energized, fresh perspective and start working on the most important item.

Remember, it is better to arrive safely 2 ½ minutes later in a calm, focused state than to arrive on time in a tense, out of focused, disheveled state which lends itself to not arriving at all because of a traffic accident. In addition, we can do the (5-7-9) Breath with meals to remind ourselves to slow down and breathe when we eat. Combining it with mindfulness and an attitude of gratitude while eating a healthy meal can result in a powerful, beneficial influence on our health.

The (5-7-9) Breath is like brushing one's teeth in that one may not see a difference after one brushing, but without it, not only oral hygiene is affected but so is overall health. Once we develop this technique by practicing it every day, it will be a very useful tool that will always be available. We can use it for mild to moderate anxiety, dealing with food cravings, whenever we become aware of internal tension or when emotions begin to get the best of us (before we react), and we can use it to fall asleep. This exercise cannot be recommended too highly, and everyone can benefit from it.

2.2.4 Mastering Conscious Breath Control

Conscious breathing reduces anxiety, agitation, and stress while promoting relaxation, calm, and inner peace, although it may take practice and requires some commitment. In the long-term, however, it is well worth the effort. A calm and relaxed mind/body is less prone to health issues and since breathing is something we can control and regulate, it is a useful tool for achieving a relaxed and clear state of mind. We can voluntarily use these techniques to disengage the conscious awareness from constant pointless mind chatter, ease stressful or discomforting situations, and deal with distractions and stress without having an inappropriate emotional or physiological response.

The research is very clear. These breathing techniques improve respiratory and cardiovascular function, decrease the effects of stress, enhance parasympathetic tone (evolve, renew, and repair mode), decrease sympathetic nervous system activity (defense mode), and improve physical and mental health. The practice of conscious breathing is foundational to feeling more calm and centered. It can help mitigate intense emotional feelings, help us sleep better, and increase our ability to bring the parasympathetic nervous system back online and de-escalate the sympathetic nervous system when the threat, task, or stressor, has passed. It opens the gate to the Subconscious Control Room of the Unconscious mind-of-the-body.

Learning to breathe consciously can modify and accelerate the body's inherent self-regulating physiological and bio-energetic mechanisms. These changes are in large part due to the fact that we are oxygenating our bodies properly as well as correcting our internal and energetic balance. It has a direct impact on the nervous system affecting the entire body and its countless cellular functions, including subtle energy systems. Deep breathing aids the digestive system by acting as a pump to massage internal organs and the endocrine system by pushing lymph throughout the body, which helps eliminate toxic waste and strengthen the immune system. The respiratory system experiences a reduction in mental and physical fatigue, as well as symptoms of asthma and bronchitis. Everything from the skin to the circulatory system is benefited by improved blood circulation and cell oxygenation throughout the body.

Setting aside several short periods each day for quiet time to practice deep breathing techniques will help us stay in touch with what is important, rather than rushing around faster and faster in response to the demands of others. When the moments seem stressful or the frustrations reach critical mass, we will "Stop, Smile, Breath, and say Thank You." We always come back to the breath. The few seconds it takes to notice our breath rise and fall can be enough to re-engage the shift from stress to gratitude. We do not have to be in any certain room or seated in a certain position. We can do it at anytime and anywhere. If we let our breath center us throughout our day, focus and come back to the breath as often as possible, we will find grounding and harmony within our own body. Everything we need is already within us.

1) Use the Bellows Breath to wake up in the morning, warm up, stimulate circulation, and heighten awareness when feeling drowsy and disconnected, or when there is a need to be particularly alert.

2) Use the first Imperative Breath, the Three-Part-Breath, when feeling sluggish or particularly fatigued to oxygenate and detoxify the cells and to dramatically increase physical energy. Practice calming and grounding the mind by filling the lungs completely.

3) Use the second Imperative Breath, the (DSCR) Breath, with the "Stop, Smile, Breathe, and say Thank You" scenario for sudden stress attacks or just when feeling over excited. It is practiced using all three of the "Breath Awareness" skills as often as possible to bring us back to the present moment where life happens. See a sticky note; breathe Deeper (into the abdomen), Slower, Calmer, and more Regular. It can be practiced while waiting in line, when stuck in traffic, or when we generally feel uptight and do not have the 2½ minutes it takes to do the (5-7-9) Breath. Before an important meeting, speech, or performance, it is helpful to Stop, Smile, do the (DSCR) Breath, and say "Thank you" three times. If time permits, one

82

can follow that with four to eight (5-7-9) Breaths and face the challenge with a clearer mind and a positive attitude.

4) Use the third Imperative Breath, the (5-7-9) Breath, with the "Slow down, Simplify, Be Grateful, Patient, and Kind" attitude every time the feeling of anxiety begins to stir, or even when just a bit uptight. It is easier to consciously regulate our breathing than to will a mood change. Practice it twice a day at specific times like just before bed and during the morning routine. The (5-7-9) Breath can be associated with things we do every day like brushing our teeth or washing our hands and can also be combined with gratitude at meal time. It is used to peel away the layers of stress that have been building up for a lifetime and has a slow cumulative effect, like chronic stress.

5) When sudden stress strikes, we visualize a Big Red Smiling Stop Sign and "Stop, Smile, Breathe, and say Thank You." We use this go-to response every time someone harms, frustrates, annoys, rejects, embarrasses us, or we feel threatened in some way. Remember to use the (DSCR) Breath here.

6) When life seems too overwhelming or complicated, we "Slow down, Simplify, and Be Grateful, Patient, and Kind." Remember to use the (5-7-9) Breath here.

7) If one can remember only one rule, let it be this: Be Kind.

2.3 Introduction to Meditation

Now that we know a little more about the power we have in our breath, we will learn something about meditation and how certain simple aspects of it are crucial to evolving from stress to gratitude. We know that this evolution requires a calm relaxed mind/body and that the best, most efficient way to do that is with the skillful application of breathing techniques. Breathing is a constant companion, a faithful friend, and a natural component of meditation. By focusing our attention on this faithful companion, we begin to relax, alter our state of consciousness, and detach from ordinary mind chatter. We have learned to visualize a Big Red Smiling Stop Sign when stress strikes, "Stop, Smile, Breathe, and say Thank You," and use the Deeper, Slower, Calmer, Regular (DSCR) Breath as an automatic "go to" in the face of sudden stressors. We have also learned that we can chip away at deep-seated (accumulated) stress with the (5-7-9) Breath and the "Slow Down, Simplify, and Be Grateful, Patient, and Kind" scenario. Now we will learn to strengthen our mind/body connections and provide the brain with vital rejuvenation and clarity by consciously using basic meditation techniques.

Meditation practices have existed for thousands of years but in the past few decades, the use of meditation has increased due to the rise of interest in the teachings of Eastern cultures, the stress and anxiety of modern life, and corroborating scientific research. Some people practice for spiritual growth or a way to enlightenment while others use meditation for stress reduction, pain relief, an antidote for disturbing mind states, and as a potent method for enhancing and developing wholesome and helpful states of mind. Meditation allows us to go beyond words and mental concepts.

Meditation is directed concentration of focused attention in order to increase awareness, reduce stress, promote relaxation, and enhance personal growth. Basic meditation is simply a matter of quieting the mind/body with focused attention, preferably on the breath, while more advanced techniques are used to target specific therapeutic needs. Meditation differs from hypnosis in that hypnosis often uses trance techniques that overload, disorganize, and trigger the fight/flight mechanism as defined by Dr. John Kappas who, in 1973, defined the profession of hypnotherapy in the Federal Dictionary of Occupational Titles. The meditator can enter the same state using stillness of mind and relaxation.

Most meditative techniques started in Eastern religious or spiritual traditions, but modern medicine has found that meditation promotes healing by eliciting the Relaxation Response and is now being used outside of its traditional religious or cultural settings. The spirit or life energy in our breath is our anchor in a turbulent world, and simple meditation techniques can help us drop down into a sense of calm and peace no matter what is going on. Some have used it to reach spiritual enlightenment by connecting to the universal rhythms and as Kabir said, "God is the breath within the breath," but that is outside the scope of this book. We will be using our breath and meditation to improve the mind/body connection by going deeper into the Subconscious mind to the Control Room of the Unconscious mind-of-the-body, and beyond to enlist the help of our own inherent connection to all that we are.

Meditation is basically a process whereby we intentionally slow down brain-wave activity from beta to alpha. Once in this state, we are able to access our Subconscious and alter (or even replace) information if we so choose.

When our minds are concentrated and focused, we are able to use our minds more effectively. Meditation allows people to use more of their potential and develop greater self-control. For our purposes, meditation is a simple mental exercise designed to deepen calmness and physical relaxation, gain control of psychophysiological functions, improve psychological balance, and enhance overall health and well-being without the nonsense. We do not go deeply into ourselves to withdraw from the world or strive to reach some exalted or higher state. We do it to enhance the free flow of chi (life force energy or spirit) and to sharpen focus, awareness, and perception of all that is.

Meditation, in one form or another, is found in all cultures and in all religions all over the world. It has survived throughout history because it works. There are hundreds of techniques, and while the forms vary, they all share a common foundation: directed concentration of focused attention. It always involves the intention to focus attention. Like a laser beam we diminish the scope while intensifying the power. We will bypass the fluff often associated with meditation by returning to this foundation and use basic proven techniques.

Meditation makes the simple but momentous shift from doing to being. It slowly but surely strengthens and stabilizes our concentration and awakens us to the present moment. Meditation does not mean sitting in a perfect state of peace while having no thoughts because that is probably not possible or even desirable. It is not spacing out in the endless fog of altered states. That's a job for the TV. It helps us live a happier, fuller, and a more stress-free life integrating mind, body, and spirit. It is about awakening and embodying wisdom and compassion; establishing a different relationship with our thoughts. Instead of attention being drawn off by whatever thought happens to present itself, in meditation we see our thoughts from a different, more stabilized perspective and then return to our focus. We are training the brain to put its attention where and when we consciously choose. This is very powerful and has profound healing implications for physical and mental health.

Thoughts are like waves in that sometimes they are agitated and sometimes they are calm. Most people spend their entire lives trying to navigate in these sometimes treacherous or even deadly waves on the surface; fighting the storms and just surviving the calm. Trying to see into the deep (which represents our inner wisdom) from above when the waves are thrashing about is next to impossible. When the waves calm down, the water begins to clear and we can almost see the deep but the view is still distorted. If we go beneath the waves as an observer, we can get a better view into the deep where our wisdom and connection to the Source of all things resides. From below the waves, we can look up and see our thoughts or look down and clearly see the light of our OM. Meditation takes us below the waves where we can observe our thoughts without getting caught up in them and at the same time, we can see and hear clearly the voice of wisdom.

Basic meditation is a state of being which brings stillness to a person, but it is not just a way to relax. It is also a very precise strategy for maintaining health and training the mind in keen observation, increased power of concentration, creativity, and emotional stability. It is a way of calming the mind and changing its focus from pesky trivial externals to a more relevant perspective. Meditation focuses the mind and keeps it from jumping around like a wild monkey. An artist focusing on the here-and-now rather than the not-yet or the already-gone or the never-to-be, immersing himself in contemplating a beautiful landscape while selecting the precise mix of paint could be meditating as deeply as any yogi.

Meditation teaches us control, focus, and gentle discipline. It teaches us to keep things simple, to relax the body and ease a busy mind, not make life more complicated or add to the list of things we should be doing. It hones one's ability to focus the mind and develop awareness without being distracted by harmful thoughts, feelings or minor physical discomforts. Concentration is far subtler and the mind rests lightly, pleasantly, and clearly upon the point of focus. When it strays, it is gently brought back to this point of focus, without irritation or frustration.

Meditation strengthens our intuition, opens the heart, and helps clear out negative emotions. It helps to purify and discipline the mind, awakening and freeing it in order to directly perceive reality and truth. Meditation helps develop detachment from physical and emotional reactions to outer events as the observer. And most importantly, meditation strengthens the integration of the mind/body/soul and helps us discover our purpose in life and develop our potential. In order to consciously choose the attitudes and beliefs which are most empowering, we need to quiet the mind/body. By eliciting the relaxation response, we can stop the mind chatter and open the heart. We take a deep breath and say, "ahhhhhh" making it a real letting go kind of breath and then say, "Thank you" to shift our attention from the storm to an attitude of gratitude. The quiet mind opens up our perceptions and frees us to make the most advantageous choices regarding our lives.

Psychoanalysts say that the capacity to spend time alone is the mark of emotional maturity and that we do not need to be in the company of others in order to feel fulfilled and happy. Meditation can develop that capacity, open our minds to an entirely new world of fulfillment and lead to better quality relationships with friends and loved ones. When we have no time to ourselves, we tend to feel overwhelmed and out of balance.

Most types of meditation have four elements in common. The first is a warm, safe, quiet location with as few distractions as possible. This can be particularly helpful for beginners. The second is a dignified but comfortable position. The third is focused attention. And the fourth is a non-judgmental, open attitude. We choose a warm, safe, quiet location with as few distractions as possible until we get good enough to welcome distractions to test and strengthen our ability to concentrate and focus. We sit in a comfortable but dignified manner because our physical position reflects and strengthens our self-image. Harvard social psychologist Amy Cuddy found that just assuming an assertive position, a "power pose," like sitting in a chair with the chest puffed out, not only affects the way we feel but actually changes hormonal levels with stress cortisol decreasing and testosterone increasing. We choose to focus our attention on the breath because it is in the present moment. It gets one's head out of one's *passt*, and since we can focus on only one thing at a time, there is no room to worry about the future. Our breath is our home base, a safe port in the storm, a reset to original settings, and provides the comfortable feeling of "arriving home." It is basic evidence of life and is always available when we need it. And having an open attitude during meditation means letting distractions come and go naturally without judging or getting caught up in them.

When practicing meditation, it helps to develop the feeling of opening one's self completely to the whole Universe with absolute simplicity and the receptive mind of a beginner. Opening up requires a non-judgmental attitude. We do not TRY to relax; we assume a non-judgmental attitude and invite the mind/body to embrace calm, comfort, and harmony. It is the paradox of Zen: Try not to try. We let go of TRYING, shift from doing to being, and allow ourselves the luxury of doing absolutely nothing, just for now. We give ourselves permission to recharge our batteries. Doing nothing on purpose is far more productive than pondering harmful thoughts or useless trivia over and over and over. It is a luxury that is as necessary as sleep.

Just like the physical body, the mind needs a rest period to evolve, renew, and repair. If we never allow our mind to rest, it becomes exhausted and foggy; thoughts are aimless and become less trustworthy. Sleep can recharge the body but is often not enough to provide sufficient mind rest. We need to consciously take the time to recharge the mind and when we get better at it, we can use that talent to consciously take control of the mind/body and our life. Those who do not consciously meditate will find themselves in some form of unconscious meditation because the brain will haphazardly shut down certain functions. If we do not do it on purpose, the mind will do it anyway (at potentially very inconvenient times) in the form of daydreaming, senior moments, brain farts, or just spacing out.

While exercise is good for us, continuous nonstop exercise becomes counterproductive. We need to rest and sleep a third of our lives to rebuild and recharge the physical body. The mind is no different but in order to survive, it is always "on" and searching for possible threats, dangers, solutions, and explanations, either real or imagined. Even while the body sleeps, the mind churns out dreams and maintains bodily functions. Meditating on the breath is a safe place to rest.

When the mind is not thinking about a particular problem or task, it is searching restlessly for something to fill the gap. All too often that gap is filled with worry, regret, or incessant mind chatter. This mind chatter can be a seemingly endless, restless stream of incomplete thoughts, anxieties, and self-talk which constantly pulses through the mind. Sometimes, because of the mind's relentless chatter, regret, and worry, we even begin to anticipate dangers or threats that do not really exist. This condition is described brilliantly by Mark Twain who said, "I've experienced many terrible things in my life, a few of which actually happened...I spent half my life worrying about things that never happened."

It is important to find a regular, comfortable place to meditate each day, where we will not be disturbed. Meditating in the same place each day builds up a vibration there and makes it easier to meditate each time. Establishing a regular rhythm is essential. Ten minutes each day is better than an hour, two or three times a week, because it creates a regular habit pattern and rhythm. Most people find mornings most conducive because they are fresher and are not yet caught up in the day's activities. Meditation in the morning sets the right tone for the day. It connects us with a higher form of energy and a sense of purpose. Beginners should proceed slowly, not try to meditate for more than a few minutes at first, and wait at least an hour after eating and several hours after drinking alcohol. Meditation should be in balance as part of the rhythm of daily living.

When our attention goes to distracting or wandering thoughts during meditation, we do not suppress them; instead, we recognize the stray thoughts, smile, say Thank You, and gently return our attention to the breath with gratitude and not frustration or annoyance of any kind. <u>Always return to the breath</u>. Avoid the tendency to get mindlessly lost in the thoughts. Simply let them come and go. We say Thank You every time we catch ourselves following a distracting thought because we are grateful for the reminder. We are pleased with ourselves because we are aware enough to realize that we have drifted. We then gently return our focus to the breath with a slight inner smile knowing that we are successfully meditating; we are doing it correctly. We might be distracted many, many times but each time we return to the breath, we experience a tiny victory and get a little stronger. <u>Recognizing the drift and returning to the breath is an integral part of a meditation done correctly</u>. As we practice being kind and patient with our mind, we naturally soften and relax into the present moment and become a kinder, more patient person.

Once we learn how to be present and aware in our daily life, we can more easily practice returning to real life when we drift into mind clutter. The practice of returning to the breath in meditation develops that skill and prevents us from falling back into old stressful habits. No matter how many other things we may be doing, we are always breathing in the present moment and returning conscious awareness to the breath provides a reliable anchor for our attention in stressful times. Always return to the breath. It's always here for us.

2.3.1 Basic Meditation

For the purposes of this program, we have chosen a path for the reader based on fundamentals and suggest that it be followed as presented. Fully mindful that there are many other methods available, returning to these basics will keep us all on the same page and make it easier to understand and practice. We can calm the mind and still the emotions by breathing in peace and stillness, and exhaling any tensions or worries. We can learn to become a detached observer noticing thoughts and emotions without getting caught up in them. As if watching a movie, we can notice what's going on, without reacting.

Before each meditation session, it is important to state one's intent (as opposed to goal) even if the intent is simply to observe inner peace, relax, or calm down after a difficult experience. The difference between INTENT and a GOAL is in the striving. An intent is simply an easy "letting it happen" while a goal involves trying too hard for meditation. An intent might be to lower blood pressure, reduce pain, or promote perfect health, happiness, vitality, and/or longevity. Whatever one feels good about feeling good about.

We begin to relax by taking a comfortable position, loosening any restricting clothing, and gently focusing on, becoming aware of, and appreciating the breath. We take three deep breaths and think, "calm, comfort, control." On one of those breaths, the eyes begin to close and take a well-deserved break. With every breath in, we breathe in relaxation to the body and positives to the mind. With every exhalation, we release any discomfort from the body and negatives from the mind. Every breath brings an even deeper calm, and greater comfort. Relaxation can be induced and senses heightened as we allow the body to let go and the mind to become quiet and still.

a) When starting a meditative practice, we first want to find a time and place where we know we will not be distracted. The time period associated with the (5-7-9) Breath usually works well and the place should be warm, safe, and quiet. Advanced students can meditate in a hurricane, but they all started with the basics. We then state our intent, (in this case it is simply to practice focusing our attention) keeping in mind that regardless of current superficial wants and desires, we all want Harmony in the end. And then, just for a moment, consider that meditation is founded on gratitude, patience, and kindness.

b) Set a timer with a pleasing tone if desired but most people simply open their eyes long enough to look at a watch or clock and gently return to their focus. Sit in a comfortable but dignified manner with the face, scalp, neck, shoulders, and body relaxed and spine straight. It is important to stay relaxed, yet aware and awake. Some students sit on a pillow with their hips slightly higher than their knees and imagine their spine is a tall, straight tree against which they can lean. With each in-breath, sit a little taller while maintaining comfort and dignity. This will ensure that the chest is out and in a good position for deep breathing. Note that meditation can be done in the prone position as well, particularly mindfulness and progressive relaxation, but is more likely to morph into sleep. Meditation requires conscious awareness, not sleep.

c) Focus attention on the breath. With our eyes closed (some feel more comfortable with eyes half closed and vision blurred) to reduce distractions, we shift from the outer world to our inner world and maintain focus and awareness on our breath. We take a deep (5-7-9) Breath with a barely audible sigh (ahhhhhh) allowing the jaw and shoulders to relax and a slight smile to form on the out-breath. Then we let the breath come naturally without trying to influence it as practiced in the "Observe the Natural Breath" skill. Observe the natural inhalation and exhalation of the breath without trying to change it.

d) Scan the mind/body from head to toe for tension or tightness. Invite it to relax as much as it wants to while remaining alert and attentive to the breath in the present moment. Assume a non-judgmental attitude, brush away stray thoughts that cloud concentration, and return to the breath. A non-judgmental attitude means we are playful, enjoy the practice, and hold a gentle inner smile as we study our breath because it keeps us from trying too hard, getting tense, or being self-critical. On the inhale, we gather up tension that we do not need to hold right now, and on each exhale, we release that tension and become more and more relaxed; a real letting go kind of breath. It is often helpful to bring the thumb and forefinger together and notice the sense of touch. When we can feel the thumb touching the forefinger, we know that we are aware and in the present moment.

e) Quietly feel the air going in and out. Notice it at the tip of the nose, back of the throat, or lower belly as practiced in the "Diaphragmatic or Abdomen Breath" skill. Notice how the temperature is cooler at the tip of the nose on the in-breath and warmer on the out-breath. Notice the rise and fall. Notice the quiet (silent peace) space between the out-breath and the in-breath. The mind/body is repairing and renewing itself on every level, and there is nothing else we have to do while it is doing that. Although doing nothing on purpose is actually doing something, we can grant ourselves the luxurious permission to have nothing else to do or nowhere else to go right now. Shift from doing to being and notice what it feels like to do absolutely nothing and have it be good for us.

f) When awareness detects a lapse in focus, silently say Thank You, smile gently and return to the breath. Always return to the basics; always return to the breath. Until we learn to use a mantra, it can be helpful to think, "Good stuff IN, bad stuff OUT" to hold attention on the breath when it begins to wander. Nothing is more important than studying the breath right now.

g) Stay focused as long as is comfortable, improving gradually. Some people set a timer (with a pleasing tone, not a shocking alarm) but most people simply open their eyes long enough to look at a watch or clock and gently return to the breath. Beginners usually start with five to ten minutes and extend it to 30 minutes as they get better at it; whatever feels right.

h) When it is time to return to the outside world, we begin to notice what is going on around us. We move our focus from the breath to the sounds, smells, shapes and colors around us. Finally, we take a comfortable energizing Three-Part-Breath and open our eyes feeling wide awake, grateful, re-energized, refreshed, happy, and ready for the remainder of the day.

One needs to look deeply into their own mind and heart to clarify the reasons that motivate them to meditate. Then they can consult this motivation when the practice inevitably seems boring, uneventful, or a waste of time. One needs to cultivate the motivation that keeps the benefits of meditation growing, week after week. Whether one is meditating to reduce stress or improve life in some way, reverse heart disease, enhance performance, or become enlightened, the deep intuition of being inextricably connected with something larger than one's self (and with every other being and thing) connects us in some way with the Source of all things.

Whatever one's Reason or Motivation for Daily Meditation, it is very important to define it clearly and make a sign that states the reason or motivation for starting the practice in the first place. Then display that sign prominently in the area normally used for meditation to serve as a reminder when motivation wanes. Unlike the need for food, water, air, or physical rest, the need for mental rest does not have an obvious unconscious alarm. We need to consciously remind ourselves that it is needed and provide it. The sign and the place of meditation are very important. Other signs will be created as we progress and the place becomes even more special. Those who are 'space challenged' can post the sign on the inside of a closet door and when it is time to meditate, open the door and sit comfortably facing it.

The physiologic benefits of practicing meditation regularly are measurable, predictable, and repeatable but not always immediately obvious. Dr. Herbert Benson likens this to brushing our teeth. We do it because we know it is good for us whether we feel it working or not. Feeling good is an added benefit. The most important thing is to cultivate the commitment necessary and actually take the time to do it. The quieting of the mind that results from eliciting the relaxation response is critical. It opens up our perceptual world, away from negativity, fear, and anxiety that so quickly narrows our perceptions and infects our beliefs with suspicion and doubt. This freedom allows us to be more awake, more aware, and more conscious of the attitudes and beliefs we choose when living our daily lives.

One deceptively simple technique often used in Zen practice is <u>Breath Counting</u>. It helps maintain focus for those who have not yet developed their awareness enough to mentally explore the intricacies of the breath: flow, apex of in-breath, space between the out-breath and the in-breath, etc. To begin the exercise, focus on the breath and count each exhale up to "five," and then start over. We do not count higher than "five," and count only on the exhale. We know that our attention has wandered when we find ourselves up to eight, twelve, or even nineteen. That's OK. Just smile, be pleased that it was noticed before the count of twenty and start another round.

Another variation of the Zen practice is to simply sit quietly and count each breath with the intention of reaching 100 without thinking about something else. Most beginners are unable to make it to 10 without being distracted by a stray thought, but the conscious realization that a thought is trying to interrupt the count is an indication that progress is being made. Simply smile, be grateful for the awareness, remember that we are not in a contest, and start over. We are honing the ability to focus and facilitate calm.

Trying a meditation for a few weeks, then discarding it as unsuitable, a waste of time, or ineffective is like being angry with a baby for not answering when asked a question. We need to let our instincts or intuition guide us, be patient, and let our health or objective have time to correct or manifest. Imagine a container that is half full of water and that our objective is to raise the level of the water to the top of the container. If we receive a pebble for each time we meditate, we can reach our objective by dropping the pebbles into the container, and depending on the size of the container, it might take a while. Becoming discouraged because we do not see any change after several pebbles, is like saying, "I don't see any muscles yet" after the first two or three workouts.

Some people foolishly believe that they do not have the time to meditate or even sit quietly for that matter. These are the people who need it the most. The fact is that we all have the time; we just choose to use our time for activities holding higher (perceived) priorities for us. Ten minutes spent sharpening the axe reduces chopping time by more than an hour. That gives us 50 minutes to do other healthy things for which we once thought we had no time. Everyone can afford 1% of their time (14.4 minutes per day) to create a healthy mind and body for the other 99%. Those who truly value their health will find the time and place to do healthy things. One busy mother found silence in her parked car, and another found privacy in a bathroom stall at work.

Some days we impatiently think that we do not have the time right now or just don't feel like doing it. When that happens, we suggest a 30 second "time out" to observe the breath. That's all; just do it for a few seconds and if that turns into a little more, all the better. At least we can say we did it, and we can do it better next time. Meditating for 30 seconds is better than not doing it at all and establishes a daily rhythm. No one can truthfully say that they do not have 30 seconds available for their own health and well-being. It is as important to good health as proper nutrition, quality sleep, and staying hydrated. The time spent meditating is not as important as quality and consistency, but it needs to be done in one form or another every day. Failure to rest the mind every day is as debilitating as failure to eat, sleep, or drink water. Try not to try. We just do it the best we can, fully mindful of the fact that nobody's perfect.

Simply by bringing our attention to the natural rhythm and flow of the breath, we can shift our mind/body toward greater calm, clarity, and balance. Breath is our constant companion and combining it with regular meditation can help us develop and carry many admirable traits over into the rest of our life. As often as possible, visit the breath and return to the present moment: Deeper, Slower, Calmer, Regular. Our breath is always with us, so we can turn to it not only during our meditation sessions but whenever we wish to calm ourselves. Each breath restores the calm intensity, harmony, and balanced presence of the meditation in the present moment. Now is good.

2.3.2 **The Magic of Incremental Steps**

The secret to mastering almost anything is to do it for a short time and then increase it as appropriate with commitment. Anyone can eat an entire five-pound roast by themselves; if taken in bite-size chunks over a period of time. Seemingly insurmountable objectives are possible when we reduce them to manageable, incremental steps with each step being big enough to matter, but small enough to manage. Anyone can meditate for 2 or 3 minutes but sitting for an hour is beyond most of us. Short stints move us through our fear and concerns in a small way, so it does not interrupt our lives or mess with our habits. This begins to establish a new habit. Everything that is ever accomplished in life is done in steps and is a process that combines choice with commitment.

As applied to meditation, a beginner might start with a 2 to 3 minute breath focus at least six days a week for the first week or two. It is best to do it every day, even if for only 30 seconds, but if one feels the need to take a day off, always take off the same day of the week. Commitment, consistency, and rhythm are key. When the student feels ready, they increase the frequency to twice a day and/or the time to 5 to 7 minutes for two weeks, then 10 to 12 minutes for two weeks, then 15 to 20 minutes for two weeks. Increasing the time or frequency beyond that is optional but beneficial. If regression occurs, we do not beat ourselves up, we just move back one step, do it for two weeks and establish it as a habit or normal routine.

Most students use a timer with a pleasant sound that will not be shocking or alarming, and when the timer goes off, they feel a sense of victory and accomplishment that can be carried into the rest of life's experiences. The emphasis is on, <u>doing what they said they would do</u>, not on how they feel about it. New beliefs and confidence build up. Time becomes less of an issue, enthusiasm builds, and self-assurance and confidence grow. We soon find that we cannot wait to get to the task and feel good about what we have accomplished.

A journey of a thousand miles <u>begins</u> with a single step and is <u>accomplished</u> by persistently taking another and another and another, focusing on the step and doing it well. It is not about feeling; it is about doing. The important thing is to stay in the doing of the thing for just the short amount of time to which one has committed, no more no less. Staying with the commitment is a victory, and a winning feeling is then appropriate. A feeling of victory and accomplishment has been earned. Over the coming days and weeks ahead, the student will notice that a growing feeling of accomplishment begins to set in, it all becomes easier, and a new habit is being created through this repetition of action. Allowing a feeling of happiness and fulfillment can be quite good and satisfying.

2.4 Summary

Part II began with a continuation of our stress management discussion and how it involves perception plasticity and the ability to accept and adapt to circumstances. We learned how it relates to breath control which in turn leads to control of the mind/body and eventually gene function. We discussed Dr. Herbert Bensons Relaxation Response, breath awareness, and practiced the three basic "Breathing Awareness" skills that form the foundation for the Three Imperative Breathing Techniques used to facilitate conscious access to the Subconscious Control Room of the Unconscious Mind-of-the-body. We learned to develop conscious control and how to expand it into areas previously ignored. With a background knowledge of the power we have in our breath, we learned how simple meditation can focus and enhance that power. We learned more about meditation itself and how to do a basic, no-nonsense meditation session. Finally, we end Part II with an Action Assignment and a visual to aid the practice.

In Part III we will discuss the power of perception, attitude, and thought and how it can be controlled to direct our lives. We will learn more about meditation and how it can be used to heal the mind, body, and soul.

2.5 Action Assignment

* Practice the Bellows Breath to wake up in the morning, warm up, stimulate circulation and awareness when feeling drowsy and disconnected, or when there is a need to be particularly alert.

* Practice the three prerequisite "Breathing Awareness" skills: the "Observe the Natural Breath, the Exhalation Focus and Squeeze, and the Diaphragmatic or Abdomen Breath," until they feel comfortable because they are the foundation of the Three Imperative Breath Techniques.

* Practice the first Imperative Breath Technique, the Three-Part-Breath when feeling sluggish or particularly fatigued to oxygenate and detoxify the cells and to dramatically increase physical energy. Practice calming and grounding the mind by filling the lungs completely.

* Associate the sudden onset of stress with a Big Red Smiling Stop Sign! "Stop, Smile, Breathe, and say Thank you, Thank you, Thank you." Breathe using the second Imperative Breath Technique, the (DSCR) Deeper, Slower, Calmer, Regular Breath. In addition to stressful moments, practice the (DSCR) Breath as many times a day as possible: in line at the supermarket, during commercials while watching TV, and at traffic lights. Placing sticky notes in areas frequented as reminders is of great help to the beginner especially.

* Associate the "Slow down, Simplify, and Be Grateful, Patient, and Kind" attitude and the third Imperative Breath Technique, the (5-7-9) Breath, with something done twice a day like brushing the teeth or washing hands before a meal because it needs to be done at least twice a day. It can also be associated with bathing or taking a shower and can be a great enhancement to the coffee break during a particularly tense day. Some students have found it helpful to write "5-7-9" on a sticky note and place it on their bathroom mirror and on the door they use to leave the house in the morning. One should never leave the house without doing the (5-7-9) Breath; it's that important.

* Meditate at least once a day, every day. It needs to be done to recharge the mind. Even a few seconds is better than not doing it at all. Never will we put so little into something and receive so much in return. We take the time to eat, brush our teeth, and sleep every day. If we put meditation on the list of things we just always do every day, we are evolving.

* Whatever one's Reason or Motivation for Daily Meditation, it is very important to define it clearly and make a sign that states that reason or motivation to serve as a reminder when motivation wanes. Place that sign prominently in the area normally used for meditation.

* Do something nice for someone and tell no one about it. It is better to know we are kinder than we say we are than to say we are kinder than we know we are.

Master the <u>Bellows Breath</u> and the Three Breath Awareness Skills

1) Observe the Natural Breath
2) Exhalation Focus and Squeeze
3) Diaphragmatic or Abdomen Breath

Three Imperative Breathing Techniques

1) Use the <u>Three-Part-Breath</u> for energy.
2) Use the <u>Deeper, Slower, Calmer, Regular Breath</u> for Sudden Stress.
3) Use the <u>(5-7-9) Breath</u> for Accumulated Stress, and Don't leave home without it.

Mute the TV and Breathe

~

Simplify
and be
Grateful, Patient, and Kind

~

<u>MEDITATE</u>
Just breathe
30 seconds to 30 minutes every day

~

<u>Make a Sign</u>
State the Reason or Motivation for Daily Meditation

PART III

Perception Lights the Way and Meditation Provides the Means

3.1 Perception, Attitude, and Thought

Perception is a mental image or concept and is what we see through our own personal experience and consciousness. Attitude is a mental state of mind or position toward the world derived from our perceptions and is how we show the world what we think about what we have seen. One might be told that he has a bad attitude at work if he complains and displays negativity caused by a perception of unfairness or overwork. Perception comes first, then the attitude and emotions reinforced by the resulting thoughts and finally, behavior. Perception is everything, and when it comes to quality of life, it is the most important word in this or any other language. The perceptions with which we approach other people each day can determine whether we experience isolation, chronic stress, suffering, and illness, or intimacy, relaxation, joy, and health. Too many people are unhappy because they are waiting for the world and others to change toward them with no thought of adapting or altering their own perceptions toward the world.

The first-century Roman philosopher Epictetus said, "Men are disturbed not by things, but by the view which they take of them," and James Allen said, "Our life is what our thoughts make it. A man will find that as he alters his thoughts toward things and other people, things and other people will alter toward him." Our perceptions form our attitudes and our attitudes determine which thoughts we choose to keep and which to dismiss. The thoughts we choose to keep, affect our feelings, and our feelings determine our actions; the way we respond to the world and the people around us. Perceptions determine our environment, from the world around us right down to the cellular level, affecting gene expression and health. In short, our perceptions determine mental and physical well-being; the direction and quality of life itself. When our perceptions are inflexible, they limit our attitudes, thoughts, feelings, actions, behaviors, and health.

There was a time when Tony feared the number 13 and associated it with bad luck. When she learned that 13 is a baker's dozen and a free gift of one, she was able to replace fear with gratitude. There was no need to leave the present and wallow in the past exploring the fear and analyzing its painful origin. There was no need to feel bad at all. She simply changed the way she looked at it in the present moment by recognizing, dismissing, and replacing dysfunctional thoughts with gratitude, patience, and kindness. Our reality is our own creation. With the right mindset, making the impossible possible becomes simple and easy. We just need to learn how to create and control our perceptions.

Sometimes we try to make even the simplest things complicated. We tend to over-analyze events and look for reasons when really it is only our perception that matters. The Taoists teach us to remain in harmony and to see things in simplicity by contemplating or even being "one" with nature (the Universe); the truest simplicity in life. Although life can be complicated, happiness is simple. Life can throw all sorts of complications at us: things break, plans go wrong, we make mistakes, people do things that are unexpected, and some can be rude and hurtful. By simply accepting and adapting to the present moment, we remain balanced and centered, happy and at peace with a sincere intent to promote harmony. We Stop, Smile, Breathe (DSCR), and say Thank you. Then with gratitude, patience, and kindness, we simply fix or replace what breaks, reformulate a better plan, avoid or neutralize rudeness, and return to our objective.

Accepting and adapting does not mean that, on the outer level, we cannot take action and change the situation. We do not need to accept an undesirable or unpleasant situation nor do we need to deceive ourselves and say that there is nothing wrong. If we recognize that we want to get out, we "accept the moment" for what it is and take positive action to get out. Positive action is more effective than negative action, which arises out of anger, despair, or frustration. It is possible to say "no" firmly and clearly or to walk away from a situation and still be in a state of complete inner non-resistance. We let it come from conscious wisdom and insight, not a mindless reaction. To be truly at peace, one needs to realize that ultimately everything is, and was as it should be. It might be that way to give us the opportunity to make things better, and had it been different, we might not exist.

Non-resistance is the key to amazing results and together with a non-judgmental attitude, and non-attachment, they are the three aspects of true freedom and harmony. It may seem as if a situation or event is the cause of suffering, but ultimately an Inflexible Perception creates resistance and the inability to adapt which leads to stress. The deep wisdom underlying the practice of Eastern martial arts exemplifies the need for non-resistance. Rather than resisting a blow, they yield to the flow of energy to overcome an opponent's force. When we push someone or a thought, they often push back. Like the weather and other things that are beyond our control, it is usually better to accept, adapt, and move out of the way. Resistance is often just misplaced unreasonable stubbornness resulting from Inflexible Perceptions. The simple act of safely letting go of control of an immovable force or the insistence upon an Inflexible Perception can become a wonderful means of stress reduction.

Just as it is not useful to identify with our own shortcomings, it is likewise not useful to judge or identify another person with their shortcomings, distortions, or afflictions. Judging a person, thing, or situation as good or bad is only seeing something from one perspective and not the whole, larger, picture. All things assume the meaning we give or attach to them. We need to remember that we see the world not as it is, but as we perceive it and recognize that we all wish to be respected, happy, safe, free, and well. When we judge others, we are not defining them; we are defining ourselves. If we see a world full of possibilities, it is because we are full of possibilities. If we see a world that is dangerous and threatening, it is because we are fearful. Kind, loving people see a kind, loving world and hostile people see a hostile world because the world and the people in it reflect us, and we reflect them. Life is our mirror. Our perceptions and resulting attitudes, thoughts, feelings, emotions, and actions create our world. We need to act toward the world and others in the same manner that we want the world and others to act toward us. People are not mean because the world is mean to them; the world is mean to them because they are mean people. There is nothing in the world that people want and need more than self-esteem; the feeling that they are important, needed and respected. Give and you shall receive.

We need to avoid getting caught up in, or attached to, anything by developing a mind that is open to everything and attached to nothing. All things are impermanent and guaranteed to change. When we detach, we gain a higher vantage point from which to view the events in our lives instead of being trapped inside them. We become like an astronaut who sees the planet Earth surrounded by the vastness of space and realizes a paradoxical truth; the Earth is precious and at the same time insignificant.

When we relax our attachment to a result, it does not decrease performance. In most situations, our effectiveness will increase because it frees us from negative emotions like apprehension, tension, anxiety, and nervousness. For example, competent surgeons conduct hundreds of operations on others, but they are unwilling to operate on their own children. They know that attachment makes them prone to error. Good business people know that if they become anxious in conducting their business, they are liable to make mistakes, and it has been said that an attorney who defends himself has a fool for a client. Thus if we can become detached from our work, we become even more effective. We become one with all that is, and our work is not all that is. It needs to be a harmonious part of the whole.

We do not try to "give up" attachment and desire rather we exchange them for acceptance and adaptability. If one objective does not work out the way it is envisioned, we adjust our vision and find another path to harmony. Whatever we fight, we will strengthen, and what we resist will persist but what we accept lightens. When the ultimate goal is harmony, these intermediate goals are just stepping stones that lead to the ultimate and can be changed and adapted. We are not married to a particular path or method. There are many paths to the top of the mountain.

Attachment to impermanent things always leads to problems and only change is permanent. Everything else is impermanent and due to this dynamic, impermanent nature of all things, even when we have some kind of happiness, it is just as impermanent and subject to change unless we are in touch with our innate inner bliss. Our fundamental nature is bliss. The happiness we mistakenly take as the result of acquiring objects of our desire does not emanate from the object itself. It occurs simply from the cessation of desire for the object. In the moments following its acquisition, the absence of desire allows the bliss that already existed to shine through. The essential nature of the Universe is harmony, let it be. True wealth is not defined by an abundance of worldly goods; it is the result of a contented mind.

We know that perceived stress can affect health and immunity. An ulcer, for example, is the result of a bacteria that is normally suppressed by the immune system. Stress inhibits the immune system and allows the bacteria to proliferate. Many other conditions such as heart disease, diabetes, and asthma have also been associated with stress inhibited immunity. The key to reducing negative stress and anxiety is to re-direct our thoughts. Once we focus on the present moment, the mind can no longer think about the past or worry about the future. When this happens, we are no longer victims of random thoughts and no longer a slave to the past or the uncertainty of the future. When we become the master of the present moment, we can master each day and avoid overwhelming stress, fear, and anxiety. Stress is a psychophysiological phenomenon that needs to be addressed both physically and emotionally. We will learn to physically feel Inflexible Perceptions, respond instead of react, and become more aware and adaptable. Reactions are mindless, preprogrammed action while responses are conscious actions of wisdom.

The art of non-reaction is the ability to postpone immediate reaction until we have had a chance to consider carefully what is happening. It is a practice that can stop negative emotions from running our lives, and help us stay calm in stressful situations. Most people can remember a time when they snapped at someone in anger and later had to apologize for it. Reactions do not always represent what we truly mean, but conscious responses do. When we feel anxiety or anger creeping into the mind, we need to remember that we have a choice. We can react in anger and complicate the situation, or we can respond in a way that encourages us and those around us to seek effective solutions. Every opportunity to develop anger is also an opportunity to develop patience. The best way to replace anger with patience is to, "Stop, Smile, Breathe (DSCR), and say Thank you." In the meantime, it is helpful to take a few minutes (at least twice a day) to breathe deeply using the (5-7-9) Breath; clear the mind of the day's worries, and relax. Do the same tomorrow and the next day, and the layers of accumulated stress will melt away. "Slow down, Simplify, and Be Grateful, Patient, and Kind."

It is often better to remain silent (with a slight smile) and not react at all than to over-react. It allows others to think well of us or just wonder what we are up to, but if someone thinks ill of us, it is still better to remain silent and let them speculate than to speak inappropriately and confirm their suspicions. Respond with conscious awareness and speak with conscious deeds. At least, let the other person finish their thought and <u>breathe before speaking</u>. When someone talks, listen to the silence as well as the words, and if one is unable to say something nice, it is best to say nothing at all. Silence is not only golden; it is sometimes the best answer. As Zen Master Dogen once said, "If you can keep your mouth as silent as your nose, you will avoid a lot of trouble." Listeners make better conversationalists and seem much smarter than interrupters.

The art of listening has the power to transform relationships. Look at the speaker, really listen, and avoid minor distractions. Show interest and give a head nod from time to time as an acknowledgment. Let the speaker finish what they are saying and <u>take a breath</u> while considering a reply. Focus on listening, avoid being judgmental while the person is speaking, and summarize what they have said to confirm understanding.

Learning to control our own mind is one of the greatest adventures we can ever encounter, and can be our greatest triumph. The mind is incredibly powerful, and its perceptions create and attract all of the conditions that occur in life, so mastery in this area should be a priority. We have heard people say for years that attitude is everything, but since our perceptions form our attitudes, perhaps we need to focus on the cause of everything: Perception.

3.1.1 Perception

We live in a world of contrasts, the Yin and the Yang, and cannot know one experience without observing the opposite experience somewhere in our lives. Without one, the other does not exist, and contained within each, is the other. When asked a question, one professor would often reply with, "Relative to what?" All things appear and disappear because of the concurrence of causes and conditions. Nothing ever exists entirely alone; everything is in relation to everything else. Most people think that the sun rises in the morning and sets in the evening, but it is only relatively true. Only from the limited perspective of an observer on or near the planet's surface does the sun rise and set. Observed from far out in space the sun neither rises nor sets, but shines continuously.

Jenna worked at a local coffee shop and was a happy, friendly person. She always had a kind word for everyone who came into the shop and almost always had a smile on her face. She had always enthusiastically volunteered to do the ordering and inventory control, made sure everyone did their share of cleaning and stocking with gentle, friendly suggestions, and enjoyed training new employees. She genuinely seemed to have fun with her work and did such a good job that the owner promoted her to manager. Suddenly the same fun job carried responsibility and perceived stress. She began to lose her delightful personality and sense of humor, and became irritable. She developed stress headaches, negativity, and felt like she was losing control. After in-depth consultations, it was determined that she was suffering from TSTSD (Taking Stuff Too Seriously Disease). If not treated, TSTSD can lead to psycho-sclerosis (hardening of the attitude), depression, and serious health problems. Jenna learned to be mindful of her symptoms and started to use the "Stop, Smile, Breathe, and say Thank You" technique when she began to feel negative stress. She began to perceive life as a fun adventure of curiosity and wonder instead of one great emergency of varying intensities. She was reminded that gratitude, patience, and kindness constitute an admirable attitude and is a powerful antidote to virtually all stress, unhappiness, and frustration. She now understands that managing a coffee shop is just a job and not her ultimate objective. A change in perception can be like walking from a dark tunnel into the bright clear light of day.

A wrong Inflexible Perception, desire, or belief that has been embedded in our cellular memories always causes immune inhibiting stress. If we can heal the wrong beliefs by Recognizing, Neutralizing, Dismissing, and Replacing them, the stress goes away, and the immune system in the body can heal everything else, even genetic illnesses and disease. Wrong beliefs cause us to be afraid when we should not be afraid, and the evidence that one has a wrong Inflexible Perception, belief, or goal is <u>anger</u>.

Angry, hostile people are five times more likely to die before the age of fifty, compared to those who are calm, adaptable, and in control. A constant state of anger causes severe physiological reactions. Hostility usually involves angry feelings, but it also involves a set of attitudes that motivate aggressive behavior directed at destroying or injuring people or objects. When a non-hostile person is aroused, the parasympathetic nervous system acts to calm things down. Reducing hostility in a constructive manner involves conscious awareness, gratitude, patience, kindness, and a clear, worthy purpose in life.

An inability to accept and adapt can lead to unpleasant inner feelings when someone opposes us. This causes us to become angry, which leads to arguments and conflict with others and this, in turn, gives rise to more problems. A two-thousand-year-old proverb states that if we hold on to anger, it's like grasping a hot coal with the intention of throwing it at someone else; we are the ones who get burned. Most political problems experienced throughout the world are caused by angry people with inflexible political, religious, and personal perspectives.

People become angry when confronted with something that blocks them from achieving a desire, and it often flares up during the very moments when clarity and objectivity are needed most. In such instances, anger is the enemy of success and perhaps even safety. The more we can stand apart from and overcome sudden anger, the greater our chance of success in any undertaking, and the greater our chance for lasting fulfillment in life. When Mohammed was asked the single most important quality that a person should have, he replied, "Be not angry."

One practitioner of Medimaginosis wrote, "I often tell people that I haven't been angry in years and upon hearing such claims, many are skeptical. They think that we need to 'be with' our anger and analyze it, delving deep into our past looking for the cause. I can accept the 'being with' thing if I only need to be with it long enough to recognize (some would say label) it, dismiss it, and replace it. And one can learn to do all that in less than three seconds if they Stop, Smile, Breathe, and say Thank you, at the first sign of the stress. We do not need to spend time wallowing in negative thoughts. I would like to note that 'never being angry' does not mean that angry thoughts do not exist, because they do. They come and go the same as thoughts of gratitude, love, and good ideas. A good idea will slip away as silently as it appeared if we don't write it down. Anger too, begins as a thought and will float away even sooner if we make a point of replacing it. I try to stand back and observe my thoughts, choosing the ones I wish to spend time with and allowing the others to float away. It's fun."

There is nothing more destructive than anger. It blocks our spiritual progress and prevents us from reaching our objectives. Anger is by nature a painful state of mind; inner peace immediately disappears and the body becomes tense and uncomfortable. We become restless and find it difficult to fall asleep, and what sleep we do manage to get is fitful and unrefreshing. We are not punished <u>for</u> our anger; we are punished <u>by</u> our anger.

Ralph Waldo Emerson said, "For every minute you are angry, you lose 60 seconds of happiness." Anger transforms even a normally attractive person into an ugly red-faced demon unable to enjoy life or even a good meal. We grow more and more miserable as it robs us of our reason and good sense. In a controversy, the instant we feel anger we stop looking for compromise and truth, and begin striving for dominance without prudence. Retaliation and petty revenge expose us to even greater danger often jeopardizing our job, our relationships, and even the well-being of our family. Habitually angry people often destroy their own happiness and are soon avoided by all who know them.

It is sometimes far better to let the other person be right, especially on minor points because being right is overrated. It's not a matter of who is right or wrong; it is a matter of finding a solution. What is real and right to one person might be bogus and wrong to another. It is simply a different opinion, and everyone has a different perception of everything. No exceptions. Different opinions, cultures or thought systems may not be right or wrong, just different. Be curious and entertain the possibility that maybe they all have a point. Those who want respect for their traditions need to show respect for the traditions of others. We do not have to agree with everyone but understanding their point of view is the mark of a civilized person. Is a man who steals a loaf of bread to feed his starving family a dangerous criminal or a brave, loving father and husband? Some people may feel like they have the right to be angry but that does not give them the right to be cruel. One who is curious and kind seems wiser and more intelligent than one who is right, angry, and critical. We can <u>reconstruct our perceptions</u>. If we look at them very carefully and alter them even a little, the different views of other people might not be as disturbing.

Fear is also a very powerful emotion that is triggered by our perceptions. When danger is real, it needs to be avoided or neutralized, while fear is an imagined mirage and needs to be replaced with gratitude, patience, and kindness. People who live in constant fear, whether from physical dangers in their environment or threats they perceive, can become incapacitated. It weakens our immune system and can interrupt processes in our brains that allow us to regulate emotions, read nonverbal cues and other information presented to us. This impacts our thinking and decision-making in negative ways, leaving us susceptible to intense emotions and impulsive reactions. Whether threats to our security are real or perceived, they impact our mental and physical well-being.

Fear and anxiety can affect all of us every now and then. It normally will last for only a short time and then pass, but some people become overwhelmed by fear and want to avoid situations that might make them frightened or anxious. Anxiety is a type of fear that is usually associated with the thought of a threat or something going wrong in the future, rather than something happening right now. It can make us sick and stop us from traveling, going to school, or even leaving the house. We can feel fear when faced with less dangerous situations like exams, public speaking, a new job, a date, or even a party. It is a natural response to something that a person feels is a threat, but when it is severe and long lasting, we need to act.

3.1.2 **Attitude**

William James of Harvard said that the greatest discovery of his generation was that human beings can alter their lives by altering their attitudes. It is our attitude at the beginning of a task that will, more than anything, determine its outcome. Our attitudes toward life and others will determine their attitudes toward us, and if we do not control our attitudes by adjusting our perceptions, our attitudes will control us.

A good attitude is not the result of success; success is the result of a good attitude. Success is the progressive realization of a worthy intent, ideal, or goal. It is more about the journey and less about the destination. It is not about being at the top of one's field and making a lot of money unless it is something that the person enjoys doing and is truly happy doing it. A success is the entrepreneur who starts his own company because that was his dream; a well-defined intent that is powered by belief. A success is the school teacher who is teaching because that is what he or she wants to do, and a success is the wife and mother who loves what she is doing and does a good job of it. A success is anyone who is realizing a worthy predetermined ideal, because that is what he or she decided to do, deliberately.

Creating a happy, harmonious life is a matter of learning to replace harmful perceptions and attitudes with healthy perceptions and attitudes. [Perception - Attitude - Thought - Feeling - Action - Result] Even our energy level is a function of belief and the associated attitudes. Energy and stamina do not come from caffeine and sugar. All the energy we need comes from within. It is generated by perception and attitude which in turn generate the thoughts, feelings, and emotions which drive us forward. Consider the seemingly lazy teenage boy who can hardly find the energy to move across the room, flops onto the couch and seems unable to even clean his room, not to mention mow the lawn. That same teenage boy turns into a human dynamo when he gets a call from a teenage girl, is getting ready for a date, or is preparing for something he is enthusiastic about. All the energy we need can be generated by the attitude.

Some people say that one person cannot change the world because no one alone is strong enough or big enough or powerful enough. That is simply not true. Everything we do, every choice we make, changes the world. When we choose to be happy with determination and conviction, we will suddenly see a changed world. The world and life itself is dull only to dull people and interesting only to interesting people. When we change our mind, we change our world.

While some people count their blessings and focus on being grateful for what they have, others focus on complaining about what they do not have. Many of them tell their friends and impressionable children how they have been cheated, treated unfairly, and should be angry about it. They become human magnets for unpleasant experiences reinforcing the poor attitude thereby attracting more problems. They create a disease that harms themselves most of all, a self-generating doom fulfilling cycle. Instead of projecting gratitude, they project anger, and since the world reflects their attitude back to them, they see an angry world. Negative thoughts are like feral cats in that if one feeds them, they will come back, and if it becomes a habit, they will stay and multiply. The same applies to blessings.

To complain is to exhibit the inability to accept and adapt (resistance) to what is and it invariably carries a negative charge. When people indulge in complaining or pointless criticizing, they give whatever is upsetting them greater control over their life. They become victims of circumstances instead of creators. A creator will actively change the situation by speaking out with gratitude, patience, and kindness to improve it, accept and adapt to it by altering their perceptions, or let it go and move out of the way. When one complains, they are implying that they are right, and the person or situation that they are complaining about or reacting against is wrong. Being righteous places them in a position of self-imagined moral superiority in relation to the person or situation that is being judged and invites the need to bring them down to the level of reality. If one is simply stating what they know to be true, however, the Ego is not involved at all and compromise is more likely. In the absence of our judgment, everything would be fine.

When confronted with a rude or overly critical person, one of our students would simply smile and show a 3x5 card with four evenly spaced words printed in very large type: Mean Nasty People Suck. It does not label, criticize, judge, or attack anyone, rather it simply states a fact and leaves it to the reader to decide whether they qualify or not. If one is not mean or nasty, the statement does not apply to them.

"The present world is a different one. Grief, calamity, and evil cause inner bitterness...there is disobedience and rebellion...Evil influences strife from early morning until late at night...they injure the mind and reduce its intellect and they also injure the muscles and the flesh." This was written by a Chinese physician 4,600 years ago but it reads like the laments of today and every day in between. People have been declaring that the world and the younger generation have been going to the dogs since the beginning of time. And still we seem to get by. With every problem, there is a solution and another problem. Accepting and adapting to the present moment with gratitude, patience, and kindness is the healthiest response.

Most people who soar to incredible heights of accomplishment in their lives do so because they limit their exposure to negative people and surround themselves with positive, encouraging people. Associating with habitual complainers makes it more difficult to maintain a positive outlook. It is usually a waste of time to complain, particularly about one's problems or poor health (with the exception of a doctor's appointment) because it bores most people and benefits no one. Negative people and insincere fake friends are more dangerous than a wild, unpredictable beast. A wild beast may attack without warning and wound the body, but a negative insincere friend will wound the mind when it is most vulnerable.

It is appropriate to note here that quite often people do not have a negative attitude because of poor health or bad luck; they have the poor health and bad luck because of a negative attitude. Negative emotions are toxic to the mind/body and interfere with its balance and harmonious functioning while positive emotions facilitate good luck, strengthen the immune system, invigorate and heal the mind/body.

Like a fertile garden, the subtle (or subconscious) mind will return, in abundance, whatever we plant. If we plant kindness, it will return kindness. If we plant hostility, it will return hostility in great abundance. We need to tend our wonderful garden and tell our subtle mind what we want it to do; plant good seeds, worthy goals, and ideals. Then nurture them, care for them, and observe what pops up. Pull out the weeds and let the seeds of our goals grow. We need to be diligent, or the weeds will take over and kill our seeds. We simply need to observe and choose our thoughts. Recognize, Neutralize, Dismiss, and Replace harmful thoughts with worthy thoughts: Gratitude, Patience, and Kindness. Man's greatest disability is pessimism, and his greatest super power is the creative integration of gratitude, patience, and kindness.

The great psychologist Abraham Maslow once said, "Think of life as a process of choices, one after another. At each point, there is a progression choice and a regression choice. To make the growth choice instead of the fear choice a dozen times a day is to move a dozen times toward self-actualization...With discipline and practice, we gradually increase our capacity to be fully present as we walk the path of life, and we will make wiser choices. A real master is not a person who is never distracted or wanders from the path; he or she is someone who is the quickest to recognize and correct their mistakes and to return to awareness when they have been momentarily distracted."

3.1.3 Thought, Feeling, and Behavior

There is a powerful connection between thought, feeling, and behavior. They intertwine very closely, and each can change the others. Feelings, or emotions, are more primitive and urgent than rational thoughts. Emotions move much more slowly, sometimes almost imperceptibly, while thoughts move like lightning. Negative thoughts have an immediate, destructive impact on our lives, is a less reasonable way of thinking and reduces clarity of mind. Sometimes we ignore how important our mind's perspective on an event is, and how our perception will affect the outcome of things we do and encounter.

Our negative and positive thoughts can also cause our beliefs to come true, a self-fulfilling prophecy, by affecting how we see things and act. When we attempt a task with negative thoughts, we probably will not feel like trying very hard and may interpret progress as unimpressive. While being a little skeptical can prevent others from taking advantage of us, taking it to the point of being pessimistic has no positive value. Not only is it unpleasant to have that perspective on life, but it can also cause us to miss numerous opportunities. Pessimistic people have been shown to have a greater chance of developing serious illnesses and the longer a person has been in that mindset, the more time and effort it will take to shift, but it is worth it. This pessimism can lead to giving up, blaming the poor outcome on a lack of ability or other circumstances. Pessimistic people often give up and make their poor expectations come true. In social settings, feeling inadequate, thinking pessimistically, and fearing inevitable rejection, we will probably mingle very little and see events in a distorted manner, assuming people do not come over to talk to us or walk away because they think ill of us. Withdrawn behavior rarely leads to friendships and can lead to the conclusion that their behavior is further proof of social ineptitude.

Negative thinking is counterproductive, self-defeating thinking that makes us feel worse, see things in a worse light, and act in ways that often interfere with goals. The more we think negatively, the worse we feel. Negative thinking sustains a bad mood and keeps us from feeling calm and content and confronting problems in constructive ways. Instead of seeing problems as normal, tolerable, manageable, or challenges to overcome, people with habits of negative thinking often overreact and blow things out of proportion. The true quality of one's character is not most evident in how one acts, but in how one has learned to react. Negative thoughts create bad feelings and cause misery and stress in even positive life circumstances. Every moment is fragile, think with care.

The negative thoughts of the critic, however, can serve a valuable purpose if we perceive them in a positive light. Things are not always rosy, and it is important to learn from mistakes. Every mistake or failure has a lesson to teach us. Take note of the lesson and then quickly discard the negative thought, replacing it with a positive perspective on the same situation. Understand that all problems can be perceived as opportunities.

Negative thinking causes changes in neurotransmitters and hormones. It impacts the health of the heart, immune system, brain, endocrine system, and digestion, as well as a person's overall risk of mortality. Deepak Chopra said, "If you want to know what your thoughts were like in the past, look at your body today. If you want to know what your body will be like in the future, look at your thoughts today." And Buddha said, "All that we are is a result of what we have thought. All that we will become is a result of what we think now. With our mind, we make the world." We become what we think about.

Much suffering in life comes from being identified with the mind and the thoughts it produces. This attachment takes us out of the present moment where life happens and puts us into the dream world of past and future. Attachment can take the form of an inflexible desire to identify with inappropriate concepts. They can take over completely, and we become them in a sense. We see through their eyes and do their will. Depending on the nature of the concepts, it can make life truly miserable. Every time we feel any sort of negative, unpleasant emotion, it is a signal that we are attached to or identifying with an inappropriate concept. Being attached to or identified with such concepts obscures our ability to see life as it is. We put more faith in our mind's convictions and projections than we do in the reality of the present moment. We need to begin the process of becoming aware of the fact that we are identified with our thoughts most of the time. We do not just use our mind for practical purposes and then set it down. Most people's minds harass them all day with pointless, repetitious or painful thoughts. The problem arises when thought becomes compulsive, and we cannot seem to stop. The fact is that most people are almost totally identified with inappropriate concepts and do not even realize it.

Some negative thoughts involve the use of negative labels. When we apply a negative label to another person in anger, we perpetuate the anger. When we habitually think of ourselves in terms of a negative label, we define ourselves in a way that reduces our hope for change. Children whose parents constantly scold and insult them often come to believe their parents' descriptions of them are true. With low self-esteem, these children have little hope of changing and put little effort into improving. This is another kind of self-fulfilling prophecy. Similarly, when adults come to think of themselves as boring, bad tempered, alcoholic, addicted, sluttish, neurotic, or criminal, they often resign themselves to the social roles these labels imply.

Most of what we experience in life depends on the focus of our attention. Some things will go right and some things will go wrong, sometimes we are lucky and sometimes we are not. If we pay more attention to the things that go right, we will experience more happiness. Today is a gift, which is why they call it the "present." We need to open our gift with joy and gratitude with the excitement we feel when opening something special on our birthday. Today is life in action and is the only time we can control how we feel, how we act, and how we think. Each moment of this life is a miracle and a mystery. Feel it, live it, love it right now and think happy thoughts. It really is the "thought" that counts. Anthony De Mello said, "If you ask the mystic why he or she is happy, the answer will be, 'why not?'."

Today is going to be a happy day,
because I am going to make it a happy day.
I will make myself happy.
I will make others happy.
When I see this again, I will still have a smile on my face.

Harboring harmful thoughts and Inflexible Perceptions throw us out of balance and harmony. They cloud our vision and allow emotions to rule our lives. The balance and harmony that the Mystics speak of has nothing to do with the mundane concepts of good and evil. It is the balance of mind/body/spirit and the attainment of harmony on all planes of our being. Maharishi Mahesh Yogi said, "Think of negativity that comes at you as a raindrop falling into the ocean of your bliss."

We cannot always control events, but the thoughts we allow ourselves to think about a situation or event produce our feelings and moods. Our feelings and moods affect our actions and reactions which in turn affect the direction and quality of life. When we develop the ability to choose our thoughts, we will be able to control our feelings, actions, circumstances, and destiny. It has been said that destiny is no matter of chance, it is a matter of choice, and our thoughts are the driving force. Another wise man once said, "If you want to be happy and at peace, then be happy and at peace. If you want to feel good, then feel good. It's your choice. Simply choose the appropriate thoughts. If you think good thoughts, you will feel good. If you think bad thoughts, you will feel bad. If you think about nothing, you feel nothing. You are only one thought away from a good feeling. Ice Cream! The smile of a happy grateful child; Chocolate; a playful puppy or a white fluffy kitten playing with a ball of yarn; a beautiful flower, fragrance or melody."

Where one person sees a dirty window, another might see a beautiful landscape. Look beyond adversity and see the innocents. We choose what we see and what we feel by choosing our thoughts. One can be miserable in paradise, while others can be happy living in an igloo. The primary cause of unhappiness is never the situation but our thoughts about it which we do not necessarily have to believe. We have thoughts, but we should not let them have us. We need to be aware of the link between our thoughts, feelings, and behavior. We need to understand that we are not our thoughts or the emotions that they create, rather we are the observer and the controller with the ability to accept or dismiss our thoughts.

We can choose to be miserable, or we can choose to be happy. When harmful thoughts pop up, we Stop, Smile, and Breathe. We say, "Thank you, thank you, thank you" as a sincere expression of gratitude for the opportunity to practice patience, kindness, and our right to choose the thoughts upon which to focus. We recognize anger, fear, guilt, worry, sadness, shame, and other harmful thoughts for what they are and neutralize them by understanding that they may have been appropriate at one time but NOT NOW. Then we replace those nasty thoughts with worthy thoughts: Gratitude, Patience, and Kindness. Worry, for example, is useless and seldom accomplishes anything. Worry replaces rational thought with irrational fears, and actually prevents us from resolving the situation that may have triggered the worry in the first place. Revenge belongs in the same trash bin as worry. Nothing positive has ever come out of a revengeful act.

Some people spend a lifetime searching for paradise and happiness, from beautiful beaches and mountain highlands to remote Pacific islands, and from the pampered life of affluence to abject poverty. If only they knew...it's already found!! It's here! It's all around us! Wherever we go, there it is. Paradise is where we make it. When faced with adversity we "Stop, Smile, Breathe and say Thank you." Confident that something good will come of the situation, we look for opportunity. As Helen Keller wrote, "When one door closes, another opens. But we often look so long and so regretfully upon the closed door that we do not see the one which has opened for us." Recognize, Neutralize, Dismiss and Replace harmful thoughts, and nurture good thoughts. Awareness allows us to see.

To really start enjoying life, we need to learn to let go of the past, stop worrying about the future, and take control of our thoughts by directing our mind to focus on what is taking place right now. Only the present moment exists. The past exists only in memory, and the future exists only in imagination. The present moment is the only thing that is real, where we live our lives, and where we need to place our attention. We need to learn to soften Inflexible Perception with conscious awareness of seven core principles contained in the roots of all major religions. We need to learn more about meditation and how it can be used to reprogram harmful perceptions that, although irrational and obviously self-defeating, often remain in control of our lives.

3.2 Develop Conscious Awareness, Gratitude, and Worthy Purpose

Developing conscious awareness is vital to developing an attitude of gratitude. Gratitude is a crucial element in stress management, and the passion we have for a worthy purpose is our motivator. Conscious awareness is the state or ability to perceive, to feel, or to be conscious of events, objects, or sensory patterns. It refers to our individual awareness of our unique thoughts, memories, feelings, sensations, and environment. Conscious awareness means that whatever is happening at the moment is happening with complete consciousness, that one is fully present. When we have little or no awareness of our inner world, we have little or no awareness of our outer world and are victims of circumstances. The automatic subconscious pre-programing runs our lives while we unconsciously walk around in a fog, operating only by reaction.

The great Renaissance painter and sculptor, Leonardo da Vinci said that the average person looks without seeing, listens without hearing, touches without feeling, eats without tasting, moves without physical awareness, inhales without awareness of odor or fragrance and talks without thinking. We need to learn to focus mindfully and practice awareness. As one fish said to the other, "What is this water I keep hearing about?" All that we sense is the Source of all things speaking. Be polite and listen. It is not difficult; all we need to do is show up, pay attention and miracles happen.

To develop conscious awareness, we start by learning to be aware of our breath, our heartbeat, and mindfulness. Being aware of our breath forces us into the present moment. We learn to spend more time in the present and less time lost in the past or future. We become more and more aware of our thoughts, emotions, and our reactions to various situations. The correlation between breathing, emotion, and thought is a perfect example of mind/body unity. We need to observe and be an intelligent witness to our actions, thoughts, and desires. Even seemingly little things like gestures, walking, talking, breathing, and eating can be an opportunity to watch and learn. We begin to realize that the more observant we are, the more clarity we gain and life becomes more manageable.

After becoming aware of our breath, we improve our ability to concentrate using meditation. We learn to catch ourselves living in the past or worrying about the future and return to the present where life really happens and can be managed. We can then bring that consciousness into everyday life. Giving our full and complete attention to a loved one, a sunset, or a flower in the present moment opens a world of beauty that cannot be seen by a scattered distracted mind. When action is required, we do not react from a conditioned mind but respond out of conscious presence.

It is helpful to note that frequent and prolonged TV watching does not improve focus and conscious awareness; it induces passivity and drains us of energy. Look away from the screen at regular intervals and return to the breath (and the present moment) so that it does not completely take possession of the visual sense. Use the mute button during commercials and don't go to sleep immediately after switching off the set. Do the (5-7-9) Breath, annotate the gratitude journal discussed later, and then go to bed.

Developing gratitude is not always easy for some people, but it is absolutely necessary for peace of mind, happiness, and harmony. Gratitude is the quality of being thankful and showing appreciation. It is a feeling, attitude, or a mindful acknowledgment of a benefit that one has received or will receive and is regarded as a virtue that shapes not only emotions and thoughts but actions and deeds as well. Gratitude is an emotion expressing appreciation for what one has as opposed to an emphasis on what one wants. Gratitude for what we have is the best insurance that it will continue while concentrating on what we do not have will ensure that we will never have enough. "He is a wise man who does not grieve for the things which he has not, but rejoices for those which he has." - Epictetus

It is easy to feel grateful when life is good, but when disaster strikes, gratitude is essential. In fact, it is under crisis conditions when we have the most to gain by a grateful perspective on life. In the face of demoralization, gratitude has the power to energize. In the face of brokenness, gratitude has the power to heal. In the face of despair, gratitude has the power to bring hope. In other words, gratitude can help us cope with hard times.

Being grateful is a choice, a prevailing attitude that endures and is relatively immune to the gains and losses that flow in and out of our lives. Gratitude can be chosen in spite of one's situation or circumstances and helps us cope with adversity. When disaster strikes, gratitude provides a perspective from which we can view life in its entirety and not be overwhelmed by temporary circumstances. If people have a grateful disposition in the face of serious trauma, adversity, and suffering, they will recover more quickly.

There is scientific evidence that grateful people are more resilient to stress, whether minor everyday hassles or major personal upheavals. Studies show that when we deliberately cultivate gratitude, we increase our levels of energy, empathy, happiness, well-being, and feelings of optimism, joy, pleasure, enthusiasm. Consciously cultivating an "attitude of gratitude" builds up a kind of psychological immune system that can cushion us when we fall.

For those who have acquired the habit of using foul language, it is suggested that they replace the curse words with, "Thank you." Replacing the need to shout profanity or some form of verbal negativity with, "Thank you" almost immediately replaces anger and hostility with gratitude. It can defuse a potentially difficult situation and usually leads to opportunity, or at least wonder, instead of stress. We have learned to visualize a Big Red Smiling Stop Sign when stress strikes but sometimes it is faster to go directly to the, "Thank you" and then back to the Stop Sign, Smile, and Breathe. Missing the nail and striking one's thumb with a hammer is one of those times.

Gratitude is an emotional and cognitive state of freedom. Holding on to anger, resentment, jealousy, and envy is poisonous to the mind/body but can be blocked by gratitude because they are incompatible and cannot exist simultaneously. Even as a situation improves, if we cling to the pain of what we do not have, or what another does have, or what we wish was different, we cannot really feel free. Gratitude is a natural skill but adversity tends to turn our focus toward skepticism, so we need to practice and develop the attitude of gratitude consciously. We start with the five steps below.

First; keep a gratitude journal. That means listing three to five things for which we are grateful every night before going to bed. When we consciously focus our attention on developing gratitude, we begin to see gifts in life as new and exciting and experience life differently than people who cheat themselves out of mindfully enjoying the gifts, grace, benefits, and good things that happened during the day. Journaling is also associated with fewer health complaints, reduced envy, feeling more spiritually connected, and a more positive attitude in general. Those who engage in this practice are more active, connected to life, and view their families more positively.

Second; do something nice for someone as often as possible and tell no one about it. Let it be a delightful little secret shared only with the Source of all things. We can make it a part of who we are and not a facade. Doing so can shift our attention away from what is stressful or unpleasant and remind us that we can be a force for positive change. Good deeds are contagious and foster a "pay it forward" environment where people are more helpful, altruistic, and compassionate. And for this, we can all be more grateful. Remember, it is better to know we are kinder than we say we are than to say we are kinder than we know we are. "Character is doing the right thing when no one is looking." J.C. Watt

Third; process life through a grateful lens. It's called reframing. Recognize the bad stuff but avoid getting caught up in it. The point is not to ignore or deny suffering but to develop a fruitful frame of reference in the present from which to view experiences and events. (Recognize, Neutralize, Dismiss, and Replace) To deny that life has its share of disappointments, frustrations, losses, hurts, setbacks, and sadness would be unrealistic and untenable. We can relive a past experience with a new perspective rather than wallowing in the same old mud. Emotional venting without a replacement perspective does not produce change, and simply rehearsing an upsetting event makes us feel worse. Processing a life experience through a grateful lens does not mean denying negativity, it means realizing the power we have to transform an obstacle into an opportunity. It means reframing a loss into a potential gain, recasting negativity into positive channels for gratitude. For example, grateful reframing might involve seeing how a stressful event has shaped who we are today and has prompted us to re-evaluate what is really important in life. This is an advantage that grateful people have and it is a skill that anyone can learn.

Fourth; develop awareness. Gratitude is a sense of appreciation and begins with awareness. We try to be more aware when something good exists or is happening and recognize the small ways that people show kindness toward us: a kind word or a warm smile. When we are not sure about their motivation, we give them the benefit of the doubt. A part of living a beautiful life is to notice the extraordinary in the ordinary. Life is made up of simple, passing moments.

Finally, it helps to, "Fake it 'til you make it." Acting grateful and going through the motions will trigger the emotion. That includes smiling, saying thank you, sending Thank You cards, and writing letters of gratitude. Actions trigger feelings just as feelings trigger actions. If we often react with an automatic "Thank you" when someone offers something kind to us, their response and our resulting feelings can trigger genuine appreciation and kindness. If we pause a moment and take time to more deeply recognize, receive, and relish the kind act or word, everyone benefits. It is a gift to the giver to let them see and feel our gratitude. If practiced consistently, we will eventually learn to pause and allow the good feeling to build or grow before responding. The deepest craving of human nature is to be loved, respected, and appreciated. We need to say "Thank you" more often and really mean it. But until then, we need to make it a point to "Stop, Smile, Breathe, and say, Think you" regardless of mood. Dale Carnegie offered some good advice when he suggested that we avoid criticizing, condemning or complaining about others and give them honest and sincere appreciation instead because everyone wants and needs to be appreciated. We need to say, "Thank you" to everyone who brightens our day, from our child's hug to a stranger who holds open a door for us. Let them know they are appreciated.

Once a precious moment is recognized, some might feel that they do not really deserve it. Self-esteem issues often clog our receptors, making us unavailable to receive graciously. We need to just recognize that someone offered a kindness, let it in, and let it be. The trick is to enjoy it without getting caught up in speculation. The Buddha is said to have said, "If you search the Universe, you will find no one more deserving of love and affection than yourself."

Developing a worthy purpose and direction is important to human beings because we are goal oriented organisms. Without a purpose, goal, or some kind of objective, we lose our will to live. We need a reason to get up in the morning: a reason to live. When we get clear about what we want, such as by setting a goal, we raise our consciousness. Before we take control of our car, we need to know where we want to go. Before we take control of our mind (thus our life) we need to know what we want to be, what we want to do, and where we want to go. The resulting clarity focuses the mind and gives us the power to think and act intelligently. We can feel this effect whenever we think about our purpose. On the other hand, when our objectives are unclear, our consciousness is muddled and our thoughts lack focus and direction. Like a ship without a rudder, we aimlessly submit to the winds and tides of the outside world.

People with a worthy purpose are more likely to succeed in life because they know where they are going, while failures believe that their lives are shaped by circumstances, exterior forces, and by things that happen to them. The opposite of courage in our society is not cowardice, it is passivity. It is habitually reacting, mindlessly doing, and following without knowing why or where it will lead. George Bernard Shaw wrote, "People are always blaming their circumstances for what they are. I don't believe in circumstances. The people who get on in this world are the people who get up and look for the circumstances they want and, if they can't find them, make them."

When we are inspired by some worthy purpose, some extraordinary project, our thoughts begin to break their bonds. The mind transcends limitations, consciousness expands in all directions, and we find ourselves in a great new wonderful world. Dormant forces, faculties, and talents come alive and we realize that we can be a far greater person than we ever dreamed. Whatever one's worthy purpose might be, it can be used as a guiding light to better see our next intermediate step.

People who are most likely to deal effectively with stress have meaning and purpose in their lives. They have worthy goals and realize that each achievement and setback is a stepping stone toward the ultimate objective of harmony and peace of mind for all beings. We have tremendous control over our lives, and purpose gives direction to the daily decisions that we all have to make. Life is not pre-planned or set, but remains a mystery that unfolds every day. We have control over our actions and if we clarify our purpose, goals, and intentions on paper, we can use it as a map to guide our steps and not be easily lost.

In the interest of clarity, we define "ultimate objective" as the dream of all humanity: Heaven, harmony, happiness, peace, and joy. A "worthy purpose" is our reason to live and our intermediate "goals" are compatible with and often support our worthy purpose. We know that the ultimate objective is harmony, happiness, peace, and joy for ourselves and all living things but we all need a worthy purpose in life. Then there are many intermediate goals that need to be attained and our immediate intentions support them.

Whether one is a truck driver, CEO, or a mother, in the end, the ultimate goal is harmony. Even the demented fanatic who strives to become a martyr by killing others is ultimately seeking harmony. They wrongly believe that the path to harmony will be enhanced or facilitated by harming the very organism that they were born to sustain. Those who create chaos and turmoil subconsciously believe that they are clearing obstacles from, and filling great potholes in the road to harmony. No matter what we have accomplished or failed to accomplish, when all is said and done, harmony is the real goal. All other goals are only intermediate steps to attaining the ultimate goal. The truck driver wants to deliver on time so he can support his family and the CEO wants to produce profit and satisfy the shareholders, but they are only intermediate steps. A mother wants to guide her child to a better life and needs to keep the ultimate goal in mind as she sets and pursues intermediate objectives to stay on track. The billionaire is no happier and healthier than the penniless Buddhist monk or Catholic nun without a greater awareness of gratitude. We and all of our toys are impermanent but harmony is eternal and we can only disrupt it for a short time. It is the natural state, let it be. Harmony for ourselves, our loved ones, and all living things is the real goal.

Objectives like earning a promotion or raising happy, responsible, well-adjusted children are often a part of life but are only intermediate goals. Making our world revolve around our job or raising children is shortsighted and limiting. We can make our purpose a job but a job is not our purpose. It is commendable to focus on the task at hand, but we need to let go when the job is done so we can move on to the next intermediate goal on our way to the ultimate objective of balance and harmony. We love our children and often refer to them as "my children" but we do not own them, they do. When we assert ownership over another human being instead of guidance, the result is usually rebellion and conflict. We are given temporary custody of them until they are able to fend for themselves, and then we let them go and continue on with our worthy purpose which may or may not include them.

A job is something we need to do and has little or no spirit in it. An occupation is something that we do to occupy our time and usually holds some spirit or emotion because it pays the bills. An occupation can be enjoyable, and when it is, the money becomes simply a by-product of having fun. In fact, the more fun we have, the more money we draw to us. The more expert in having fun we become, the more people will ask for our enjoyable service. A worthy purpose is a "calling" and can draw us in to immersion where we joyfully lose all track of time. Confucius said, "If you choose to do what you love for a career, you will never have to work another day in your life." Life can be fun, challenging, and interesting, rather than stressful and harassing.

We do not ask what the Universe has to offer instead we ask what we have to offer into the universal energy. What are our skills and talents? What would we enjoy doing all day long for free? An occupation that makes us smile means that we are on the right path. We are all special and gifted in our own unique way and have something which when shared, improves the world around us.

A purpose in life is a reason to get out of bed in the morning, but too often we are not sure what that purpose is. We suggest that everyone make a concerted effort to define their worthy purpose, intermediate goals, and intentions with the ultimate objective in mind. Having a one-sentence "Worthy Purpose Statement" can give us clarity, direction, and fulfillment.

The process begins by first discerning what we are most passionate about, and then listing specific goals and intentions to which we can commit. Note that goals and objectives focus on a stated outcome in the future while intentions focus on the present. When we break down our purpose into a list of goals and intentions, we can align our conduct and actions with what matters most in our life. People who have a clear purpose in life deal more effectively with stress and see achievement as well as setbacks as a stepping stone toward their ultimate objective.

The first step is to find a quiet place, get comfortable, breathe and allow the mind to be open. We then write down two or more of our most dominant unique personal qualities. For example, words like organized, creative, giving, courageous, empowering, etc. If nothing immediately comes to mind, ask three close friends or relatives to summarize two or more top strengths and qualities.

The second step is to make a list of the things we want, fantasize about, or need that elicit positive feelings and enthusiasm. Next, we list the things we want to reduce, get rid of, or avoid that provoke negative feelings. Then we write down at least two ways that we enjoy expressing these improvements and personal qualities when interacting with people such as volunteering, writing, or teaching. It might be helpful to remember that the foolish do what they like while the successful like what they do. Then, in present tense, write a description of what a perfect world is like in as much sensory detail as possible.

The third step is to write the word HARMONY at the top of a blank sheet of paper. Then write the question, "What is my worthy purpose?" As fast as possible, write down any words, images, phrases or sentences that come to mind without judgment or analysis. It is important to relax, visualize, and list exactly what we want out of life, and describe in multisensory detail what we want in the present tense as if we already have it. Details left out of the description, by default, will be indiscriminately determined by the Subconscious mind and may not be compatible.

The fourth step is to combine all of these steps into a written single statement starting with, "My worthy purpose is..." Some examples might be: to create opportunity for others: to make people happy: teach others how to evolve from stress to gratitude: to reduce suffering, etc. One might ask themselves, "For what would I like to be remembered?" or "What work would I do for free?" and then evolve in that direction. Some people may get clarity in one sitting while others will need to learn more about Creative meditation in Part VI, which will answer a lot of questions.

Once we have a clear, simply stated one-sentence worthy purpose, we need a plan. Ask what needs to be done to make that vision a reality and call it "My Mission Statement." This is a progressive list of intentions, supporting goals, and intermediate objectives that may need to be done before the worthy purpose can be realized.

Be aware that there may be people in our lives who want to discourage us or make fun of our objectives. If they cannot be convinced to alter their attitude to one of support, we need to stop talking with them about our goals. If they continue to discourage us, we may need to consider avoiding these people. Letting go of friends and people in our lives that do not support us is often a necessary part of achieving our goals. We can make new friends who are positive and happy to support us in the achievement of our objectives.

Remember that our worthy purpose, calling, or destiny is not a matter of chance, it is a matter of choice. One can look for a worthy purpose and make it their passion or look for a passion and make it their worthy purpose. Either way, we can choose to make our worthy purpose anything we want but the greater the passion, the greater the fulfillment. Just as one can create the emotion of fear by thinking about scary things or create the feeling of pleasure by thinking about pleasurable things, we can create a passion for anything by choosing the appropriate thoughts. Think about how much better life is for those who enjoy getting up and heading out the door each day. Consider how much the people around them benefit by simply being in the company of a happy, enthusiastic person who enjoys life and seems to just be having a wonderful time and accomplishing more in a year than most people do in a lifetime.

And then, when that's done, go out and do something special. Don't overlook life's small joys while searching for the big ones. Even if it is only gazing at a blue sky or smelling a rose, experience joy every day. Spend some time making the memories that are fun to recall. Few people have ever gone to their grave wishing that they had spent more time working or watching TV. Go to the zoo, walk in a park, get an ice cream cone, plant a tomato seed, look at the stars, take a hot bath, snuggle, listen to a favorite album, or start a hobby. Sir Winston Churchill loved to paint, and it is said that he never traveled to meet another world leader without his paints. Hobbies are delightful mindful experiences that prevent us from becoming obsessed or controlled by our objectives. They are little vacations that expand our awareness while practicing mindfulness and maintaining our ability to focus. Learn to play the guitar, juggle, learn a new computer program, another language, or start a terrarium. There is a link between learning and happiness. Life is fun. We can dream like we will live forever, live like the world will explode next week, and play like nobody's watching.

3.3 The Seven Principles of Harmony "I am We"

We learned that perception is everything and that we need to Recognize, Neutralize, Dismiss, and Replace harmful perceptions, attitudes, and thoughts with worthy perceptions, attitudes, and thoughts. We understand that a harmful perception creates stress, and if it is uncompromising or inflexible, it can destroy harmony and eventually the perceiver. Worthy perceptions, attitudes, and thoughts open our awareness, and when energized by the emotion inherent in belief and spirituality, super-human events can occur. Our study of spirituality and the power of belief confirmed that it is fundamental to our evolution from stress to gratitude.

Although spirituality and religion were once synonymous, spirituality has come to be associated more with an intimate pursuit of personal growth and the feelings, thoughts, and behaviors that often arise from the search for a higher power as perceived by the individual. Spirituality does not depend on collective or institutional context whereas religion is associated with membership in a formal institution, rituals, and adherence to official denominational doctrines. One can be spiritual without being religious or religious without being spiritual.

Religions tend to collect add-ons and rituals that often symbolize a core truth but just as often obscure it. They are often complicated and conflicting, but with only a few minor semantic exceptions due to translation ambiguity, all major religions agree on the Seven Principles of Harmony. For that reason, our study of spirituality, faith, and belief will not focus on any religion or doctrine but on the seven principles that are common to them all and have survived the stormy manmade political power struggles. Ancient mystical, esoteric and secret teachings dating back over 5,000 years including ancient Egyptian, Greek, and Indian Vedic traditions, all have as their common thread these seven principles. Once we understand, apply and align ourselves with these principles, we will experience growth in every area of life.

Regardless of one's religious preference, our discussions of spirituality should be compatible and even complementary. Tapping the awesome nature of the human mind is enhanced dramatically when accompanied by a deep wisdom and belief that stimulates emotion which is the driving force of action. Because the *Imagine Harmony* program uses fundamentals common to all major religions, we can explore spirituality at its basic level without modern religious constraints. This adds the power of core wisdom and belief to our objectives, creating harmony and resulting in their attainment. Spirituality exists when we imagine a meaning or power beyond our visible world, and it is an essential component of deep wisdom. It is the power of that deep wisdom and belief that spirituality brings to the *Imagine Harmony* program. When spirituality, imagination, and deep wisdom are integrated, they manifest deeper conviction, growth, and evolution. We can do anything if we are willing to give up the belief that we can't. As you believe, so shall it be done.

Dr. Herbert Benson demonstrated that, with deep belief, conscious human beings can change the chemical composition of their blood, which in turn regulates genetics, psychophysiology, and behavior (the way we respond to the world). He referred to it as the "Faith Factor" and it was found that we can replace even Inflexible Perceptions. By eliciting the relaxation response in conjunction with deep wisdom and belief, we can bypass the Ego and discover the exciting and powerful forces of the mind. We can take the placebo effect to new highs, but we need worthy concepts to support such belief.

We went back to the roots of religion and found that they all have a common spiritual foundation: seven simple principles that were known to exist over 5000 years ago. Before Hinduism, Abraham, Jesus, Buddha, Muhammad, or Guru Nanak, the Seven Principles of Harmony were universal and remain so today. It is not a religion in itself but rather a philosophy or an attitude.

There are many paths to the top of the mountain: The Kingdom of God, Nirvana, Jannah, Heaven, Sukhavati, Shangri-La, Paradise, Great Spirit Happy Hunting Ground, etc. It seems that every religion professes to be The Way; (the only way) and that is not in conflict with universal harmony until they declare that all who do not believe as they do will go to hell and "live a horrible, tormented eternity; while believers will live an eternity of bliss." Some even feel that infidels should all be killed. Many of these add-ons obscure, or completely contradict, the original teachings.

The great religions of the world are like branches of the same tree in that they are all different but are all attached to the same trunk and draw sustenance from the same roots. Their inherent similarities are deep and show a profound unanimity of the human spirit while differences are superficial. Harmony is generated by focusing on these profound commonalities. The Principles of Harmony are the roots from which the dogma of all major religions has evolved.

PRINCIPLES OF HARMONY

1) Be one with all that is, with reverence, love, and kindness.
2) Be aware in the present moment, accepting and adapting with wisdom and curiosity.
3) Recognize, neutralize, dismiss, and replace anger, fear, guilt, worry and other harmful thoughts with gratitude, patience, and kindness, the wonder of life, and the beauty of the gift of breath.
4) Be a happy, healthy, calm mind at peace, in balance and harmony with the Universe.
5) Be free of the past with acceptance and forgiveness, as only change is permanent.
6) Pursue life diligently with integrity, purpose, sincerity, and joy.

7) Understand that harmony is the real goal, the ultimate objective of all pursuits. Imagine harmony, be harmony, live harmony.

Just as orators often use a single word or phrase to trigger the recall of an entire subject, we often use the words, "Be grateful, patient, and kind" to bring the concepts of all seven principles to mind. We have found that it can be simplified even further: Be Kind.

That's all. Everything is there. All the laws, rules, books, commandments, and teachings of all the great teachers, prophets and gurus are saying the same thing: Be kind. That's IT! The rest is just commentary and elaborations in varying degrees of detail. The explanations, fables, proverbs, anecdotes, symbols, rituals, add-ons, and multiple translations of translations of verbal teachings committed to imperfect human memories for decades, even centuries, before being written down are often more confusing than enlightening. If everyone would just be kind, harmony would surface and there would be no crime or need for law libraries.

With the delineation of the core universal truths, we can use them as guidelines and a foundation to support our belief in our new worthy perceptions, attitudes, thoughts, feelings, behaviors and responses that will replace the old harmful and formerly Inflexible Perceptions. We can feel confident that our worthy purpose and compatible deep beliefs are supported by universal truth. Managing stress, happiness, harmony, and controlling the mind/body with the Conscious mind can only be realized with the help of that deep wisdom and belief.

The "Principles of Harmony" is an attitude at the deepest level and is part of all that IS. We are part of all that IS. Therefore, we are The Principles of Harmony at the deepest level. In some people, it is so deep and buried under so many layers of randomly acquired programs that their lives operate on these superficial programs, many of which are harmful.

The Principles of Harmony is a simple philosophy that leads to and sustains our vision of perfect health, happiness, vitality, longevity, and harmony. The principles are interconnected, support and moderate each other, and are not to be understood as stages in which each stage is completed before moving on to the next. They are to be understood as seven significant dimensions of one's behavior, operate together, and define a complete path, or way of living.

We will learn to use the relaxation response and the parasympathetic nervous system to replace harmful perceptions later, but first, we need to learn more about affirmations. To bring our inherent harmony to the surface, we redirect our thoughts from the harmful to the worthy, avoid waking the "I" centered Ego by referring to ourselves as "we", and focus on the positive nature of the Principles of Harmony. Note that the words "anger, fear, guilt and worry" have been deleted to direct the focus to the positive. It is suggested that an attempt be made to commit the affirmations to memory so they can be used during Contemplation meditation later.

Principles of Harmony
(I am We Affirmations)

1) We are one with all that is, with reverence, love, and kindness.
2) We are aware in the present moment, accepting and adapting with wisdom and curiosity.
3) We recognize, neutralize, dismiss, and replace harmful thoughts with gratitude, patience, and kindness, the wonder of life and the beauty of the gift of breath.
4) We are a happy, healthy, calm mind at peace, in balance and harmony with the Universe.
5) We are free of the past with acceptance and forgiveness, as only change is permanent.
6) We pursue life diligently with integrity, purpose, sincerity, and joy.
7) We understand that harmony is the real goal, the ultimate objective of all pursuits. We imagine harmony, we are harmony, we live harmony.

The very FIRST PRINCIPLE states that we are one with all that is; an inseparable part of the Source of all things; a member of the Kingdom of God; a single cell in the body of the Universe. From the smallest microorganism to vast galaxies, all things form a part of a web of interconnected multidimensional phenomena. With a sense of oneness, there is always an innate goodness and appropriateness of action. Our two fingers do not behave inappropriately toward each other because they are part of the same body. When most people think "I am" it is the Ego speaking, not the whole self. The Ego foolishly thinks that it alone is "I" and the stronger the Ego, the stronger the sense of separateness. The truth is that I am WE. We are a drop in the ocean and an ocean within the drop.

I cannot exist without my body or my mind or my soul, just as water cannot exist without the elements of oxygen or hydrogen. And as water is not oxygen and it is not hydrogen, I am not my body, I am not my thoughts, and I am not an invisible soul. Body is only a vessel, thoughts are only tools that I can choose to use or dismiss, and soul is only my incorporeal life force connection to the source of all creation. I am we.

We are the body, the Conscious mind, the Subconscious (or subtle) mind, and a very subtle light that was before the body existed and will be after it dies. (Some call it the soul, the spirit, or life force energy) The body provides a physical being and represents us to others. The mind holds only one thought at a time but jumps around like a wild monkey from one picture to another to another providing us with an endless stream of thoughts, ideas, and past experiences wrapped in the emotion of the time. It can be guided by the Conscious mind as a gardener tends a fertile garden, or it can be allowed to run wild indiscriminately reacting to egotistical whims. And soul is our life force energy, a timeless connection to all that is, providing the true self, the observer, the interpreter, and the witness beyond the self-image. We are one cohesive, synergistic unit greater than the sum of the parts. I am we.

We are awareness, consciousness, wisdom, and loving-kindness in a form that thinks. We are a piece of the source of all things, and all things are of the source. It is like we are all holding hands as universal chi. We acknowledge our ego but identify with, and speak from our true self, the light within, the soul, the spirit, the wisdom and loving-kindness that is of the source of all things, to which we are all connected. I am we.

As two fingers of the same hand are separate, they are of the hand, which is of the body, which is of the source of all things, of which we are all a part, uniting us all as one. We are like a single cell in the body of the Universe, nourished by the same life force energy source, separated only by an invisible ego. I am we.

Our essence is a field of awareness that is consciousness and universal intelligence that conceives, manifests, and governs the body and mind. The essential we is inseparable from our source, and all that is. I am we.

We are one with all that IS.
Harmony IS an attitude at the deepest level.
Therefore,
I am Harmony at the deepest level.

"A human being is part of the whole called by us Universe, a part limited in time and space. We experience ourselves, our thoughts and feelings as something separate from the rest; a kind of optical delusion of consciousness. This delusion is a kind of prison for us, restricting us to our personal desires and to affection for a few persons nearest to us. Our task must be to free ourselves from the prison by widening our circle of compassion to embrace all living creatures and the whole of nature in its beauty...We shall require a substantially new manner of thinking if mankind is to survive." Albert Einstein

The SECOND PRINCIPLE reminds us to be aware in the present moment, the NOW, and that if we do not accept what is, we are accepting what is not. The past no longer exists except in memory, and the future does not exist except in imagination. Past and future have no reality of their own. Only Now exists, only Now is real. Once the present moment is accepted, we can more easily adapt to it, fix it, or move out of the way. That requires wisdom from within, and curiosity is preferable to irrational emotional reactions. If others annoy, disapprove or disagree with us, curiosity opens the door to learning and facilitates the use of our wisdom. Every problem has at least three solutions: 1) Fix it with kindness. We can change those things that are within our control. 2) Accept, adapt perceptions, and look for opportunity. We can change our perceptions and attitudes toward those things that are beyond our control and look for opportunity. 3) Walk away or around it, let it go, let it be, and move on.

The greatest oak was once a NUT that lived in the present moment. She adapted to change from scorching summer heat to subzero winter cold and prevailed by bending with the storms while others rigidly resisted and broke. She was unable to change the events or move away, but she could accept and adapt. The United States Marines have adopted this concept as an unofficial motto "adapt, improvise, overcome."

The THIRD PRINCIPLE states that we acknowledge our thoughts and recognize those that are harmful just long enough to label them as anger, fear, guilt, worry etc., and immediately proceed to neutralize them with the awareness that they are no longer appropriate; they might have been at one time but not NOW. Once the harmful thoughts are neutralized or proven wrong, they are dismissed and replaced with worthy thoughts that are more compatible with our objective. Worthy thoughts usually have roots in gratitude, patience, and/or kindness. When harmful thoughts are replaced with an appreciation for the wonder of life, harmony dominates. And if one doubts for a second, the majesty of breath, try living without it for a few minutes. When breath finally returns, the body will be emotionally grateful, and the beauty of the gift of breath will be more obvious.

The FOURTH PRINCIPLE states that we are a happy, healthy, calm mind at peace, in balance and harmony with the Universe. James Allen wrote, "The more tranquil a man becomes, the greater is his success, his influence, his power for good. Calmness of mind is one of the beautiful jewels of wisdom." It is our birthright. We were born with an endless reservoir of bliss, the flow of which seems to get blocked by Inflexible Perceptions that we pick up along the way. Health and happiness are inherent, and when either one is threatened, the mind/body springs into action to restore homeostasis unless blocked by those pesky Inflexible Perceptions. When we are able to get through the accumulated diversions and reconnect with our OM, or inner light, it reopens the flow, and the wisdom of the Universe refills our being with natural balance and the elegance of universal harmony.

The FIFTH PRINCIPLE states that acceptance and forgiveness allow us to let go of the past. The past exists only in memory, but haunts us if we do not acknowledge it, label it, learn what we can from it and let it go. Although the past is gone, without acceptance and forgiveness its memory and effects can take over our lives. Delving into the past to find ourselves or the origin of a problem is a bottomless pit. We cannot find ourselves in the past because life and all that we are is in the present. We learn from the past and plan for the future, but live in the present. Remember in the present, plan in the present, BE in the present. Now is good. Forgiving one's self or others does not mean condoning harmful actions or forgetting, but it does entail defining the lessons learned and "letting go" of anger toward past hurts. Forgiveness replaces blame and is absolutely essential for complete healing.

The nature of all things is dynamic vibrating energy that is constantly rearranging and changing form. "As with all things, this too shall pass." All things change, all things are impermanent. Our bodies, the bodies of people we love, material possessions, emotions and situations will all change. Acting like nothing will ever change is foolish. If we accept, forgive, and let go, harmony will resurface freeing us from the yoke of righteous indignation, another poisonous Inflexible Perception. Holding on to the past will only result in rope burns.

The SIXTH PRINCIPLE reminds us that life is not a passive endeavor. Man is a goal oriented organism and needs a purpose but without integrity and sincerity, our ultimate objective (harmony) cannot be attained. Our little projects are important to our state of mind but if contaminated by harmful perceptions, they threaten happiness. Life is a fun, joyful adventure of curiosity and wonder, not a stressful, corrupt exercise in greed to acquire things. Regardless of earthly treasures, our mind and body are our most precious possessions, and their health is our most valuable asset. When we pursue life diligently with integrity, purpose, sincerity, and joy, it will manifest gratitude, patience, kindness, and ultimately, natural harmony.

The SEVENTH PRINCIPLE reminds us that harmony is the ultimate objective of all pursuits and that we need to consciously understand that all other goals are subordinate to and either directly or indirectly in support of the dissolution of chaos and the restoration of harmony. There is no goal or objective more paramount. The natural order of the Universe is innately harmonious and elegant and to act against it creates turmoil and stress in our lives. When people live according to the laws of the Universe, they live in harmony with the natural environment. They can elicit the "evolve, renew, and repair mode" at will and take conscious control of the mind/body and gene expression. They evolve from stress to gratitude.

These principles already exist within us all, but we need to bring them out, articulate them, and integrate them into all that we are and all that we do. They are so important that we ask our students to print, laminate, and display them in prominent places. They are asked to memorize them as affirmations and review them in Contemplation meditation as outlined in the next section. We need to understand, memorize, and make them a part of our lives. We also use a shorter version as a mantra when we are jogging, walking a long boring distance, or get stuck in a long line. With each step we say or think, "I am we - we are one - with all that is - Be Grateful - Patient - Kind - Happy - Healthy - Calm mind at peace - in Balance - and Harmony - with the Universe" repeat. It is sometimes done as an add-on to (DSCR) practice discussed in Part I when high stress is not an immediate factor.

3.4 The Healing Power of Meditation

Humans have tried to fix their problems with everything from psychotherapy and drugs to positive thinking and politics with only a passing interest in meditation. The great master teachers of meditation have recognized its miraculous potential for centuries and finally, the rest of us are beginning to realize its integral nature. With the recent advances in neurophysiology, scientists are now identifying some of the psychophysiological benefits. They are becoming more and more aware of the minds enormous potential for impacting health and well-being. We are beginning to explore the healing power of meditation to counterbalance a life that is over-stimulated, stressed, and outer-directed by turning to something as simple as our own breath and inner silence. People from executives striving for peak performance, harried mothers needing serenity, and athletes aiming for the "zone," are finding that meditation can be their best friend.

We use Concentration meditation to focus, Mindfulness meditation to descend into a deeper level of relaxation and cultivate awareness, Contemplation meditation to separate delusion from truth, and Creative meditation to establish a dialogue with our true self, our Soul, our OM and our inner connection to the vast wisdom of the Source of all things.

Basic meditation is simply a matter of quieting the mind/body with focused attention, preferably the breath, while more advanced techniques are used to target specific therapeutic needs. We can also add visualization, or combine breathing and movements like that of chi gong. Energy flows where awareness goes. We can use one, or a combination of meditation categories in sequence or integrated. An example of integration might be when contemplation is used in Mindfulness meditation to investigate the mind/body, our feelings as they relate to our senses, and the various mind states and emotions that we experience. After we learn to still and concentrate the mind, we contemplate a predetermined subject allowing thoughts to flow freely using an investigative quality that is without judgment or criticism. This allows one to view their thoughts in the present without reviewing the past or planning for the future. We can be consciously aware of our thoughts and emotions and choose not to identify with them. By doing this, we can eventually gain the insight necessary to see all things as they truly are; temporary and impermanent. Only change is permanent. This can be very liberating in that it takes the edge off of the need for us to cling to anything. It is as if we become freed from a bad addiction and realize that we now have a new lease on life.

Dr. Herbert Benson found that the relaxation response can be used to turn off or at least moderate even a chronic fight-or-flight response and bring the body back to pre-stress levels. Dr. Benson describes the relaxation response as a physical state of deep relaxation which engages the parasympathetic nervous system. The two main branches of the autonomic nervous system (the sympathetic and parasympathetic) need to be balanced and work together. The sympathetic nervous system is necessary to our survival because it enables us to respond quickly with the "defense mode" when there is a threat. When the threat passes, the parasympathetic nervous system is supposed to return the mind/body to "evolve, renew, and repair mode" and a feeling of relaxation and calm. When the sympathetic nervous system is over stimulated, we experience the "fight-or-flight" response, and if this imbalance is allowed to continue for long periods of time or reoccur too frequently, the nervous system gets stuck in high alert or "defense mode" even though there is no immediate threat. Over stimulation of the sympathetic nervous system is caused by harmful perceptions and is exacerbated by time restraints, multitasking, and the media's relentless distorted suggestions that danger lurks around every corner, and that we have dangerous diseases that only the toxic, side-effect laden pills of their sponsors can cure.

To restore balance, we use the breathing techniques outlined in Part I and II to slow breathing, meditation to focus attention, and peaceful imagery of a mountain stream, forest or perhaps a secluded beach to engage the senses. Research has shown that regular use of the relaxation response can help any health problem that is caused or aggravated by chronic stress and according to Dr. Benson, one of the most valuable things we can do in life is to learn deep relaxation. We need to make an effort to spend some time every day quieting our minds in order to create inner peace and better health. Patients have experienced profound results. Just as the athlete takes a deep breath before competing, the evolving person pauses to meditate before heading off to work. Learning to meditate is a great skill that can help us to be better equipped to deal with life's unexpected stressors, heal ourselves, and achieve better health.

Regular practice offers dozens of scientifically proven benefits both physical and emotional. They include keeping depression and anxiety at bay, lower stress levels, better and deeper sleep, improved flow of air to the lungs, improved circulation, lower blood pressure, lower heart and metabolic rates, lower cholesterol levels, enhanced immune system, greater empathy, decreased irritability and moodiness, calmer outlook, more patience, and gives a person more control over their mind/body, especially in the area of pain, alertness, and healing. Meditation enhances memory, insight, clarity, creativity, and emotional stability. It produces a sense of well-being and communion with the cosmos as well as feelings of peace, joy, vitality and happiness. Meditation is used for overall wellness and because people tend to heal faster with meditation, it leads to reduced costs of medical treatment.

Recent studies show that long-term practice changes the body on a cellular level that actually slows down and may reverse aging. One study in Japan measured levels of the enzyme telomerase in a group attending a meditation retreat for three months. Telomerase repairs the caps at the ends of chromosomes, called telomeres. Fraying telomeres are one of the main genetic causes of aging, but meditators showed a huge increase in reparative telomerase at the end of their retreat, physical proof of reverse aging. These studies have found that meditation actually causes our DNA to heal itself, repairing our cells from a genetic level.

When studying the brain waves of meditators, Dr. Richard Davidson, director of the Laboratory for Affective Neuroscience at the University of Wisconsin, found that brain circuitry can be rewired. For a long time, scientists thought that each individual was wired with certain "set-points" for happiness, depression, and so on. This study shows that the brain can rewire itself and alter its set points simply by the self-healing power of thought. Over time, sustained practice rewires and increases the capacity of our nervous system. We develop a quality of lucid, loving, peaceful, radiant presence that we can then carry over into every moment and activity of our lives. As the day progresses, we can consciously recall and re-energize the feeling of peace, clarity, understanding, kindness, and vitality that we brought alive in our meditation.

Like master computer programmers, the great meditation masters throughout history have developed the capacity to program their bodies, minds, and hearts to experience highly refined states of being and an unshakable inner peace that external circumstances cannot disturb. They have demonstrated the ability to control bodily functions that are usually considered involuntary, such as heart rate, body temperature, and metabolism. Practicing meditation can result in a state of greater calmness, physical relaxation, psychological balance, and change how a person relates to the flow of emotions and thoughts. The more consciousness we bring into the body, the stronger the immune system becomes and is a potent form of self-healing. This begins with training in Concentration meditation.

The most convenient and basic focus point or "point of concentration" is one's breath. When attention wanders off into thoughts or memories, the participant gently returns attention to breathing.

Though most meditative practices provide relaxation, decades of research show that different techniques produce different physiological, psychological or behavioral effects. Concentration techniques improve focusing ability while Mindfulness practices involve watching or actively paying attention to experiences without judging, reacting, or holding on. Non-judgmental observation increases even-mindedness in daily life, facilitates better pain management, and reduces negative rumination (depression). Letting go and reducing mental resistance deepens relaxation, calms the sympathetic nervous system, restores psychophysiological balance, lowers blood pressure, alleviates chronic anxiety, and reduces stress hormones such as cortisol.

The more we identify with our thinking, our likes and dislikes, judgments and interpretations, the less present we are as the conscious controller. We need to become present, and know what IS before any effective attempt can be made to control or alter IS. That starts with becoming the observer of the mind/body and the watcher of thought. Much of our emotional pain is from an unconscious resistance to what IS, but we can heal physical tension and pain by recognizing it, and neutralizing or dissolving harmful thoughts and emotions by using the breath. We observe the waves and smile at them.

We are not victims of pain; we are an observer of it. We recognize it, breathe "into" it and replace it with gratitude and other worthy thoughts. Whether physical or emotional, we understand that there is the pain, and then there are our thoughts about the pain which can feed the pain and make it bigger. Pain and suffering are inevitable, but misery is optional.

The secret to coping with tension and pain is to soften around it, rather than resist it, and to expand our awareness to include it, rather than tighten, contract, and fight it. That with which we are familiar has a tendency to let go and release while that which we resist tends to persist. Pain is a result of conscious or unconscious tension and most people do not feel this tension, or notice the contractions, until it becomes pain. Unless we recognize and relax it, tension will accumulate and become pain. Chronic unconscious tension causes or worsens every kind of illness, injury and disease. Even our breath is restricted becoming shallow, rapid, tense, and irregular. The ability to breathe fully and freely is important because it gives us a way to dissolve or burn away physical tension as well as psychological and emotional pain.

Everyone has a resting level of muscle tension. Some people have a great amount of tension at rest, others less. When people are under acute stress, their muscles tend to have higher levels of resting tension that can be painful and fatiguing. Mindfulness meditation has been shown to relax the mind/body without the use of drugs, by breathing "into" and expanding the muscle groups. Breathing "into" it means we imagine the air expanding the muscle groups, gathering up as much tension as possible while holding it for a couple of seconds, focusing on how it feels, and then letting the tension go out with the breath while focusing on the sensations of relaxation. With each breath, the pain and tension lessen until it is eventually gone. We feel the tissue expand, loosen, and absorb fresh oxygen, nutrients, and vitality while expelling toxins and waste material. We feel the breath collect as much tension as possible on the inhale and letting it go with the exhale. Then we go back for more in the same area or move on to the next area when we are ready.

To medicate or meditate, that is the question. Those who adopt the philosophy of "Meditation before Medication" will quickly learn that meditation has no side effects, is far less expensive, and usually more effective than medication, especially in the long term. Few doctors are integrating meditation into their practice because it takes time, and time is money. They find it easier, faster, and more profitable to dispense a prescription than to teach their patients the techniques that allow them to substitute skills for pills.

With meditation, we can open the ego gate, enter the Subconscious, and take control of the Unconscious mind-of the-body. If we go deeper and become one with our OM, the mind/body/soul becomes a powerful force far beyond anything we could have believed possible; greater than the sum of the parts is an understatement. The OM is our direct connection to the Source of all things and is part of the same phenomenon that created the Universe, its galaxies, stars, Earth, water, fire, air, and the mind/body we currently inhabit. We were born with genes that cause disease, genes that cause perfect health, genes that destroy defective cells, and by using only a tiny bit of this universal power, we can reconfigure these genes. We can turn off gene functions that are harmful while activating or reactivating, and energizing gene functions that are beneficial. From the Subconscious

Control Room of the Unconscious mind-of-the-body and our OM generated energy, we can create a mind/body of balance and harmony.

The Buddha figured it out more than twenty-five hundred years ago: "The secret of health for both mind and body is not to mourn for the past, worry about the future, or anticipate troubles, but to live in the present moment wisely and earnestly...breathing in, I relax my whole body; breathing out, I smile to my whole body." Practicing meditation for about twenty minutes every day improves the body's capacity to heal itself. When the mind/body is calm, we also improve our ability to listen, speak gentle words, and re-establish communication with our own soul as well as other people.

3.5 Meditation Practice

When first learning a formal technique for quieting the mind, we need to be patient with ourselves. Effectiveness comes from repetition and practice, and we need to learn these techniques when things are calm. Just as it is difficult to learn how to swim in a stormy ocean, it is difficult to learn to elicit the relaxation response in the midst of emotional, psychological or social storms. We need to learn the techniques in calm waters. Then, when the rains come, we can use them to help us stay afloat in stormy seas. Relaxation is a learned skill but with practice, quieting our restless thoughts becomes automatic. When we become aware that we are rushing in our heads, we stop, smile, breathe, and take a quiet moment of reflection with an attitude of gratitude. A quiet mind follows awareness and attention.

Meditation develops the art of letting go of intrusive thoughts and returning to our focus. It develops our ability to forgive and is an exercise in dismissing harmful thoughts like worry, fear, and anger. Dr. Benson says "to summon the healing effects of the relaxation response, you need to surrender everyday worries and tensions." Meditation involves stripping away the veils that keep us from seeing what has been true all along and gets our harried minds out of the way of our body's natural ability to heal. Relaxation is a basic innate life skill and is the key to ending much of our suffering. The ability to relax and the willingness to let go are vital and a crucial part of forgiveness. It opens our hearts and allows us to learn from the painful lessons of the past in order to move into the future unhindered. Happiness in life depends on our ability to let go and relax especially in those moments when it is the last thing that we would think to do.

Mastering the art of letting go begins with learning to let go of the breath and set it free. When we master the art of letting go of the breath quickly and completely, we find that we are also able to let go of pain and tension, fear, anxiety, disturbing thoughts, negative feelings, and even the past, quickly and easily. If one is unable to let go of an exhale fully and freely, quickly and completely, we should not be surprised if we cannot let go of physical pain, painful thoughts, fear, anxiety, or habits and patterns from the past. However, when we master the skill of letting go of the exhale, we will surprise ourselves at how easily we can let go of many other things on many other levels. To practice using the exhale to trigger relaxation we practice releasing the breath. It helps to take a full, deep, expansive inhale in order to trigger a powerful reflexive release on the exhale. It looks, sounds, and feels like an exaggerated sigh of relief.

The idea is not to control the exhale, but instead to <u>let it go</u> quickly and completely. When we learn to let go of the exhale easily and freely, we also learn that life is a continuous process of letting go; letting go of each passing moment with each breath, and any physical tension or muscular contractions that we do not need to hold on to right now. We learn to let go of the need to be right all the time, hard feelings, harmful emotions, negative thoughts, and rigid opinions.

Meditation synchronizes three elements as one. The first is the mind, the second is the body, and the third is the chi: life force energy, OM, Soul, or Spirit. Sometimes the mind forgets about unity, fragments and runs off to the future or the past where it gets caught up in anger, fear, guilt, worry, sadness, shame, and jealousy. There is no peace or stillness until we bring the mind back to the breath, the present, the now, and then reunite the mind, body, and soul as one elegant, far more powerful whole: mind/body/soul.

Meditation offers an inner ground and balance that external circumstances cannot destroy. When we practice returning to our breath, it is like arriving home, and eventually, we grow to understand that we are always home, no matter where we go. Following the breath brings us home and units mind/body and the OM or Spirit within. It sheds new light on the old adage, "Home is where the heart is." When we make friends with ourselves, warts and all, and have a worthy destination in mind, we always have a comfortable place to be and do not get pushed so far off course that we become lost. Without the fear of getting lost, we can open our minds to what IS without judgment or aversion. The heart begins to open to all that we are and see the world with fresh eyes, free from the usual projections and expectation.

Because we need to check the memory banks from time to time and analyze possible future scenarios, it is not practical or even desirable to stay in the present all of the time. Getting stuck in an unreal world all of the time, however, is a problem. Our challenge is to stay in the present for as long as we can. If we keep our attention in the present as much as possible, we will be anchored in the "Now" and eliminate most of our stress and anxiety. We will not lose ourselves in the external world or get lost in the past or future. Thoughts and emotions, fears and desires, will still be there, but they will not take over. If we can stay deeply rooted within, nothing can shake us. It helps to check in from time to time by asking, "Am I still breathing?" It returns our attention back to the inner energy field of the body, and body awareness keeps us present.

If we could click a timer "on" every time the mind began to daydream or dwell on pointless repetitive thoughts, and click it "off" when the mind returns to the present or mindful, meaningful thoughts, at the end of the day, we would find that much of our day was spent in scattered mindless, pointless, repetitive daydreaming. Some of this mindlessness happens when we are attempting to operate a several-thousand-pound, multifaceted metal machine (that the law considers to be a lethal weapon) as it speeds down a crowded roadway at a hundred feet per second.

To remain grounded in the present, we make it a point to focus on our breath 25% of the time instead of daydreaming, and 75% on consciousness of the space around us, what we are doing, and an openness (accepting and adapting) to receive what IS. Like returning to the breath in our basic meditation, we learn to return to the present in our daily life. Remembering to use our breath awareness to focus on the present 25% of the time instead of daydreaming, we stay in contact with life and start to feel calmer even in the face of catastrophe. Physically we feel stronger because our mind/body is free from the affliction of stress and anxiety, and our thoughts are clearer instead of jumbled and racing.

There are really only five things to remember when preparing to meditate: 1) Find a quiet place. 2) Sit in a dignified but comfortable position with eyes closed or half closed. 3) Breathe easily and naturally through the nose, concentrating attention on a single predetermined point, allowing the mind to be still and focused. Some can even feel their heart beat and their blood flow during the silence after the out-breath. 4) Maintain a non-judgmental attitude without worrying about attaining a particular level of relaxation or whether it is being done correctly. Just observe and let it be, inviting relaxation to occur at its own pace. Replace judgment and criticism with acceptance and curiosity. 5) When the mind wanders or intrusive thoughts pop up, simply smile and silently say, "Thank you" as a sincere expression of gratitude for the awareness that the mind has wandered and gently return to the chosen object of focus without judgment or aversion. This wandering is normal. In fact, students should be pleased with themselves when they realize that the mind has wandered because noticing the drift and returning to the focus is an integral part of a meditation done correctly.

Meditation always involves the intention to focus attention and is a state of wholeness and harmony. This definition of meditation can be categorized into one or some combination of four approaches: Concentration meditation, Mindfulness meditation, Contemplation meditation, and Creative meditation. Many forms of prayer use one or more of the four categories listed or have been considered a separate category of meditation with the focus on God or some spiritual topic but that is beyond the scope of this book. We will be tapping into our inner healer, OM, Soul, or true self using an interactive dialogue to enhance our intention to take control of our own mind/body and affect gene expression but we will not be referencing any particular religious tradition. In most cases, we are all saying the same thing anyway, just using different words.

Concentration meditation activates the parasympathetic nervous system, focuses attention on a single point, and emphasizes the conscious return to that point of concentration each time the mind wanders. By repeatedly refocusing on one point of concentration, the meditator develops discipline, the ability to focus, and gains control of the mind. Mindfulness meditation observes a predetermined image without judgment or attachment and develops our ability to let it go. The image can be a sense, action, thing, the mind/body whole or part, word or words. Rather than a single point of concentration, mindfulness develops awareness: a clear and single-minded awareness of what actually happens to us and in us, at the successive moments of perception. Contemplation meditation focuses on the mysteries of life, reflects upon the interdependent nature of things, develops understanding and insight, facilitates in-depth study with the aid of great wisdom, and provides a better understanding of predetermined subjects. It reflects on the deeper meaning of a seed thought, strengthens our resolve, vision, and clarity and is what we do when we want to "meditate on it." <u>Creative meditation</u> develops our ability to control our evolution and elicits one of the greatest gifts of our humanity. It uses visualization and the power of imagination and reason, to conceive, plan, rehearse, and stimulate the belief, emotion, and energy required to manifest great things, solve problems, and visit any corner of the Universe.

Before beginning a meditation journey, it is helpful to determine one's <u>intent</u> and which <u>type</u> of meditation to use. The intent might be to reduce stress, renew, re-energize, lower blood pressure, or just relax. The type is limited to basic meditation at this point but we will discuss Concentration meditation in the next section and the other three types in greater detail later. The array of choices may seem confusing unless the student consciously chooses the type that is most compatible with their intent before they begin. Meditation practitioners are like good pilots in that they know where they want to go before they set a course and start the engines.

The best time to practice meditation is first thing in the morning but should be done once or twice every day for ten to twenty minutes to produce the maximum benefit. Those who think that they do not have time are the ones who need it the most and should just sit down for 30 seconds, breathe, force a smile, and then if they feel like doing more that's great, but if they do not, at least they can say that they did it. As opposed to spending the same 30 seconds mindlessly rushing around (trying to chop wood with a dull axe) it provides composure and a sharper axe.

Our students practice meditation after doing the <u>(5-7-9) Breath</u> that they have associated with their morning hygiene routine. Most do not use an alarm because alarms are usually too alarming, rather they open their eyes to check the time and return to their focus. If one feels that they need an alarm, find one with a pleasing tone. When finished, they take a few deep breaths, smile and sit quietly for a moment or two to avoid harshing their mellow. Eliciting the relaxation response delivers physiologic and emotional benefits as predictably as flipping a light switch causes the light bulb to shine. Using deep breathing and meditation, we can learn to respond effectively to the stresses in life instead of overreacting to them.

A beginner does not sit down and attempt to meditate for an hour or even 30 minutes. That's like trying to run a marathon the day after deciding to take up running. Referring to "The Magic of Incremental Steps" in Part II

Section 2.3.2, most people start with a 2 to 3 minute breath focus at least six days a week for the first week or two. It is important to do it every day, even if for only 30 seconds, but if one feels the need to take a day off, always take off the same day of the week. Commitment, consistency, and rhythm are key. When the student feels ready, they increase the frequency to twice a day and/or the time to 5 to 7 minutes for two weeks, then 10 to 12 minutes for two weeks, then 15 to 20 minutes for two weeks. Increasing the time or frequency beyond that is optional but beneficial. If regression occurs, we do not beat ourselves up, we just move back one step, do it for two weeks and then establish a habit or normal routine. As one young lady put it, "Kissing a guy who does not brush his teeth every day is like licking a garbage disposal, and dealing with people who do not meditate every day is like working with a mental zombie to those who do."

Meditation has no single all-inclusive definition because it means something different to every perceiver but for our purposes, it is directed concentration of focused attention. We do not need to clutter our minds with complicated explanations and concepts; we just need to control our focus. We simply want to feel harmony. Albert Einstein taught us that any fool can make things bigger, more complex, and more violent. It takes a touch of genius and a lot of courage to move in the opposite direction.

"Every breath we take, every step we make, can be filled with peace, joy, and serenity. We need only to be awake; alive in the present moment …we practice to be happy right in the present moment. When we're sitting, we should have happiness as we are sitting. When we are walking, we should have happiness as we are walking. When we practice correctly, there's peace and happiness today; we don't have to wait until tomorrow. " Thich Nhat Hanh

3.6 Concentration Meditation 1

Concentration meditation focuses one's attention on a single, relatively stable object, word or phrase, while other forms of meditation assume a more dynamic, inclusive field of observation. We have defined meditation in general as directed concentration of focused attention which implies that all of the meditation techniques we use have their origins in Concentration meditation. Traditionally, one first practices Concentration meditation for some time to still and focus the wandering and undisciplined mind. Then this strong concentration is directed to look deeper.

We need to train the mind to concentrate and focus attention on the object of meditation and hold it there without distraction. Whenever the mind wanders, simply return it, again and again, to the object of meditation. No matter which form of meditation one uses, this principle always applies. It allows the mind to be calm and awaken beyond thought, elaboration, and the Ego's sense of self. With patience and practice, the mind will become calmer, more powerful, and able to apply itself to any task with precision and understanding.

Through the power of concentration, we build our capacity to overcome distraction and to sustain mental focus. The power of a scattered mind is very limited. But the power of a concentrated mind can be focused effectively to enhance and deepen insight into other meditative intents. It is important to note here that an intention can be to focus attention on the experience of having no intention. Like an adjustable flash light or laser beam, the tighter the focus, the brighter and more powerful the beam. Such is the difference in illuminating power of the concentrated mind to the ordinary, scattered, and fragmentary flow of attention that most people bring to everyday living.

By learning how to bring the stream of our attention into a laser-like beam of one-pointed concentration, we can train the mind to become a highly useful instrument for penetrating the ego gate into the Subconscious Control Room of the Unconscious mind-of-the-body. A concentrated mind is a prerequisite for the development of conscious control of gene expression and the precursor of great wisdom and harmony.

There are many ways to elicit the psychophysiological benefits of meditation, but the easiest is the "Observe the Natural Breath" exercise described in Part II. When combined with a mantra, one can attain results, not unlike those described in Dr. Benson's studies, and they become more and more profound with practice. Mantras can dominate the full scope of our focus and prevent distracting thoughts from entering the mind, help us achieve a state of relaxed awareness, and have the benefit of allowing the mind to enter a subtler level.

A mantra is a word or short phrase repeated over and over to calm and center the mind. It provides immediate help and long term benefits that accumulate the more it is used. The more one uses it, the more effective it will be. It can be used while walking, jogging, or waiting in line. It is not used when mindful attention is required such as when one is chopping vegetables or operating machinery, but most ordinary repetitive activities can be easily integrated into a meditation practice.

When choosing a mantra, it is helpful to use one that is time tested and has been found to be effective in the past. Almost any one or two word phrase that has a positive tone (or no meaning at all) will work but soothing, mellifluous sounding words will avoid stimulating associated stray thoughts. Making up a word is not recommended but words like love, peace, harmony, lahm, yang-chi, so-hum, I am-we, rah-ma, haum-sah, om, or one, have been used for centuries. Choose a mantra that feels right and preferably has no emotional meaning that might cause a distraction during meditation. No one mantra is better than another if it feels right but once it is chosen, it is best to stick with it. Dr. Benson used the one-word mantra "One" in his studies, and many of our students use One-Om, lahm, or so-hum. It can be used as the sole focus of attention or in harmony with the breath and/or heartbeat. When using a two-word mantra like "so-hum" in harmony with the breath, we silently chant "so" on the in-breath and "hum" on the out-breath and sometimes listen for our heartbeat during the pause between the in-breath and the out-breath. A single word mantra is chanted on the out-breath. With experience, we learn to choose our intent before beginning, but the novice learns faster by using the same intent and focus each time until it becomes comfortable. We still begin our meditation by focusing on the breath but shift to the mantra when it feels right.

a) We first find a time and place where we know we will not be distracted. The time period associated with the (5-7-9) Breath usually works well and the place should be warm, safe, and quiet. We then state our intent, (in this case, it is to cultivate the ability to concentrate) keeping in mind that we all want the same thing in the end. Regardless of current superficial wants and desires, harmony is the real goal. And then, just for a moment, consider that meditation is founded on gratitude, patience, and kindness.

b) Set a timer with a pleasing tone if desired, but most people simply open their eyes long enough to look at a watch or clock and gently return to their focus. Sit in a comfortable but dignified manner with the face, scalp, neck, shoulders, and body relaxed and spine straight. It is important to stay relaxed, yet aware and awake. Some students sit on a pillow with their hips slightly higher than their knees and imagine their spine is a tall, straight tree against which they can lean. Note that meditation can be done in the prone position as well, particularly mindfulness and progressive relaxation, but is more likely to morph into sleep. Meditation requires conscious awareness, not sleep.

c) Focus attention on the breath. With our eyes closed or half closed to reduce distractions, we shift from the outer world to our inner world and maintain focus and awareness on our breath. We take a deep (5-7-9) Breath with a barely audible sigh (ahhhhhh) allowing the jaw and shoulders to relax and a slight smile to form on the out-breath. Then we allow the mind/body to become still and focus our attention on the natural tidal rhythm of the breath, feeling the rise and fall of the inhalation and exhalation without trying to influence it.

d) Scan the mind/body from head to toe and back again for tension or tightness inviting it to relax as much as it wants to while remaining alert and attentive to the breath in the present moment. Assume a non-judgmental attitude, brush away stray thoughts that cloud concentration, and return to the breath. On the inhale, we gather up tension that we do not need to hold right now, and on each exhale, we release that tension and become more and more relaxed; a real letting go kind of breath. It is often helpful to bring the thumb and forefinger together and notice the sense of touch. When we can feel the thumb touching the forefinger, we know that we are aware and in the present moment.

e) As our focus settles on the breath, we begin to employ a simple predetermined mantra like "so-hum." With each inhale, we silently say "so" and with the exhale, we say "hum," and then listen for our heartbeat during the pause between the in-breath and the out-breath. We do not worry about how quickly or deeply the body relaxes; we just invite it to relax in its own way in its own time without trying to force or fix anything. We find that the body really likes to relax and let waves of spacious awareness wash gently through us. Awareness of the breath anchors our attention in the present moment.

f) When awareness detects a lapse in focus or an unrelated thought arises, silently say thank you, smile gently and return to the breath. Always return to the breath and continue the mantra, "so-hum." We hold a gentle inner smile because it keeps us from trying too hard, getting tense, or being self-critical. The mind/body is repairing and renewing itself on every level, and there is nothing else we have to do while it is doing that. Although doing nothing on purpose is actually doing something, we can grant ourselves the luxurious permission to have nothing else to do or nowhere else to go right now. Shift from doing to being and notice what it feels like to do absolutely nothing and have it be good for us. Stay focused as long as is comfortable, improving gradually. Beginners start with two to five minutes and extend it to 20-30 minutes as they get better at it.

g) When it is time to return to the outside world, we return to the breath and become aware of this calmness and centeredness, commit it to memory for future use, and allow the benefits of this practice to expand into every aspect of life. Feeling secure and a wonderful sense of well-being, we become more alert and aware in every way. We begin to notice what is going on around us, wiggle our fingers and toes, smile because we feel so good, and move our focus from our inner world to the sounds, smells, shapes and colors around us. Finally, we take a comfortable energizing Three-Part-Breath and open our eyes feeling wide awake, grateful, re-energized, refreshed, happy, and ready for the remainder of the day.

h) Some find it helpful to bring the hands together (the gasho or prayer position) and close the moment with gratitude and reflection. It is helpful to sit still for a moment or two with the intention of incorporating the benefits into our daily lives. To keep us in the present moment, we continue to keep 25% of our attention on our breath (DSCR) replacing pointless repetitive daydreaming. With the other 75% on what we are doing and what really matters in life, we check in from time to time by asking, "Am I still breathing?"

The mantra can also be combined with the Zen practice of Walking meditation. We incorporate a simplified version of the Principles of Harmony Affirmations explored in Section 3.3 by holding one concept of an affirmation in mind with each step as follows: "I am we - we are one - with all that is - Be Grateful - Patient - Kind - Happy - Healthy - Calm mind at peace - in Balance - and Harmony - with the Universe." It is repeated over and over as we walk, breathing a little deeper and standing a little taller, sporting a slight smile and enjoying the present moment. This is an add-on to (DSCR) practice discussed in Part I when high stress is not a factor. Life is good and with each step, we reinforce our attitude of harmony. It replaces pointless, negative, or worrisome thinking with constructive character building. Anytime one needs to walk more than a few steps, employing this technique embeds a positive attitude deeper into the Subconscious.

Some forms of mantra meditation involve audible chanting and use the sound as the object of their focus. In yoga, the mantra "Om" is regularly used since it delivers a deep vibration that makes it easy for the mind to concentrate on that particular sound. It, however, is not as socially acceptable in normal daily life as following one's breath with a silent mantra and slight smile.

When we follow our breath, repeat a mantra, or practice some other basic technique every day, the mind begins to settle down naturally, while thoughts and feelings spontaneously bubble up and release any negative energy they might be holding.

3.7 Summary

In Part III, we learned that perception and attitude determine the direction and quality of our lives and that it is possible to control and direct them. We explored the powerful connection between thought, feeling, emotion, and behavior. We are not victims of our circumstances, anger, or fear and are not controlled by the past or uncertain future unless we allow it. We learned the art of non-reaction, non-resistance, non-judgment, non-attachment, how to develop conscious awareness, the five steps to gratitude, and how to find a worthy purpose in life. We learned to tap into the motivating power of spirituality and seven basic principles that form the foundation of all major religions. Finally, we discussed the healing power of meditation and how it works, the secret to controlling tension and pain, the art of letting go, how to choose a mantra, and Concentration meditation. We end Part III with an Action Assignment that reminds us what to work on and what needs to be part of our lives.

Part IV will expand the student's knowledge of relevant concepts, justify the statement that everything we need to evolve from stress to gratitude is already within us, and that we can get there from here. It will cover Mindfulness meditation and Contemplation meditation, and how we use them to make our journey more fruitful and enjoyable.

3.8 Action Assignment

* Understand that perception is the root of all that we are and all that we do, and that we can control it. View problems as an astronaut viewing the Earth from outer space.

* Develop a mind that is open to everything and attached to nothing.

* Be aware that every problem has at least three solutions: 1) Fix it with kindness. 2) Accept, adapt perceptions, and look for opportunity. 3) Walk away or around it, let it go, let it be, and move on.

* Define a personal purpose that begins with "My worthy purpose is..." Simplify it down to one single sentence and let it light the way. Write a more detailed "Mission Statement" and plan a path that includes intermediate intentions, supporting goals, and objectives. Then smile, breath, and enjoy the trip. All things are POSSIBLE.

* Review the five steps to developing Gratitude and above all; Be Kind, no matter what, Be Kind.

* Commit the Seven Principles of Harmony (I am We affirmations) to memory.

* When jogging, walking, or waiting in line, say or think, "I am we - we are one - with all that is - Be Grateful - Patient - Kind - Happy - Healthy - Calm mind at peace - in Balance - and Harmony - with the Universe." This can also be an add-on to (DSCR) practice discussed in Part II when high stress is not an immediate factor.

* Practice letting go, starting with the exhale: Take a deep breath IN and let it go as an exaggerated sigh of relief.

* Understand the healing power of meditation and the importance of being present with the breath 25% of the time instead of pointless repetitive daydreaming. Practice returning to the breath as often as possible by asking, "Am I still breathing?"

* Choose a mantra that feels right and preferably has no distracting emotional meaning. Begin Concentration meditation by focusing on the breath and then expand it to harmoniously include the mantra.

* Note the sign created in Part II stating the Reason or Motivation for Daily Meditation and choose an intent for each meditation: to de-stress, renew, re-energize, lower blood pressure, or just to relax.

* Meditate every day, preferably after doing the (5-7-9) Breath. Do not start the day without at least doing the (5-7-9) Breath.

* Adopt an attitude of gratitude, smile, and do something new as often as possible.

"My Worthy Purpose is……"

"My Mission Statement is…..."

Review the five steps to developing Gratitude

Principles of Harmony

(I am We Affirmations)

1) We are one with all that is, with reverence, love, and kindness.

2) We are aware in the present moment, accepting and adapting with wisdom and curiosity.

3) We recognize, neutralize, dismiss, and replace harmful thoughts with gratitude, patience, and kindness, the wonder of life and the beauty of the gift of breath.

4) We are a happy, healthy, calm mind at peace, in balance and harmony with the Universe.

5) We are free of the past with acceptance and forgiveness, as only change is permanent.

6) We pursue life diligently with integrity, purpose, sincerity, and joy.

7) We understand that harmony is the real goal, the ultimate objective of all pursuits. We imagine harmony, we are harmony, we live harmony.

Every problem has at least three solutions:

1) Fix it with kindness.

2) Accept, adapt perceptions, and look for opportunity.

3) Walk away or around it, let it go, let it be, and move on.

Make it a habit to:

Be present at least 25% of the time by asking…Am I still breathing?

Use the (5-7-9) Breath before leaving the house

Practice the Grateful, Patient, Kind Walk

MEDITATE

Check the "Reason or Motivation for Daily Meditation" sign, choose an intent, mantra, and breathe!

30 seconds to 30 minutes every day

Be Kind no matter what Be Kind

**Where there is life,
there is hope.
(Cicero)**

PART IV

Evolving from Stress to Gratitude
Meditation 2 & 3

4.1 Everything We Need Is Already Within Us

Like a fertile garden, the subtle (or Subconscious) mind will return, in abundance, whatever we plant. If we plant kindness, it will return kindness. If we plant hostility, it will return hostility. If we choose to plant corn in our garden, water and care for it, it will return hundreds of corn kernels for every one that we plant. If we choose to plant nightshade, it will return poison in just as wonderful abundance. It is impersonal. It does not care what we plant. It will return an abundance of what we plant but it will not judge what we plant. Judgment is a function of Ego and the Conscious mind, not the subtle or Subconscious mind. Things are always popping up from the subtle mind, some good and some not so good, and it is the job of the Conscious mind to observe and weed the garden by identifying and discarding harmful thoughts while allowing worthy thoughts to grow and flourish.

Some people are inner-directed and feel that we create our reality by what we think and imagine, while others are outer-directed and believe that they are controlled by exterior forces. The inner-directed person is guided by the spirit within while the outer-directed person is pushed and controlled by circumstances, demands, and opinions of other people. Outer-directed people have never learned that positive feelings are created within. They are shackled by the subconscious belief and expectation that well-being, or happy, positive feelings are dependent on outside forces. This undermining dependency of fear, stress, and anxiety is a self-limiting system. Moving forward in life calls for meeting challenges and taking on new opportunities with calm, comfortable control. The days of thinking that the body is only controlled by exterior forces and operates independently of our beliefs is fading away.

As we learned in PART I, the Conscious mind knows that feelings are not facts, thinks abstractly, and provides us with logic, reason, willpower, language, decision-making, and superior judgment. It sets goals, judges results, likes to try new things, has a short-term memory, and is conceptually based. It is only about 12% of our brain, has a limited processing capacity, has a short attention span, and is time bound, that is, uses past, present, and future concepts. The Conscious mind is only a small percentage of the whole, is slow so it cannot be everywhere, and needs the subconscious automatic reactions and programs to run thing while it is busy thinking about something else. The problem is that some of those programs are defective or wrong and need to be turned OFF or replaced.

Our Conscious mind is miraculous and a unique gift, but it cannot directly control the body; it needs to check all instructions or commands it wishes to manifest with the Ego at the ego gate between the Conscious and Subconscious mind. Then, if approved, the order is passed on into the Subconscious Control Room where the right switches are thrown and the Unconscious responds without question like a great impersonal computer.

The Subconscious mind is habitual, monitors operation of the body, likes the familiar, thinks literally like an impersonal computer, holds our long-term memory (stores past experiences, attitudes, and values) and is sensory based. It has an expanded processing capacity and uses only the present moment. It does not understand future rather it sees stored memories and future images from the Conscious mind in the present. The Subconscious mind receives all physical and sensory input and stores everything with all past input. It can add to or alter memories but (barring physical damage) all input will remain until death. When recalled, this stored data is sent back to the Conscious mind through the ego gate where it is again filtered by the ego's perceptions. The Subconscious is easily accessible through meditation, uses imagery to communicate, and is ruled by beliefs resulting from its own perception of reality or Conscious instructions that get past the ego gate. It will leave evaluating and choosing of what is best to the Conscious mind if it is awake and aware, but most of the time it is allowed to control autonomic physical functions, our actions, and emotions based on its programs. It tends to have dominant control over life experience and can organize choices and decisions, but the Subconscious has neither free will nor goals, only the Conscious does.

Ego has one foot in the Conscious mind and one foot in the Subconscious mind and stands at the gate between the two functions filtering and allowing only that information it feels is appropriate to pass. It filters sensory and stored information from the Subconscious going to the Conscious as well as all imagined instructions and objectives formed in the Conscious going to the Subconscious. It allows only those instructions that it deems safe and appropriate to pass through the gate and on to the Subconscious for action in the Control Room. It tries to protect the Subconscious from non-conforming beliefs and thoughts from the Conscious mind and the outside world. It can be easily overwhelmed by too much information that can result in anxiety and stress or bypassed by meditation, both of which cause the distracted gatekeeper to abandon the gate to the Subconscious and allow unchallenged concepts to enter and be readily accepted whether they are true or not.

Ego is not evil or even bad, just wrong a lot and although it is a tiny part of the whole, Ego thinks that IT alone represents "I" and believes it must fight for itself in the world. Ego is an expression of separateness, the affirmation of being separate from others. It is often associated with compulsive thinking in order to be assured of its future existence, automatically reacting from past programming rather than responding from wisdom.

The Unconscious mind is the mind-of-the-body and controls the autonomic nervous system, heart rate, breathing, temperature control, blood pressure, digestion, fear, anger, sex drive, and all those things that we incorrectly assume are beyond our conscious control. Most of the time the Subconscious, the largest portion of the brain, is controlling the Unconscious with pre-learned or preprogrammed instructions stored in its memory. But sometimes the Conscious mind will actually wake up and make a decision or learn a new program and then let the new program run things while it worries about something or hangs out in a past event. That is why we miss our exit on the freeway sometimes.

OM (spirit, soul, life force energy) is our connection to the Source of all things. It is our connection to a vast, possibly infinite, repository of universal wisdom made up of incomprehensible, dynamic, constantly changing forms of vibrating energy. Our Conscious mind has access to this wisdom; Ego does not. Consciousness has access to imagination and awareness while ego uses only current sensory perceptions and preprogrammed responses. When consciousness is able to bypass or slip by the Ego at the gate and consult the vast universal wisdom through OM, it is far more qualified to run the show with a greater purpose in mind and awareness of what we are doing and where we are going. Bypassing the Ego and learning to access the OM at will is a key part of Medimaginosis.

Our natural wisdom, or intuition, exists beyond the confines of our Conscious mind. We gain access to it when we quiet down and listen for inspiration or insight. Unlike ordinary thoughts or knowledge, wisdom is a silent voice that exists only when the mind is calm. There is always a part of us that knows exactly what to do, if we listen. It is the ability to step back from our usual way of seeing life and of doing things. This becomes easier as the mind quiets. According to Miles Kingston, the difference between knowledge and wisdom is that knowledge is knowing that a tomato is a fruit while wisdom keeps them out of our fruit salad. Knowledge is knowing what to say, and wisdom is knowing when to say it.

Decisions and mental patterns we create can alter and change our emotional and physical reality dramatically. For example, we can cultivate contentment by consciously choosing to give our happiness priority over being right. Being right or making someone else wrong is worthless if it requires energy that could be better spent enjoying life. If we let someone else be right sometimes (especially on minor points), choose our battles carefully, and allow ourselves the luxury of feeling happy, the resultant harmony is real music. We are conscious co-creators of our universe. When the mind, body, and soul are effectively integrated, with adaptation, all things are possible and miracles happen. Everything we need is already within us.

4.1.1 **Psychoneuroimmunology and Epigenetics**

The rapidly expanding fields of psychoneuroimmunology and epigenetics have sound answers to healing the root cause of disease. In times of stress, a negative message absorbs into our Subconscious mind and is reinforced every time we recall and focus on it. When we negatively judge ourselves we are reinforcing, even instructing our Subconscious mind to persist with the behavior. Research tells us that this information is then transmitted to every cell in the body. Our cellular intelligence is designed to adapt to its perceived environment, but most people are not aware of this fact and that every time they think about something they do not want, they actually draw it closer.

Psychoneuroimmunology (PNI) is a relatively new science named in 1980 at the University of Rochester medical school by psychologist Robert Ader. It is the investigation (ology) of the interaction between the mind (psycho), the brain and nervous system (neuro), and the body's biochemical resistance to disease and abnormal cell development (immun). It might also be called psycho-endo-neuro-immunology because it also includes the study of the (endocrine system) or hormonal system and integrates several other disciplines including genetics, pharmacology, and molecular biology.

The focus of researchers in this field is on both the illness-causing and healing effects the mind can have on the body. They study stress and how the body's stress response relates to the emotions of anxiety, anger, fear, guilt, worry, sadness, shame, and jealousy, how it weakens the immune system, interferes with healing, and even causes disease. For physical health and well-being, we need to be able to effectively neutralize stressful emotions and cultivate a more balanced state.

In biology, epigenetics is the study of changes in gene expression caused by mechanisms other than changes in the underlying DNA sequence and introduces the concept of conscious control into genetics. The discovery that cells are responding to the internal environment of our thoughts, beliefs, and feelings confirms the contention that changing our perceptions produces biological changes on the cellular level. Epigenetic research reveals that genetics are controlled by perception of our environment and adapt to our beliefs and identities. Genes cannot turn themselves ON or OFF; rather the organism changes to adapt to its perceived environment.

Our genes are reconfigured through external, environmental stimuli, a discovery that runs contrary to the long-held assumptions of genetic determinism (life is controlled by genetics).

Traditional science has believed that our genes are fixed and that nothing can change genetic determinism. Conversely, epigenetic research indicates that cells have a dynamic cellular intelligence and that gene functions are being turned ON and OFF based on external perceptions. Our perceptions of the external environment alter the electrochemical environment of the cells and sensors on the cell's exterior send instructions that alter gene functions to adapt. What is most exciting and empowering is that if the environment that supports a disease is eliminated, and a new healthier environment replaces it, the predisposition for the genetic disease will not be supported, and it will not manifest.

The epigenetic theorems were slow to evolve and integrate into the mainstream of academia, partly due to the fact that the training of health professionals is deeply vested by the pharmaceutical industry and the even greater promise of lucrative gene therapies. Our innate ability to impact gene expression is still ignored by many contemporary medical textbooks and clinical practitioners, but the old model of genetic determinism is slowly being replaced with the new model of epigenetics.

The difference between these two models is significant because genetic determinism assumes that we are victims of our genetic code, that the illnesses and diseases that run in families are propagated through the passing of genes associated with those attributes. Buying into genetic determinism leaves one utterly powerless to do anything about the health of the body because it implies that life is driven by our genetic code, which we were born with and locked into. Scientists have completely shattered this dogma and proven it false. We actually have a tremendous amount of control over how our genetic traits are expressed through our perceptions.

The mass media continues to promulgate the belief that we are victims and need to be rescued from outside. This is where the pharmaceutical and medical community has inserted itself. They try to sell the idea that genes determine our future when in actuality, that technology has no more scientific value than a palm reading. Epigenetic control reveals that environmental information alters the function or expression of the genes without changing the underlying DNA sequenced code. Each and every cell in our bodies has a type of intelligence. Genes change their expression depending on what is happening outside the cell and even outside the body. Environmental factors such as nutrients, attitude, conscious thoughts, emotions, and subconscious beliefs, all affect the environment of the cell.

Scientists undertook the "Genome Project", which was launched in 1990 and completed in 2003, to map out all human genes and their interactions. They began with the belief that the human DNA consisted of about 150,000 genes and that their work would be the basis for curing virtually any disease. They discovered that genes do not operate as previously predicted and that the human body consists of only about 23,000 genes. Since then, we have come to understand that epigenetic regulation can provide for more than 30,000 different variations of expression. To understand the potential variations of genetic expression we can multiply each gene by 30,000 possibilities and when associated with other genes that also have as many variations, the number of integrated expressions is mindboggling. So rather than try to figure it out, we just tell the Subconscious mind what we want it to do and let it do its job. Just as the many adjustments on a television can alter the picture, the model of epigenetics allows for adjustment of the genes. It can be turned ON and OFF, change the color, tint, contrast, horizontal, and vertical without altering the original DNA or broadcast signal. We do not need to know how it works, we just need to adjust the controls.

Our genes are the fundamental programmers that take the fertilized egg to the stage where the developing cells begin to look like a human. From the fetal stage on, the modifications are epigenetically controlled, meaning, they are influenced by the environment. Sperm and eggs are generic. They form a human, but they do not determine wheather that human is going to develop big muscles or study medicine. That is the job of the Conscious human mind. Once the human form is made, development could become anything from a bodybuilder to a scientist. The information from the environment, such as a mentor emphasizing learning over physical workouts, will shape perceptions and beliefs. The Subconscious mind reads environmental signals, integrates them with stored programs and then regulates the body's chemistry that controls the genetic expression of the cells which then impacts the selection of proteins our bodies use to build tissue which then impacts our health and the quality of our lives, which then impacts our environment.

Perception is critical because our senses read the environmental but have no opinion as to what they mean until subconscious programming or the Conscious mind interprets the environmental signals based upon the flexibility of our perceptions. To the degree a situation is perceived as threatening the Unconscious will release neurochemicals that control cell behavior and gene activity to coordinate a protection response versus the perception of a pleasant image.

The new knowledge of how perception controls biology reveals that we can be active participants in controlling the character of our health and behavior. Our ability to consciously control our perceptions and environment has a profound influence on our lives, versus the old belief system where we are victims of forces beyond our control. When we live in the here and now, present as much as possible, and actively use our Conscious mind to run the show, we create harmony. We are what we think, not what our Ego thinks we are. We are not victims of fate, but prisoners of our own delusions. It is like standing on the bridge of a ship at sea, watching it head toward a large iceberg. All that is required to correct the course is a turn of the wheel, but too many people are unable or unwilling to take control, usually as a result of ignorance.

We are all like the captain of a beautiful yacht. We can take care of it, keep it clean and shiny or let it deteriorate from lack of maintenance. We can take control of the helm or simply turn on the engines and let it go. The aware captain efficiently sails from port to port successfully navigating all sorts of storms and obstacles while the unaware captain either does not care to take control or does not know how the controls work. The aware captain has a voyage mapped out and planned while the unaware captain allows external forces like the tide and wind to guide the ship and wonders why he never seems to arrive at his desired port. If fact, if he gets out of the harbor at all, he will either sink or run aground.

Science has indeed taken us far beyond Newtonian physics, which says we live in a mechanical universe. According to this belief, the body is just a biological machine and by modifying the parts, we modify health. As a biological machine, the body will respond to physical things like drugs, and by adjusting the drugs that modify the machinery, doctors can modify and control health. However, with the evolution of quantum physics, scientists have realized the flaws in Newtonian physics. Quantum physics shows us that the invisible, immaterial realm is actually far more important than the material realm and that our thoughts may shape our environment far more than physical things.

The true secret to health and happiness does not lie within our DNA, but rather the environment we create with our minds. Our cells will read or not read the genetic blueprint depending on the signals being received from the environment. Having a "cancer program" in one's DNA does not automatically mean one is destined to get cancer. This genetic information does not ever have to be expressed. What this all means is that we are not controlled by our genetic makeup. Instead, our genetic expression (which gene functions are turned ON and which are turned OFF) is primarily determined by our perceptions.

We can control our genes and alter them on a regular basis, depending on the foods we eat, the air we breathe, and the thoughts we think. It is our perceptions of the environment and the resulting lifestyle that dictates our tendency to express disease, and this new realization is set to make major waves in the future of disease prevention. When a disease occurs, the solution is simply to "remind" the affected cells of their healthy function, so they can go back to being normal cells instead of diseased cells. We change their environmental instructions.

Drugs affect many genes other than just the targeted gene and can be like trying to kill a mosquito with a shotgun, or eradicate a rat population in an ecosystem by introducing a large number of poisonous snakes that like to eat rats. The mind, on the other hand, coordinates the genes it needs to accomplish its assigned objective. Without integration, a single gene may have little effect on the body, and there is no such thing as THE cancer gene. Physiological change can require the influence of many genes in a specific configuration. Some need to be deactivated while others need to be activated, integrated, and fine-tuned. Just because a person has a specific gene does not mean it will manifest its associated effect unless numerous other genes (associated or not) are in the exact activation sequence to enable the change. Association does not necessarily mean causation.

Just because one has a gene common in those who have a particular condition does NOT mean the condition will manifest. Telling a person that they need to have expensive bariatric (weight-loss) surgery because they have THE fat gene or telling a woman that she is brave and calling her a hero for having her breasts and ovaries removed because she has THE cancer gene reeks of ignorance. It is like sacrificing a virgin to the volcano god to prevent an eruption or cutting off the hands of a young boy because his father stole a loaf of bread and his grandfather was a pickpocket. It was professed that the boy obviously had a gene common to criminal behavior and the only way to avoid a life of crime was to cut off his hands before he begins to steal. Submitting to the amputation willingly does not make the boy a hero, it makes him a victim of barbaric ignorance or even greed if the victim had to pay money for the procedure. Was the surgeon motivated by genuine concern for the patient or the mercilessly inflated fee?

There is no need to know which genes are supposed to do what or understand the intricacies of the genetic changes to control them. Rather than attempting to learn the how-and-why of gene expression with the intention of controlling what <u>appears</u> to be the key genes, we let the mind do what it does best. We give it a task and let it make the needed changes. It already has the code. We do not need to know how every computer chip works, just what buttons to push.

The major problem with believing the myth that our genes control our lives is that we become victims of our heredity. Some who present themselves as authority figures tell vulnerable patients that they have a single gene that has been associated with breast cancer and that a mastectomy is needed to avert the threat. They are told how brave they are for submitting to their expensive procedures and should also have their ovaries removed for good measure. This myth essentially says that our lives are predetermined, and therefore we have very little control over our health. It limits us to the hope that modern medicine will find a way to alter the gene responsible, or develop drugs to modify our chemistry. The new science, however, reveals that our perceptions control our biology, and this places us in the driver's seat, because if we can change our perceptions, we can shape and direct our own genetic function. We all have tumor suppressor genes, and these genes are capable of stopping cancer cells in their tracks. These genes are present in every cell in the body, but if they are turned OFF, cancer cells can proliferate. The best, most effective cancer drugs are created from within.

4.2 Mass Cognitive Manipulation

When we forget that we can take control of our perceptions, we are vulnerable to those who would manipulate our thoughts and feelings for their own benefit and profit. Our modern world has taken "marketing" to the extreme, using wonderfully imaginative ad campaigns to sell their goods. The power of suggestion and the psychology of compliance are used every day in mass-marketing strategies to sell everything from drugs and illness to cars, insurance, and God. Every day, advertisers attempt to influence or even alter our perceptions with endless sales promotions for toxic medications with dangerous and potentially deadly side effect or unhealthy junk food. They tell us that we are deficient and that we need their products to be complete. But wait, there's more! They invent diseases and imply personal attachment or ownership by referring to "your" medication, "your" disease and that you need to urgently ask "your" doctor for drugs at an exorbitantly inflated price. Today! The same drug in almost any other country would sell for a fraction of the price.

Pharmaceutical manufacturers make a lot of money by convincing us that we have a disease and then selling us their remedy. Their TV commercials invent diseases and conditions that we did not realize we had and refer to them as "your" awful disease and air them every few minutes, loading our favorite entertainment programs with subliminal anxiety producing fears. They are seldom interested in the cause, only the opportunity to sell more drugs and often refer to common conditions or symptoms as a disease and attempt to make us own this hideous new disease.

The same brain-wave state we associate with hypnosis, known as alpha, is the state we all go into when we watch television. The average person will slip into alpha within minutes, and many in a matter of seconds. This is a state of hyper-suggestibility where we are prone to accept suggestions to buy products and alter perceptions. Advertisers urge us to "Ask your doctor." She can find a disease for you, arrange for unnecessary surgery, recommend expensive procedures, and sell you all the pills you and your insurance company can afford, and more.

Simple conditions that the body can handle on its own are often inappropriately referred to as diseases and prognoses are exaggerated to ensure that we are frightened enough to purchase the prescribed medication at shamefully inflated prices. Any side effects caused by the original medication are often treated with a second prescription and a third to handle problems that inexplicably appear as a result of mixing medications. Doctors and pharmacists often know the effect of mixing two drugs, but few studies have been conducted to determine the side effects of medicating the side effects of two or more drugs. More than seventy-five percent of all doctor visits are for ailments that the body can handle on its own or imagined diseases that came to the patient's attention while watching TV, but almost all such doctor visits end with a drug sale.

It is the job of the immune system to seek out and destroy foreign germs, harmful mutant cells, aberrations, and disease-causing organisms and substances. But, when the outside world refers to a condition or symptom as "your disease" and the Subconscious begins to accept it as "my disease," the immune systems start to accept them as if they belong. If the Subconscious mind thinks they are "mine," and not foreign invaders, it may actually protect and feed them rather than destroy them.

Television has probably the single largest impact on people today, and we wondered how much sickness is sold by the media manipulating and distorting our attitudes and beliefs. How much illness is sold in order to create a market for medication? Advertising people and pharmaceutical advocates manipulate our perceptions or trick us into becoming attached to them, their products, and identifying with or owning a disease for which they claim to have a cure. They are promoting a form of ownership like "my heart" or "my hair." We own and care for our heart, hair, mind, and body, but we do not want to own a disease, we want to defeat it.

The medical community likes to refer to even a temporary imbalance in one's health as "your disease, or your pain" rather than "the problem, or the pain." Using terms like "the cancer" rather than "my cancer" or referring to a medication by its name or "the medication" rather than "my medication" or "my pills" forms a perception more conducive to defeating the aberration and avoiding the manufactured desire to hold on to a condition or a medication with toxic and potentially deadly side effects. Destabilizing medication and diseases do not belong to us. They are malfunctions and foreign invaders that need to be broken up, dissolved and floated away to restore harmony and balance.

164

Advertisers try to trick us into using ownership terms like; my yahoo, my eBay, my dentist, my disease, my fibromyalgia, my doctor, my depression, my diabetes, my medication, or my pills. This is an attempt to manipulate our perceptions and make us feel like we own a disease. They are shamelessly exploiting a subconscious desire to hold on to what we feel is ours, form an attachment, maintain a need, and buy more pills.

If we think we own a thing, the Subconscious mind will try to keep it (like "my keys"), but if we think the thing is a foreign invader, the Subconscious mind will reject it. We will feel better about getting rid of this abnormality because it does not belong instead of harboring a subconscious need to hold on to a thing that we unconsciously feel is ours. As one astute student noted, "It is NOT <u>MY</u> disease and should never be referred to as such because it implies ownership. MY strong immune system protects and restores MY body by repelling and protecting against <u>foreign invaders</u> and alien discomforts that do not belong in MY body and certainly do not belong to me."

The Subconscious translates our spoken language into images, feelings, and emotions and is quite literal. That's why "losing weight" seldom translates into optimum health and the reduction of an overweight condition for more than a few months if at all. The Subconscious hears the words "lost weight" and sees something that belongs to it as lost like car keys and feels the need to find it again, and usually does. In fact, it usually picks up a few extra pounds in case it happens again. Many dieters have lost, and subsequently found again, a thousand pounds or more. If advertisers can get us to accept their product or service as something that belongs to us, we will hold on to it and resist losing it whether it is good for us or not.

According to the A.C.Nielsen Company, most estimates find that by the time young people are 18 years old, they have seen some 200,000 commercials and the purpose of all of these commercials is to convince them that they are deficient in some way. They are convinced that they are too fat, their complexion is poor, their hair isn't soft and full enough, or that they have an awful disease. Advertisers know that before we will buy a product, we must feel a need for it. They cannot sell a life vest to someone who has no fear of drowning, so they create the fear.

One can almost hear the TV network executives thinking, "We gave them more than 2 ½ minutes of news, now they owe us the right to sell them more pills." Advertisers are trying to convince the Subconscious that a disorder of some kind and their product or service is a part of our being or identity. The object is to foster attachment and desire in the name of profit, and not our benefit. They employ actors to pretend that they are doctors, authority figures, and patients with fake testimonials telling us to, "Hurry! Call NOW! Ask your doctor; she can sell you pills, TODAY!" Supplies are limited! Medimaginosis provides the means to discuss it with our mind/body first and tap into a vast reservoir of wisdom that may or may not suggest pharmaceutical or surgical intervention.

One of our studies found that a typical TV program is only about 67 percent of the air time. More than 30 percent is advertising. Our research included a study of TV commercials for pharmaceuticals, which usually occur within the first few minutes of watching and often dominate the last half of most national news broadcasts. We recorded the percent of each commercial devoted to listing side effects and made note of how they tried to gloss over the disclaimer and distract the viewer with visuals and misleading phrases. Often as much as half of the ad was spent listing side effects, and most were quite serious, even deadly, but they have ways of diverting our attention from them and highlighting the miracles they supposedly provide. The list of side effects is more depressing than the diseases that they want us to believe are a part of our identity. Listen carefully to the side effects listed on drug commercials. It could be a life-saving epiphany.

All drugs come with stressful side effects, and they might include, nausea, headaches, vomiting, diarrhea, swelling of the lips tongue or throat, anxiety, insomnia, drowsiness, anal leakage, internal bleeding, skin rash and blistering, mood swings, mouth ulcers or infection, excessive sweating, jaundice, itching, hives, respiratory failure, stroke, heart attack, blood in stool or urine, suicidal thoughts, birth defects, ringing in the ears or hearing loss, seizure, shallow breathing or breathing that stops, dry mouth, cough, fever, feeling unsteady, loss of coordination, trouble concentrating, memory problems, weakness, confusion, hallucinations, amnesia, loss of smell and taste, blurred or double vision, dry eyes, night terrors and sleep walking, erectile dysfunction, fecal incontinence or bowel control problems, compulsive behavior, bodily aches and pains, abdominal pain, nightmares, abnormal tongue coating, hair loss, blindness, anemia, chest pains, anorexia, back pain, vaginal infection, hemorrhage, blood clots, bone pain, irregular heart rate, breast enlargement in men, intestinal inflammation, loss of sex drive, difficulty or discomfort in breathing, loss of appetite, indigestion, fluid retention, fatigue, eye pain or swelling, fainting, high blood sugar, joint pain or swelling, menstrual problems, leg cramps, liver failure, lung inflammation or infection, nosebleeds, nerve pain or damage, numbness, palpitations, tingling, sensitivity to light, wheezing, tremors, urinary tract swelling or infection, abnormal vaginal discharge, and death…just to name a few. There are some remedies worse than the disease.

Too many medical professionals, advertisers, and pharmaceutical companies have a financial interest in convincing us that we have afflictions, and they like to use the terror imbued word "DISEASE" because it instills fear and congers up visions of the black plague, the sick and dying, and indeed the diseased. They spend billions of dollars annually on advertising, particularly TV ads, trying to convince us that we have a disease and need to buy their pills. With the fear of DISEASE paralyzing our judgment, we are motivated to pay whatever it takes to treat it. The first rule in sales is to find (or create) a need and then fill it.

According to the federal government transparency initiative, drug and medical-device companies pay billions (not just millions) of dollars to U.S. physicians and teaching hospitals every year, that some critics say have compromised medical care. The payments and so-called transfers of value to hundreds of thousands of doctors and 1,360 teaching hospitals include such items as free meals, favors, gifts that company sales representatives bring to physicians' offices, and fees paid to doctors for "consulting." Some doctors receive tens of thousands of dollars annually from drug companies while surgeons have received even larger amounts from medical-device makers, partly from royalties on products they helped develop and promote.

Famous celebrities have been called heroes for submitting to radical surgery to remove perfectly healthy breasts and ovaries because medical professionals found the presence of a gene that they think might be associated with breast and ovary cancer. Then the news is released to their adoring public as a noble thing to do. Such radical surgery to remove healthy tissue is unnecessary and even foolish, but lucrative, and that is what motivates condolence and concurrence. These celebrities were motivated by fear not altruism, and that fear was cultivated by ignorance, or profit oriented medical professionals, not compassionate humanitarians.

We are in no way diminishing the importance of allopathic or conventional medicine. We are, however, concerned about the lopsided emphasis on the physical while ignoring the mental, emotional, and spiritual aspects of healing the whole person. Antibiotics and vaccines save lives when the immune system is overwhelmed, doctors set broken bones and sew up wounds, and surgeons reattach severed limbs and correct abnormalities that no amount of mental intervention can equal.

We are advocating Integrative Medicine; the working together of every applicable modality in varying degrees as the condition warrants. There are many people who would not be alive today without good allopathic Western medicine. Some have new organs, others have been brought back to life after a heart attack, and many have taken some kind of medicine which has aided the eradication of an infectious disease. The forte of Western medicine is in acute, life-threatening, emergency situations. It is not, however, as helpful in the treatment of chronic illnesses and the most prevalent, expensive, and life-debilitating kinds of stress-related diseases.

We are adamant about the fact that the art of healing needs to be integrated without prejudice to include any modality that does not harm, and that anyone who claims to have a cure-all or all the answers in one modality needs to be avoided. <u>With integration, most of the problems that Western doctors treat today would not have developed in the first place</u>.

There is a common parallel in regard to today's world energy crisis. For instance, there are other ways of creating energy that are more efficient and effective than burning fossil fuels. The fact is that it is not in the interest of the fossil fuel industry to embrace other technologies. This is the same situation in the medical industry. Since non-allopathic healing does not serve the financial interests of the chemical-selling pharmaceutical industry, conventional medicine has little interest in endorsing other healing modalities.

More doctors are beginning to understand that they only have some of the answers and need to acknowledge and accept integration while others rely too much on drugs and not enough on healing. There are other tools that can be far more effective considering most of our ills start in the mind. It is the greedy focus on increasing already egregious profits that are snubbing reasonable integration of our diverse forms of healing. Eventually, there will come a time when today's medical treatments with toxic chemicals (pharmaceuticals) will be as archaic as the four humors and as barbaric and primitive as lobotomy, leeches, and bloodletting. Scientists once believed that the world was flat. Everyone believed that. Holding on to outdated, erroneous belief is another example of an Inflexible Perception. We need plasticity and cooperation, less greed and more awareness of the greater good.

People are so careful to buy organic, eat healthy, and avoid salt, fat, pesticides or other elements thought to be unhealthy, but will ingest large quantities of toxic drugs advertised on TV or prescribed by a doctor. The *Journal of the American Medical Association* reported recently that iatrogenic disease (physician induced disease or illness caused by medical treatment) is a leading cause of death in this country.

An American is more than three times more likely to be killed by a drug side effect than a firearm, and overall, the medical profession kills more than 24 times more people in the US than guns. Hundreds of people are killed every single day as a result of pharmaceutical side effects alone. According to US government statistics, FDA approved prescription drugs kill more than 100,000 people every year. When other medical related deaths were included, like medical errors, failed procedures, and surgery gone wrong, that number was 783,936 in 2011 while, in the same year, 31,940 people were killed by guns in the USA.

A more recent study based on the results of a ten-year survey of government statistics showed that nearly 800,000 people die every year in the USA from iatrogenic diseases and that reaction to prescription drugs are responsible for over 300,000 deaths per year. Due to the power and influence of the medical community, this information is not widely publicized until someone high profile like Michael Jackson or Joan Rivers becomes one of the statistics. And even then, reporters are hesitant to go into too much detail for fear of incurring the wrath of this powerful, affluent group.

On March 29, 2016, Daisy Lynn Torres (a 14-month-old girl) was taken to her dentist in Austin, Texas for a "routine" dental procedure. Her mother, Betty, was told that her little girl had two cavities and that she needed two crowns for which they had to put her under anesthesia. After the little girl was anesthetized and the procedure was underway, the dentist saw an opportunity, told Betty that he was going to put six crowns in that tiny little mouth instead of the two originally planned. Then when they were about halfway through, Betty was informed that "a complication" had occurred and that her daughter would be taken to the hospital. In Betty's own words, "When they finished half of the crowns, she went into cardiac arrest...one of the workers came over and told me to give her a kiss goodbye...so I laid my head on her forehead and gave her a kiss. But I could tell it was already too late. I kissed her forehead, but she was already gone. I could see it. But no one wanted to tell me." Unlike medicine, meditation has never killed anyone.

Throughout history, mass cognitive manipulation has also been an integral part of organized religion. Polls cited in *Newsweek,* however, indicate that more and more Americans are beginning to question the need for rituals and consider themselves spiritual but not necessarily religious. They sometimes find organized religion too limited by rituals and belief systems, too focused on archaic symbols and stories, and not sufficiently concerned with supporting them in their search for direct spiritual experience. Religions generally begin with vital spiritual principles but often grow rigid and authoritative over the centuries. Sadly, some religions have even begun to thrive on demonizing those of other faiths and then these self-proclaimed religious people make war and kill their fellow humans with the insane belief that the Source of the Universe is on their side and condones their egotistical madness.

The Chinese communist government has considered religion to be a remnant of old China used by the ruling classes to keep power and is based on superstitious mumbo jumbo and outrageously improbable unverifiable stories. They contend that most (holy books) are collections of inaccurate translations, exaggerations, antediluvian metaphors, fairytales, myths and legends that were written by biased human beings with egos and agendas. Like Mohamed and Socrates, Jesus, Buddha, and Confusions never wrote a word. The insightful teachings of these men were committed to imperfect human memories and passed on by word of mouth, sometimes for decades or even centuries before being written down and translated and retranslated again by different people with different agendas and perspectives. It has been said that truth is relative, and hearsay is inadmissible in a court of law for good reason. Every time a message passes from one person to another, it changes by the degree of perception variance.

Our study of religion found that there are as many concepts of God as there are human beings. Some may get spiritual experiences when they watch a sunset, walk along the beach, or play with their children. Everyone has a different concept of everything, no exceptions. Kabir referred to God as the breath within the breath, simply put, God is energy. Decades ago, Albert Einstein proved that everything is energy. All that we know to be matter is, in fact, rapidly moving particles of energy. This concept is hard for our minds to fathom since we experience it as substance.

Some say that God made man in His own image, but others say that man made God in his own image. They have given the Source of all things a name and a face, reducing an unfathomable entity to a mental idol that they can believe in and worship, a vision of their own image. In the opinion of many visionaries and highly evolved conscious people, this anthropomorphizing of God is a primitive, misleading concept in dealing with things outside the human sphere. They contend that these people imagine and then pray to some old guy with a beard sitting on a throne up in the sky someplace, judging everything we do and handing out rewards and punishments for good and bad behavior. We can safely assume that people have created God in their own image when it turns out that God hates all the same people they do.

Other people feel that God is pure energy that cannot be created or destroyed, only changed into an infinite number of forms, of which we are one. They believe that the Source of all things has endowed humans with unique gifts, and it is what we choose to do with these gifts that will determine our rewards and punishments, not a vindictive, jealous, judgmental old man in the sky who professes to love us. Albert Einstein said, "I cannot imagine a God who rewards and punishes the objects of his creation, whose purposes are modeled after our own—a God, in short, who is but a reflection of human frailty." The way is not in the sky. The way is within.

We were asked by one scholar to imagine billions of galaxies, the billions of stars in each galaxy, the planets they contain, and then to imagine some old guy with a beard sitting on a throne hovering above this insignificant little planet. We cannot be so arrogant as to think that we can comprehend or even define the infinite Source of all things when our trivial intellect and limited ability to preserve can barely grasp our own little problems or the nature of the Universe. She went on to say that referring to God as He or She is like assuming God has a nose, ears, and genitals, which seems a bit preposterous, illogical and egotistical. She stated that it could be something a human might make up to inspire fear of a power beyond his own to manipulate the beliefs and behavior of a flock that could not comprehend the enormity of the cosmos or even that the Sun does not orbit the Earth. She conceded, however, that if this is the image a person needs to hold in mind to inspire harmony and balance; it's a good thing as long as superstitious, antediluvian perceptions are not forced upon others as *The Only Truth* that must be adopted by all humans that deserve to live.

We found that God is a term used by many to represent their infinite, incomprehensible, eternal deity: the Source of all things. This "Source" formed the billions of galaxies scattered across the Universe, each with billions of stars and planets. It formed (and is in) the subtle subatomic particles which cannot be seen even with our most powerful microscopes. We will use the term "Source of all things" instead of the word "God" because the word, like "love", has lost its original meaning through thousands of years of misperception and misuse, but also because it implies separation from, or an entity other than the whole that includes us. It tends to reduce a cosmic force beyond human comprehension, description, and definition to a finite entity. We will represent this "Source" as Being itself, not a being; a verb, not a noun. But no matter what term is use, it will be inadequate. If, however, a mental image of an old man sitting on a throne in the sky, responsible for all creation, controlling, judging, and handing out rewards and punishments for good and bad behavior helps someone relate to the Source, oneness, and all that is - it should be tempered with gratitude, patience, and kindness and then encouraged.

It has been said that the meek shall inherit the Earth, but that assumes that the meek cooperate with each other and celebrate the indomitable human spirit. Like the cells in the body, we can think of humanity as a huge superorganism of several billion people. When the cells fight one another, we call that autoimmune disease, and it looks a lot like our species has a bad case of autoimmune disease. To survive, we need to work together toward mutually beneficial objectives. All of which lead to the ultimate objective of harmony. Harmony requires a balance between cooperation and competition, plasticity of perception, gratitude, patience, and kindness.

We need to defend against attack but reject revenge or the urge to attack in anger or fear of an imagined threat or react impulsively. If we study the history of a person and walk a mile in their shoes before criticizing or judging, we will begin to understand. Respond with conscious compassion for all that IS, and that includes one's tormentor or attacker. "If we could read the secret history of our enemies we should find sorrow and suffering enough to disarm all hostility." (Longfellow)

4.2.1 **Paradigm Change**

Allopathic paradigms are beginning to changing from a focus on illness to a focus on wellness, and psychological paradigms are changing from a focus on mental illness, unhappiness, fear, and anger to mental health, happiness, gratitude, and conscious awareness. A focus on diagnosing and analyzing the past and wallowing in a pit of woes is changing to observing and choosing one's thoughts in the present with appreciation and gratitude.

Too many so-called experts prefer that their clients keep their anger and stay in counseling for years, taking their money and helping them discover all kinds of causes for their problems. The cure, however, requires a focus on where we are, and where we are going instead of where we have been. Some people spend years going to counselors or therapists to look for the cause of problems only to end up finding more real or imagined roadblocks from the past to justify holding on to their problems. Unless we explore the past with the intention of learning from our mistakes, releasing it and letting it go, we risk falling into the self-pity pit.

All unhappiness stems from the negative thoughts that we have about our lives, not from life itself. When a person is already feeling threatened, angry, or insecure, focusing on the problem almost always results in greater insecurity and a lower emotional state. After years of weekly therapy and thousands of dollars, the therapist has a new swimming pool and the client can articulate his problems better than he could when he started, but still feels stressed out and frustrated. There is a clear difference between learning from the past and becoming immersed in (or getting caught up in) a problem or issue.

The old paradigms focus on the past and are often designed to get us even more caught up in what is wrong with our lives. They sometimes drag a single phobia out for years in endless analysis, getting lost in the details of the issue. They assume that our problems are deeply rooted and extremely complex, and that the only way to deal with them is with intense analysis. Many therapists encourage clients to "feel their fear or anger" and then think about the issue over and over again, creating more negative thoughts and worse feelings (sometimes referred to as analysis paralysis). And then they wonder why their clients never seem to feel better. People who wallow around in suffering under the guise of "being with" or "experiencing" their pain are simply feeding their self-centered Ego and a "poor me" attitude.

The new paradigm is focused on the present and goes far beyond superficial positive thinking. It teaches us to live in the present, how to avoid getting caught up in negative thought, and makes the link between thought, feeling, and behavior clearer. It assumes that the Conscious mind is in control and is an observer of the Subconscious as it jumps from one thought or memory (wrapped in the emotion of the time) to the next, that we become attached to a thought only if we choose to. It teaches people to mindfully observe their thoughts in the present like watching TV. We <u>recognize</u> negative thoughts and <u>neutralize</u> them by understanding that they might have been appropriate in the past but not now. We <u>dismiss</u> those thoughts that are destructive or inappropriate and <u>replace</u> them with thoughts that are of our choosing and worthy of our time. It is our thinking about our circumstances, not the circumstances themselves, that determines how we feel. In the absence of thoughts about "what's wrong," the ill feelings disappear, even if the circumstance remains.

The events that cause stress all have one thing in common: we have to think about those events. If we do not think about them, we do not experience stress. When we are depressed, our thoughts are usually in the past. When we are anxious, our thoughts are usually in the future. It is the single act of thinking about them and not the present that causes stress. Inflexible Perceptions lead to chronic thought which creates chronic stress. Now is usually good. The present moment is always available for us to form whatever perspective we choose. Stress is not in the situation or event; it is in the mind.

Some have tried to say that the new paradigm is denial but denial is a refusal to acknowledge. When we consciously recognize a harmful thought and put it in perspective with the present moment, we are able to neutralize it with the realization that it is obsolete, inappropriate, or simply wrong. We begin to understand the powerful connection between the thoughts and feelings, consciously choose to dismiss them, and then move on to more useful thoughts. That is the opposite of denial. A wider more positive view of everything is not putting one's head in the sand; it allows us to see the wonder and be curious.

Others have said that the new paradigm leads to complacency, but Individuals who master the art of living in the present moment are aware and sensitive to their own problems as well as the problems of others without becoming immobilized by them. They see opportunity where others see problems. They care about issues but realize that staying upset does nothing to improve a situation. They are passionate about certain topics but maintain just enough distance to keep a sense of perspective, and they do not lose sight of their major goal; to be happy and at peace with a sincere intent to promote Harmony. As an end in themselves, worldly attainments are only intermediate goals. Harmony is the real goal of human life.

4.3 **We Can Get There from Here**

While traveling the path of Evolution, change begins to take place inside our being, mentally, physically, and spiritually. We begin to see and experience life from a greater vantage point, from a greater depth of meaning, and from an inner place of belonging. The miraculous mind of man has the ability to steer its ship toward health or illness. Unlike other forms of life on earth, we can consciously control our gene expression. We can reconfigure and adjust our genes, turning ON advantageous function while turning OFF detrimental functions. Without changing the DNA, we can change the way it responds.

Before the 1940s, it was widely believed that such functions as heart rate, blood pressure, and brain activity were beyond our conscious control. But during that decade, biofeedback machines were developed that permitted laboratory subjects to become self-aware of these body processes. To the surprise of researchers, it was learned that far from being out of our control, such process can be altered, when we are made aware of what our body is doing. It was not that they were unable to control their blood pressure, they just had no way of instantaneously knowing exactly how it reacted to whatever they were doing to change it. "Seeing" our heart rate on a monitor makes it possible for us to learn to change its rhythm.

Without delving into how aging or genetic change occurs, we know that it involves the switching OFF of some gene functions and the switching ON of others. Recent research on neuroplasticity proves unequivocally that there is no such thing as "too late" where the brain is concerned. What this means is even if we are very used to feeling stressed and overwhelmed and even if we are rarely present and empowered, it is never too late. We can regrow, or grow for the first time, these brain connections. It is just about using our brain differently.

A case study: Henry evolved from a grumpy burned out physical disaster area on the verge of a heart attack, to a happy, energetic executive in perfect health and having a wonderful time. He was a store manager for a large retail chain with the hope of being promoted to upper management and perhaps the executive level. He was making good money but worked 12-14 hour days, six days a week and stopped in on his day off to keep everyone on their toes. Upper management was always pushing for more sales and no matter how well he did; they always wanted more. He had no control over advertising and marketing but was expected to sell more and more regardless of store traffic. First, it was chronic heartburn, high cholesterol and high blood pressure, then a skin rash, tinnitus, dry mouth, ear infections, gingivitis, tooth loss, joint pain, hair loss, coughing spells, asthma, angina and, of course, insomnia and anxiety. He was seeing a primary physician and two specialists all of whom had no idea what the cause was and treated each symptom as it occurred resulting in nine medications per day. Each time a medication was added, another side effect appeared and was treated with another drug. His healthcare plan provided for an annual physical which he failed miserably. It served as a wake-up call and motivated him to begin the Medimaginosis Program and within a matter of weeks, he had eliminated all but one of the prescribed medications, and even that one was a radically reduced dosage. He is now a happy, healthy kid again, doing cannon balls in the pool and learning to juggle. We can choose our thoughts, and become what we think about.

Stress Management Consultants offer a plethora of solutions to prevent stress naturally such as time management, situation management, sound sleep, smiling, driving, reading a good book, watching a comedy, playing with animals, and worry alternatives. While these are wonderful activities in their own right, as solutions they all have one shortcoming. They deal with the symptoms of stress without tackling the cause. When pharmaceuticals are used, it is like suppressing fever without treating the typhoid within, or disconnecting the oil light instead of adding oil. If we wish to control stress, we need to treat the root cause; Inflexible Perceptions. The cure comes only through the mind being open, flexible, and receptive; <u>blind belief</u> is not enough. It is not the mind which has fixed views and prejudices and thinks it knows it all or which just takes what other people say as being the truth; it is the mind that is open to plasticity of perception that is the way to peace and harmony. This mental state is very important.

When things go wrong in our life and we encounter difficult situations, we tend to regard the situation itself as our problem but in reality whatever problems we experience come from the mind. If we were to respond to difficult situations with a peaceful, positive attitude of mind they would not be problems for us, even regarding them as challenges or opportunities for growth and development. Problems arise only when we react to difficulties with an inflexible or negative state of mind. In meditation, the inflexibility softens and becomes pliable. Plasticity of perception allows the wisdom of the OM, creativity, and adaptability into circumstances or events.

From a neuroplasticity perspective, the negative thinking circuits that we have set up in our brain will not necessarily fade by establishing further positive thought circuits alone because it is the negative circuits that need to be altered or neutralized. We can control what we think about, yet deeply ingrained negative thought, emotion or behavior patterns are often so persistent that they are very difficult to shut off. As a result, they constantly reinforce the dysfunctional wiring that supports them. The first step in changing our thoughts is identifying the negative thought. Stopping to identify or label negative thoughts gives us the opportunity to neutralize, dismiss, and replace them and make rational decisions. This includes avoiding negative people because they can be very contagious.

Life itself can help us learn to release attachments and stop clinging. For example, when anger takes control of our mind, we need to "Stop, Smile, Breathe, and say Thank you." We need to take the time to recognize or identify the thought, become aware of how much control it has over us, and neutralize it by understanding that it is no longer appropriate. Then we simply dismiss it or let it go and replace it with a more appropriate thought. (Recognize, Neutralize, Dismiss, and Replace) Doing so without Medimaginosis can be extremely difficult especially when the anger is great, but firmly taking control, releasing, and replacing the hold on the emotion is necessary. Medimaginosis allows us to relax the ties that drag us down, relax the attitude, and release our grip on rigidity. Letting go of anger, fear, and greed is also an essential part of respecting one's self.

There is nothing in the body that the mind does not influence. Most of us know how a negative thought or worry can cause an upset stomach, and this is just one example of how the body is affected by the mind. Perception (belief, attitude, thought) changes lifestyle affecting diet and activity patterns which intern further alters gene expression. When we imagine a healthy lifestyle in as much detail as possible, gene expression will begin to change to manifest the image. All perceptions are relative and can be directed. We need to learn to manage our mind, thoughts, and attitudes, or they will manage us. Perception is everything and with Medimaginosis, we can create new perceptions and alter old ones.

After studying many of the non-allopathic forms of healing, we began to see common traits shared by all of the most successful modalities. Overall, genomic pattern changes have been shown to occur in practitioners of several mind/body techniques utilizing different meditative practices including Vipassana, mantra, mindfulness or transcendental meditation, breathing focus, Kripalu or Kundalini Yoga, and repetitive prayer. These modalities are accompanied by focused attention, awareness, and slower brain waves that produce relaxation all the way down to the cellular level. The cells move out of the "defense mode" and into the "evolve, renew, and repair mode" facilitating healing. Relaxing the cells with some form of meditation dramatically improves just about anything. Discordant energy in a cell is almost always caused by beliefs or thoughts associated with an event. With meditation, we can direct our thoughts to relax the cells and neutralize harmful negative energy with a positive form of energy.

Many people incorrectly believe that by simply improving external conditions, we can create happiness. It has produced remarkable material progress but has not made us happier or reduced our problems. They are just different. We have polluted our environment, become obese, and spread disease throughout the world. Our lives are now more complicated, and mentally we are becoming unhappy and worried. There are now more problems and greater dangers than ever before. We need basic human comforts but simply improving external conditions can only make us happy if our mind is peaceful. If our mind is not peaceful, we will not be happy, even if our external conditions are perfect. The more we control our mind, the more our inner peace increases and the happier we become. The most effective method to restore the sense of happiness is to control our own mind, beginning with anger and attachment. Peace within makes beauty without. True peace is to know one's self as an inseparable part of the timeless, formless, Source from which all that exists derives its being.

Problems, suffering, and unhappiness do not exist outside the mind; they are feelings and thus part of the mind. When we change our mind, our mind will change our world. Dr. Wayne Dyer said, "When you change the way you look at things, the things you look at change." Abraham Lincoln said, "People will be just about as happy as they allow themselves to be." And on her 103rd birthday, Maybelle Behrens said, "Life is a hoot when ya never mind the crap." The most profound answers in life may be the simplest.

4.3.1 Conscious Awareness in the Present Moment

Just as people chose to see the world as "flat" in the past because they had no experience of its roundness, people see their consciousness in a very narrow or flat way due to lack of experience. Awareness means we consciously choose to let go of our attachment to past and future and make "Now" the main focus of life. It means choosing to live in the state of presence rather than floating around in time. It means accepting and adapting to what is. Whenever the mind slips away from the present, two problems loom. Unless we are reminiscing about the wonderful times we had or dreaming about an exciting, positive future, our mind will likely be regretting something that has already happened and cannot be changed or worrying about something that has not yet happened and probably never will. Every personal goal can be enhanced by learning to live in the present. Awareness means responding with thought rather than automatically reacting on blind impulse or ego programming. Whenever we are really effective at achieving anything, we are fully engaged in what we are doing, concentrating on the here and now. That is mindfulness and awareness. The positive aspects of life, happiness, relaxation, satisfaction, effectiveness, and compassion, are all found in the present moment. Live in the present; everything else is just imaginary. For thousands of years, mystics have affirmed that no one can be denied peace, calm, silence, the fullness of joy, and reverence for life. Inner peace is a natural state of mind, but it can be found only in the absence of negative thinking. Without inner peace, there is no real happiness at all. People who live in the present know that a contented state of mind not only feels better than any other state but also that a levelheaded, contented mind is more effective and honest than a disturbed, frantic one. People who constantly feel dissatisfied, distressed, struggling with the past and worrying about the future are usually unable to be kind and compassionate toward others. They are too consumed with their own wants and needs. The past, while real at the time, is now only a thought that is being carried through time via one's own mind; nothing more, nothing less.

Now is good.

Now has no room for past or future, guilt or worry.

Past no longer exists except in memory.

Future does not exist except in imagination.

Past and future have no reality of their own.

Only Now exists, only Now is real.

Now is good.

Look around you.

Now we are safe.

Now we are warm.

Now we are free of the past with acceptance and forgiveness.

Now is good.

Now we are grateful, patient, and kind.

Now we are a calm mind at peace,

in balance and harmony with the Universe.

Now is real life,

a fun adventure of curiosity and wonder.

Now is a friend.

Now is all that IS, and a wonderful place to BE.
If we do not accept what IS,
we are accepting what is not.

Now is good.

Life is always now and constantly unfolding in the present moment. Even past or future moments only exist when we remember or anticipate them in the present moment. As negative thoughts enter the mind, we can dismiss them and choose more pleasant thoughts. If we fail to learn the art of living in the present, we can turn even beautiful everyday experiences into negative situations. When we live in the present moment, ordinary, everyday life takes on a new significance. Taking walks, watching a sunset, gardening, reading a book, all begin to feel special. When our attention is brought back to the here and now, we <u>engage</u> in life rather than just thinking about it; and ordinary life becomes extraordinary life. It is most important to spend the majority of our time being present and focused on the actual world around us. Life is right here, right now and attention to the present will foster a rich, full life. We need to learn from the past and plan for the future, but live in the present. Remember in the present, plan in the present, BE in the present.

"The greatest weapon against stress is our ability to choose one thought over another…The world we see that seems so insane is the result of a belief system that is not working. To perceive the world differently, we must be willing to change our belief system, let the past slip away, expand our sense of now, and dissolve the fear in our minds." William James

4.3.2 Adversity is Inevitable, but Stress is Optional

The Taoists teach that all ill health emanates from stress or tension, and this view is gaining more and more credibility in the Western world. In fact, many of the top medics and scientists now put stress as the number one killer. This is particularly obvious in the case of heart disease, which is still the main cause of death in many parts of the world.

The evil dragons of stress are being addressed only superficially by both the medical and psychological communities. The medical community tends to focus mainly on the physical, such as stimulants, toxins, trans fats, sugar, and dehydration. The psychological community tends to focus on other people as the cause, for example, difficult children, demanding bosses, or inconsiderate co-workers. This approach allows us to stay in a victim position and supports us in pointing the finger. When we point the finger outside ourselves, it leads to a comfortable but disempowered state.

Inner-directed people listen to their own heart while outer-directed people follow advice and instructions from outside sources. They relinquish their control over their own life to another source. To be inner-directed means to look within for our own answers, to trust our own intuition and wisdom over and above anyone else's opinion, and to follow our own instincts. If we are inner-directed, we do not rely on another person to make us happy and do not give someone else the power to control our emotions. It is important to seek the words and opinions of others, but they need to be filtered by our own natural wisdom before being applied to life. Inner-directed people are happy because they know that their life is a series of choices and that they are in control of those choices. Exterior events and circumstances do not determine their behavior; their inner conciseness does. When we lose sight of the fact that we are the ones doing the thinking that upsets us, it can appear as though our circumstances create our feelings. This encourages us to blame our unhappiness on our circumstances.

Some reflection on both positive and negative aspects of one's past can be an important teacher, but the key is to remain aware, avoid getting caught up in irrelevant details, and understand that an excessive focus on the negative is an obstacle to life-enhancing insights. An unfortunate incident might last only a few seconds, but the negative feeling will go on as long as we hold the thought. When we let go of the thought or change the channel, the feeling will disappear. Our thoughts make us angry, our past does not. That was then. This is now. Now is good.

If we can begin to "catch ourselves" in the act as we are thinking negative, self-defeating thoughts, we learn to notice when we are getting too analytical and caught up in pointless detail. When we learn to avoid getting caught up, two things happen. First, our experience of life will begin to change. We feel happier, more satisfied, and more joyful. Second, as we avoid getting too caught up in our thinking, we will begin to access our own natural wisdom on a far more regular basis. We will begin to see answers, access and maintain our own wisdom. When we catch ourselves thinking our way into a negative state of mind, it is easy to stop doing it. (Recognize, Neutralize, Dismiss, and Replace with Gratitude, Patience, and Kindness.) Many traditional therapists, however, encourage clients to pay attention to specific thoughts and inner mental experiences in great detail and the focus is almost always on the negative.

The fact that one is caught up in their thinking is far more relevant to the way they currently feel than are the details of what they are caught up in. Anytime we can be aware of and witness our own thoughts, instead of becoming lost or absorbed in them, we are in a position to grow from our experience rather than being immobilized by it. Feeling stressed is a tip-off that one is caught up in thoughts. When we watch our thoughts like a TV with remote control, we can change channels and choose what we want to watch. When we watch TV, we are aware that we are separate from what is happening on the screen. Learning to watch our own thoughts works in a similar manner. We create some distance between our self and our thoughts, and this sense of distance allows us to consciously watch our thoughts in the same way we might watch a movie, and it can be very entertaining. The distance we create when we watch our thoughts protects us from any negative effects.

We feel the way we do because of the thoughts we think. Just as our feelings create thoughts, thoughts create feelings and lead to various types of behavior. There is a space between thought and feeling, and another between feeling and behavior. The spaces represent where our potential wisdom lies. There is a moment after each thought, and between series of thoughts, in which we have the opportunity to respond or not respond to what just occurred. Sometimes people respond to each thought as if it were an emergency while others acknowledge their thoughts with the knowledge that they now have the chance to act on it, dismiss it, or just make a note of it and think about it later. Those who believe that every thought needs to be taken seriously should reconsider. If we can learn that thoughts do not need to be taken too seriously, and can be looked at with perspective, from a distance, we can regain control over our own lives, and gratitude will emerge. We sometimes have little control over which thoughts enter our minds, but have enormous control over which thoughts we take seriously and which ones we dismiss.

We may feel that if we could only find the right place to live, the right possessions, the right work, the right friends, the right partner – the right everything – we would be truly happy. Consequently, we put most of our time and energy into trying to rearrange the outside world to accommodate our Inflexible Perceptions rather than rearranging, or managing our perceptions. Sometimes this works out for us but only up to a point, and only for a short while. If we want to be truly happy and free from chronic stress, we need to learn to loosen our grip on Inflexible Perceptions, take control of our mind, and adopt an attitude of Gratitude, Patience, and Kindness. That is a natural state for those who start every day with the (5-7-9) Breath and a short meditation. Our fundamental nature is bliss and the happiness we mistakenly take as the result of finding the right stuff occurs, not from getting our way, but simply from the cessation of desire that allows the bliss that already existed to shine through. True happiness is not the result of getting our way; it is from a contented mind.

As we learned in Part III, the four general categories of meditation are Concentration meditation, Mindfulness meditation, Contemplation meditation, and Creative meditation. We learned to practice basic meditation which is the simplest form of Concentration meditation and choose a mantra to hone our ability to focus. Now we will move on to the second category and learn more about Mindfulness meditation.

4.4 Mindfulness Meditation 2

Mindfulness is simply the state of conscious awareness in the present moment where life happens and Mindfulness meditation is the state of conscious awareness in the present moment, consciously directed and focused. The state of mindfulness feels like learning something new and involves "observing" or "noticing" things. By noticing our experience without judging or evaluating whether it is good or bad, we tap into a source of active, mindful meditation that elicits the relaxation response. Instead of having one single focus object, word or phrase, the world around us and the world of thoughts and feelings within us become our focus.

According to Forbes, Sara Lazar and her team at Harvard found that Mindfulness meditation can actually change the structure of the brain. They found an increase in the cortical thickness in the hippocampus, which governs learning and memory, and in certain areas of the brain that play roles in emotion regulation and self-referential processing. There were also decreases in brain cell volume in the amygdala, which is responsible for fear, anxiety, and stress corroborating the participants' self-reports of reduced stress level. They were able to show that meditation not only changes the brain, but it changes our subjective perception and feelings as well. A follow-up study by Lazar's team found that after meditation training, changes in brain areas linked to mood and arousal were also linked to improvements in psychological well-being.

The Forbes article went on to say that a growing number of studies have shown that meditation can be very effective in helping people recover from various types of addiction. One study, for example, pitted mindfulness training against the American Lung Association's freedom from smoking (FFS) program and found that people who learned mindfulness were many times more likely to have quit smoking by the end of the training and at the 17-week follow-up, than those in the conventional treatment.

At those times in our lives when we are in the "zone," wrapped in wonder, listening intently, watching a sunset, ocean waves, fish in a fish tank, or marveling at the beauty of nature, we are experiencing this type of meditation naturally. If we close our eyes and listen, listen very carefully, those who are indoors might hear the hum of a machine in the same room, something happening in the next room, or they might hear some muffled noises from the street. Those who are outside might hear birds, cars, or a lawn mower. No matter where we are, we will probably hear ourselves: tummy gurgling, heart beating, or the sound of our breath. If we expand our sphere of awareness to other senses, we might notice the touch of the forefinger to the thumb, the pressure of our weight on the chair, the temperature in the room, the smell of the morning air, or the fabric softener used to wash our clothes. With our eyes closed, we can get in touch with other senses. Our eyes see a lot of wonder, but if we give our other senses a chance, life will seem so much richer. Some of us have placed "DSCR" sticky notes in strategic places to remind us to pause and use the Deeper, Slower, Calmer, Regular Breath (from the abdomen) whenever it is convenient until it becomes an inherent part of life. With the skills learned in Mindfulness meditation, we can do it with a clearer brighter awareness of where we are, what we are doing, and how we are feeling.

Mindfulness is a non-judgmental attention to the details of our experience as it arises and subsides, and does not reject anything. A non-judgmental detachment frees us from emotional bonds and Inflexible Perceptions. Detaching the mind from all preconceived opinions, thoughts and personal reactions imposed by our background, traditions, social groups, and environment free us to build clear and unprejudiced thought patterns, and receive the present moment without coloring or distorting it. We show up for life, and if something needs to be changed, we are present enough to understand what needs to be done. We notice the present moment and breathe a bit deeper, slower, calmer, and regular. We accept what IS and then fix it with kindness if it is broken, adapt to it by changing our perception of it, or let it go, let it be, and move on.

Mindfulness meditation strengthens our sense of wonder and appreciation, enabling us to effortlessly attend to the totality of our experience as it happens, and enhances our ability to enjoy the present moment. It emphasizes a highly receptive mindful attention toward an action or objects within one's sphere of awareness and is one of the most powerful techniques available. This type of meditation is used to cultivate receptiveness, mindful attention toward daily life, provide pain relief, and help for those suffering from anxiety and depression. Because stress is often caused by a preoccupation with the past (guilt, shame, regret) or with the future (fear of upcoming events), mindfulness is also an excellent way to help manage stress.

Busy people often think that they have too many things to do but focusing on the task at hand can give them a sense of control and completing the task reduces anxiety and promotes a sense of accomplishment. Those mindful people who have learned to prioritize their do-list are always working on the most important tasks and seem to be the most productive. When things get really complicated, then it is time to make them simple. When we are being pulled in many directions at once, then it is time to move to the middle. The mindfulness meditator can see things as they are without the need to control them, can let them go their own way, and live in the center of the circle. From the center of the circle, all of the craziness of the world falls into perspective. Things that really are not important lose their power to command our attention and we are free to concentrate our efforts on the things that are relevant to our predetermined worthy objectives.

Little problems sometimes seem quite imposing when we are oblivious to the whole and have no worthy intent or objective to guide us. Getting lost in irrational worry or petty details can be likened to holding a small coin so close to the eye that it blocks out all of creation causing us to lose all sense of direction. The closer we look at something, the larger it becomes. The Sun is actually 1.3 million times larger than the Earth, but something as tiny as a dime can seem even larger than the Sun if we hold it too close and lose sight of the whole. If we are looking at the present, larger is beneficial as long as we are mindful and aware of the whole, but if we are looking at the past, larger means wallowing in the often toxic juices of the unreal without direction. We learn from the past, let it go, and live in the present accepting and adapting to what IS. We just need to be anchored by the breath, aware and focused on what we are doing while being mindful of the whole and our worthy intent.

Mindfulness means doing a task consciously as opposed to doing it subconsciously or allowing the subconscious programming, or habit, to do it automatically. One can drive to work and not remember it or eat and entire meal and not remember how it tasted. We might not even be able to remember what we had for dinner because the Conscious mind was busy thinking about something else and let the Subconscious mind take over the task of eating. It might have been a tasty, enjoyable experience but if the Conscious mind is not present to experience it, life passes us by.

Eating mindfully means taking the time to enjoy the flavor of each bite and eating more slowly. Savoring and varying the type of food with each bit results in the consumption of less food and greater satisfaction. Actively using the senses radically improves the experience. Enjoy the aroma, color, texture, and accompanying music if available. Our senses perceive and create our world and by actively using them to our best advantage we bring more of our world to life. We can enhance life, become healthier, and feel more alive than ever before by learning to focus mindfully. Every experience becomes a cornucopia of memorable sensations. Every situation has something to teach us as long as we do not assume that we already know everything. In the beginner's mind, there are many possibilities while the experts mind is limited, unless they also understand how little they know.

Mindfulness means checking in with each and every one of the senses and taking the time to really focus on them in the present where past troubles and imagined future problems cannot interfere with our health. It is being conscious and aware of every action and decision because they come from the Conscious mind, not our subconscious autopilot. It is noticing each one of the six senses, sight, smell, hearing, touch, taste, and intuition.

The subtle movements and sensations connected to the flow of breath provide the perfect means and method of developing mindfulness. Mindfulness meditation often begins with bringing attention to the sensation of the flow of the breath in and out of the body. The meditator learns to focus attention on what is being experienced, without reacting to or judging it. This is seen as helping the meditator learn to experience thoughts and emotions in normal daily life with greater balance and acceptance. We become aware of the whole, and the relevance of the task at hand, making even a dull job interesting by focusing on it, studying it, and looking for details with the whole as a reference. Like a laser beam, the tighter the focus, the greater the effect, and being aware of the whole as well as our intent or objective, we can better guide the laser beam. As the meditator progresses in the ability to concentrate, mindfulness practice may begin.

Practicing mindfulness anchors us in the present moment, fosters a non-judgmental stance, and can help us maintain awareness. Without awareness, the Subconscious mind will automatically attach values to everything, call things good and bad, ugly and beautiful, and look for reasons to criticize, complain, and always be offended. Mindfulness teaches us to recognize, and wake up from, the daydreams and worries the mind fabricates and returns us to the clarity, precision, and simplicity of the present, where life actually takes place. With mindfulness and a compassionate, patient smile, one can choose which thoughts to follow and which to merely let pass by. The smile will protect us from taking any of these thoughts too seriously, trying too hard, or being too judgmental.

Mindfulness meditation is unique in that it is not directed toward getting us to be different from how we already are. Instead, it helps us become aware of what is already true moment by moment. It helps us be present with whatever is happening, no matter what it is. The practice of Mindfulness meditation gives us the opportunity to become more present with ourselves just as we are, shows us our inherent wisdom, and teaches us how to stop perpetuating the unnecessary suffering that results from trying to make the world conform to an arbitrary Inflexible Perception.

Mindfulness meditation is about the practice of being aware and mindful of whatever happens and NOT about getting ourselves to stop thinking. We just let the mind be fluid and flow from one thought to the next without getting caught up in any one particular thing. Meditators who live in a noisy city do not have to block out the outside sirens and screaming children; they let the mind be aware of the sounds without becoming critical or disturbed; a non-judgmental observer. No judgments of good, bad, right, wrong, lazy, weak, strong, kind, mean, etc. are given any attention. Learning to let go is similar to dismissing intrusive thoughts in Concentration meditation. Any judgments about our feelings are to be passively detached with a return of one's mental focus of observation.

Like watching a nature documentary, it is often helpful to see our thoughts from below the surface as waves in a vast ocean that well up, peak and fall back into the vastness. If we can identify with the whole ocean, we will not get caught up in, possessed by, attached to, or begin to identify with a thought that may not be advantageous to our worthy objectives. Sometimes the observation leads to a general labeling of waves as a thought, feeling (emotion), or an image without judging them as good or bad. This labeling is a neutral observation and not a judgment. A more detailed label, however, can lead to judgment and the intent here is to cultivate conscious awareness, the ability to let go, and a detached non-judgmental attitude. We assume a non-judgmental attitude by giving ourselves permission to be happy and to let go of the delusion that we need to be right all the time, or the need to judge and control everyone and everything based on our dubious personal perceptions. We are free of the past with acceptance and forgiveness, aware that all things change. We accept and adapt to the present moment with gratitude, patience, and kindness.

There have been many techniques developed throughout the centuries but the Progressive Relaxation body scan is one of the most effective. It is intended to help us enter a very deep state of relaxation, but it is important to remain alert, aware, and relaxed without trying. Trying just creates more tension while simply "inviting and allowing" the mind/body to relax opens our awareness to each passing moment. We let go of judgmental and critical thoughts when they arise, and just accept what is happening within us, seeing it as it is. We begin with the breath, expand our awareness to the body, and finally into our daily lives.

Practice the Mindfulness meditation using the Progressive Relaxation body scan in as much detail as possible the first few times. When the body gets used to relaxing on command, a less detailed scan can be used.

a) We first find a time and place where we know we will not be distracted. The time period associated with the (5-7-9) Breath usually works well and the place should be warm, safe, and quiet. We then state our intent, (in this case, it is to develop the ability to let go and awareness without judgment) keeping in mind that we all want the same thing in the end. Regardless of current superficial wants and desires, harmony is the real goal. And then, just for a moment, consider that meditation is founded on gratitude, patience, and kindness.

b) Set a timer with a pleasing tone if desired, but most people simply open their eyes long enough to look at a watch or clock and gently return to their focus. Sit in a comfortable but dignified manner with the face, scalp, neck, shoulders, and body relaxed and spine straight. It is important to stay relaxed, yet aware and awake. Some students sit on a pillow with their hips slightly higher than their knees and imagine their spine is a tall, straight tree against which they can lean. Note that meditation can be done in the prone position as well, particularly mindfulness and progressive relaxation, but is more likely to morph into sleep. Meditation requires conscious awareness, not sleep.

c) Focus attention on the breath. With our eyes closed or half closed to reduce distractions, we shift from the outer world to our inner world and maintain focus and awareness on our breath. We take a deep (5-7-9) Breath with a barely audible sigh (ahhhhhh) allowing the jaw and shoulders to relax and a slight smile to form on the out-breath. Then we allow the mind/body to become still and focus our attention on the natural tidal rhythm of the breath, feeling the rise and fall of the inhalation and exhalation without trying to influence it.

d) Scan the mind/body from head to toe and back again for tension or tightness inviting it to relax as much as it wants to while remaining alert and attentive to the breath in the present moment. Assume a non-judgmental attitude, brush away stray thoughts that cloud concentration, and return to the breath. On the inhale, we gather up tension that we do not need to hold right now, and on each exhale, we release that tension and become more and more relaxed; a real letting go kind of breath. It is often helpful to bring the thumb and forefinger together and notice the sense of touch. When we can feel the thumb touching the forefinger, we know that we are aware and in the present moment.

e) Return to the breath, letting it get a little easier and deeper. Feel the air move in and out at the tip of the nose. Notice how the temperature is cooler on the in-breath and warmer on the out-breath. We feel the air enter the nostrils, lungs, and expand the diaphragm. With each in-breath, we bring in fresh energy, vitality, and oxygen. We can feel it mix with the blood and flow easily, naturally, and bountifully to every part of the mind/body. With each out-breath, we release a bit more of any accumulated tension.

190

We do not worry about how quickly or deeply the body relaxes; we just invite it to relax in its own way in its own time without trying to force or fix anything. We find that the body really likes to relax and let waves of spacious awareness wash gently through us. Awareness of the breath anchors our attention in the present moment.

f) We sit for a few minutes in this environment moving from the usual mode of doing to a mode of non-doing or simply being. The mind/body is repairing and renewing itself on every level, and there is nothing else we have to do while it is doing that. Although doing nothing on purpose is actually doing something, we give ourselves the luxurious permission to do absolutely nothing else right now. Just for now, we are on a well-deserved mini vacation where there is no trying, no place to go, no one to impress, and nothing to do. Just be with the breath and the feelings associated with it. We become aware of the movement of the breath as it comes in and out of the body without trying to change it. We observe the breath deep down in the belly, feeling the abdomen as it expands gently on the in-breath and falls back toward the spine on the out-breath; letting go. Let the body sink a little bit deeper into relaxation with each exhalation.

g) Whenever we notice that the mind is distracted, we return to the breath. Without judging, we smile, say Thank You and gently return to the breath in the present moment. Always return to the breath. We hold a gentle inner smile because it keeps us from trying too hard, getting tense, or being self-critical. Just allow a deep connection to the calm and peacefulness that is here and just breathe with ease and comfort. All we have to do is watch and feel our breath.

h) As we maintain awareness of our breathing we begin to expand the field of our awareness so that it includes a sense of our body as a whole; feeling the body from head to toe. Imagine a wave of relaxation and comfort starting at the tips of the toes and moving all the way up to the top of the head, and back down again to the tips of the toes. Allow the wave of relaxation and comfort to cycle up and back down again for a few more moments and notice a feeling of being warm, safe, and completely at ease. With 25% of our attention on the breath and the rest of our attention naturally on our body, we observe whatever feelings and sensations come up without judging them, without reacting to them, just being fully aware in the present moment.

i) When we have established an expanded sense of the body, we allow the sense of the whole body to fade into the background and refocus on our feet with the breath still 25% of our attention. Become aware of whatever sensations are there. Even if a blank is registered, we experience the nothing as something. We "breathe into" our feet. That means imagining the breath moving from the nose, into the lungs where it mixes oxygen with the nutrient-rich blood and flows down to the feet. We imagine the breath permeating and loosening the muscles around the joints, allowing the joints to relax and separate, creating space for the oxygen-rich blood to flow into and around them. Imagine the cells relaxing, loosening, and hungrily soaking up the oxygen and nutrients like tiny sponges, repairing, healing, and rebuilding. Feel the warmth of new energy returning and restoring perfect function. Nourish the feet and expel any tension that might still be there with the out-breath. We just notice the sensations without judgment and when it is time, allow our focus on the feet to dissolve in the mind's eye and move on to the muscles and sensations in the lower legs.

j) Feel the lower legs from the surface right down into the bones, experiencing and accepting whatever feelings exist here. Breathe into them, collect any remaining tension and breathe it out. When it feels right, let go of the focus on the lower legs, relax deeply and move on to the thighs, then the pelvis, and then the abdomen and lower back. Breathe into them, notice any feelings, collect any remaining tension or tightness that might still be there, and send it out with the breath. Then let each region dissolve into relaxation and move on.

Continue to move the focus up the body just experiencing each part as it is, letting the breath penetrate and expand on the in-breath. As the cells relax, they absorb fresh oxygen and vital nutrients while expelling waste products and toxins. On the out-breath, let these toxins, any tension, tightness, or "holding on" to just flow out as much as it will. Expand each part of the body on the in-breath gathering up any tightness, fatigue or discomfort and expelling it on the out-breath. Then when it feels right, let the image of each part dissolve with the out-breath and let go, sinking even deeper into stillness and relaxation.

One might notice a tingling, warmth, the blood surging through the veins, or just nothing. If there is nothing, notice <u>that</u>, because nothing is something that needs to be noticed here with 75% of our attention. The other 25% is observing and feeling the movements of the diaphragm, that umbrella-like muscle that separates the belly from the chest. Experience the lower rib cage as it expands on the in-breath, deflates on the out-breath, and tune into the rhythmic beating of the heart. Observe whatever sensations, or lack of sensations, are experienced. Let them soften and release all tension as the body sinks even deeper into a state of relaxed awareness and stillness: content to just be here, right now.

Moving the focus of awareness on to the hands and fingertips, we become aware of the sensations now in the tips of the fingers and thumbs where it might be possible to feel some pulsations from the blood flow, dampness or warmth. Feeling all sensations regardless of what they are, breathing into any tension and letting that tension dissolve with the out-breath, we let go of whatever thoughts come up, return to the breath, and just experience ourselves in this moment. Continue moving this process up the body, breathing into, sensing, relaxing and letting go of each part. Just observing and experiencing the arms, shoulders, neck, face, jaw, chin, lips, eyes, and forehead just as they are, allowing any tension to leave with the out-breath.

Finally, with all muscles from head to toe in a deep state of relaxation we now experience the entire body breathing. Sinking deeper and deeper into a state of stillness and deep relaxation, we allow ourselves to feel whole; in touch with our essential self in a realm of silence, stillness, and peace. We allow the world to be as it is, beyond our personal fears, concerns, and the tendencies to want everything to be a certain way. Enjoy this moment as long as desired, with 25% of attention on the breath and the other 75% on a peaceful mind/body.

k) When it is time to return to the outside world, we take special notice of this calmness and centeredness, committing the images, feelings, and emotions to memory for future use and allowing the benefits of this practice to expand into every aspect of life. We begin to notice what is going on around us, wiggle our fingers and toes, smile because we feel so good, and move our focus from our inner world to the sounds, smells, shapes and colors around us. Finally, we take a comfortable energizing Three-Part-Breath and open our eyes feeling wide awake, grateful, re-energized, refreshed, happy, and ready for the remainder of the day.

l) Some find it helpful to bring the hands together (the gasho or prayer position) and close the moment with gratitude and reflection. It is helpful to sit still for a moment or two to review the experience and annotate any ideas, visions, or inner guidance received in meditation with the intention of incorporating the benefits into our daily lives. To keep us in the present moment, we continue to keep 25% of our attention on our breath (<u>DSCR</u>) replacing pointless repetitive daydreaming. With the other 75% on what we are doing and what really matters in life, we check in from time to time by asking, "Am I still breathing?"

We can lengthen this meditation by first focusing on the right foot and leg and then the left, focusing on smaller parts of the body. To shorten this meditation, we focus on larger portions of the body. Rather than focusing on the foot, ankle, the calf, knee, and thigh individually, we expand the focus to include the entire leg. The focus might move from the legs to the hips, torso, neck, and head with a little extra time spent on any area that is holding an inordinate amount of tension. The more detailed the focus, the longer the meditation will be.

Every time we take a breath, we have the opportunity to return to the present: mindfully inhaling and mindfully exhaling with a gentle smile and full awareness. Focusing on the rising and falling movement of the abdomen is especially effective. With mindfulness of breathing as our home base, we can focus our attention and direct it to observe anything or to perform any action with greater presence. The awareness that we apply to our breath can be expanded to include all physical and mental processes. Any activity can be done with mindfulness.

Associating mindfulness and being present with the first beverage of the day, every coffee break, and every shower makes life far more interesting. At the first beverage of the day and at each coffee break during the day, notice the color, shape, what the surface of the liquid looks like in the cup, any reflections of shadow and light. Feel the cup. Is it cool, warm, or room temperature? Use all senses and notice the texture, depth of color, sounds, smells, and taste. We can apply mindfulness to any task or event to make it more interesting and fulfilling. Carrying mindfulness and awareness into everyday life makes even the most mundane events interesting. The colors are brighter, sounds are clearer, the air smells better, and the world seems more like a treasure chest full of goodies.

4.5 Contemplation Meditation 3

Contemplative (reflective or analytical) meditation is almost certainly the oldest form of meditation and involves predetermining an object, theme, principle, inspirational words, question or topic upon which to focus our reflection, or analysis. The meditator becomes immersed in the subject and becomes one with it allowing images and trains of ideas and thought to come to mind, revealing its true nature. It has a calming effect on the mind while stimulating transformative power and provides us with great conviction and strength to influence the course of our lives. The emotional equilibrium, clear intelligence, clairvoyance, and penetrating insights that develop can then be applied to investigating the very subtle phenomena within, the dynamic interrelatedness of everything, and provides us with a sense of ourselves as co-creators of our world.

Traditionally, Contemplative meditation was used to gain insight into the meaning of life, death, interrelationships, and social conscience, or to come to a conclusive insight regarding some key idea in science, philosophy, or prayer to arrive at a conclusion. It can also be used to improve self-awareness or self-realization and provide us with a powerful and effective tool for focusing our attention on personal or professional questions enabling us to discover creative solutions or breakthrough insights. Contemplative meditation helps reconnect the individual with the whole and understand the inner technology necessary to fulfill virtually any developmental aspiration we may have. It can help us in opening the heart and remove any negative energy that exists, deepen our empathy and forgiveness, and teach us to live in kinder ways.

Contemplation meditation is an opportunity to reflect upon the interdependent nature of all phenomena revealed by the sages and confirmed by contemporary physics. In addition to artists of all genres, mathematicians and theoretical physicists regularly employ contemplation in their research with great success. This practice integrates gratitude, patience, and kindness into a world obsessed with conflict and the latest scientific advancement without dogmatic allegiances. It is a form of knowing arrived at by the silent perception of reality, intuition and visualization, not thinking.

While scientists have primarily focused their attention on the external world, there is no aspect of reality more pertinent to health, genuine happiness and harmony than the nature of human identity. We will contemplate "I am," the Principles of Harmony, our attitudes at the deepest level, and any subject that needs a deeper understanding.

Contemplation begins with a thought that attracts us. The process is spontaneous and takes place in its own timing. We read our affirmations, sit for a few minutes to reflect on them, letting our mind go where it will without trying to force the words to create an immediate shift inside. Whatever we feel, we let the words incubate, stay with us for a while, and remain patient. As we consider our affirmations, their attraction expands and deepens. As it does, a feeling emerges from the idea or original image. Whatever the feeling, if we stay with it long enough, a change occurs. By subtle degrees the feeling becomes impersonal. It is no longer suffused with personal associations and memories. We return from contemplation as a knower, rather than a person with an opinion. We may not argue for it or even be prepared to discuss it, but we would indeed know it to be so.

Benefits are often gradual and from the inside out. Gentle nudges from the inner mind begin to guide one's choices. We act differently because we are thinking differently. The fear of public speaking, for example, might be so great that one might do almost anything and invent almost any excuse just to avoid it. Then one day it seems tolerable. And then one day the opportunity to share with others is exciting. What we believe in our Subconscious is who and what we become. In order to evolve, we need to enhance the way we think. Speaking directly to the Subconscious alters old inner beliefs about ourselves and the world around us. It seems to almost magically manifest our goals and ideas, and it happens without doubt or fear.

We learned to focus using Concentration meditation, and how to expand our awareness with Mindfulness meditation. Here we will learn to transform an everyday idea into wisdom, rarefied and pure. At the deeper levels of contemplation, the idea or image we begin with leads to silence, awareness, curiosity, truth, and wonder. We always know where we are and what we are doing but allow ourselves to become more focused, calm, relaxed, and at peace. We become so wonderfully absorbed in our study that the opportunities and the truths within our thoughts and ideas begin to stand out and merge with our own natural wisdom.

In the beginning, we can experience "I" as conscious awareness, or the Conscious mind, instead of a reflection in a mirror. Then we mindfully expand our awareness to include the Subconscious and Unconscious mind realizing that this too is "I." With further expansion of our awareness, "I" becomes a whole mind/body and then a mind/body/soul. We can feel our connection to the Source of all things and realize that we are a part of a vast, possibly infinite Universe. We understand that we are like a single cell in the body of the Universe, nourished by the same elegant energy source and separated only by invisible egos. I am we. We are one with all that IS.

Before beginning a contemplation session, we need to preselect our subject or object of focus. Our students are asked to make three signs and tape them to the wall at eye level in the area normally used for meditation. The first sign is a two-part sign and goes in the center. The top half was introduced in Part II and states the practitioners "Reason or Motivation for Daily Meditation." The bottom half is a one-sentence statement of the practitioners "Worthy Purpose" (determined in Part III) followed by a more detailed "Mission Statement" that supports and develops the worthy purpose with secondary objectives: The Plan. The second sign is a copy of the numbered "Seven Stages of Adversity" and is taped to one side of the first (center) sign. The third sign is taped to the other side and is a copy of the "Seven Principles of Harmony (I am We Affirmations) with the addition of the practitioners (8th Affirmation), determined in the next section. Use the signs to review these critical bits of wisdom and commit them to memory for a more fluent meditation. There is, however, no shame in opening one's eyes during a Contemplation meditation to check the exact wording.

The First sign was created in Part II and III and goes in the center.

The Second sign shown below is taped to one side of the First and is also reprinted in Appendix D:

1) Situation or event.
2) STOP, SMILE, BREATHE, and say, "Thank you, Thank you, Thank you," as a sincere expression of Gratitude for the opportunity to practice Patience, Kindness, and our right to choose the thoughts upon which to focus.
3) Recognize, neutralize, dismiss, and replace harmful thoughts with Gratitude, Patience, and Kindness, knowing that something good will come of this. Be Grateful that it was not worse and feel Compassion for those who are worse off.
4) Accept and adapt to the present moment with Patient positive thought, wisdom, and curiosity.
5) Ask if the problem can be resolved, and look for opportunity.
6) With a calm, peaceful mind, we allow our own natural wisdom to determine the best course of action.
7) Remain balanced and centered, happy and at peace, with a sincere intent to promote Harmony.

The Third sign shown below is taped to the other side of the First and is also reprinted in Appendix G:

I am we.
We are one with all that IS.
Harmony IS an attitude at the deepest level.
Therefore,
I am Harmony at the deepest level.

Principles of Harmony (I am We Affirmations)

1) We are one with all that is, with reverence, love, and kindness.
2) We are aware in the present moment, accepting and adapting with wisdom and curiosity.
3) We recognize, neutralize, dismiss, and replace harmful thoughts with gratitude, patience, and kindness, the wonder of life and the beauty of the gift of breath.
4) We are a happy, healthy, calm mind at peace, in balance and harmony with the Universe.
5) We are free of the past with acceptance and forgiveness, as only change is permanent.
6) We pursue life diligently with integrity, purpose, sincerity, and joy.
7) We understand that harmony is the real goal, the ultimate objective of all pursuits. We imagine harmony, we are harmony, we live harmony.
8) My 8th Affirmation

Most students select only one of the principles per session for an in-depth contemplation of each word.

4.5.1 The 8th Affirmation

The (8th Affirmation) is an integral part of the foundation of the Imagine Harmony Program. Whatever one thinks their intermediate goal or purpose is in life (amass a fortune, raise a happy family, promote world peace, or simply serve humanity in some well-defined way), it is far more likely to manifest with the consistent use of the (8th Affirmation).

In Part III, we determined our "worthy purpose" and "mission statement" with the ultimate goal in mind. Now we need to express them in the form of our own personal (8th Affirmation). Keep the affirmation simple and short enough to memorize, vivid and clear enough to facilitate immersion, and make it personal. Own it by starting it with "I" or "My." Because the

Subconscious operates in the present, we need to keep our affirmations in the present tense, "I am creating" and avoid "I will create." The word "will" implies future giving the Subconscious mind the option to procrastinate or find reasons to not do it now, or ever. Statements like "I want" or "I need" also imply a future fix while "I am creating" refers to now. Become immersed in the image and make it as vivid and clear as possible. Imagine achieving worthy objectives and goals in the present. See it as already completed or in progress, how it feels, and how it is affecting friends and relatives. Stating that "I will lose 20 pounds by July" is even more counterproductive because it adds the dimension of time restraints beyond the subconscious realm of the present. Also, when the Subconscious loses something that it thinks belongs to it, it will do all it can to get it back.

In addition to simplicity, clarity, present tense, and immersion, two important laws need to be understood when making affirmations: the Law of Reverse Effect and the Law of Awareness. The Law of Reverse Effect reverses statements that use NO, NOT or any conjunction that includes NOT such as DON'T. Because the Subconscious deals in images rather than words and does not have an image for NOTHING or the NOTS, it just ignores them focusing on the remaining images reversing the original intent. Consider the statement, "I am not fat." The Subconscious ignores "not" and sees an image for "I am" and "fat" which reverses the original statement that uses the word NOT and sees, "I am fat." The Law of Awareness states that we tend to attract subconscious attention and action to whatever dominates the mind. It is imperative to use affirmations that focus the Subconscious on the desired result and avoid negatives. Rather than focusing on a problem, it is better to focus on the solution and the Subconscious mind will support the image. Focus the statement on the positive aspects and not the thing to be replaced, that is, rather than "I feel less fat" we need to focus on the solution, "I am fit and healthy." It says to the Subconscious that "fit and healthy" belong to us and needs to be manifest. Understand that affirming perfect health, happiness, vitality, and harmony for one's self first is not a selfish act. We must first be what we want to see in others. That is why airlines tell mothers to place the first available oxygen mask on themselves in an emergency and then attend to their children.

And finally, speak the affirmation out loud and repeat it several times. After four or five times, the degree of commitment will be obvious in the voice. If there is some resistance holding it back, we will form an image of it, find out what the problem is, and replace it in Part V.

An example of a personal affirmation might be: I am providing a happy, comfortable life for my family: Even though I am always growing, learning and getting better, I am satisfied and content right now, I am OK now: I am Evolving my mind, body, and soul as one cohesive, synergistic unit with Perfect Health, Happiness, Vitality, Longevity, and Harmony: All of my biological systems are functioning perfectly: I am altering gene expression by reconfiguring genes to shut down or turn OFF those gene functions that are detrimental to Perfect Health, Happiness, Vitality, Longevity, and Harmony while activating or reactivating, and energizing those gene functions that are advantageous to Perfect Health, Happiness, Vitality, Longevity, and Harmony.

Other affirmations that might be used, even in the Beta or normal awake state, might be simple derivations of the Principles of Harmony such as:

I am Kind.

I am Grateful, Patient, and Kind.

I am Grateful, Patient, Kind, Happy, Healthy, and a Calm mind at peace, in

Balance and Harmony with the Universe.

I am Evolving Perfect Health, Happiness, Vitality, Longevity, and Harmony.

I am the Principles of Harmony, an attitude at the deepest level.

Contemplation meditation:

a) We first find a time and place where we know we will not be distracted. The time period associated with the (5-7-9) Breath usually works well and the place should be warm, safe, and quiet. We then state our intent, (in this case, it is to develop a better understanding and insight into a predetermined thought) keeping in mind that we all want the same thing in the end. Regardless of current superficial wants and desires, harmony is the real goal. And then, just for a moment, consider that meditation is founded on gratitude, patience, and kindness.

b) Set a timer with a pleasing tone if desired, but most people simply open their eyes long enough to look at a watch or clock and gently return to their focus. Sit in a comfortable but dignified manner with the face, scalp, neck, shoulders, and body relaxed and spine straight. It is important to stay relaxed, yet aware and awake. Some students sit on a pillow with their hips slightly higher than their knees and imagine their spine is a tall, straight tree against which they can lean. Note that meditation can be done in the prone position as well, particularly mindfulness and progressive relaxation, but is more likely to morph into sleep. Meditation requires conscious awareness, not sleep.

c) Focus attention on the breath. With our eyes closed or half closed to reduce distractions, we shift from the outer world to our inner world and maintain focus and awareness on our breath. We take a deep (5-7-9) Breath with a barely audible sigh (ahhhhhh) allowing the jaw and shoulders to relax and a slight smile to form on the out-breath. Then we allow the mind/body to become still and focus our attention on the natural tidal rhythm of the breath, feeling the rise and fall of the inhalation and exhalation without trying to influence it. The mind/body is repairing and renewing itself on every level, and there is nothing else we have to do while it is doing that. Although doing nothing on purpose is actually doing something, we can grant ourselves the luxurious permission to have nothing else to do or nowhere else to go right now. Shift from doing to being and notice what it feels like to do absolutely nothing and have it be good for us.

d) Scan the mind/body from head to toe and back again for tension or tightness. Invite it to relax as much as it wants to while remaining alert and attentive to the breath in the present moment. Assume a non-judgmental attitude, brush away stray thoughts that cloud concentration, and return to the breath. On the inhale, we gather up tension that we do not need to hold right now, and on each exhale, we release that tension and become more and more relaxed; a real letting go kind of breath. It is often helpful to bring the thumb and forefinger together and notice the sense of touch. When we can feel the thumb touching the forefinger, we know that we are aware and in the present moment.

e) As our focus settles on the breath, we begin to employ a simple predetermined mantra like "so-hum." With each inhale, we silently say "so" and with the exhale, we say "hum," and then listen for our heartbeat during the pause between the in-breath and the out-breath. We do not worry about how quickly or deeply the body relaxes; we just invite it to relax in its own way in its own time without trying to force or fix anything. We find that the body really likes to relax and let waves of spacious awareness wash gently through us.

f) When awareness detects a lapse in focus or an unrelated thought arises, silently say Thank You, smile gently and return to the breath. Always return to the breath and continue the mantra, "so-hum." Awareness of the breath anchors our attention in the present moment, and we hold a gentle inner smile because it keeps us from trying too hard, getting tense, or being self-critical.

g) We sit for a few minutes in this environment becoming one with the breath and our mantra. Then, when we are ready, we expand our field of awareness to include our predetermined focus. In the case of a text, we read it through completely coordinating it with the rhythm of our breath. Ideally, it is memorized and recited line by line, relaxing a bit in between each line so that we can let the meaning sink in and become one with it. When our attention wanders to unrelated thoughts, we smile, use the "always return to the breath" skill that we learned in basic meditation, and return to our chosen topic. Each out-breath releases a bit more stress and tension from the mind/body allowing us to let go of any tightness within. Letting go of tension and stress morphs into comfort, freeing the Subconscious to accept our worthy affirmations.

h) Focus on one word at a time; contemplate each individual word. We imagine that the Universe is about to whisper the answer to our deepest questions, and we listen carefully because we do not want to miss it. It whispers words of wisdom, let it be. We try not to try or worry if nothing comes up. If we feel stuck, we just return to our breath for a moment and then come back to the object of our meditation again when it feels right.

i) If we discover an answer, let it be and relax. It is likely to be experienced as a fresh discovery or something new, and the tendency is to jump up and get excited about it. If we can relax with it, more will come, but if we get too enthusiastic about the answer and start thinking about it, the experience can dissipate. Our students meditate with a pen and paper next to them so they can open their eyes, calmly make a note and return to their meditation. They can THINK about it later.

j) When it is time to return to the outside world, we return to the breath and become aware of this calmness and centeredness, commit it to memory for future use, and allow the benefits of this practice to expand into every aspect of life. Feeling secure and a wonderful sense of well-being, we become more alert and aware in every way. We begin to notice what is going on around us, wiggle our fingers and toes, smile because we feel so good, and move our focus from our inner world to the sounds, smells, shapes and colors around us. Finally, we take a comfortable energizing Three-Part-Breath and open our eyes feeling wide awake, grateful, re-energized, refreshed, happy, and ready for the remainder of the day.

k) Some find it helpful to bring the hands together (the gasho or prayer position) and close the moment with gratitude and reflection. It is helpful to sit still for a moment or two to review the experience and annotate any ideas, visions, or inner guidance received in meditation with the intention of incorporating the benefits into our daily lives. To keep us in the present moment, we continue to keep 25% of our attention on our breath (DSCR) replacing pointless repetitive daydreaming. With the other 75% on what we are doing and what really matters in life, we check in from time to time by asking, "Am I still breathing?"

Other worthy subjects for contemplation are:

* For what am I most grateful now? Or What does my body need now?

* Being aware of the needs (as opposed to wants) of others, how can I help? The answer to that one always seems to come up the same. Become the Principles of Harmony first and the answers will appear.

* Evolve both mind and body with perfect health, happiness, vitality, longevity, and harmony, accepting and adapting to the present moment with gratitude, patience, and kindness.

* Contemplate favorite gems from the Appendix section, especially A and H.

4.6 **Summary**

The first half of Part IV is a more in-depth study of how the mind, body, and soul work together and how they handle thoughts and use wisdom. We examined discoveries made in the field of psychoneuroimmunology and epigenetics supporting our contention that human beings can control their gene function if they choose to. We studied the attempts by the outside world to control our thoughts, feelings, spending habits, and life itself. We examined the deceptions advertisers use, how profit manipulates perception, and revisited our study of spirituality and religion. We explained how dangerous it is to allow the outside world to control our lives, how the paradigms are changing for the better, and that we can get there from here. We can evolve from stress to gratitude. We discussed conscious awareness and that being alive is being in the present moment where life is, and although adversity happens, stress is optional.

In the second half of Part IV, we learned more about Mindfulness meditation and how to develop conscious awareness and deep relaxation. Then we studied Contemplation meditation and learned to solve problems and turn ordinary thoughts and ideas into simple, pure, natural wisdom without the fluff and attachments. We learned to create our own affirmations based on our personal worthy purpose making it feel more real and part of our being. Finally, we close Part IV with an Action Assignment and visual to aid practice.

In Part V, we will learn more about Creative meditation, the fourth category of meditation. Then we will learn to apply it and discover the power of Medimaginosis.

4.7 **Action Assignment**

* Understand that conscious human beings can create their own reality and take control of their lives when the mind, body, and soul work together as one cohesive, synergistic unit.

* Understand that we are controlled by outside forces, circumstances, or our genes, only if we allow it.

* Learn from the past and plan for the future, but live in the present. Remember in the present, plan in the present, BE in the present. Now is good.

* Know that, rich or poor, no one is immune to adversity, but everyone has the right to choose their own thoughts, create their own perceptions, and control their own life. All human beings have the right to evolve from stress to gratitude.

* Practice Mindfulness meditation using the Progressive Relaxation body scan in as much detail as possible the first few times. When the body gets used to relaxing on command, a less detailed scan can be used.

* Choose a task and do it mindfully, in the present moment, using all six senses. At first, use each sense, one at a time, and then combine them for an overall mindful experience. Experience life.

* Write a personal (8th Affirmation). Establish at least one personal affirmation that embodies the "Reason or Motivation for Daily Meditation" and the "Worthy Purpose" created in Part III. Use the seven rules of affirmations: 1) Simple and short enough to memorize. 2) Vivid and clear enough to facilitate immersion. 3) Personal enough to own using "I" or "My." 4) Use present tense avoiding the words, will, want, and need. 5) Avoid the NOTS. 6) Focus on the solution instead of the problem. 7) Speak it out loud.

* Make three signs and tape them to the wall at eye level in the area normally used for meditation. The first sign is a two-part sign and goes in the center. The top half was introduced in Part II and states the practitioners "Reason or Motivation for Daily Meditation" and the bottom half is a one-sentence statement of the practitioners "Worthy Purpose" followed by a more detailed "Mission Statement" that supports and develops the worthy purpose with secondary objectives: The Plan. The second sign is a copy of the numbered "Seven Stages of Adversity" and is taped to one side of the first (center) sign. The third sign is taped to the other side and is a copy of the "Seven Principles of Harmony (I am We Affirmations) with the addition of the practitioners (8th Affirmation). Use the signs to review these critical bits of wisdom and commit them to memory for a more fluent meditation. There is no shame in opening one's eyes during a Contemplation meditation to check the exact wording.

* Practice Contemplation meditation using all, or a part, of the three signs.

* Practice Contemplation meditation using a predetermined theme, subject, or problem and note any ideas, visions, or epiphanies.

* Re-read APPENDIX D through H.

* Continue using the stress busters practiced in Part I, II, and III on the next page.

Stop, Smile, Breathe, and say Thank you - when stress strikes.

Recognize, Neutralize, Dismiss, and Replace harmful thoughts with Gratitude, Patience, and Kindness.

Breathe Deeper, Slower, Calmer, and Regular as often as possible. "Am I still breathing?"

 Slow down, Simplify, and be Grateful, Patient, and Kind - all the time.

Practice the (5-7-9) Breath at least twice a day every day, and never leave home without it.

Practice the (Grateful, Patient, Kind) mantra walk.

<u>MEDITATE</u>

Review all three signs, choose an intent and breathe.

30 seconds to 30 minutes every day

PART V

Medimaginosis

5.1 Medimaginosis - A gentle journey to the real self

Medimaginosis is an omni-denominational meditation/imagery/wisdom driven wellness practice that directs the mind, body, and soul to manifest harmony and to evolve as one cohesive, synergistic unit with perfect health, happiness, vitality, and longevity. Medimaginosis is made up of three syllables: Medi – for meditation, focused attention, and directed concentration: Imagi – for imagine, visualize, pretend, and immerse or assimilate: And Nosis – for knowledge, belief, and wisdom. Nosis is a Greek word meaning, "to know" or believe as used in the words prognosis and diagnosis. It is the power source that supplies the energy to act on imagined concepts. Medimaginosis differs from relaxation and basic meditation in that each is a progressively deeper state with progressively greater efficacy respectively. Medimaginosis combines all four types of meditation using the best, most effective aspects of each with imagery and belief in a worthy objective or intention. It uses powerful subconscious journeys and processes that bring about evolution in subtle ways and illuminates the path to physical, mental, emotional, financial, and spiritual harmony.

Medimaginosis involves achieving a state of relaxation fostering a state of deep calm. We can create images that protect, comfort, advise, solve problems, guide us toward our objective, and produce healing. Imagery is not just visual, but rather the use of all the senses making everything more vivid, bright, and clear. An effort is made to actually hear, feel, smell, and even taste the imagined event. How <u>long</u> we focus on them is less important than how _regularly_ we practice. A few minutes every day can reap greater benefits than an hour twice a week.

Three vital ingredients make Medimaginosis effective and aid in the accomplishment of almost anything. It combines meditation, imagery, and wisdom to produce our ultimate goal and all those intermediate goals that lead to it. Imagery journeys and processes explore images that arise freely from the Subconscious revealing valuable information. Medimaginosis facilitates the deliberate intensification of the imagery experience, slows it down and deepens connections which reinforce and associate new positives, help create new beliefs, and simultaneously desensitize old negatives. The belief in a worthy goal or purpose from deep within can provide the motivation to move mountains.

We all have conscious goals and Medimaginosis creates conditions within the Subconscious for positive progress. First, meditation is employed to establish balance, focus, calm, comfort, and control. Second, imagination is used to manifest positive outcomes in the areas of physical health, emotional fulfillment, financial balance, and spiritual harmony. Third, the profound depth and wisdom of our connection to the Source of all things is tapped for inspiration and information to maximize the use of those talents that will be most helpful in healing all areas of life. Repeated use of this approach will integrate the various parts of life and heal the whole person.

Medimaginosis involves relaxation and a process for engaging universal wisdom to provide information, guidance, and positive evolution. It integrates several dimensions of perception, including physical senses, feelings, and experiences as well as dynamic processes that embrace each individual as a whole person, rather than simply identifying them as a mom, teacher, carpenter, smoker, or victim. As opposed to allowing external forces to control us, Medimaginosis connects the mind, body, and soul providing guidance and a catalyst to heal and integrate the various parts of the individual, forming the whole Self from within. One who practices Medimaginosis is never bored or angry for more than an instant.

Medimaginosis enables a better understanding of ourselves as individuals and as an integral part of the universal consciousness. The individual perceptions, thoughts, dreams, and awareness of the person blend together. All aspects are harmoniously integrated and synergistically create a single Self greater than the various parts. The _physical_ is seen as happy, healthy, vibrant, and radiant. The _emotional_ is peaceful, thankful, and willing to give and to receive love. The _financial_ experiences monetary healing, definition, and is balanced with generosity and financial intelligence. The _spiritual_ energizes and integrates all the parts together as a whole continuous dynamic flow.

Understanding that every mental image directly influences our body, new dimensions of self-mastery or self-sabotage become clear to us. Although an actual or imagined experience may last only a minute, our innate capacity to remember or anticipate the experience may trigger similar mental, emotional, and physiological reactions again and again. Bringing these emotionally charged images to conscious awareness, we learn to creatively and productively control our imagination and even alter memories. We not only master the psychosomatic symptoms associated with distress and anxiety but also energize and strengthen positive, healing qualities of mind.

Dr. Andrew Weil teaches us that the mind reacts with the body in ways more creative and complex than we can begin to specify. We cannot separate our physical health from our emotional, mental, and spiritual states of being. All levels are interconnected, and a state of "dis-ease" in the body is often a reflection of conflict, tension, anxiety, or disharmony on other levels of being as well. Anywhere that there are nerves in the body, there is the potential for the mind to go and influence.

The body does not speak English or any other spoken language, but it does respond to images and visualization as if they were sensory. Learning the inner language of "listening" to spontaneous imagery and "speaking" with creative visualization, we equip ourselves with critical skills for optimizing many of the functions of our mind/body and realizing extraordinary levels of health and performance. Visualizing the image of a healthy body is often enough for the body to understand it as truth, so we generate an image or idea in mind before beginning visualization. Any function of the body can be influenced by the mind and the power of the imagination. Any interactive communication requires imagery, and although imagery does not always involve meditation, meditation almost always involves imagery in some form or another and is the best way to connect.

We have learned how to facilitate our journey from stress to gratitude with various forms of conscious manipulation of the mind/body but have only touched the surface of humanities greatest gift: the human imagination and our ability to communicate with all that IS including the Source. In Part III, we introduced Concentration meditation and developed our ability to focus.

In Part IV, we developed our ability to observe without judgment or attachment and let go of a thought or image with Mindfulness meditation. Then we began to use our imagination and natural wisdom with Contemplation meditation. The Medi of Medimaginosis will be explored in more depth in our discussion of Creative meditation, the fourth category, but first, we will learn more about the Imagi or the power of imagination in Medimaginosis and then the Nosis or knowledge, belief, wisdom, and perception.

5.2 Imagi – Imagination

Everything that has become manifest because of humanity, began in the imagination. It can help us set goals, focus intention, change physiology, help imagine possible futures, and help create and activate a plan. It can help us learn about our inner world of feelings, thoughts, and body sensations. We can travel in time and space going anywhere, anytime.

All humans have an imagination; we are born with it, but we all imagine in different ways. All ways of imagining are highly individualized but equally effective and powerful. We visualize, imagine, picture, or pretend with any or all of our senses. Some people see with the mind's eye while others hear, feel, smell, and/or sense the message with equal depth and richness. We do not waste a lot of time and energy trying to imagine in a different way. Each person just needs to notice how they imagine things, accept it, know that it is perfectly ok to do it that way, and develop it.

To improve one's awareness of their ability to visualize, we start by choosing a topic and taking a few deep, slow breaths to calm the mind. Some people like to count or just observe the breath for a time to hone their focus. It is no different than daydreaming except that this time the topic was chosen intentionally. Imagine achieving or demonstrating an objective and remember to include as much detail as possible. Really get into it and keep the experience 100% positive. Visualization is a way of convincing the Subconscious that an affirmation is already a reality. Beliefs that do not support the visualization will start to fade away, and new beliefs will begin to develop. It is daydreaming on purpose.

Many people assume that pretending is just for children, but pretending is a valuable skill. Albert Einstein used to say that the pursuit of truth and beauty is a sphere of activity in which we are permitted to remain children all our lives. When we pretend that something will happen, what we pretend has a far better chance of manifesting than when we do not imagine anything at all. If we consciously pretend or imagine that something is already accomplished, the Subconscious mind perceives it as accomplished because it operates only in the present, and the body tends to respond accordingly. Our imagination is not a magic spell to take us away from a world of possibilities. It is a powerful modality for attaining our goals and maintaining our balance, although an occasional relaxing mini-vacation can be most beneficial.

The uniquely human gift of imagination affords us the ability to replace or morph wrong belief and establish worthy objectives. Imagination is a birthright and can change the way we see things, our emotions, the way we feel and perceive reality. It can literally change our physiology. Research has demonstrated a real physical advantage to imagining exercise. Because the Subconscious mind does not differentiate between what is real and what is imagined in vivid detail, a mental muscle workout begins to tone the body.

What we habitually imagine, recall, or think about, such as an affirmation, becomes anchored in the Subconscious, is translated into images wrapped in the emotion of the moment and significantly affects the body. Every cell of the body has an innate intelligence. Cells live together, cooperate, sense each other, and constantly communicate. When we feel depressed or have a bright idea or think we are in danger, our cells join in. If the mind is full of thoughts of danger, the nervous system will prepare to meet that danger by initiating the stress response, a high level of arousal and tension. If we imagine peaceful, relaxing scenes instead, it sends out an "all-clear" signal, and the body relaxes. Consciously controlling those habitual thoughts is the key to controlling the mind/body and gene expression.

Imagination can make or break our success in goal achievement. Athletes are taught to visualize a successful outcome and become one with the task and sales trainers teach their students to sell the sizzle and not the steak. See success and feel the benefits. Imagine the benefits and what life would be like when accomplished and allow the Subconscious mind to be persuaded to accept the desired change by getting involved in the benefits. It is far easier to hit a target that we can see.

As with PTSD or a bad dream, we have the power to alter the image and become the hero. We can imagine vanquishing the villain by whatever means necessary, saving the town, and gaining the admiration of the townspeople. The image is then returned to memory, and when recalled again, it will include the new information and emotions. Anything can happen in the imagination if we choose to allow it.

5.2.1 Imagery

Imagery is a thought in the mind that we can see, hear, taste, smell, or experience in some combination of these things. Imagery is subjective, very individualized, and comes alive from a complex mix within. An image may not be visual. It can be a feeling, or come through to the imagination as a sound, or any other sensory experience. The range of effective imagery experience is unlimited, and there is no right or wrong way about it.

While the central nervous system governs voluntary movement, the autonomic nervous system regulates physiological functions that normally operate without conscious control. The autonomic nervous system does not readily respond to ordinary words or thoughts like "salivate." But it does respond to imagery. Relax for a moment and imagine biting into a juicy yellow lemon. That image can cause salivation but the word or command does not.

Images arise from experiences, combinations of experiences that merge into new unexpected images, and new mysterious images from somewhere mystical, spiritual, ancient, universal, eternal, or metaphysical. At first, some students say that they see or even sense NOTHING. Understand that nothing IS something. They learn to observe it close enough to determine whether it is trying to send a message, whether it is black or blue, scented or odorless, making a noise or silent, warm, cold or room temperature. Nothing is something. In the realm of an imagery journey, whatever is there or is not there IS an image.

Imagery is not mythology. It has been shown to be extremely effective in eliciting either the relaxation response or great stress. Conditions that are caused or aggravated by stress often respond very well to imagery techniques, and they help us learn to relax and be more comfortable in any situation, whether we are ill or well. Imagery is a process of self-awareness and exploration that facilitates our ability to connect the Conscious mind to the Subconscious mind engendering creativity, inspiration, and new solutions to old problems. It is how the Subconscious mind expresses information, and speaks to the whole self. It is the symbolic language of the deeper self and allows us to communicate with our mind/body in its native tongue. It is a rich, symbolic, and highly personal language, and the more we use it, the more quickly and effectively we will use it to improve our health. We all understand and use conscious language and logic, but most of us are relatively unfamiliar with our unconscious needs and desires. Imagery gives the silent Subconscious a chance to bring its needs to light and to contribute its special qualities to the healing process.

Healing imagery has powerful direct effects on physiology. We can reduce, modify, or eliminate pain and stimulate changes in many bodily functions usually considered inaccessible to conscious influence. It may not always completely eliminate pain, but it can make changes in pain perception and let it go. The emotional aspects of any illness can often be helped through imagery, and relieving the emotional distress may, in turn, encourage physical healing.

All imagery is desensitizing and can be used to face a feared entity, and to realize that it is not the boggy man we once thought it was. Whatever the issue, there is usually some type of fear underneath it all. When new information is different from the subconscious programs and beliefs that we are used to, fear, anxiety, and stress is the result. Sometimes, fear erodes hopes and dreams, and we feel like we have lost our way. What we want seems impossible, or it feels as if it would take magic powers to open the door to our dreams. By recognizing, neutralizing, dismissing and replacing it, homeostasis is restored and adaptation redefines POSSIBLE.

It is our imagination that allows us to react not only to current stressors but to anticipate danger and remembered griefs. Uncontrolled imagination gives human beings the unique ability to compress a lifetime of stress into every passing moment. It is an excellent example of the psychophysiological power of imagery.

The most common form of imagery that affects our health is worry. Worry focuses on thoughts of danger and disaster, which may or may not come to pass, causing the body to becomes tense and aroused, anticipating a threat or challenge. The fight-or-flight response is activated, initiating a chain of physiologic changes that ready the body for intense physical activity. The body is on alert and prepared for the worst.

Imagined threats almost never materialize, and worse, they may never go away. A habitual worrier replaces one worry with another, and the cycle never ends. They are unable to release their pent-up energy or take the opportunity to relax, and their system cannot rebuild its depleted reserves.

Eventually, they become exhausted, "stressed out," "burned out," sick, and tired. The only threats have been the thoughts themselves, though the responses and the physiologic toll they have taken have been quite real.

Imagery of various types has been shown to affect all the major control systems of the body, but the healing potentials of imagery go far beyond its simple effects on physiology. Recovering from a serious or chronic illness may require changes in our lifestyle, attitudes, relationships, or emotional state. Imagery can be an effective tool for helping us see what changes need to be made and how we can go about making them. We just need to learn how to communicate with it.

5.2.2 **Interactive imagery**

Interactive imagery is a two-way medium of communication between the silent Subconscious mind and the verbal, thinking Conscious mind. It is a conversation or sensory communication with the body, a body part, or a problem by forming an image of it and communicating with it to resolve an issue or improve something. It can be used both to illuminate and recognize patterns that affect our health and to focus energy that can alter those patterns. Interactive imagery helps us become aware of subconscious patterns, needs, and potentials for change while communicating our conscious intentions or requests to our Subconscious mind and all it controls.

Interactive imagery is a simple process that involves paying attention to the imagery that arises in response to the questions we ask and imagining our desired goals as if they are already achieved while maintaining a positive, relaxed state of mind. We can move our consciousness to any part of the body and carry on a conversation with it. We can form an image of a symptom, feeling, or body part, acknowledge its intelligence, and speak to it, asking it what it needs and be receptive to the answers that come from deep within. Discover what it wants, what it needs, what it will take to succeed, and what it has to offer if its needs are met. Doing this is the essence of the inner-dialogue process, and adopting an attitude free of judgment will facilitate this conversation. Rest assured that the same intelligence that created the body also knows what it needs to be healthy.

We are not usually taught that our bodies are intelligent and that we can communicate with it. Many people have become disconnected from their body language and have somehow given away their birthright in the area of health and healing assuming that a symptom is a superficial signal to take a pill or run to the doctor instead of an attempt to be heard.

While symptoms and resistance are usually unpleasant, they are not the enemy. In fact, they serve as a natural warning system that, seen in the right perspective, can help keep us in the best possible health. Symptoms are like warning lights or gauges in a car. When the oil light goes on, we do not disable the light or tape over it so we can go about our business. Similarly, we do not go to a doctor and ask only for relief of the symptoms. We need to understand what the symptom is trying to tell us. Our immediate goal is relief of the symptom or healing of the illness, but our approach will be negotiation rather than conflict because, like people in general, the Subconscious responds better to persuasion than to force. Maintain a non-judgmental, curious attitude of harmony.

Sometimes, even negative images can be useful because a frightening image often represents one's own fears, an angry image might represent one's own anger, and a sad image often represents one's own sadness. This gives us the opportunity to deal with these important, perhaps controlling aspects of our lives. It gives us the opportunity to speak directly with them and negotiate a resolution.

5.3 Nosis – Knowledge, Belief, Wisdom, and Perception

Perception is our way of regarding, the way that we notice, interpret, think about or understand something using our six senses: touch, smell, sight, hearing, taste, and intuition or wisdom. That leads to belief when confirmed, which becomes Nosis or knowledge. Belief is the blending of perception, wisdom, logic and emotions that provide the power to move an intention or an idea from the imagination to reality. It is the blending of these major components that form the basic structure of our personal beliefs. Through the window of these beliefs, we make sense out of the things going on around us, call it knowledge, and use it to form assumptions about probable future results. A new belief can start out as a theory or an emotional perception that seems to be supported by logic and wisdom, many of which were established in childhood and have outlived their usefulness. Others are leftovers from situations and circumstances that are no longer relevant, but still influence how we evaluate everything in our lives.

Most beliefs are felt or learned through experience over the course of time and train us to think about things a certain way, while other beliefs are the result of conscious choice. We can deliberately create our beliefs instead of just waiting for them to show up. Doing this helps us focus, leads to passion and we can use this passion to power our intentions. We can reinforce new beliefs by spending more time with them and learning more about them. Acquiring corroborating evidence and expert opinions help firm up a new belief. Reinforcing beliefs will lead to a deeper understanding and a stronger foundation for a belief as it is harder to sway a belief that is well known and understood. When we build deep belief based on confirmed truth, we move forward with confidence and use emotion or passion for the outcome as the driving power. Also, people who consciously learn and pursue new information, tend to be happier because there is a feeling of growth and of success that comes with learning. People pursuing new information are opening their minds to be amazed and enthralled with everything around them, whether it's a new language and culture or an unknown micro-organism.

Belief driven emotion powers behavior, affects gene expression, and supplies the energy to act. To create and control this power, we first need to take control of our thoughts and define our goals as worthy and true. Thoughts create emotions just as emotions create thoughts. We determine a worthy objective, decide where we are going, what we want to do, and then think the thoughts that will create the emotions needed to move in that direction at the desired speed and intensity. One can become a servant to their subconscious thoughts and emotions, but controlled thoughts and emotions become our servants. We need to learn to manage our mind, thoughts, beliefs, and attitudes, or they will manage us.

Belief is the absence of doubt and is a mental representation of one's attitude toward the likelihood or truth of something. Doubt, on the other hand, is the greatest inhibitor of all pursuits. Where there is doubt, there is hesitation and timid progress, but where we are sure of our beliefs and self, we move forward with commitment. No matter what the undertaking, if we can suspend the DISBELIEF, we can succeed at anything. If we consciously create beliefs built on the pillars of gratitude, patience, and kindness, we will be able to pursue life eagerly with integrity, purpose, sincerity, and joy.

The greater the belief, the greater the probability of success. A belief is an idea one usually holds with conviction, importance, confidence, faith, and perceived trust. Belief is not necessarily "the" truth or reality but is accepted as true, like the Easter bunny or tooth fairy. The degree to which one believes a perception determines its emotional energy and impact on daily life. Whether we believe we can or believe we cannot, so shall it be. Because everything we do or do not do is because of our beliefs, to improve the quality of life and get better results, we need to update our beliefs.

With or without logic or empirical evidence, the drive and energy that fuels motivation is the emotion of fervent belief. It almost does not matter what one believes in, a religious belief, a doctor, or in nature itself, the belief can heal. We all have a belief in something, and we can boost the power of the body to heal with what we believe, which is different from person to person.

No two people have the same thoughts, beliefs, and perceptions and will evolve in different ways. Even identical twins, born with the same genes, will have very different patterns of gene activity, or gene expression. At age seventy, their bodies can be dramatically different as a result of perceptions and lifestyle choices. Diet, activity, stress, relationships, work, and physical environment can change the way a gene functions, expresses itself, or interacts with other genes. Identical twins that are born with the same DNA will have completely different genetic profiles at age seventy. Their chromosomes do not change but decades of life experience will have caused the activity of their genes to be switched ON and OFF in a mind-boggling myriad of unique patterns. <u>Our beliefs control our genes, and we control our beliefs</u>.

Our original perceptions, beliefs, and behaviors are programmed in early childhood but as we get older, we learn that some of these original perceptions are obsolete or just plain wrong. We learn that we can rewrite the software and change our perceptions of the environment. When we change our perceptions of the environment, the environment changes. When we treat the environment differently, the environment treats us differently.

5.3.1 Placebo, Health, and Chi

The placebo effect is the result of an individual expecting or believing in a positive outcome and getting it regardless of the potency of the drug administered. It is real, and it can be used to our advantage. Having a belief and energizing it with emotion will inevitably make that outcome more likely. Belief causes change, and emotion (or spirit) energizes it. It has been determined that the placebo effect is responsible for over half the action of some of our most powerful and trusted drugs and much of the action of any therapy, whether it is alternative or conventional, medical, surgical, or psychological.

The placebo effect refers to the phenomenon in which some people experience emotional or physical improvement after an inert treatment that they believe is effective. Pain and other symptoms often improve when researchers mislead patients by treating them with placebos, inactive imitations of medicines such as sugar pills, or injections of saltwater. The simple belief that one took a potent drug causes these reactions. The placebo effect has been shown to dilate bronchi, heal ulcers, make warts disappear, lower blood pressure, and even make bald men who think they are getting Rogaine grow hair. Psychologists often take advantage of the placebo effect by giving glowing testimonials about the effectiveness of their techniques because they know making believers of their clients will result in more cures.

Placebos can also cause strong negative reactions called the "nocebo" effect. As opposed to positive effects of placebo, the nocebo is equally powerful and has negative effects regardless of the potency of the drug administered. When patients stop taking the placebo, the side effects disappear. These nocebo complaints are not random; they tend to arise in response to the side effect warnings on the actual drug or treatment. The mere suggestion that a patient may experience negative symptoms in response to a medication (or a sugar pill) may be a self-fulfilling prophecy. For example, if a patient treated with a placebo is told that he might experience nausea and headache, he is likely to feel nauseous and get a headache. Patients given nothing but saline, who thought it was chemotherapy, actually threw up and lost their hair.

The placebo and nocebo response is developed and enhanced by Beliefs and Expectations one has about a thought, event, or treatment and is purely psychogenic in nature. Empirical evidence has shown that a person's positive beliefs are a strong influence for good on their health, and almost any physiologic function can be influenced by imagery, belief system, and/or emotional change triggered by thought. Similarly, automatic negative thoughts, bad moods, and compulsive worrying eventually take up physical residence in our bodies and agitated minds can inappropriately trigger the fight-or-flight response in the body. People who dwell on worst-case scenarios, who exaggerate risks, or who project doubt and undue worry keep the nocebo effect busy in their physiologies. They signal their brains to send help when no physical sickness is present, persuading the body to get sick when there is no biological reason for sickness to occur. One could even die because of belief.

The nocebo effect is probably most obvious in "voodoo death," when a person is cursed, told they will die, and then dies. Voodoo deaths seem to come from the great anxiety and loss of hope in the cursed person caused by an overwhelming belief that death is imminent. The notion of voodoo death does not just apply to witch doctors in tribal cultures. Documented cases of patients believed to be terminal were mistakenly told that they had only a few months to live actually died within their given time frame, even when autopsy findings reveal no physiological explanation for the early death. Voodoo deaths, faith cures, the placebo effect, and hypnosis all provide dramatic evidence for the power of belief.

Some people think that a draft will cause them to get sick, and if one is unable to control stress, such a belief will indeed produce illness. It is thought that a draft causes a rapid temperature change which causes discomfort. Discomfort is stressful and, as we know, stress inhibits the immune system allowing germs, which would otherwise be contained, to proliferate and cause illness. A good antidote is to use the Bellows Breath to warm up and energize the system.

Due to profit and time restraints of incorporated medicine, physicians frequently have busy clinic schedules and need to make sure that they get the information to the patients as succinctly and accurately as possible. When doctors tell patients that they have an "incurable" illness or that they will be on medication for the rest of their lives, they are essentially cursing the patient with a form of "medical hexing." They think that they are being realistic and that the patient deserves to know so they can make necessary arrangements. But they have instilled in the Conscious and Subconscious mind a belief that they will not get well, and as long as the mind holds this negative belief, it becomes a self-fulfilling prophecy. If we believe we will never recover, we won't.

Faith cures by charismatic healers may come from a newly acquired serenity, acceptance, confidence, and vigor due to belief in the cure that reduces helplessness and allows one to notice small improvements and pay less attention to symptoms or problems. Faith in the cure may help some people to stop gaining sympathy and attention for the sick role. Perhaps believing in the cure or the healer reduces anxiety and the experience of pain. Such changes may alleviate an emotional problem or overcome a physical one. Perhaps these improved feelings and behaviors produce beneficial effects on the disease processes. Hippocrates said, "...some patients, though conscious that their condition is perilous, recover their health simply through their contentment with the goodness of the physician."

Ignoring or minimizing the power of belief or the placebo effect, medical research and some doctors in practice have lost one of the most powerful therapeutic forces available to man. The placebo effect can present us with some of the most dramatic examples of the power of the mind over the body and of the use of personal belief to heal a huge variety of physical maladies, and cancer is no exception. Everyone has tumor-suppressing genes and our immune system eliminates thousands of abnormal cells every day, we need to learn how to avoid inhibiting them and optimize their effectiveness.

Scientific research is demonstrating ever more clearly that the things we can touch, taste, and measure may frequently have to take a backseat to what we perceive or believe to be real. It is how we interpret reality or how our body "sees" the concrete world around us that is important. Our personal power and potential for well-being are shaped by the negative or positive ways we think and perceive. Belief can be translated into physical reality in the body. One can turn ON a whole host of symptoms and diseases by simply believing them, and similarly, they can be relieved.

Hippocrates said, "Natural forces within us are the true healers of disease." When the natural forces of the body are inhibited by stress of some kind and become overwhelmed by infection, doctors treat them with drugs and we tend to think that the drugs healed the patient. A better perception might be that the drugs were used as a tool to help reduce the infection to the point where the natural force could regain control and effectively heal the patient. Drugs do not heal, nature does. When they are not causing more harm than good, drugs simply assist the true healers of disease.

One example of the power of expectation and belief was shown to affect surgical outcomes in the 1950s. An operation that was believed to be quite successful in relieving chest pain (angina pectoris) and improving heart function in men with blockage in their coronary arteries gained popularity. The operation involved making an incision next to the breastbone and tying off a relatively superficial artery. Most of the patients who underwent this procedure improved dramatically, experiencing both relief of pain and an improvement in heart function. Then, in 1961, a controlled study was done on the operation and published in the Journal of the American Medical Association. A matched group of men with similar angina were brought to the operating room, they were anesthetized, and a surgical incision was made. Half of these men, however, were sewn up again without having anything else done. After surgery, they experienced the same dramatic relief of angina pain and enjoyed the same improvement in heart muscle function as the men who underwent the real operation.

In another study, patients about to undergo surgery, who were "convinced" of their impending death, were compared to another group of patients who were merely "unusually apprehensive" about death. While the apprehensive bunch fared pretty well, those who were convinced they were going to die usually did. Similarly, women who believed they were prone to heart disease were four times more likely to die. It is not because these women had poorer diets, higher blood pressure, higher cholesterol, or stronger family histories than the women who did not get heart disease. The only difference between the two groups was their beliefs.

Also, there was an interesting 2002 Baylor College of Medicine study of three groups with osteoarthritis in the knee. One group had one form of arthroscopic knee surgery, one group had another form of arthroscopic knee surgery, and the third group had incisions but no procedure. At the end of one year, all the groups had the identical results of less pain and better movement in the knee. All participants believed they had received a complete knee surgery even though the 3rd group had not. At the end of a two-year follow-up, there was still the same level of improvement across all three groups. This result was duplicated in two other studied at other institutions. Belief is powerful.

One does not have to figure out what the mind/body has to do, only how to conceptualize the intent or imagine the end result in a quiet, positive manner. The mind/body will take care of the rest. Healing is inherent and is as natural as breathing but a positive mindset can optimize what the body is already doing. Anything we believe in can act as a placebo and we do not need to believe that healing will happen, just that it can happen. The mind simply needs to be convinced that healing is possible and about to occur. The phenomenon that created this miraculous biological entity in the first place, surly has the ability to repair it.

The Spontaneous Remission Project, which was compiled by the Institute of Noetic Sciences, has documented over 3,500 case studies of "chronic," "incurable," or "terminal" illnesses that were cured or reversed. There is no such thing as an incurable illness. To optimize the probability of spontaneous remission, we have to start by relaxing the mind/body, softening Inflexible Perceptions, and replacing negative beliefs that sabotage self-healing efforts.

Traditional Chinese Medicine includes acupuncture, herbal therapy, nutrition, massage, meditation, and the martial art called Tai Chi to balance the body and direct the healing power of one's vital life energy, or chi. Chi is an invisible force within our bodies and within the Universe that engenders life. There are 49 cultures around the world that understand the concept of chi in one form or another and sadly, ours is not one of them. Western conventional medicine recognizes the role of energy at the molecular level and is extremely effective for treating acute disease and traumatic injuries. In treating chronic illnesses, however, the absence of this "life force energy" concept limits its effectiveness. Fortunately, some medical professionals are beginning to recognize this colossal omission.

Throughout China and many other parts of the world, people are learning to use meditation, imagery, and belief to activate and direct Chi energy for many health issues. Meditative practices calm and focus the mind, direct one's intention and concentration on the body, and can awaken and direct our chi. Some people feel their chi as warmth or tingling, while others simply visualize it moving as a glowing ball. Whether or not one can actually sense chi, the body will still benefit by becoming calm, focused, and present. Once becoming aware of one's chi, however, it becomes easier to notice it, feel it, and direct healing energy to help relieve physical or emotional stress in minutes.

Advanced meditation masters can alter their involuntary responses at will, such as lowering their heart rate and breathing to very low levels, or increase skin temperature in a very precise way. We all have the same abilities, although we do not consciously use them. With a little practice, almost anyone can focus on a spot on the palm of the hand and make it grow warmer. Even if that ability has never been used before, it will happen.

Tibetan Buddhist monks use this phenomenon in an advanced meditation technique known as *tumo* to warm their entire bodies. This technique is so effective that monks who use it can sit in freezing ice caves meditating overnight while wearing nothing more than their silk saffron robes. What we can induce merely by intending it may only be limited by belief and Inflexible Perceptions.

Studies have shown that when subjects in a deep relaxed state are informed that they are being burned by the touch of an ice cube or something that they <u>believe</u> is very hot, a blister arises. And when some multiple personality disorder patients switch personalities, their blood-sugar level, eye color, and other physical attributes begin to change.

Humanity is unique in that we have a Conscious mind that can control physical functions whereas an animal simply reacts. The Conscious mind of man can control his own evolution and direct the Subconscious to instruct the Unconscious mind-of-the-body to respond in a desired direction by adjusting perceptions and beliefs. It is not the DNA or its genes that determine the cell's future function. It is the cell's environment or the dynamic electrochemical soup in which it lives that determines its characteristics, function, and overall health. Our cells adapt to the soup in which they live and belief determines the ingredients of the soup. When we learn to control our perceptions and beliefs, we will be able to control our own gene expression.

New discoveries will continue to astound us regarding the ability of the mind/body/spirit to regenerate, rewire its circuitry, and evolve. That evolution is physical, but it happens in response to mental intentions. We need to sell the Subconscious on the worthiness of a conceived idea, believe it is possible, and then it will achieve, create, and manifest the idea.

5.3.2 **Affirmations – resistance**

Affirmations, especially when combined with strong emotions, are used to reinforce both existing and new beliefs. They have been shown to be far more effective than knowledge, persuasion, good communication, or other such techniques used to change habits and behavior. Exceptional results require exceptional beliefs, but we may need to be patient with ourselves because it can take a while for some new beliefs to take hold. Unlike a computer, we cannot easily erase subconscious programs. We can, however, alter them or replace them with a more appropriate program. We just need to find a way to get it accepted.

Many problems which cannot be solved at the level of action can be readily solved at the level of belief. When trying different actions, systems, or methods, and nothing seems to work, a new belief will often enable us to take different actions, thereby producing different results. Our beliefs have consequences just as our actions do, and those consequences are not always positive. New beliefs guide us to think about the world differently, causes us to look at situations from a new perspective, and take different actions. Even if we think that someone else is responsible for throwing obstacles in our path, we need to remember that WE are responsible for the way we respond to others and that most people respond better to persuasion than to force. Seeing the world from a new perspective is often very enlightening.

Limiting beliefs have a profound effect on our lives and come from a variety of sources: friends, family, teachers, neighbors, the media, and our own interpretation of the world and the events in our lives. The people around us have a significant effect on us and in many cases, the source of the limiting belief truly had our best interests at heart, but sometimes we learn things that are inaccurate. Keep in mind that no matter what other people say or do, it is our perception that creates the belief.

Most people will not spend a lot of time on something that they believe is doomed to failure. They will be less motivated to create a healthy mind/body if they genuinely believed that everyone in their family was destined to be overweight. Sometimes we believe things with a lot of conviction, but when we really think about it, we are not sure why we believe it. Speak the belief aloud and a feeling that it might not be completely true gives us permission, subconsciously, to examine the belief more objectively. Imagine altering or replacing the old belief, and imagine what life would be like without it.

Imagine being free from an old inaccurate belief or habit, update it or find another belief that counteracts the old belief, and find evidence that this new belief is valid. Keep adding evidence until the new belief feels comfortable. Then observe the new feelings, behavior, and results after replacing the belief. Installing a new empowering belief is similar to learning a limiting belief, except that the process has intention behind it. Most new beliefs need evidence to support them before they can be accepted so we need to find it. It has been said that sometimes all it takes to change a life is to decide which beliefs do not serve us and to literally change our mind about them.

Doubt and fear are the Devils most valuable tools, and if we can eliminate just a few of them and replace them with beliefs that empower us, life will forever change for the better. It is our fears and resistance that stop us from achieving great things, and it is our doubts that stop us from even trying. It's very difficult to fail if we have a worthy purpose and continue toward it until it is accomplished.

We have the ability to use our imagination as a rehearsal room to practice being the person we wish to be. We can be anywhere or do anything we wish. As stated in Part IV Section 4.5.1, the seven rules of affirmations are: 1) Simple and short enough to memorize. 2) Vivid and clear enough to facilitate immersion. 3) Personal enough to own using "I" or "My." 4) Use present tense avoiding the words, will, want, and need. 5) Avoid the NOTS. 6) Focus on the solution and not the problem. 7) Speak it out loud.

A good affirmation is simple and clear enough that we can feel the end result. We allow the Subconscious to own it using the words "I" or "My" and using as many senses as possible to become immersed in fulfillment physically, mentally, and emotionally. Notice how it feels to have already accomplished the goal. Notice how it feels as friends and loved ones hear about this fulfillment. We can view ourselves as healthy, happy, and enjoying life to its fullest. We can create a mental picture of rejuvenation, looking younger with sparkling eyes and shiny hair, feeling younger, forgiving others, and forgiving ourselves. We can place ourselves prominently at the center of a life that is joyful, active, spiritually balanced, and full of purpose.

We use the present tense because the Subconscious sees and acts on every image as if it were occurring now. It tends to ignore words that refer to the future like will, want, and need. Similarly, it ignores negative terms like Not, No, Never, Nothing, and conjunctions that include Not like Can't or Don't because the Subconscious does not have an image for the NOTS. When it receives the statement, "Do not think of a dog," it loses something in the translation into its language of images. The Subconscious has an image for do, think, and dog, which reverses the original statement that uses the word NOT and sees, "Do think of a dog." That's why we immediacy think of a pink elephant when someone says, "Do NOT think of a pink elephant." At the

Subconscious level, "I am not timid" is understood as, "I am timid" and focuses on the problem which is, "timid." To successfully get that point into the Subconscious, one needs to use a phrase that does not include the NOTS and names only the desired result: "I am confident." Then we need to say it out loud and feel the emotion.

Belief in an affirmation focuses on what one is becoming. It does not mean that we are blind to our shortcomings, just that we do not focus on or identify with them. We recognize negative events and beliefs just long enough to learn from them, realize that they no longer apply, let them go, and look for opportunity. It gives us the freedom to make mistakes and cope with setbacks by seeing them as temporary setbacks, not the end of the world. Like any other obstacle, we accept and adapt to our situation and create the circumstances we need to reach our next intermediate goal.

Affirmations can put energy behind our choices, transforming positive thoughts and good feelings into positive actions. When we think positive thoughts, when we feel happy feelings, and when we allow our actions to be positive, the mind/body/soul is in balance and harmony. It is often helpful to say what we want to do out loud and repeat it several times. We can frequently get a sense of how much energy we can really commit to this choice by the sound of our voice. By the time we repeat this affirmation four or five times, we should be able to say it whole-heartedly unless there is some part of us resisting or holding back. Like symptoms, this resistance is not necessarily a bad thing.

This resistance just lets us know that there is something about it that does not quite fit, and we need to know more about it before it can be accepted. Resistance can be psychological defenses and are necessary components of healthy psychological functioning. Defenses maintain a barrier between our conscious awareness and our unconscious processes. We need to take the time to explore them respectfully, and find out why it is there using interactive imagery. In Part VI, at the 3rd essential journey, we will learn to let an image of the resistance form, have a conversation with it, and find out whether there is a way to meet its needs yet allow the change to happen. With this process, we can learn more about any inner concern or objection to proceeding on our current path. Subconscious images, resistance, and symptoms are valuable teachers, and we need to treat them all with great respect and consideration in the Conscious mind.

5.3.3 **Replacing Negatives**

It has been said that old habits die hard, but they are almost always open to modification or improvement by learning new information. Habits are automatic behaviors that can be empowering or inhibiting. They remove the need to consciously make a choice every time we do something. Positive habits help us get what we need while negative habits hold us back, preventing whatever we want from ever happening. The Subconscious resists attempts to <u>break</u> habits but <u>altering or replacing</u> them is natural and easy. Developing the ability to recognize negative habits and consciously alter or replace them with positive habits can help us accomplish great things. Charles Dickens said, "I never could have done what I have done without the habits of punctuality, order, and diligence, without the determination to concentrate myself on one subject at a time."

We feel and believe what we have determined to be true in the past using logic and reason. Once in the mind, it is there forever, but it can be altered or neutralized by new information that labels it obsolete or incorrect. It is far easier to alter or replace a belief or habit than to ignore or get rid of it. We do not need to change everything or spend thousands of dollars on therapy to understand everything or rip ourselves apart emotionally. Dwelling on the past or digging for the <u>reason</u> a harmful feeling or thought keeps popping up is usually not only a waste of time but can be quite harmful because that effort generally stimulates those old feelings that were so powerful and brings them back to life again along with many other reasons to keep them. A more effective course of action is to Recognize, Neutralize, Dismiss, and Replace them. Our whole system recognizes negative feeling as toxic. Bottling them up and ignoring them poisons the system and blocks our progress. We need to focus on rewriting those subconscious behavioral programs that interfere with realizing our predetermined worthy objectives.

<u>Recognizing</u> harmful thoughts or feelings that are no longer needed or wanted and <u>neutralizing</u> or desensitizing them is essential and should be followed by <u>dismissal</u> or "letting go" when they are determined to be false, no longer applicable, obsolete, or limiting. And finally, they need to be <u>replaced</u> by more appropriate and useful thoughts or feelings framed in gratitude, patience, and <u>kindness</u>. Some have said, theologians in particular, that "love" is the magic word and that all of our problems will be solved if we just learn to love one another, but some people are <u>really hard to love</u>.

We can still show them kindness, however, and be grateful for the lessons they have taught us.

Our memories are wrapped in the emotion of the moment, and when they are recalled and consciously mixed with the emotions and events of the present, they are returned to memory slightly altered. A memory with a highly charged emotion recalled and felt with the present conscious emotion of "even though this happened, I love and respect myself anyway" then returned to memory, will include the statement with its new positive emotions and have a kinder impact the next time it is recalled. A memory can be disarmed and desensitized in the safety of the present. We need to make sure that the alteration is done consciously and is accompanied by a more appropriate emotion for the next time it comes up. One can also review recurring bad dreams and change them. A disturbing old memory or dream that keeps popping up is desensitized by viewing the footage with different emotions like gratitude, forgiveness, and self-respect instead if anger, blame, fear, guilt, and shame. Recall, review, and edit the emotion until it feels better. Then let it return to memory for later use in its altered state.

Losing a loved one can be difficult, and it is completely natural to feel angry and hurt from time to time but holding on to these feelings for years will make it impossible to move into a healthier relationship or even function effectively. Bottling up negative emotions can lead to rashes, nausea, constipation, dry throat, bloating, headaches, sleep disorders, and other problems as a result of reduced immune function. Anger and fear make the heart beat faster and neck muscles tense up. Arguing with someone for a long time can lead to exhaustion, high blood pressure, and many other stress-related problems. When these symptoms first appear, we need to listen to our mind/body and identify (recognize) corrosive negative emotions that have been ignored or put on the back burner. People suffering from these ailments often take them as a signal to run to the doctor but very seldom is there an identifiable pathological cause for these symptoms. When anger, fear, guilt, worry, sadness, shame, depression, or anxiety is recognized, it is important to neutralize them as soon as possible.

The Subconscious mind stores all sensory information with their accompanying emotions and psychophysiological responses. If muscles get tense during an argument with someone, they will probably tend to do so in the future when the memory is recalled and become a habit associated with arguments. Those who are listening to their mind/body will recognize the signal and notice the anger in plenty of time to neutralize it before it gets out of hand. Delving into a detailed analysis to determine why we are angry is usually of little value and wastes a lot of time and therapy. Simply understand that it no longer applies. The past no longer exists except in memory and is obsolete. If it persists, recall it, alter the image to reflect resolution, and return the altered image to memory.

When we change the way we think or look at things, the things we look at change and affect our emotions. We look for the thinking errors and ask if there is a better way to look at them. To cognitively challenge thinking errors, we start by listing the evidence for and against this idea, notice whether it is based on fact or habit and whether the origin is from a reliable source, and has been confirmed. Notice whether extreme, exaggerated, or all-or-none words are distorting thought. Some examples are never, always, forever, must, should, can't, everything, and everyone.

Turning a bad thing into a good thing is possible but the world "out there" will not shift until the world "in here" does. With Medimaginosis, we can replace old habits, negative emotions, physical pain, or anything one no longer needs or wants, with a new image of something better. We can redirect emotional energy of bad or unhealthy behavior, and increase the passion to create good or healthy habits, behavior or objectives.

5.4 Medi – Creative Meditation 4

Creative meditation is the fourth category of meditation, and when combined with the three other categories (Concentration meditation, Mindfulness meditation, and Contemplation meditation) it is the Medi of Medimaginosis. Creative visualization is magic in the truest and highest meaning of the word. Because the Subconscious mind is not able to tell the difference between a vividly visualized thing and the real life concrete thing, we can go anywhere and do anything we like. Vivid visualization can stimulate the release of certain hormones and impulses, recreate certain brain functions, increase the number of nerve ending and junctions in certain areas, and even increase the brain's ability to shape itself and how it functions. Imagery can be used to help refocus on everyday blessings and shrink negative internal images down to size. Additionally, these tools have been shown to help in the management of pain, nausea and other unpleasant sensations and emotions. This means that our vivid visualizations can make us happier and more productive or stressed and miserable.

We learned to focus energy and attention using Concentration meditation and how to expand our awareness, let go, detach and observe with Mindfulness meditation. Then we learned to investigate and transform an everyday idea into wisdom, and insight into understanding the nature of reality with Contemplation meditation. Here, we will learn to use Creative meditation to build positive pictures and give them life and direction using the thought energy of the mind. Later, we will put them all together invoking the energy of belief, inner listening to receive impressions and inner guidance, and calling on the power of visualization for healing and beneficial epigenetic gene expression. With focus, concentration, awareness, contemplation and a clear perception, we can consciously and carefully use thought, belief, visualization, imagination, affirmation, and intent to evolve.

Meditative practices that are thousands of years old teach us to quiet the mind and the body through methods that are highly effective yet gentle and use attention and imagination to create the changes we desire. We learn to relax and distract the Ego (or put it to sleep) to gain access to the deep Subconscious. Creative meditation and imagery is a powerful way of lowering stress, lowering anxiety, revealing negative subconscious beliefs, loosening old bonds, and opening the pathway to new positive associations with acceptance rather than fear. It is not the solution to all of our problems, but it gives us the opportunity to speak with the wisest person that ever lived and ask them what they would do.

Creative meditation focuses on images and creativity as opposed to Contemplation meditation which is more of an investigative reflection on the nature of what IS and draws upon new adaptive attitudes and intuitive resources. Creative meditation is more than fantasy or a substitute for unpleasant realities; it develops our ability to control our evolution and elicits one of the greatest gifts of our humanity. It uses visualization and the uniquely human power of imagination to conceive, plan, rehearse, and stimulate the belief, emotion, and energy required to manifest great things, solve problems, and visit any corner of the Universe. It uses these gifts to consciously cultivate and strengthen specific qualities of mind, to align or even interact with the great enlightened healers or teachers, and be receptive to impressions or guidance.

All great achievements of mankind first appear in the imagination culminating in all the creative wonders of our modern civilization. According to Albert Einstein, imagination is more important than knowledge. It took imagination to discover and use fire, create weapons, cultivate crops, construct buildings, and invent cars, airplanes, television, computers, and space travel. Imagination not only prompts great works of art and discoveries in science, but it also has the power to influence the mind/body. We have only to look at the process by which man creates everything around him to see the role of this great gift. First is the idea, then development by following a line of related thought. Planning is next followed by giving it the energy of emotion and intention until it eventually emerges in a tangible form. Without imagination, humanity would have become extinct long ago.

The most effective way to use creative visualization is by "going with the flow." We do not need to exert a lot of effort to get where we want to go; we simply keep clearly in mind where we would like to go, and then patiently and harmoniously follow the flow of the river of life, vigilantly using a well-maintained rudder to miss the rocks and sandbars. It is a more effortless and harmonious way to get there than through struggling, striving, fighting, and resisting. We need to trust ourselves and our own deepest intuitive feelings. If it feels like we are forcing, pushing, straining, or struggling, we are doing something wrong. If it feels helpful, releasing, opening, strengthening, enlivening, or inspiring, it probably is. Unless they are hostile, trust the thoughts, feelings, or pictures that first come. Relax, breathe naturally, and always remember to return to the breath. It is almost never a bad idea to return to the basics and review the principles, even for advanced practitioners of Medimaginosis.

Focused visualization is very powerful. In the past, many of us have used our power of creative visualization in a relatively unconscious way. Although the power of thought and creative imagery is becoming more recognized, it is still usually employed in unconscious and haphazard ways. Learning to use it in the most conscious and creative way involves understanding and aligning one's self with the vast wisdom of the Universe.

5.4.1 Personal Place of Peace

One of the first things we need to do when we start using creative visualization is to create a Personal Place of Peace within ourselves where we can go anytime we want. It has been called the Happy Place, Personal

Sanctuary, and Inner Retreat among other things but it is a place that is wholly owned by the individual and can never be taken away from us. It is the 1st of five essential journeys and is the jumping off point for many other creative adventures. We can create our Personal Place of Peace exactly as we want it to be; an ideal place of calm, comfort, and control where we feel good. As Hermann Hesse once said, "Within you there is a stillness and sanctuary to which you can retreat at any time and be yourself."

A Personal Place of Peace is a relaxed state of mind, a visualized tranquil place that calms us down and allows us to restore balance. It is a beautiful, comfortable, calm, serene, safe, secure, peaceful, quiet place to play and express one's self; a personal creation that may change on its own, or by our design, as our conscious awareness evolves. It is a mental vacation spot. It allows us to go there as needed to be alone or with a friend, an inner advisor, inner healer, or spirit to help us through the rough times we all face. Some people use meditative techniques to get there while others can just close their eyes, relax and be there instantly because they have been there many times before.

Going to one's imaginary sanctuary or Personal Place of Peace is an incredibly powerful technique. It is a place to begin relaxing the mind/body, replace pointless or repetitive harmful images, and to break free of inhibiting stress. It really doesn't matter what kind of place we imagine as long as we feel particularly at ease there. It may be a place one has been to before, a place seen in a picture, movie, a dream, or an original creation. We can choose to linger there a while, just enjoying the peacefulness and serenity and leave whenever we want, simply by opening our eyes and being aware of where we are now.

Our imagination can take us anywhere we choose. The peaceful image of a mountain stream, secret garden, forest, a field of flowers, or any body of water can symbolize calm, peace, and harmony. People choose serene places such as a den, sewing room, man cave, an isolated spot in the woods, a hiking trail, river bank, a mountain retreat, peaceful seaside cove, secluded beach, one's own back yard, a fishing pond, a warm fireplace, a favorite restaurant, a computer-generated virtual reality, a room filled with soft blue light and gentle green foliage, or even the womb. It often includes a pool of healing waters or a warm healing light that penetrates the muscles and heals all disharmony. Whatever the choice, it needs to be safe, peaceful, and calming.

The place gives relief just by being there, a stress-free haven in which one feels connected, renewed, strengthened, free, respected and loved; a place where the natural healing abilities of the body can operate at top efficiency; a feel-good place of calm and security, where one is relaxed, comfortable, loved, admired, and respected. It might be a real place from memory, a new creation, or a place no one else would choose. It might change from time to time, and one might have more than one Personal Place of Peace. It is always exactly the way we want it to be, and it always feels the way we want it to feel. It can be an adventure of fun and wonder or a place to rest, recharge, restore, renew, rejuvenate, and ready one's self to go forward again. It is a place within that one can go to anytime, where all is always well, and a space of well-being from which one can jump off into other journeys.

Imagine whatever is most comfortable, pleasing, and calming, using all the senses to give the experience greater depth making it more memorable and real. Imagination and visualization can include hearing jingle bells, or feeling the warmth of a campfire and smelling the smoke. We can make the experience stronger and more memorable than reality by focusing on the scene and immersing ourselves in a sensory rich environment. Better than a detailed hologram, we can hear the surf, smell the ocean mist, and feel the warm breeze, the texture of the sand between our toes, a cool rain, or the warmth of the Sun. We become one with the scene, creating the feeling that we are there and that wherever we look we see the beauty and wonder of our own personal sanctuary; our own Personal Place of Peace.

We have the option of either sticking to one Personal Place of Peace or create one for every mood. If we stick to one place, we can develop greater detail and feel more at home. Creating several scenarios might not be as concrete, but it will likely evoke wonder, curiosity, and the joy of examining and discovering new things. It is a personal place to create as we wish. As one student exclaimed, "It's my island, and I have decided that it will have no snakes, bugs, or animals that aren't cute, fluffy, sweet, and adorable." In the imagination, travel is cheap, and we can afford to visit a vineyard in Italy, vacation at a mansion in the south of France, or relax on a beautiful tropical island anytime we like. One may find it more comfortable to use different inner places for different purposes, such as a sunny beach for rest and relaxation, and a mountaintop to get an overview of a situation. Most students are more comfortable using one special place consistently and using it as a home port from which other journeys begin. The most important thing is to respect what feels best.

With practice, one can enter their Personal Place of Peace just about anytime they like, literally altering brain function, restoring mood and balance, and clearing a path through chaos. It is the basis for controlled mental travel that we will use to communicate with that part of us that is directly connected to the Source of all things, tap into universal wisdom, and bring it into our daily lives.

Before starting, we need to decide where we want to go with our imagery. We will determine intent, focus on the breath, use Progressive Relaxation, find our Personal Place of Peace, and create a signal to anchor the experience in the Subconscious for Rapid Return. Progressive Relaxation is a shorter form of the Mindfulness meditation and is the most successful technique for slowing down brain-wave activity when originally learning to use Creative meditation. This process can be simple "focused attention," an imagined light, or warm energy filling the body as practiced in Part IV. It starts by relaxing the mind and all the muscles one by one, from the toes to the nose, slowly moving up until it fills the entire body.

With Mindfulness meditation, we spend more time with each body part, breathing into it with no attempt to change or control anything. The intent is to observe and experience the sensations we find, if any, and practice "letting them go" by moving our focus to the next area. With Creative meditation, we focus on the body part and breathe into it with the intention of allowing greater relaxation, comfort, and control. The difference is intent.

Personal Place of Peace journey:

a) We first find a time and place where we know we will not be distracted. The time period associated with the (5-7-9) Breath usually works well and the place should be warm, safe, and quiet. We then state our intent, (in this case, it is to develop the power of imagination, find our Personal Place of Peace, and create a Rapid Return signal) keeping in mind that we all want the same thing in the end. Regardless of current superficial wants and desires, harmony is the real goal. And then, just for a moment, consider that meditation is founded on gratitude, patience, and kindness.

b) Set a timer with a pleasing tone if desired, but most people simply open their eyes long enough to look at a watch or clock and gently return to their focus. Sit in a comfortable but dignified manner with the face, scalp, neck, shoulders, and body relaxed and spine straight. It is important to stay relaxed, yet aware and awake. Some students sit on a pillow with their hips slightly higher than their knees and imagine their spine is a tall, straight tree against which they can lean. Note that meditation can be done in the prone position as well, particularly mindfulness and progressive relaxation, but is more likely to morph into sleep. Meditation requires conscious awareness, not sleep.

c) Focus attention on the breath. With our eyes closed or half closed to reduce distractions, we shift from the outer world to our inner world and maintain focus and awareness on our breath. We take a deep (5-7-9) Breath with a barely audible sigh (ahhhhhh) allowing the jaw and shoulders to relax and a slight smile to form on the out-breath. Then we allow the mind/body to become still and focus our attention on the natural tidal rhythm of the breath, feeling the rise and fall of the inhalation and exhalation without trying to influence it.

d) Scan the mind/body from head to toe and back again for tension or tightness. Invite it to relax as much as it wants to while remaining alert and attentive to the breath in the present moment. Assume a non-judgmental attitude, brush away stray thoughts that cloud concentration, and return to the breath. On the inhale, we gather up tension that we do not need to hold right now, and on each exhale, we release that tension and become more and more relaxed; a real letting go kind of breath. It is often helpful to bring the thumb and forefinger together and notice the sense of touch. When we can feel the thumb touching the forefinger, we know that we are aware and in the present moment.

e) As our focus settles on the breath again, we let it get a little easier and deeper. Feel the air move in and out at the tip of the nose. Notice how the temperature is cooler on the in-breath and warmer on the out-breath. We feel the air enter the nostrils, lungs, and expand the diaphragm. With each in-breath, we bring in fresh energy, vitality, and oxygen. We can feel it mix with the blood and flow easily, naturally, and bountifully to every part of the mind/body. With each out-breath, we release a bit more of any accumulated tension. We do not worry about how quickly or deeply the body relaxes; we just invite it to relax in its own way in its own time without trying to force or fix anything. We find that the body really likes to relax and let waves of spacious awareness wash gently through us. Awareness of the breath anchors our attention in the present moment.

f) When awareness detects a lapse in focus or an unrelated thought arises, we return to the breath. Without judging, we smile, say Thank You and gently return to the breath in the present moment. Always return to the breath. We hold a gentle inner smile because it keeps us from trying too hard, getting tense, or being self-critical. Just allow a deep connection to the calm and peacefulness that is here and just breathe with ease and comfort. All we have to do is breathe.

g) We sit for a few minutes in this environment switching from the usual mode of doing to a mode of non-doing or simply being. The mind/body is repairing and renewing itself on every level, and there is nothing else we have to do while it is doing that. Although doing nothing on purpose is actually doing something, we can grant ourselves the luxurious permission to do absolutely nothing else right now. Just for now, we are on a well-deserved mini vacation where there is no trying, no place to go, no one to impress, and nothing to do. Just be with the breath and let the body sink a little bit deeper into relaxation with each exhalation.

h) We begin Progressive Relaxation by focusing on the normal, natural rhythm of the breath and following it as it moves from the nostrils to the diaphragm, through the hips, thighs, knees, lower legs and all the way down to the toes. We visualize, sense or imagine in our own personal way, the cells in our feet relaxing and bathing in the oxygen-rich blood. With every breath, we give ourselves permission to allow this warm comforting sensation to slowly flow with the breath, through the toes into the heels, then with the next breath, it flows into the ankles. Each breath progressively relaxes the next area, moving from the ankles to the lower legs, then the knees, the thighs, hips, and mid-section. We become aware of, and absorbed in, this comfortable sensation. With every breath, we continue to imagine, allow, and sense a warm and nurturing sensation penetrating every cell. The entire body is letting go and becoming even more comfortable as a deep inner calm begins to form. As all of the senses begin to heighten there is a greater awareness of calm, comfort, and control. Breathing easily and effortlessly, we continue to feel even calmer as this comfortable sensation of warm energy or light fills the chest and makes its way to the shoulders, neck, and head. With each breath, it progresses through every muscle in the face, lips, eyes, and forehead. When it fills the entire body, we expand the whole being with the next breath. We feel the entire body breathe in all that is good, and any tension that might remain, is now just slipping off in easy release.

i) Then, when we are ready, we shift our focus to creating our Personal Place of Peace. We identify a path along which we will travel as we journey through this serene inner place. We take a few deep breaths and enjoy the sweet smell of tranquility. We feel calm, safe, and secure as our journey takes us deeper and deeper into our image. Like trying to focus on an island shrouded in fog, we can gradually begin to enhance the vivid clarity of the image. As we get closer, we become more keenly aware of the sights, new sounds, texture of things that we can examine and touch, the smells, tastes, and the feelings under our feet. Using all six senses, we follow our path until we find the place of richest sensory comfort. This is our private place; our own Personal Place of Peace.

j) Once we reach our private place we look around and take several additional deep breaths. It makes us feel calm, peaceful, and filled with freedom and joy. We notice every detail of this beautiful place, soaking it all in, smelling the smells, listening to the birds or petting the puppies; exploring whatever sensory pleasures we might find. It is a place that we love to be in because it is very beautiful, very safe, very secure, and powerful. Take some time to look around and notice the colors, listen to the sounds or notice that it is very quiet. Notice what the air is like in this special place, what the temperature feels like, what time of day or night it is, what the light is like, and what time of year it seems to be. Sense the peaceful beauty, relax, and enjoy it.

k) Imagine choosing a particular spot in this beautiful place to relax into an even deeper feeling of all is well. It is quiet, peaceful, secure, very beautiful and serene, where one can be completely relaxed. It is the most comfortable, most empowering connected spot in all of creation. We stay in our private place as long as we like, allowing our imagination to run free with pleasant images. We notice how our body feels and review the best aspects of our journey and our Personal Place of Peace so we can more easily return to it in the future.

l) Now that we know where this beautiful, peaceful place is, we need to anchor it in our Subconscious so we can quickly return to it anytime we like. The most effective way to do that is to create a physical signal associated only with this special place; a signal to the Subconscious mind that we want to return to our Personal Place of Peace in all its glory as if we had never left. Our signal is a (5-9-9>1) count similar to the (5-7-9) Breath but incorporates a finger signal, a count up to nine instead of seven, and a reverse count from nine down to one. While still basking in our Personal Place of Peace, we take special note of all that it offers and associate it with our signal. With the thumb and forefinger together on the writing hand, take an especially deep Three-Part-Breath IN to the count of five. Then hold it for a slower than normal count, past the usual 7 to 9 (5-9), while squeezing the thumb and forefinger together a little tighter with each ascending number, feeling the pressure build and increase a little more with each count. Then at nine, release both the breath and the tension between the thumb and forefinger, and begin a reverse count from nine down to one (9>1). With each descending number, the vision of our Personal Place of Peace becomes more and more clear and anchored into the Subconscious. Using all six senses we recall our special place of peace in every detail and from this point on, anytime we wish to return to this place, we simply signal the mind/body with the thumb and forefinger (5-9-9>1) count in. It will all come rushing back as if we had never left. It can be used to quickly shift focus, de-stress, desensitize to discomfort, quiet the mind, calm the breathing, lower anxiety, and to take back control. We continue to imagine and visualize being in our Personal Place of Peace and how it feels for as long as we like, knowing that we can come back again anytime we want.

m) When it is time to return to the outside world, we become aware of this calmness and centeredness, commit it to memory for future use, and return to the breath. We take a big deep cleansing breath IN, and let it go with the images but bring back the good peaceful feelings. We allow the benefits and what has been most meaningful and important from this journey to become solidified in the Subconscious and prepare to bring it into the conscious outside world to improve every aspect of daily life. Feeling secure and a wonderful sense of well-being, we become more alert and aware in every way. We begin to notice what is going on around us, wiggle our fingers and toes, smile because we feel so good, and move our focus from our inner world to the sounds, smells, shapes and colors around us. Finally, we take a comfortable energizing Three-Part-Breath and open our eyes feeling wide awake, grateful, re-energized, refreshed, happy, and ready for the remainder of the day.

n) Some find it helpful to bring the hands together (the gasho or prayer position) and close the moment with gratitude and reflection. It is helpful to sit still for a moment or two to review the experience and annotate any ideas, visions, or inner guidance received in meditation with the intention of incorporating the benefits into our daily lives. To keep us in the present moment, we continue to keep 25% of our attention on our breath (DSCR) replacing pointless repetitive daydreaming. With the other 75% on what we are doing and what really matters in life, we check in from time to time by asking, "Am I still breathing?"

Sometimes we may not feel like going through the mental process that accompanies a journey, even though it is enjoyable. Sometimes we just feel a bit spent and need to recharge our batteries. In that event, we simply relax and imagine that the Universe is recharging our chi. We might imagine an inexhaustible beam of light or energy coming from the Source of all things, like the warmth of the Sun inundating the entire mind/body. Just relax, breathe, and let the Universe recharge the trillions of tiny batteries in every cell. Breathe in chi and exhale all that is limiting. We allow the Universe to breathe for us and absorb all the energy we need from the same inexhaustible Source that created and feeds a possibly infinite array of galaxies and suns. We have access to a virtually unlimited source energy and tapping in to it is a matter of mind.

5.5 Journeys of Wisdom and Wonder

We learned to use the 1st of five essential journeys in the previous section where we created our own Personal Place of Peace. It is the first level of Creative meditation. The 2nd essential journey will take us a little deeper into the Subconscious where we will meet our Personal Mentor or inner advisor; a protective and compassionate, wise and trusted counselor, guide, coach, teacher, and healer, all in one. The 3rd essential journey is that of Discovery and goes even deeper into the Subconscious mind. We build on our Contemplation meditation practice and learn to investigate an issue, topic, subject, feeling, emotion, desire, or belief by forming an image of it, viewing it from different perspectives and carrying on a conversation with it. The 4th essential journey is to the Control Room and takes us even deeper than the Discovery Journey. It is a place deep in the Subconscious mind where the Unconscious mind-of-the-body is controlled. For most people, this controlling is done by prerecorded subconscious programs, but we can learn to take control and direct mind/body functions that were previously thought to be strictly autonomic. The 5th essential journey takes us to the deepest level and the center of our true self where we will meet and speak with our OM, or our connection to the Source of all things, to access unlimited wisdom. It is our personal liaison to a vast, possibly infinite, repository of wisdom and love that some call God, The Great Spirit, Allah,

Yahweh, or Jehovah. These techniques are free, fun to practice, and can be used as many times as we like.

There is no limit to the imagination as far as we know, and there is no limit to the secondary journeys we can create. Anytime we find ourselves in our Personal Place of Peace, we can create other special places where miraculous things happen and invoking the assistance of a deep spiritual belief has been shown to supercharge the effect. The right journey is a way to experience our goals and accelerate the subconscious acceptance of a new positive concept, create a new association, or desensitize an old negative program. Outside the boundary of time and space, anything becomes possible.

These journeys immerse us in new images in powerful ways. Most of them use the Personal Place of Peace as a jumping off point because it is safe, comfortable, and familiar. After we have been there a few times and know how it feels, we can use the (5-9-9>1) Rapid Return technique instead of the more extensive Progressive Relaxation process. After a long hard day, however, some people like to take the long way to their Personal Place of Peace. For those who have learned other effective methods of returning quickly to the meditative state, we suggest that they use the method with which they are most comfortable, but know that cutting corners reduces efficacy.

A simplified basic outline of a Medimaginosis journey makes the process clearer and more logical, especially to a new practitioner. Even experienced practitioners of Medimaginosis refer to this outline like a pilot uses a checklist. No matter how many times a pilot has flown an airplane, the checklist is always used to ensure that no item is ever forgotten. Consciously omitting a step or two for good reason is perfectly acceptable but mindlessly forgetting them can lead to apathy and reduced effect.

Meditation checklist:

Before
1) State the predetermined intention, Relax, and Breathe.
2) Scan the mind/body and release any tension into the breath.

Warm Up
3) Use the Progressive Relaxation technique and/or the (5-9-9>1) Rapid Return signal to return to the Personal Place of Peace.
4) Relax even deeper with a Mantra and breath focus.

Main Event
5) Meditate on a predetermined intention.

Cool Down
6) Return to the breath and return to the outside world slowly with the Three-Part-Breath.

After
7) Annotate insights, evaluate them consciously, and safely carry them into daily life.

The most common secondary journeys are stress busters and begin by focusing on the breath, relaxing and letting go. They are most effective from the deeper level of our Personal Place of Peace, but we can also just visualize or imagine moving to a place of deep relaxation, gather up all or part of the stress and tension into a deep breath and blowing it into a passing cloud in the sky with the out-breath. Then we watch it float away feeling completely refreshed on all levels.

Two other useful methods of letting go of harmful stress in a matter of seconds include the bubble image and the backpack journey. The bubble image starts by taking three deep breaths and imagining, visualizing, or pretending that we are blowing the stress into a bubble ring and the stress is trapped in the bubble, floats away, disappears into the sky or pops and disburses into the atmosphere.

The backpack journey begins by imagining that one is carrying a heavy backpack filled with the negative beliefs and events from the past. We can feel how heavy it is on our shoulders. Now at the top of a staircase, we stop and open the backpack. We take out the heavy boulders of past events and beliefs that we no longer need and leave them at the top of the staircase. After putting the backpack back on, we can feel how light it is and notice the change in our shoulders, neck, and back. Even our mood is lighter. Now walk down the stairs celebrating that the old ideas and beliefs have been left behind feeling lighter and happier with each step. At the bottom of the stairs, we can fill our backpack with good stuff, tasty nutritious foods that build a healthier mind and body, deep restful sleep, and the comforting feeling of simplicity and control in the present.

The healing light journey starts at our Personal Place of Peace as do most of the other journeys. In this serene sacred place, we can enter a deeply relaxed state and notice that our senses are sharper and more acute as images come forward easily and naturally. The stillness of it seems to speak and radiate a sacred kind of energy. We choose a particular spot that seems most comfortable and calming; a comfortable spot that radiates a warm healing light that seems to glow and flow. We invite and allow this healing energy to come forward to relax, rejuvenate, and restore. Let the new image grow and expand and fill the whole being. Allow this positive healing energy, a light of warmth and healing, to penetrate deep into every muscle, tissue, fiber, organ, and bone in the body right down to the cellular layer. This warm, positive healing light is doing its good work as we begin to notice that it concentrates energy in particular areas of the body where it is needed most.

An ancient healing practice that has always been quite effective is the idea of healing hands, and it feels somehow quite familiar. We sense and imagine that warm, loving, healing hands are resting lightly on just the right places, emanating the warmth, the flow, the healing light, and the understanding that healing happens. Experiencing these journeys can take us beyond thinking to being, and the more sensory rich a journey is, the more memorable and effective it will be. Most of our students also find that their Personal Place of Peace has a pool of warm healing water in which they can immerse their entire body. It can be a truly enjoyable process and a magnificent adventure.

The "Glove Anesthesia" is another useful technique that deals with pain or discomfort. We start by focusing attention on the right hand. Feel a slight ripple of cool air across the hand and notice how it begins to feel different than the left hand. The cool ripple of air allows the hand to begin to feel cooler. Feel the coolness in the air transfer into the hand. As the hand becomes cooler, we seem to drift deeper into this calm relaxation and comfort. As the coolness begins to increase, memories of another time when the hand was very cool or cold come to mind; a time when the hand was covered in snow or in a cold stream of water. Now the feeling continues to change as the cold feeling becomes a feeling of numbness; a numb feeling that has been felt before, perhaps in different parts of the body. Remember the cold, numb feeling and allow it to develop in the hand. Allow that cold, numb feeling to grow even stronger by focusing and feeling the sensation. The words cold and numb become more powerful, and it becomes easier to feel with practice whether the eyes are open or closed. Now take that cold hand and place it over the area where there has been discomfort. Feel the cold, numb feeling begin to flow from the hand into that area. Feel it flow like a cold flowing energy that begins to surround and flow through the area bringing the cold, numb feeling. With this wonderful feeling of numb and coolness, freedom, and relief, a smile begins to come up as well. Allow the smile, continue to flow those feelings of numb and cold, and witness the numbness flowing easily and effortlessly.

5.5.1 **Personal Mentor – A wise and trusted guide & inner healer**

After establishing a Personal Place of Peace, the 2nd essential journey is meeting one's Personal Mentor or inner advisor; a protective and compassionate, wise and trusted counselor, guide, coach, teacher, and healer, all in one. This all-important image of natural wisdom, caring, and support is so personal and connected to our essence, that this is the only image that we allow into our Personal Place of Peace. Our Personal Mentor has direct access to all memories, experiences, emotions, and knowledge of the Subconscious mind and loves us as much as, or more than, we do with our well-being and harmony as their ONLY goal. It knows us better than we do because it has been with us since our birth, seeing and hearing everything that has ever happened to us. To find it, we go to our Personal Place of Peace and invite our Personal Mentor to join us.

A Personal Mentor within can be something imagined from familiar sources in fact or fiction, or something surprising and new, ordinary or supernatural. A wise loving guide and protector, it might be one's own wisdom within or an older wiser sense of self. It can appear as a representation of another being, dog, cat, thing, or perhaps a religious or spiritual figure. Anything might arise from the Subconscious to answer the call. A Personal Mentor often appears in the form of the classic "wise old man" or "wise old woman," but they come in many other forms as well. Sometimes they come in the form of a person we know, a trusted friend or relative who has fulfilled this function in real life. People sometimes encounter their Personal Mentor as a natural force like the wind or the ocean, an angel, fairy, leprechaun, a light or a translucent, ethereal spirit, and it is not uncommon to simply experience a sense of something calming, strong, and wise, without any visual image at all.

Our Personal Mentor is also a wise, caring, kind, and knowledgeable healer. People who have an illness that is chronic or severe have probably consulted many doctors, whose highly educated, logical analysis may have led to a diagnosis. Yet the diagnosis may not have led to a cure, or even relief. If good logical thinking has come up empty, it may be time to get a "second opinion" from within. Our Personal Mentor knows more about our body, feelings, and life than anyone on Earth. It is a part of us that is usually hidden from our conscious awareness, but Medimaginosis gives it the ability to communicate. It might offer advice in areas as diverse as nutrition, posture, exercise, environment, attitude, emotions, and faith. We can recognize emotions like anger, fear, guilt, shame, sadness, and worry, and discuss them openly with a wise, understanding counselor. Our Personal Mentor wants to help, believes in us, and is always on-call to consult, protect, assist, and help with any situation. The wisdom to answer questions, resolve a dilemma, make a decision, and feel support, is as close as the imagination.

It is not necessary to have any particular belief about an inner advisor in order to use it, but it helps if it makes sense. Whether one believes that their advisor is a spirit, a guardian angel, communication from outer space, a messenger from God, a hallucination, or a symbolic representation of their own inner wisdom, it will be just as effective. Clinically and practically it just does not seem to matter.

While most people have one Personal Mentor or inner advisor that is a protective and compassionate, wise and trusted counselor, guide, coach, teacher, and healer, all in one, it is also perfectly acceptable to have more than one Personal Mentor. Some people have whole communities of advisors, each with a different gift: a wise teacher who provides advice, guidance, and clear thinking; a wise elder who provides compassion, understanding, and a sense of loving; a healer with intimate knowledge of our psychophysiology; and perhaps a child who teaches playfulness and trust. If one if these advisors is unable to help, we simply ask it to "refer" us to another inner figure who knows more about the issue at hand.

We have much more information within us than we commonly use, and a Personal Mentor is a symbolic representation of that inner wisdom and experience. Our Personal Mentor should be thought of as a friendly guide to these valuable subconscious stores and an inner ally who can help us understand ourselves more deeply. It is a matter of relaxing, getting quiet, going to a quiet, peaceful place, and then imagining being with a wise, loving figure that knows us intimately. It is a way to get in touch with the vast store of information and knowledge that we rarely if ever use and it is a way to get to another perspective about ourselves.

Albert Einstein taught us that we cannot solve our problems with the same level of thinking that created them, and that the level of the solution is never at the level of the problem. At the level of the problem is repetitive thinking that gets nowhere, old conditioning that keeps applying yesterday's worn-out choices, unproductive, obsessive behavior, and stalled action. But at a deeper level, we have untapped creativity and insight.

Everyone has struggled with a problem and ultimately come to terms with it by acting on a gut feeling, a good hunch, a flash of insight, or perhaps an enlightening dream. It is usually hidden from conscious awareness and comes from something deep inside. Imagining this guidance as a figure with which we can communicate helps to make it more accessible. Having a talk with an imaginary wise figure is one of the most powerful techniques for helping us understand the relationships between our thoughts, feelings, actions, and health. Confiding in a Personal Mentor is safe and confidential while confiding in other people, especially people who depend on us for money, status, or advancement is not always a good idea.

Our Personal Mentor can help us understand more about the nature of a condition or situation and the part we might play in affecting it. It can act as a source of support and comfort, a sense of peacefulness, of inner calm and compassion. Especially if one has been feeling depressed, panicky, or just confused, checking in with a Personal Mentor can be an important step toward healing. Direct relief of symptoms and recovery from illness often comes as a result of realizing the function of a symptom and making changes so that the mind/body no longer needs to create the symptom.

There are three problems that surface frequently enough to merit special attention here. The FIRST is that sometimes no image appears, the SECOND is that the image is hostile or critical, and the THIRD is a failure to evaluate the advice we receive consciously.

FIRST…Some people do not find a Personal Mentor, or even a Personal Place of Peace, on the first journey and that is perfectly alright. There is no need to force it because the essential image will arise when the time is right. Be patient. A Personal Mentor might turn out to be something that was there all along that was not recognized at first because something else was expected. Working with imagery successfully is more a matter of allowing than creating. It seems that the harder one tries, the less likely it is that we will succeed. The more deeply we relax, and the more receptive we are to accepting whatever comes, the more likely we are to have a good meeting with our Personal Mentor. As with any skill, we need to be patient and practice.

When a Personal Mentor or Personal Place of Peace is a no show, avoid letting the journey build into frustration and anxiety. There is no need to force it. Like trying to produce a urine sample on command at the doctor's office, trying too hard can be a show stopper. Just let go and let it be, like watching an enjoyable movie, the image will arise freely when the time is right. Eventually, it will come into being in an easy and effortless way. Until that time, maintain a positive subconscious attitude and belief while practicing basic meditation. Always return to the breath and that which we seek will simply show up.

Physical stress blocks conscious awareness, so we need to back off, relax, and listen with an intention that is focused and clear. We detach from instinctive emotional reactions by returning to the breath until our mind/body begins to calm down. Answers always come eventually, because the mind is never at a loss for channels of communication. Generations of wisdom support the notion that creative solutions arise spontaneously.

Sometimes it helps to imagine what a Personal Mentor would look like if we had one or imagine having a talk with a very good friend. Imagine telling a close friend, in detail without holding anything back, about an illness, thoughts, feelings, and any questions that no one has been able to answer. Tell the friend everything that is related, including things never revealed to anyone ever. Imagine this friend listening with compassion and then responding. Remember that our imaginary friend already knows everything about us so there is no need to be afraid to tell them something for fear of embarrassment or disappointment.

SECOND...It is possible to learn something important from encountering and dealing with a hostile or critical image but understand that it is NOT a Personal Mentor. A Personal Mentor is characterized by being both wise and caring. While our inner Personal Mentor may sometimes point out changes that need to be made, the advice comes from a stance of being helpful and compassionate, not coercive or blaming. An imposter might be reminiscent of a negative, overly critical authority figure from the outer world, and simply needs to be sent away. Then invite the real thing to replace it.

Some images that pop up from the Subconscious can be blocking, negative, challenging, mean, critical, or scary. We need to understand that it is just an image in the imagination and that it can be dissolved by imagining a positive counter or simply opening one's eyes. Other responses might be to consult with one's Personal Mentor about it, confront the negative image, turn it into a positive relationship, just let it go and move on, or simply send the negative image away and bring in a positive replacement image. We can also roll it up into a ball, toss it into the deep blue of the Universe where it transforms into positive energy, or put it into a passing cloud and watch it float away. Some people bring in a protector-image with unlimited powers and abilities that comes forward to help, or become the hero themselves, vanquishing the negative image and moving on.

The simplest way to deal with an imposter is to assert one's self. We tell it that we are in our quiet place to meet with our Personal Mentor, a loving, caring figure, and that, in this special inner place, we are in control. We let it know that we are looking for ways to become healthier and happier, that only our Personal Mentor is allowed in this Personal Place of Peace, and that we will not tolerate harping or criticism that does not lead toward growing and healing. Recognizing and standing up to an inner critic is important because the self-image it generates often becomes a self-fulfilling prophecy. Remember, we have complete control and any hostile of scary images can be "dematerialized" by replacing it or simply opening our eyes. If an image does not feel right, just send it away and invite another more appropriate image to form.

THIRD...Failure to evaluate the advice consciously can lead to even bigger problems. Evaluating the advice we receive is a critical aspect of working with subconscious imagery. Our Personal Mentor is one of many aspects of our Subconscious mind, and it is possible for us to receive information from other inner sources. Weighing the potential benefits and risks of what has been suggested allows us to analyze what we have learned and consciously discriminate between potentially useful and potentially risky actions.

While we do want to know what our images have to say, we do not have to do everything they recommend. The Conscious mind is in control. Whatever comes from a talk with an image needs to be considered consciously to determine what it might mean to act on the advice. We need to evaluate the risks and benefits of following the advice and make our own decision about whether or not to follow it. Consider what it has to say but any action needs to be based on a conscious decision. Using logic and the superior judgment of the Conscious mind, we can weed out obvious mistakes.

An image might suggest a course of action that involves some risk. They might say we need to talk more frankly with a spouse, let ourselves be more assertive and express our emotions, or move on in life. They might suggest that we change our job or occupation in order to feel better or improve our health. Typically, there is some resistance to this kind of advice, but if there was no resistance to it, there would not be a problem, symptom, or an illness. We can tell our Personal Mentor that we are considering the advice it has given us and are experiencing resistance. Discuss fears or concerns thoroughly, and ask for help understanding more deeply and perhaps suggest a course of action that takes these concerns into account.

Imagery work involves keeping this dialogue going, bringing advice back, taking a conscious look at it, and noticing what would happen if acted upon in real life. List the risks, benefits, and potential barriers. It requires consciously assessing possible adaptations and other ways of dealing with the situation and whether it is compatible with our true beliefs and ethics. We can also explore additional options through imagery and have further discussions with our Personal Mentor about the best and safest way to do what needs doing. Then make a choice from honest assessments. Imagine doing it and noticing what happened as a result.

We seek the words of others and believe them only when they are in harmony with our own natural wisdom. Seek balance and the middle path, avoiding extremes: not too much and not too little is just right. It is that balance between keeping our destination clearly in mind, enjoying all the beautiful scenes we encounter along the way, and being willing to change our direction if life starts taking us in a harmful direction that keeps us on track. It means being firm yet flexible, open but not gullible, skeptical but not cynical. It is the plasticity of perception that facilitates our evolution from stress to gratitude, perfect health, happiness, vitality, longevity, and harmony.

Turning insight into action is dependent upon remembering the insight, so our students keep a pen and paper at the ready during meditation. Our epiphanies might remain mere fantasy if we do not take steps to make them real. With Medimaginosis, we can direct the Unconscious mind-of-the-body to manifest psychophysiological evolution, but conscious action is required to effect the outside world. While still relaxed and comfortable, we can easily open our eyes just wide enough to see and record our thoughts for later evaluation and return to state. After a Medimaginosis journey, it is also helpful to immediately take some time to write down or record whatever happened in the experience because, like a dream, it fades rapidly from the memory and is often completely forgotten after returning to the outside world. Write down any ideas or epiphanies that were not written down during the session, what was learned, and any questions, resistance or obstacles that might need to be discussed in the next session. After using the Medimaginosis program for three or four months, most people express astonishment over the vast increase in the number of ideas, epiphanies, and inspirations they have received from their own mind.

Clarify insights, state them clearly and simply, put energy and resolve behind them by establishing clear, concise affirmations and make a plan. Rehearse the plan in the imagination, imagine actually carrying out the plan, become aware of obstacles, adjust the plan to account for them, and if needed, break it down into smaller steps to make it happen.

Meeting our Personal Mentor is simple. The first step is to let ourselves relax and go to our Personal Place of Peace where we are calm, comfortable, and relaxed. Then we allow an image to appear for our Personal Mentor accepting whatever image comes whether it is familiar or not, as long as it is wise, caring, and supportive. Preconceived expectations can stand in the way of our benefiting from the experience.

Personal Mentor Journey:

a) We first find a time and place where we know we will not be distracted. The time period associated with the (5-7-9) Breath usually works well and the place should be warm, safe, and quiet. We then state our intent, (in this case, to meet our Personal Mentor) keeping in mind that we all want the same thing in the end. Regardless of current superficial wants and desires, harmony is the real goal. And then, just for a moment, consider that meditation is founded on gratitude, patience, and kindness.

b) Set a timer with a pleasing tone if desired, but most people simply open their eyes long enough to look at a watch or clock and gently return to their focus. Sit in a comfortable but dignified manner with the face, scalp, neck, shoulders, and body relaxed and spine straight. It is important to stay relaxed, yet aware and awake. Some students sit on a pillow with their hips slightly higher than their knees and imagine their spine is a tall, straight tree against which they can lean. Note that meditation can be done in the prone position as well, particularly mindfulness and progressive relaxation, but is more likely to morph into sleep. Meditation requires conscious awareness, not sleep.

c) Focus attention on the breath. With our eyes closed or half closed to reduce distractions, we shift from the outer world to our inner world and maintain focus and awareness on our breath. We take a deep (5-7-9) Breath with a barely audible sigh (ahhhhhh) allowing the jaw and shoulders to relax and a slight smile to form on the out-breath. Then we allow the mind/body to become still and focus our attention on the natural tidal rhythm of the breath, feeling the rise and fall of the inhalation and exhalation without trying to influence it.

d) Scan the mind/body from head to toe and back again for tension or tightness. Invite it to relax as much as it wants to while remaining alert and attentive to the breath in the present moment. Assume a non-judgmental attitude, brush away stray thoughts that cloud concentration, and return to the breath. On the inhale, we gather up tension that we do not need to hold right now, and on each exhale, we release that tension and become more and more relaxed; a real letting go kind of breath. It is often helpful to bring the thumb and forefinger together and notice the sense of touch. When we can feel the thumb touching the forefinger, we know that we are aware and in the present moment.

e) As our focus settles on the breath, we begin to employ the Progressive Relaxation process or the thumb and forefinger Rapid Return signal that we established in a previous journey to our Personal Place of Peace. To begin the Rapid Return process, it helps to sit a little taller and look up as if there was a movie screen on the inside of the forehead. Take a deep Three-Part-Breath to the count of five and hold it for an ascending count from one up to nine while pressing the thumb and forefinger together a little tighter (creating tension) with each ascending number. Then release the tension and the breath to a descending count down from nine to one. With each descending number, our Personal Place of Peace comes into greater and clearer focus, and at "one" we find ourselves basking in the beauty and comfort of our Personal Place of Peace as if we had never left.

f) We sit for a few minutes in this environment becoming one with the breath and soaking up the beauty, serenity, and wonder that is this place. At this point, spending a few minutes with one's mantra can noticeably deepen the feeling of relaxation. Then, when we are ready, we expand our field of awareness to include our predetermined intent which is to meet our Personal Mentor in this case. Some people walk down a hallway and find a door labeled "Personal Advisor" or "Advisory Council" while others follow a path to a secret garden where they meet their Personal Mentor. Most people simply invite their Personal Mentor to appear in a special spot within their Personal Place of Peace where they can both feel comfortable and at ease; an ideal spot where it would be most conducive to meet with a Personal Mentor. It is the most empowering and connected spot in all of creation to have an easy, comfortable conversation with a trusted, loving friend.

g) Invite an image to form or allow a sense of all the great wisdom within to freely come to life that represents the kind, loving, trusted and supportive Personal Mentor; a wise teacher that knows us better than we do because it has been with us since our birth. It is an intuitive genius that has seen and heard everything that has ever happened to us, and has access to all the experiences, memories, and knowledge we have within us. Freely bringing it to life and let it arise naturally. Welcome the advisor that comes and get to know it as it is. One image is no better than another, and there is no best way for them to communicate. Some advisors talk, others communicate their messages through their expressions or actions or by changing their forms completely. Sometimes people just "get the message" without really knowing how, while others don't see an advisor at all and don't hear anything, but they do know what is being communicated. Let it be what it is for now, a light or a feeling or a wise old man or woman, and know that any image is fine as long as it feels safe and comfortable. But if for some reason, the image does not feel right or we sense anything but complete devotion to our well-being, we send the imposter away and replace it with an image that is friendly, helpful, and healing. The real Personal Mentor feels comfortable and is an image that we can trust in all ways. This is our place and we alone have complete control.

h) We need to take some time to get to know this awesome phenomenon and notice how it feels to connect with it and feel its energy. A Personal Mentor is often quite happy to finally be able to communicate directly because, until now, it has been only sporadic communication through gut feelings or intuition. Notice that it is a trustworthy image that would give guidance for whatever seems important and help figure things out in a caring, wise, concerned, and loving way, with our well-being as its highest priority. When we can feel a distinct sense of caring and wisdom, we begin a polite conversation with it and accept what comes. We can ask our wise inner advisor for general guidance or for advice on a particular issue or health concern. We can tell it about a problem and ask any questions we have concerning an event or situation, taking all the time we need. We tell our mentor what is uppermost in our mind, how we feel about it and listen carefully to the answer as we would to a wise and respected teacher. Allow it to communicate in whatever way seems natural. If there is some uncertainty about the meaning of the advice or if there are other questions that need to be asked, continue the conversation until it feels complete. Ask questions, be open to the responses that come back, and consider them carefully. We continue to imagine and visualize being with this loving mentor and continue the conversation as long as we like. We explore the subject in whatever depth feels right, keeping in mind that we can come back again anytime we want and that our friend will always be here for us.

i) As we consider what our advisor has told us, we imagine what life would be like if we took the advice we have received and put it into action. If there seems to be a problem or obstacles standing in the way, we can ask our Personal Mentor how we might deal with them in a healthy, constructive way. Because our advisor knows everything about us, it is sometimes unwilling to tell us something. This is usually to protect us from information that we may not be ready to handle. When this occurs, we ask our advisor what we need to do in order to make this information available, and our advisor will usually show us the way. Like a real relationship, we need to treat it with respect and be receptive to whatever comes up. It is far more powerful than most people know.

j) When it is time to return to the outside world, we thank our Personal Mentor for meeting with us and say goodbye for now in whatever way seems appropriate. Realizing that we can return and meet with our advisor again whenever the need arises, we let the images go, and return to the breath. We take a big deep cleansing breath IN, and let it go with the images but bring back from this journey the good, the positive, and the true to our conscious outer awake life or outer world. We allow the benefits and what has been most meaningful and important from this journey to become solidified in the Subconscious and prepare to bring it into the conscious outside world to improve every aspect of daily life. Feeling secure and a wonderful sense of well-being, we become more alert and aware in every way. We begin to notice what is going on around us, wiggle our fingers and toes, smile because we feel so good, and move our focus from our inner world to the sounds, smells, shapes and colors around us. Finally, we take a comfortable energizing <u>Three-Part-Breath</u> and open our eyes feeling wide awake, grateful, re-energized, refreshed, happy, and ready for the remainder of the day.

k) Some find it helpful to bring the hands together (the gasho or prayer position) and close the moment with gratitude and reflection. It is helpful to sit still for a moment or two to review the experience and annotate any ideas, visions, or inner guidance received in meditation with the intention of incorporating the benefits into our daily lives. To keep us in the present moment, we continue to keep 25% of our attention on our breath (<u>DSCR</u>) replacing pointless repetitive daydreaming. With the other 75% on what we are doing and what really matters in life, we check in from time to time by asking, "Am I still breathing?"

5.6 Summary

The first half of Part V was an in-depth explanation of Medimaginosis, how it works, and its many effects. We learned to use the fourth category of meditation, Creative meditation, to develop our uniquely human gift of imagination and the power of belief and wisdom. We discussed the relationships between Interactive Imagery, the placebo effect, and affirmations, how to control them, and how to deal with resistance.

In the second half of Part V, we learned to travel without having to pack a bag. We embarked upon the 1st of five essential journeys to the most beautiful place in all of creation, where we can be safe, happy, and well. We went to our own Personal Place of Peace and learned how to return to it anytime we like in a matter of seconds. We learned to relax and let go there, how to unload unwanted stress, discomfort, and pain. From there, we set out on the 2nd essential journey where we met our own Personal Mentor or inner advisor; a protective and compassionate, wise and trusted counselor, guide, coach, teacher, and healer, all in one; a kind, caring knowledgeable healer within whom we can confide because it already knows us better than we do. We learned to evaluate and turn the new insights into action and safely carry them into daily life. Part V ends with an Action Assignment and visual aid page.

Part VI takes us on the 3rd, 4th, and 5th essential journeys where we learn to expand on the Contemplative meditation and enhance Creative meditation using Interactive Imagery. We learn to take control of mind/body functions and gene expression using universal wisdom and belief as a power booster. Then we move beyond thought with action to create our reality. Finally, we summarize the program and integrate Medimaginosis with diet and activity concerns that balance harmony.

5.7 **Action Assignment**

* Understand that Medimaginosis is a powerful synergistic integration of meditation, imagery, and wisdom that illuminates the path to physical, mental, emotional, financial, and spiritual evolution and harmony.

* Review the "Principles of Harmony (I am We Affirmations) including the personal (8th Affirmation) and list any resistance or doubt that is felt when stating an affirmation out loud. We will learn to deal with them in Part VI but we first need to be conscious of them here.

* List unwanted habits or problems and then write the desired solution or alternative. Let the negative go and focus on the solution or desired result by creating an affirmation for it.

* Practice Creative meditation first by creating a Personal Place of Peace and a Rapid Return signal. Develop it in the greatest detail possible and practice both the Progressive Relaxation Return and the thumb and forefinger (5-9-9>1) Rapid Return technique.

* Review the stress busters including the cloud, bubble, backpack technique, healing light, healing hands, and the glove anesthesia. Practice one or two of them and choose a favorite.

* Review the seven basic meditation steps using the checklist on the visual aid page.

* Students need to return to their Personal Place of Peace and invite their Personal Mentor to join them, spend some time with it and get to know it intimately. When it feels right, we ask our Personal Mentor to comment on the affirmations created from the list above.

* Annotate insights, evaluate them <u>consciously</u>, and safely carry them into daily life.

Medimaginosis

Create your Personal Place of Peace and Rapid Return Signal.

Create your own Personal Mentor and get to Know it.

Meditation checklist:

Before
1) State the predetermined intention, Relax, and Breathe.
2) Scan the mind/body and release any tension into the breath.

Warm Up
3) Use the Progressive Relaxation technique and/or the (5-9-9>1) Rapid Return signal to return to the Personal Place of Peace.
4) Relax even deeper with a Mantra and breath focus.

Main Event
5) Meditate on a predetermined intention.

Cool Down
6) Return to the breath and return to the outside world slowly with the Three-Part-Breath.

After
7) Annotate insights, evaluate them consciously, and safely carry them into daily life.

Promote Harmony with Gratitude, Patience, and Kindness

He who avoids extremes
wins balance, peace, and joy.
(Bhagavad Gita 6:16-17)

PART VI

Creating Perfect Health, Happiness, Vitality, Longevity, and Harmony

6.1 **Journeys of Discovery and Control**

We began our discussion of the 'five essential journeys' of wisdom and wonder in Part IV when we created our Personal Place of Peace and went on to meet our Personal Mentor in Part V with the 2nd essential journey. Here we will experience the 3rd essential journey of Discovery and the 4th essential journey to the Subconscious Control Room of the Unconscious mind-of-the-body. In the next section, we will experience the 5th essential journey and go to the deepest level of mind, the center of our chi, where we will meet our connection to the Source of all things. These processes give us an increased awareness of our personal power, enhance our creativity, and disperse energy blockages.

When heavy-duty emotions are too much for the mind to handle, the body often reacts with pain. We can use Medimaginosis to explore an image that represents the pain, feeling, emotion, or an image of the positive feeling we would like to have. A symptom, resistance, or negative emotion is a signal from within that something needs attention and that something needs to change. In our society, we are programed to run to the doctor or take a pill when we notice a symptom, and while diagnosis and knowing treatment options is important, a symptom is a message from our own system that is trying to tell us something, and we need a way to hear it. Imagery can be a way to get in touch with that symptom, our body, feelings, and spirit by giving them a voice, and dialoguing with them. We can learn to quiet the mind and form images of symptoms, and then fix the picture. We enter the

Subconscious Control Room of the Unconscious mind-of-the-body, observer any mental or physical functions that may need attention on a huge screen, and make adjustments as needed. We allow the body to express itself by asking it to convert any issue into a mental image and speak to us.

6.1.1 Discovery – the 3rd Essential Journey

The 3rd essential journey is the process of discovery. A discovery journey can be used to investigate an issue, topic, subject, feeling, emotion, desire, belief, known, unknown, concern, symptom, resistance, question, uncertainty, confusion, or curiosity. It can be a certain definite thing or a mystery, and a subconscious friendly way to understand our beliefs and how they relate to life. We change the subject matter into an image or symbol because, as an image, it is a little easier to deal with. The journey allows us to investigate the image and find out what we need to know in a comfortable, positive way. A perspective shift helps us see it differently, allows for desensitization of negatives, and builds new positives.

We first go to our Personal Place of Peace and linger for a time, filling our senses and immersing ourselves in the calm relaxation and sensing the security, comfort, and control that is ours. When we are ready, we turn our attention to the object of the 3rd essential journey and set off to find our Place of Discovery. Some people walk along a path in the woods to a beautiful garden, stream, or clearing, while others walk down a hallway that leads to a door marked "Discovery Room." Everyone has a different Place of Discovery, but they can all be equally effective.

After arriving, we make ourselves comfortable, with a cup of our favorite beverage perhaps, and begin to form an image of whatever we need to learn more about. This process is especially helpful for emotions like anger, fear, guilt, grief, and worry because it allows us to recognize them, form an image of them in the safety of our Place of Discovery and begin a dialogue with the image. While in our Place of Discovery, we always feel free to invite our Personal Mentor to join us for support, to help guide the discussion, and to resolve resistance.

The discovery process uses imagery that gives us an opportunity to look at a symptom, problem, thing, or question in a different way, to get closer, view it from a distance, speak to it, get familiar with it, and exchange places with it to see things from its point of view for a better perspective and understanding. The Subconscious is a place that is not restricted by a sense of order, sequence, or time and can be anywhere at any time. We can communicate with it by asking the image to speak, see it from the vantage point of an onlooker watching ourselves, or become immersed as a participant. Learning to communicate with these images can build confidence, take us to a higher level of consciousness, resolve problems, redirect and re-program old inappropriate responses, and fashion new healthier, more suitable functions. We can free up and optimize our beliefs to allow us to create new choices and possibilities.

We start by stating our intention which might be anything from, "form an image of a symptom and ask it what it is trying to tell me" to "form an image of a bad habit and ask it what it needs to morph into a good habit." Then, as usual, we relax, breathe, and begin to shift our awareness from the outside world to our inner world. Using the (5-9-9>1) Rapid Return signal, we go to our Personal Place of Peace where we are calm, comfortable, and relaxed. Then we go to our Place of Discovery and allow an image to form that represents or gives a sense of the thing we wish to explore, accepting whatever image comes whether it is familiar or not. If it seems hostile or scary in any way, we invite our Personal Mentor to join us for support, ideas, and perhaps security or arbitration if needed. We observe the image from as many perspectives as needed to get a clear view and notice what it feels like to be in its presence. Then, with the help of our Personal Mentor, if needed, we begin a dialogue with the image and ask whatever questions are appropriate. We discussed the importance of a simply stated worthy purpose in life in Part III and for those who were unable to complete that task at that time, NOW is the time and place to do that.

Discovery Journey:

a) We first find a time and place where we know we won't be distracted. The time period associated with the (5-7-9) Breath usually works well and the place should be warm, safe, and quiet. We then state our intent (in this case, to form an image of and speak with a symptom or problem), keeping in mind that we all want the same thing in the end. Regardless of current superficial wants and desires, harmony is the real goal. And then, just for a moment, consider that meditation is founded on gratitude, patience, and kindness.

b) Set a timer with a pleasing tone if desired, but most people simply open their eyes long enough to look at a watch or clock and gently return to their focus. Sit in a comfortable but dignified manner with the face, scalp, neck, shoulders, and body relaxed and spine straight. It's important to stay relaxed, yet aware and awake. Some students sit on a pillow with their hips slightly higher than their knees and imagine their spine is a tall, straight tree against which they can lean. Note that meditation can be done in the prone position as well, particularly mindfulness and progressive relaxation, but is more likely to morph into sleep. Meditation requires conscious awareness, not sleep.

c) Focus attention on the breath. With our eyes closed or half closed to reduce distractions, we shift from the outer world to our inner world and maintain focus and awareness on our breath. We take a deep (5-7-9) Breath with a barely audible sigh (ahhhhhh) allowing the jaw and shoulders to relax and a slight smile to form on the out-breath. Then we allow the mind/body to become still and focus our attention on the natural tidal rhythm of the breath, feeling the rise and fall of the inhalation and exhalation without trying to influence it.

d) Scan the mind/body from head to toe and back again for tension or tightness. Invite it to relax as much as it wants to while remaining alert and attentive to the breath in the present moment. Assume a non-judgmental attitude, brush away stray thoughts that cloud concentration, and return to the breath. On the inhale, we gather up tension that we do not need to hold right now, and on each exhale, we release that tension and become more and more relaxed; a real letting go kind of breath. It is often helpful to bring the thumb and forefinger together and notice the sense of touch. When we can feel the thumb touching the forefinger, we know that we are aware and in the present moment.

e) As our focus settles on the breath, we begin to employ the Progressive Relaxation process or the thumb and forefinger Rapid Return signal that we established in a previous journey to our Personal Place of Peace. To begin the Rapid Return process, it helps to sit a little taller and look up as if there was a movie screen on the inside of the forehead. Take a deep Three-Part-Breath to the count of five and hold it for an ascending count from one up to nine while pressing the thumb and forefinger together a little tighter (creating tension) with each ascending number. Then release the tension and the breath to a descending count down from nine to one. With each descending number, our Personal Place of Peace comes into greater and clearer focus, and at "one" we find ourselves basking in the beauty and comfort of our Personal Place of Peace as if we had never left.

f) We sit for a few minutes in this environment becoming one with the breath and soaking up the beauty, serenity, and wonder that is this place. Then, when we are ready, we expand our field of awareness to include our predetermined intent which is to find our Place of Discovery and form an image of whatever we need to learn more about. Some people walk down a hallway and find a door labeled "Discovery Room" or "Place of Discovery" while others follow a path to an area where it seems most conducive to an investigative meeting. It is the most empowering and connected place in all of creation to have an easy, comfortable conversation with the image of a symptom or problem. Most people invite their Personal Mentor to accompany them for support like a wise and intuitive attorney.

g) We then settle into our Place of Discovery and when we feel comfortable and at ease, we allow an image of the symptom or problem to form and let it arise naturally. Welcome the image that comes and get to know it as it is. Let it be what it is for now, but always remember that this is our creation, and we alone have complete control. We visualize, imagine, or simply sense a representative of our predetermined subject, easily and freely bringing the image to life, and let it come forward. Notice how close it is and examine it from multiple angles, floating above it, below it, and all around it. Notice its color, shape, size, and energy using as many senses as possible. Notice how it feels to be in its company.

h) For a deeper understanding, we imagine connecting with it and establish communication. We greet the image and thank it for showing up, tell it how we feel, and let the communication come about naturally. We ask the image what it wants, what matters most to it, and tell the image what we want. Ask the image what needs to happen to improve the situation, or what inappropriate beliefs need to be amended to move forward. We can trade places with it knowing that we can easily trade back to ourselves again anytime. We can become the image and explore its viewpoint, looking into the world and noticing what seems different from this point of view. When we trade back to ourselves again, we take notice of any changes. Allow it to communicate in whatever way seems natural. If there is some uncertainty about the meaning of the message or if there are other questions that need to be asked, continue the conversation until it feels complete. Ask questions, be open to the responses that come back, and consider them carefully. We continue to imagine and visualize being with this image and continuing the conversation as long as we like, exploring the subject in whatever depth feels right, keeping in mind that we can come back again anytime we want.

i) If this is an image that needs to be fixed or modified, this is the time to do it because this is the time it is most receptive to change. If there seems to be a problem or obstacles standing in the way, our Personal Mentor is always available to assist and advise us on how we might deal with it in a healthy, constructive way.

j) When it is time to return to the outside world, we thank the image and our Personal Mentor for meeting with us and say goodbye for now in whatever way seems appropriate. Realizing that we can return and meet with them again whenever the need arises, we return to our Personal Place of Peace where we sit for a moment and contemplate what we have accomplished. We take a big deep cleansing breath IN, and let it go with the images but bring back from this journey the good, the positive and the true. We allow the benefits and what has been most meaningful and important from this journey to become solidified in the Subconscious and prepare to bring it into the conscious outside world to improve every aspect of daily life. Feeling secure and a wonderful sense of well-being, we become more alert and aware in every way. We begin to notice what is going on around us, wiggle our fingers and toes, smile because we feel so good, and move our focus from our inner world to the sounds, smells, shapes and colors around us. Finally, we take a comfortable energizing Three-Part-Breath and open our eyes feeling wide awake, grateful, re-energized, refreshed, happy, and ready for the remainder of the day.

k) Some find it helpful to bring the hands together (the gasho or prayer position) and close the moment with gratitude and reflection. It is helpful to sit still for a moment or two to review the experience and annotate any ideas, visions, or inner guidance received in meditation with the intention of incorporating the benefits into our daily lives. To keep us in the present moment, we continue to keep 25% of our attention on our breath (DSCR) replacing pointless repetitive daydreaming. With the other 75% on what we are doing and what really matters in life, we check in from time to time by asking, "Am I still breathing?"

6.1.2 Control Room – the 4th Essential Journey

The 4th essential journey is a trip to "The Control Room" located deep in the Subconscious mind from which the Unconscious mind-of-the-body receives its orders. This is the place where millions of mind/body functions are miraculously monitored and integrated, and where we learn to operate the controls. Most of these functions are automated, preprogrammed, and function without conscious attention. Some were present at birth, but many more were acquired as a result of perception and experience with the environment. It is our objective to take control of these automated programs and update them in accordance with the life we consciously choose using conscious logic, reason, and balanced judgment that the Subconscious does not have.

If the Control Room is likened to the command post of a vast army, the Conscious mind would be its Commanding General receiving feedback from troops in the field. The Commander does not need to know how to fly an aircraft or calibrate its instruments but has the power to not only control its maintenance schedules but have it flown into combat, grounded, or replaced by a better model. Like the Captain of a huge ocean liner that hosts, feeds and fills the needs of thousands of passengers, the Conscious mind is not the source of power but has the ability to command its crew, control velocity and hold or change its course. Learning how to master our own thoughts and responses is critical but we do not need to know how everything works because the Unconscious mind already knows. As we change the dial settings in the Control Room, the instructions for the change speed to the appropriate areas of need and the changes just happen.

The Control Room directs all physical and mental functions from simple body functions, feelings, and desires to complex processes of internal healing, blood flow, immune cell intervention, behaviors, thoughts and information processing. Emotions like anger, fear, guilt, grief, and worry, can also be adjusted from the Control Room but it seems to be more effective to first recognize them and discuss them with our Personal Mentor and/or form an image of them in our Place of Discovery and initiate a dialogue with them one at a time. Then if an adjustment from the Control Room is needed, it can be included in the next trip.

As with all other journeys, everyone experiences the Control Room differently. Many people imagine or sense a huge monitor or movie screen with thousands of tiny windows around the perimeter. Each tiny window is monitoring a different part of the mind/body and can be moved to the main screen when focus is needed. For example, one can find the screen that represents the immune system, select it, and send it to the main screen by just thinking about it. When it pops up on the main screen, the appropriate controls also move into place allowing us to make adjustments. Our attention is like a guided beam of potentially unlimited energy and intelligence that can be focused and directed to any place that needs healing. It is connected to a Source of Chi energy that is virtually unlimited, and the inner intelligence of the body can put that energy to good use.

Some students find that it is better for them to limit this process to one item per day to concentrate the effect but others find it just as effective to treat a list of problems every day for several days in a row. When we identify another area that needs positive change, we can move our attention to the tiny window on the perimeter of the main screen that is monitoring it. That image then pops up on the main screen, and the controls appear at our fingertips where we will make the adjustments. If it feels right, continue on to other areas that need attention and continue to do this with all the things that need to be modified. Those who choose to work on one problem at a time focus on intensifying the change. Even after our Conscious mind has left the Control Room, the Unconscious mind will continue the process of change in all the important areas associated with our orders. They have become its new program, and controlling physical feelings and functions becomes more and more familiar and responsive with practice. This level of control and greater well-being continues into daily life.

Everyone has a different concept of what the Control Room looks like and the journey below is only one example of what might form. As with the other essential journeys, we have found it to be most effective to begin it from our Personal Place of Peace. With a calm, peaceful mind/body, one might follow a path or a hallway to a special place of empowerment and connection or a room labeled "Control Room." It often helps to invite our Personal Mentor to be there with us to resolve resistance or deal with any questions.

Control Room Journey:

a) We first find a time and place where we know we will not be distracted. The time period associated with the (5-7-9) Breath usually works well and the place should be warm, safe, and quiet. We then state our intent (in this case, to find our Control Room and take control of a symptom or problem), keeping in mind that we all want the same thing in the end. Regardless of current superficial wants and desires, harmony is the real goal. And then, just for a moment, consider that meditation is founded on gratitude, patience, and kindness.

b) Set a timer with a pleasing tone if desired, but most people simply open their eyes long enough to look at a watch or clock and gently return to their focus. Sit in a comfortable but dignified manner with the face, scalp, neck, shoulders, and body relaxed and spine straight. It's important to stay relaxed, yet aware and awake. Some students sit on a pillow with their hips slightly higher than their knees and imagine their spine is a tall, straight tree against which they can lean. Note that meditation can be done in the prone position as well, particularly mindfulness and progressive relaxation, but is more likely to morph into sleep. Meditation requires conscious awareness, not sleep.

c) Focus attention on the breath. With our eyes closed or half closed to reduce distractions, we shift from the outer world to our inner world and maintain focus and awareness on our breath. We take a deep (5-7-9) Breath with a barely audible sigh (ahhhhhh) allowing the jaw and shoulders to relax and a slight smile to form on the out-breath. Then we allow the mind/body to become still and focus our attention on the natural tidal rhythm of the breath, feeling the rise and fall of the inhalation and exhalation without trying to influence it.

d) Scan the mind/body from head to toe and back again for tension or tightness. Invite it to relax as much as it wants to while remaining alert and attentive to the breath in the present moment. Assume a non-judgmental attitude, brush away stray thoughts that cloud concentration, and return to the breath. On the inhale, we gather up tension that we do not need to hold right now, and on each exhale, we release that tension and become more and more relaxed; a real letting go kind of breath. It is often helpful to bring the thumb and forefinger together and notice the sense of touch. When we can feel the thumb touching the forefinger, we know that we are aware and in the present moment.

e) As our focus settles on the breath, we begin to employ the Progressive Relaxation process or the thumb and forefinger Rapid Return signal that we established in a previous journey to our Personal Place of Peace. To begin the Rapid Return process, it helps to sit a little taller and look up as if there was a movie screen on the inside of the forehead. Take a deep Three-Part-Breath to the count of five and hold it for an ascending count from one up to nine while pressing the thumb and forefinger together a little tighter (creating tension) with each ascending number. Then <u>release</u> the tension and the breath to a <u>descending</u> count down from nine to one. With each descending number, our Personal Place of Peace comes into greater and clearer focus, and at "one" we find ourselves basking in the beauty and comfort of our Personal Place of Peace as if we had never left.

f) We sit for a few minutes in this environment becoming one with the breath and soaking up the beauty, serenity, and wonder that is this place. Notice this profound state of relaxation and become aware of how good it feels to take control. Then, when we are ready, we expand our field of awareness to include our predetermined intent which is to find our Control Room and take control of a symptom or problem. Some people follow a path to this secret place where they feel most empowered and connected. Others visualize or imagine walking down a hallway and find a door labeled "Control Room" and when it senses the energy of its own Conscious mind, the door slides open quickly and easily. It often helps to invite our Personal Mentor to be there with us to resolve resistance or deal with any questions.

g) Inside this amazing room, some have found a huge monitor with thousands of tiny windows all around the perimeter of a giant highly sensitive neuro-chemical 3-D screen. Each window around the edges of the main screen is monitoring some function of the mind/body and can be expanded to the main screen if conscious attention is focused on it. The image can zoom in or out, and the view moved around at will. We can choose a part of the mind/body that we want to work with and bring it up on the main screen. We can choose a shoulder, foot, a particular muscle, an organ, feeling, desire, thought, or the process of healing, blood flow, or immune cell intervention. As we focus in on it, the control device that can help us the most right now miraculously appears at our fingertips. It might be a dial, a lever, or some other kind of control device. There might even be an auto-repair button that activates or stimulates repair.

h) As we get a closer look at the control device, we might notice numbers from 1-10 or just low, medium, and high. We notice where the device is currently set and how we feel now. Then we visualize or imagine that we can reach out and turn the control down by half. We can see and sense our hand on the control and, just like turning down the volume on an old radio, we can turn down discomfort, reduce inflammation, increase blood flow, or even direct immune cells to vanquished foreign invaders. Notice the change in comfort level as it is turned down.

266

To test the control, we can turn it back up to the starting point and notice the change. If we can turn it up, we can also turn it down again. The idea of turning it down becomes something that the Subconscious embraces and turning it down becomes easy and effortless. As comfort fills the area, we continue turning it down until it is just the right level and set it there for now. Our Subconscious knows now that we have the ability to use the controls to turn down discomfort for greater relaxation and relief. Now we can let ourselves feel the good qualities of our images and appreciate the inner Control Room for all that it can bring.

i) We can apply this control to any one of the countless monitors around the main screen to cut off the blood supply to a wart, tumor, or other foreign invader. We can dial down a headache, heal a rash, and even shut down harmful gene functions. We do not need to know which genes need to be reconfigured or where they are located because our Unconscious mind-of-the-body already knows.

We can communicate with the Unconscious mind-of-the-body by using affirmations and projecting a detailed 3-D image of our desired result on to the main screen, and it obeys. Repeating the affirmation and holding the image of the desired end result communicates the order to our vast Unconscious mind that knows when to breathe, where to maintain our body temperature, where to send immune cells, how to create a headache, and how to heal a wound. It will begin to create the projected image and automatically shut down gene functions that are detrimental to that objective. It will know which genes or combination of genes are advantageous to that objective and begin to activate those genes that are latent and energize those that are weakening.

j) When it is time to return to the outside world, we express our gratitude and appreciation for this awesome Room and thank our Personal Mentor for assisting. As the feeling of comfort still lingers, recognize the good qualities of these images and the wonder of imagination. We say goodbye for now in whatever way seems appropriate and move back through the doorway as it closes securely behind us. We return to our Personal Place of Peace where we sit for a moment and contemplate what we have accomplished. Realizing that we can return again whenever the need arises, we let the images go and return to the breath. We take a big deep cleansing breath IN, and let it go with the images but bring back from this journey the good, the positive and the true to our conscious outer awake life or outer world. We allow the benefits and what has been most meaningful and important from this journey to become solidified in the Subconscious and prepare to bring it into the conscious outside world to improve every aspect of daily life. Feeling secure and a wonderful sense of well-being, we become more alert and aware in every way. We begin to notice what is going on around us, wiggle our fingers and toes, smile because we feel so good, and move our focus from our inner world to the sounds, smells, shapes and colors around us. Finally, we take a comfortable energizing Three-Part-Breath and open our eyes feeling wide awake, grateful, re-energized, refreshed, happy, and ready for the remainder of the day.

k) Some find it helpful to bring the hands together (the gasho or prayer position) and close the moment with gratitude and reflection. Then they review the experience with the intention of incorporating the benefits into their daily lives. To keep us in the present moment, we continue to keep 25% of our attention on our breath (DSCR) replacing pointless repetitive daydreaming. With the other 75% on what we are doing and what really matters in life, we check in from time to time by asking, "Am I still breathing?"

l) At the end of a meditation session, it is helpful to sit still for a moment or two to review what just happened and annotate any ideas, visions, or inner guidance received in meditation so it can be applied to daily life.

6.2 Journey to the Center of Chi – The Magic of OM

Up to this point, we have been dealing mainly with the mind/body, but the whole human being is a mind/body/soul; one cohesive, synergistic unit that science has only recently acknowledged. What some call Soul, Spirit, Chi, or the very subtle mind, is not yet measurable but it unquestionably exists. By working together, mind, body, and soul form a oneness that is far greater than the various parts. We become one with all that is, and when we are one with all that is, we are never alone. Learning how the mind, body, and spirit work together is one of the most important things we can do to stimulate healing, enhance the quality of life, and evolve as a species. We learned to relax the Ego and put it to sleep, so as to allow conscious messages to pass through the unguarded ego gate and into the deep Subconscious where we learned to control the Unconscious mind-of-the-body. Now we will learn to integrate the power of the OM.

We explained the mind/body in five basic levels; the Conscious Mind, Ego, Subconscious Mind, Unconscious Mind, and the OM. Refer to the diagram in Appendix "B" and the Introduction Section 1.5. The Conscious Mind or self-aware mind is the thinker and is most highly developed in humans. It is our logic, reason, willpower, language, decision maker, and superior judgment. It analyzes the past, imagines the future, can express free will, and is aware of itself and the present. The Ego is like a guard at the gate between the Conscious and Subconscious mind that censors all information in both directions. It acts like it alone represents "I" and wants to be our primary protector. The Subconscious Mind is concerned with all sensory information, emotions, and memory. It acts habitually without conscious thought and runs our lives most of the time. The Unconscious Mind is the mind-of-the-body and is concerned mainly with survival, sex, food, and social acceptance. It has no ulterior motives or will of its own and facilitates all mind/body functions while existing in the dark with only the Subconscious to guide it and tell it what the environment is like and what needs to be done. OM is that very subtle light at the center of our chi (life force energy). It exists in every living cell, radiating in all directions, and is the difference between life and death. OM has been called the Soul or Spirit, and is centered slightly below the physical heart and above the solar plexus at the middle dantian. OM is an extension of the Source of all things and is one's personal connection to a vast, possibly infinite, repository of wisdom made up of incomprehensible, dynamic, constantly changing forms of vibrating energy.

If we could put a living human being into a huge blender and turn it on, we would end up with a soup consisting of all the necessary atoms to make a living person; they would just be rearranged. The great mystery is how these atoms were arranged and blessed with life, intelligence, consciousness, imagination, and a spirit. It reveals our feeble capacity and our need for consultation and guidance from a higher power. We do not need to create life from soup, but we do need help finding a way to live together and function as a whole.

Spirituality is not necessarily tied to any particular belief and requires no outside organization to validate it. Though spirituality is often associated with religion, it does not require religion and belief may or may not be religious. It might even be a belief in a physician, a drug, procedure, or a relationship. In addition to one's belief in a caregiver or a modality, however, there are extra benefits when integrated with belief of a spiritual nature. Whether it is a belief in God or a magic potion, this spirituality appears to be wired into us, is very powerful, and can heal or even kill. Invoking the placebo or nocebo effect with a spiritual passion maximizes physical and mental responses and the degree of belief controls intensity. We will use the inherent power of belief, spirituality, and Benson's Faith Factor to strengthen our resolve, vision, and clarity. The subject of contemplative prayer, however, will be left to the clergy and personal preference because everyone has their own concept of prayer.

When the Conscious mind holds a predetermined intent with a non-judgmental attitude, and the Soul replaces a feeble want or willpower with belief, passion, and determination, the body begins to evolve into the vessel needed to successfully navigate the course and adapt to the environment. The body will evolve naturally on its own, but when an unencumbered conscious intent is energized by the power of the OM, the randomness is replaced with an efficient supercharged adaptation. As far as we know, the genes we are born with is all we have to work with but our OM provides the power to reconfigure the functions of the genes we have.

We can turn off those genes that are detrimental to our intent while activating and energizing advantageous genes or combinations of genes that have been slowing down. Genes that might be associated with cancer, obesity, or immune disorders can be shut down while latent genes or combinations of genes that have been weakening or have never been used can be activated and energized. This is the domain of the Unconscious mind-of the-body, and all it needs is the order from the Control Room and an energizing belief to make it happen. The Conscious mind provides the order (assuming that it gets through the ego gate) and the OM provides the power to evolve mind, body, and soul.

6.2.1 **OM - the 5th Essential Journey**

The 5th essential journey is a gentle adventure into the center of our essence, chi, or life force energy. We call it the OM, but others call it the center of the Soul with a direct connection to the Source of all things. At the center, everything is more balanced. OM is that part of us that is infinite, eternal, and directly connected to all that IS, making us a part of one big harmonious symphony. It is the stillness underneath the mental noise, the love and joy underneath the emotional pain and stress, and our direct line of communication to what some call God. Our OM, Spirt, or Soul, is our life force or essence without which we would be inanimate. By whatever name it is called, OM is that invisible mystery that brings life.

We have learned to communicate with our Subconscious mind and access the Control Room of the Unconscious mind-of-the-body. Now we will learn to communicate with our Soul at an even deeper level and to elicit the aid of a power beyond our comprehension. The most exciting use of deep meditation is to access information and energy from one's higher self and beyond. The ability to consciously alter gene expression by turning off harmful functions and turning on advantageous functions is powered by this phenomenon. All things are possible when the Soul is willing to believe we can. It might require some adaptation, but all things are possible.

OM is not our Personal Mentor. Our Personal Mentor is limited to our subconscious knowledge and natural wisdom while OM has access to all universal wisdom, physical and spiritual, known and unknown, and is directly connected to the Source of all things. OM is omni-dimentional and radiates beyond the body, but originates from a place that is far deeper and is not as accessible as our Personal Mentor. It is the true self at the deepest level and learning to communicate with it gives us the ability to tap into limitless creativity.

Everyone experiences the Medimaginosis journeys differently, but most begin at their Personal Place of Peace where they can best visualize, imagine or sense moving beyond the place where they confer with their Personal Mentor. Then they go deeper than their Place of Discovery, and on past their Control Room where a great bright light can be seen in the distance that seems to be emanating from an even deeper level. It seems to be accessed by a beautiful staircase that descends into the center of Chi. The staircase symbolizes, enhances, and deepens our immersion into the meditative state by associating a greater sense of well-being, calm, comfort, control, love, and compassion, with each descending step. Wonder gives way to a sense of lightness or floating and signals our approach into the deep universal wisdom. Far below the waves of thought, we glimpse a sense that we have entered a deeper reality; a hidden presence that cannot be described but can still be felt. Some feel their entire body light up and begin to glow from within. It is an image and a feeling not unlike invincibility that goes with them throughout their day. No problem or circumstance is unmanageable. There is a sense of unity with all that is and the Source of all things.

At the level of OM, there are no imposters but the journey is deep, and the Conscious mind can be misled into believing that it has arrived or can take a wrong turn that leads to an imposter. The same imposters that impersonate our Personal Mentor and impart negative or harmful advice can show up along the path to the Deep and can be mistaken for our OM. The first clue is that the imposter lacks the compassion, love, and positive energy that fills us when we meet our OM. If it doesn't feel right, it probably isn't. Also, if the journey seems too easy or short, we need to evaluate the advice and make our own decision about whether or not to follow it using logic and the superior judgment of the Conscious mind. We have complete control, and if an image doesn't feel right, we just send it away and continue the journey or vanquish it by replacing it or simply opening our eyes.

Sometimes we ask questions of our OM and receive answers but other times we just enjoy a deep sense of peacefulness and a promise of support. There may be times when our OM may not be willing to give us immediate resolution because it is too soon, it is not the right time, or we are not ready. Like the man who said to the stove, "Give me heat, and then I will put in the wood," it might be that something else needs to happen, or something else needs to be done first. If that is the case, we ask what needs to happen first, and we will usually be put on a road that eventually leads to the resolution we seek.

OM Journey:

a) We first find a time and place where we know we will not be distracted. The time period associated with the (5-7-9) Breath usually works well and the place should be warm, safe, and quiet. We then state our intent (in this case, to journey to the deepest level of self and meld with the greatest power that mankind has ever known). Preparing to meet our OM is like preparing for an audience with a messenger from God and should not be taken lightly. Then, just for a moment, consider that meditation is founded on gratitude, patience, and kindness.

b) Set a timer with a pleasing tone if desired, but most people simply open their eyes long enough to look at a watch or clock and gently return to their focus. Sit in a comfortable but dignified manner with the face, scalp, neck, shoulders, and body relaxed and spine straight. It's important to stay relaxed, yet aware and awake. Some students sit on a pillow with their hips slightly higher than their knees and imagine their spine is a tall, straight tree against which they can lean. Note that meditation can be done in the prone position as well, particularly mindfulness and progressive relaxation, but is more likely to morph into sleep. Meditation requires conscious awareness, not sleep.

c) Focus attention on the breath. With our eyes closed or half closed to reduce distractions, we shift from the outer world to our inner world and maintain focus and awareness on our breath. We take a deep (5-7-9) Breath with a barely audible sigh (ahhhhhh) allowing the jaw and shoulders to relax and a slight smile to form on the out-breath. Then we allow the mind/body to become still and focus our attention on the natural tidal rhythm of the breath, feeling the rise and fall of the inhalation and exhalation without trying to influence it.

d) Scan the mind/body from head to toe and back again for tension or tightness. Invite it to relax as much as it wants to while remaining alert and attentive to the breath in the present moment. Assume a non-judgmental attitude, brush away stray thoughts that cloud concentration, and return to the breath. On the inhale, we gather up tension that we do not need to hold right now, and on each exhale, we release that tension and become more and more relaxed; a real letting go kind of breath. It is often helpful to bring the thumb and forefinger together and notice the sense of touch. When we can feel the thumb touching the forefinger, we know that we are aware and in the present moment.

e) As our focus settles on the breath, we begin to employ the Progressive Relaxation process or the thumb and forefinger Rapid Return signal that we established in a previous journey to our Personal Place of Peace. To begin the Rapid Return process, it helps to sit a little taller and look up as if there was a movie screen on the inside of the forehead. Take a deep Three-Part-Breath to the count of five and hold it for an ascending count from one up to nine while pressing the thumb and forefinger together a little tighter (creating tension) with each ascending number. Then release the tension and the breath to a descending count down from nine to one. With each descending number, our Personal Place of Peace comes into greater and clearer focus, and at "one" we find ourselves basking in the beauty and comfort of our Personal Place of Peace as if we had never left.

f) We sit for a few minutes in this environment becoming one with the breath and soaking up the beauty, serenity, and wonder that is this place. Notice this profound state of relaxation and become aware of how good it feels to take control. Then, when we are ready, we expand our field of awareness to include our predetermined intent which is to journey to the deepest level of self and elicit a power beyond the comprehension of mankind. We visualize, imagine or sense moving beyond the place where we confer with our Personal Mentor, past our Place of Discovery, and beyond our Control Room where a great bright light can be seen in the distance. It seems to be emanating from a deeper level and is accessed by a beautiful staircase.

g) As we get closer, the image gets clearer, and standing at the top of the staircase, we feel calm, safe, comfortable, and in control. We notice the staircase in more detail, and the great bright light below seems warmer and more inviting. We visualize, imagine, or sense a set of ten stairs covered with a thick, fluffy white carpet that is like a cloud beneath the feet and perhaps a brass handrail or walnut banister. The great bright light beckons and although the source is not yet visible, we intuitively know the stairs lead to a very safe magnificent place. It is a staircase that takes us deeper into this quiet, serene, inner place and into the center of Chi as we feel ourselves descending the ten softly carpeted stairs. We associate each step with a greater sense of well-being, relaxation, calm, comfort, control, love, and compassion. 10...9 deeper and more relaxed, 8...7 easily and naturally, 6...5 deeper and more comfortably at ease, 4...3 the mind is quiet and still, but alert, 2...and...1 At the bottom of the stairs, we become aware that we are in the presence of a vast infinite love. Some see what might resemble an angel, a soft-spoken figure with a gentle smile that radiates truth, kindness, and gratitude, or a warm brilliant light, but all feel a deep sense of love and compassion from the image. It is that part of "We" that loves us unconditionally.

h) With great reverence, we express our gratitude for the opportunity to unite mind, body, and soul in dialogue and synergistic harmony; to coordinate conscious intent with spiritual energy. Our OM radiates a warm, deep sense of love and is pleased to finally meet and communicate directly. Although OM already knows what we want to say, we communicate our predetermined intent which might be to heal an affliction, evolve from stress to gratitude, or manifest perfect health, happiness, vitality, longevity, and harmony. We explain our reason for the request which might be to better provide for our family, to facilitate and energize our worthy objective, or to promote harmony in specific ways. If the request is truly associated with a worthy objective and is not from hostility or negativity, OM will reply with instructions as to what we need to do next, and provide the power of intense belief, passion, and enthusiasm to our actions. As a united force, mind, body, and soul work together at a dramatically increased level to manifest our worth objective with the ultimate objective of harmony firmly in mind.

i) We continue our conversation for as long as we like, asking questions and resolving potential problems. We begin to understand that we now have an invincible ally that is an integral part of the team and is always with us, ready to guide and energize the mind/body/soul as a far more powerful unit.

j) When it is time to return to the outside world, we express our gratitude and appreciation for this experience and as the feeling of comfort still lingers, we say goodbye for now in whatever way seems appropriate and begin to ascend the staircase. We return to our Personal Place of Peace where we sit for a moment and contemplate what we have experienced. Realizing that we can return again whenever the need arises, we let the images go, and return to the breath. We take a big deep cleansing breath IN, and let it go with the images but bring back from this journey the good, the positive and the true to our conscious outer awake life or outer world. We allow the benefits and what has been most meaningful and important from this journey to become solidified in the Subconscious and prepare to bring it into the conscious outside world to improve every aspect of daily life. Feeling secure and a wonderful sense of well-being, we become more alert and aware in every way. We begin to notice what is going on around us, wiggle our fingers and toes, smile because we feel so good, and move our focus from our inner world to the sounds, smells, shapes and colors around us. Finally, we take a comfortable energizing Three-Part-Breath and open our eyes feeling wide awake, grateful, re-energized, refreshed, happy, and ready for the remainder of the day.

k) Some find it helpful to bring the hands together (the gasho or prayer position) and close the moment with gratitude and reflection. Then they review the experience with the intention of incorporating the benefits into their daily lives. To keep us in the present moment, we continue to keep 25% of our attention on our breath (DSCR) replacing pointless repetitive daydreaming. With the other 75% on what we are doing and what really matters in life, we check in from time to time by asking, "Am I still breathing?"

l) At the end of a meditation session, it is helpful to sit still for a moment or two to review what just happened and annotate any ideas, visions, or inner guidance received in meditation so it can be applied to daily life.

6.3 Thought and Belief to Doing and Being

Marcus Aurelius, the great Roman Emperor, said, "A man's life is what his thoughts make of it," Shakespeare wrote, "There is nothing either good or bad, but thinking makes it so," and James Allen wrote, "As a man thinks, so is he." Our physical universe is built on the foundation of thought, and all stress is created by our thoughts and will not come to us without our consent. Everything of Man is and was created through thought, belief, and meaningful action.

Belief is fundamental to our evolution from stress to gratitude, and absolutely essential in learning to consciously control the mind/body and alter gene expression. When thought and meaningful action are energized by the emotion inherent in spirituality or fervent belief, super-human events can occur. Enthusiasm wanes after a time but a passion sustained by belief and an "I Can" attitude is a glowing ember that endures and is available to reignite the flames of enthusiasm again at any time. Like the little engine that could, we can reach our objectives by focusing on a worthy purpose that is powered by an intense belief. "I think I can, I think I can." The drive and energy that fuels motivation is the emotion of belief and when that energy is applied to the realization of a worthy purpose, the mind/body is at its happiest and most fit.

Ralph Waldo Emerson wrote that nothing great has ever been achieved without enthusiasm. At the height of creative activity fueled by enthusiasm, there will be enormous intensity and energy behind what we do. We feel like an arrow moving toward our target and enjoying the journey. When enthusiasm tempered by an attitude of Gratitude, Patience, and Kindness encounters obstacles in the form of adverse situations or uncooperative people, it does not attack rather it turns the opposing energy into an asset, accepts and adapts to it by altering its own perception or steps around them.

What people believe about themselves is extremely important, and a deeper spiritual belief is more powerful than most people know. In a study conducted at the University of Texas, elderly people were asked before they underwent heart bypass operations whether they drew strength and comfort from their religious or spiritual faith. The study showed that those who answered "no" were three times more likely to die in the six months after surgery. Along with administering proper medical treatments, a good physician respects, and is able to mobilize, the invisible, intangible aspects of healing that come from belief, trust, and forces beyond our current understanding.

Some people do not believe in a spiritual entity, but they can still believe in science and the proven power of their own body to heal more effectively when they believe it can. A growing body of challenging modern research shows that our thoughts, beliefs, prayers, spirituality, and passion have significant effects on health and quality of life. An increase in spirituality grounds us in positive dynamism and purges negativity which can have a positive impact on all that we do and all that we are. We are not interested in promoting one religious system over another; we are concerned with the scientifically observable phenomena and forces that accompany thought, belief, spirituality, passion, and the resulting actions.

Passion is a heart and soul feeling that produces the enthusiasm and energy that is the source of our finest moments. It is the power that can transform a mental blueprint into the physical dimension but without action, it is incomplete and wasted. Rather than sitting around fanaticizing about how nice it would be if we could find a way to make it happen, we make a plan, imagine its fulfillment, apply passion, and act. Plans begin as thoughts and then with action driven by passion, they manifest physically. A dream is just a fantasy without subconscious acceptance and action. Medimaginosis can direct the Unconscious mind-of-the-body to manifest psychophysiological evolution, but conscious action is required to effect the outside world. Feel the power that comes from absorbing, controlling, and focusing the energy of passion. Action fuels even more passion. The more action one takes toward a worthy purpose, the more passion one feels for it.

Everyone has a spiritual belief system, even if it is that "there is no such thing as spirit." Defining and following a personal spiritual path can change one's life, relationships, ability to love, and overall health, as well as providing the power needed to evolve. It is not enough to use willpower or just to have a weak superficial belief. Ardent belief trumps willpower every time. People have to make the conscious link between a heartfelt belief and their objective for the magic to happen. But first, we may need to cultivate the receptiveness needed by opening and quieting the mind. Meditative practices that are thousands of years old teach us to quiet the mind and the body through methods that are highly effective yet gentle and that use attention and imagination more than willpower to create the growth we desire.

Meditation, imagery, and belief are quite effective on their own but when combined, produce a synergistic result not unlike like combining 2 + 3 + 4 to equal 67. Like gravity, Medimaginosis will have strong positive physiological effects whether the practitioner understands how it works or not. Focusing on a deep positive belief powered by the passion and energy provided by OM enhances evolution dramatically. It enhances states of health and well-being and quiets worries and fears significantly better than meditation alone. The process becomes very natural and produces not only the physiological effect but helps us make a more powerful contact with our spiritual beliefs. Those who affirm profound beliefs directed by a quiet creative mind have exhibited incredible physical and mental powers, and the limits of their potential currently seem boundless.

Sometimes people know that they need to make a change and believe in the worthiness of their purpose but see too many complications and feel overtaken by inertia. William James of Harvard University wrote, "We need only in cold blood act as if the thing in question were real, and it will become infallibly real by growing into such a connection with our life that it will become real." What he was saying is that if we want to feel happier, act happier. If we want to feel more confident, act more confident. There is a back-and-forth relationship between cause and effect. We can "fake" our emotions to kick-start them for real. When we act out the change we want, before we know it the change will be real.

It is not helpful to spend time bemoaning the current situation and wishing for more stuff; we need to do something every day to bring worthy objectives and desired qualities into the present. We do not worry about whether we are doing it exactly right, but if one wants to evolve, it needs to be done. There is no TRY, just do it or not. Our thoughts are powerful, especially when energized by emotion, but it is what we do with them that moves the outside world. The world steps aside for those who know where they are going.

6.4 Perfect Health, Happiness, Vitality, Longevity, and Harmony

With consistent practice, Medimaginosis can enable the Conscious mind to alter perceptions and habits related to every aspect of life including stress, sleep, food, and physical activity as it takes control of the mind/body and gene expression. Those who refuse to find time for improving the mind/body will sooner need to find time for illness. Meditation does not replace a good night's sleep or physical activity, but it does reduce the amount of sleep a person requires and helps us to shed those unwanted pounds much easier and more effortlessly. It instructs the Unconscious mind to regulate hormones and metabolism by sending it a healthy mind/body image. If such problems as body weight or insomnia become troublesome, Medimaginosis provides the means to visit the Discovery Room and have a chat with an image of the problem and/or discuss it with a Personal Mentor. We can ask an image of insomnia what it needs to morph into peaceful, comfortable sleep, or we can ask an image representing a weight problem what it needs to create a strong, healthy body.

Improving our outer world starts by improving our inner world. When we have a healthy image of our mind/body, the Unconscious will automatically create it relentlessly correcting unhealthy habits. We can imagine how good it feels to wash a flat stomach in the shower and evolve to conform to our new self-image. A healthy diet, physical activity, and sound sleep are just a part of the person we become. Our mind and body are our most precious possessions, and their health is our most valuable asset. Treat them with care. Eubie Blake once said, "If I knew I was going to live this long, I would have taken better care of myself."

Avoid obsessive thoughts of diet or exercise and focus on an image of health. When a worthy objective is visualized, imagined, or sensed in great detail, there is no room for a compulsive obsession with food or exercise. Healthy eating and activity habits will just naturally fall into place. If the mind thinks it is healthy, it will just naturally do what a healthy person does. "I am a healthy person, and a healthy person would not eat that" or "If I was a smoker, I would have a cigarette here, but I am a non-smoker now, and I feel good about that."

With a positive mental image, diet, physical activity, and sound sleep will <u>naturally</u> become a part of life to the extent that they are needed to produce the image. The Subconscious will begin to observe the beauty of our world more mindfully and find activity enjoyable whether it is swimming, dancing, hiking, walking, yoga or Tia Chi. Like a puppy, happy, healthy people are playful and active. They do not mope around, pout, ruminate, criticize, and complain. They begin to see colorful, healthy fruit as desirable and enjoy the smell of a fresh cantaloupe. Junk food begins to taste too salty, sit heavy in the stomach, and just feel wrong. Be aware, however; it will still smell really good, even though it is literally poison for a healthy evolving person. For best results, food should not be a source of entertainment, but activity should be.

To assist this process, we can consciously do a few things that are more compatible with our image. We can create an environment in the home or office that makes it feel secure, safe, and balanced. We can eat healthy, stay active, and live within our income. We need to live within our means and feel the relief it brings, make time to love, and feel the harmony of a balanced life. Remember that a job or even an occupation is not one's life, rather it is only one of many temporary tools used to build a happy, harmonious life. Leaving our job at the workplace frees us to pursue a real life and practice using some of the other tools. We do not allow it to take over our entire life.

Decorate with healthy live plants, cheerful colors, pictures, and uplifting objects to relieve stress and create a soothing environment. Wilted flowers and plants, clutter and drab surroundings represent tension. An organized living or working space promotes calmness and peace. Arrange furniture to facilitate easy access without bumping into things (feug shui) removing as many sharp objects and corners as possible. When everything is in order and we can find what we need without feeling rushed, it facilitates a feeling of peace. Scents or aromatherapy can also be used to improve an environment, complement comfort, and enhance a good mood, or reverse a bad one.

Research has long shown that music can enhance health, brain power, and a sense of well-being. This phenomenon is known as "The Mozart Effect." Much of Mozart's music mimics the rhythmic pulses of Alpha brainwaves, known to be experienced during meditation, a creative act, or relaxation and has been shown to improve concentration. Instead of watching TV for hours, spend some time listening to beautiful music while relaxing, working on a hobby, or enjoying the company of family or friends.

Life is a great adventure of curiosity and wonder if we can keep it simple and mindfully live all the days of our lives. Have fun, be happy, and play nice with the other kids. Take a fun walk. Look up and out, breathe deeply and enjoy the view. Our bodies are marvelous self-healing mechanisms constantly busy with self-repair and greater balance. They want to be lean, clean, healing machines that deserve TLC, and we need to practice loving ourselves and all the life around us.

6.4.1 Stress, Mirth, and Restful Sleep

A program for reducing stress needs to cultivate the desire for independence and control of one's own destiny and foster a willingness to re-engineer one's perceptions, beliefs, and actions. We learned that we need to Stop, Smile, Breathe (DSCR), and say Thank You when stress strikes suddenly and to Slow down, Simplify and be Grateful, Patient, and Kind when chronic stress builds. But the greatest tool we have is meditation because it can help us loosen our Inflexible Perceptions and take control of our mind, our body, and our entire life. Harmony and stress are states of mind and so their causes are not to be found outside the mind. Our problems do not exist outside our minds.

When we have bills to pay, a family to feed and a job that we hate, we are not stressed because of the circumstances, we are stressed because we think we cannot pay the bills, feed our family or see our job getting any better. No person, situation, or event can make us feel badly without our permission, but many people still think that their happiness is contingent upon external circumstances and situations, rather than upon their own inner attitude toward things, or toward life in general. And blaming others for our problems just makes them worse. If we refuse to give the outside world our permission, we are the master of our own reality.

The world can get to us, but only if we let it. We need to take a moment to breathe, think "Slow down, Simplify, and be Gratitude, Patience, and Kind," and then return to reality more balanced and centered. Research has shown that people who practice the "Slow down, Simplify, and be Grateful, Patent, and Kind" technique actually accomplish more than those who are stuck in high gear. Take some time to sharpen the axe, have real fun with loved ones and enjoy life. Naturally serious people in particular need to be playful and silly sometimes to avoid letting little things get them down in a big way. It's easy, even a child can do it.

Adults just don't laugh enough. Laughter is one of the best emotional and physical therapies for anyone under stress and one of the best ways to connect with other people. In a difficult situation, a sense of humor can help everyone keep a positive outlook, and just a little bit of shared happiness can help lift moods and improve self-esteem. Laughing releases happy endorphins into the brain that serve to reduce harmful chemicals in the mind/body that are stress-related. There are some times that do call for seriousness, but most of the time, a little laughter seasoned with Gratitude, Patience, and Kindness can be quite beneficial. When everyone is thinking the worst or feeling anxious about a situation, laughter can dissipate tension just enough to give them a more manageable perspective on an issue. Serious issues deserve a focused approach but whenever laughter can be introduced, the resulting release of tension can be a tremendous opportunity to lift the mood, clarify minds, and lead to more open communication. We can then think more effectively about solutions for the problem at hand. A simple smile can make a huge difference in stress levels even over the phone; people will hear it.

Getting in touch with nature is also a wonderful way to reduce stress and create peace. Trees and greenery, clouds passing overhead and stargazing have a very soothing effect on people, calm the sole, and lower blood pressure. Imagine being surrounded by gentle green foliage and a soft blue sky. These colors are known to be very relaxing. Watching fish in as fish tank or waves lap on shore are simple pleasures that can help us live longer and enjoy it more. Visit a local zoo or a pet shop and watch the fish as they gently swim through the water. Almost any body of water can have a calming effect on stressed people. The sight and sound of a fountain in a city park can melt away tension and provide the opportunity to take a Three-Part-Breath and relax. Go swimming, or at least wading in shoulder deep water. Water calms the mind and the buoyancy relieves physical stress pent up in the muscles. At the end of a stressful day, water can be even more relaxing than music, but together it's bliss.

Many studies have shown that the therapeutic nature of touch is far more powerful than many people realize. Even petting a kitten or a friendly touch of the hand can reduce stress and stimulate the immune system. Gently touching the lips with one or two fingers is a technique that often helps to initiate relaxation. The lips contain a large number of parasympathetic nerve fibers and touching them can produce relaxation and an instant calm. Touch relieves pain by stimulating nerve endings and a hug is a great anti-depressant. In one interesting study, librarians lightly touched the hands of some students as they handed back their library cards and avoided touching others. The students who had been touched reported feelings that were more positive about the librarians, themselves, and the library. The Subconscious mind picked up on the briefest contact which most of the students did not even recall. A hug is a transfer of positive energy and always makes a difference. According to scientists, hugging stimulates the vagus nerve in the middle of the chest. (The vagus nerve is the tenth cranial nerve and interfaces with parasympathetic control of the heart, lungs, upper digestive tract, and other organs of the chest and abdomen.) Hugging someone or even a pet strengthens the immune system and promotes positive feelings.

To turn lunch time into a healthier stress-buster, one can make a healthy smoothie the night before and take it to work in a thermos the next morning. When it's time for lunch, relax for a few minutes with a (5-7-9) Breath, half of the healthy drink, a piece of fruit, carrot sticks and celery, instead of chips, soda, and a processed meat sandwich. Then take a meditation walk as described at the end of Section 3.3, return refreshed, and finish the healthy drink with a smile and a calm mind at peace.

Sound, restful sleep is as important as healthy food and activity, but it is sometimes elusive to people who think about stressful moments over and over again or worry about things over which they have no control. Focusing on the breath and thinking "Deeper, Slower, Calmer, Regular" replaces re-runs of the day's events and pointless repetitive thoughts. The (5-7-9) Breathing technique and/or Progressive Relaxation can often morph into sleep but if results are not immediate or seem to have little effect, do not give up. To form a subconscious habit, establish a routine using some of the techniques in this section, and practice that routine consistently for several nights. Eventually, the Subconscious will get the idea, create a program (or habit), and calm, peaceful sleep will just happen as it should. Sleep problems will happen less and less often until they are no longer a concern.

Avoid watching negative or violent TV programs before going to bed and mute the commercials because they are designed to get us excited about their products, not induce sleep. It is helpful to take a warm bath, create a dark, comfortable environment for sleep to encourage the production of melatonin, and go to bed at about the same time every night. Get comfortable with a cup of caffeine free herbal tea that has been shown to induce calm, and annotate the gratitude journal discussed in Part III. We have suggested that people do something nice for someone every day, tell no one about it, and write down their feelings about that before they go to bed. Then if sleep is still elusive, plan a good deed for tomorrow and go to bed with that deed in mind. Such thoughts have been linked to sounder sleep and better dreams. An attitude of Gratitude, Patience, and Kindness brought up from the deepest level with Medimaginosis is a powerful antidote for all forms of adversity. Adults who frequently feel grateful sleep more soundly, are more physically active, and have greater resistance to all forms of illness.

6.4.2 **Diet**

Diet seems to be an area of much controversy because of the many claims and weight loss theories being sold by so many different gurus, but eating right does not have to be complicated or even a project. An effective diet might be as basic as substituting a piece of fruit or an activity of some kind for snacking on unhealthy food. It could be something as simple as mindfully eating the foods that we know are good for us and limiting the bad stuff. Varying one's diet and replacing white foods with more colorful foods has also been shown to be a simple, effective strategy. There are so many micronutrients, vitamins, and minerals that we cannot expect to get everything we need by eating the same things all the time. If a diet does not contain enough of an essential nutrient, the body will be slower to send the 'full' signal to the brain and may even ask for more until it gets what it needs.

When the Medimaginosis program is practiced regularly, a healthy diet and activity level just seem to fall into balance as a natural part of the lifestyle. With a healthy mental image, we simply feel like eating properly and in proportion to our activity level without obsessing over it or even giving it any thought at all. We find that both diet and exercise simply fall in line with our image of balance and harmony.

Unless a person is training for a bodybuilding contest or the Olympics, they probably already know enough about nutrition to maintain good health. Most people know that no unhealthy person is unhealthy because he or she eats too many fruits and vegetables and that there is no sane diet that tells us that eating doughnuts and chips is the way to a healthier body. The problem is not usually a lack of knowledge; it is usually Inflexible Perceptions, habits, and mental attitudes. Generally, we already know what is good for us and what is not but if we need to learn more, our new perspectives make further research interesting and enjoyable. Because there is no shortage of available information about either subject, there is no need to include it in a book about stress management and conscious control of psychophysiology. That said, we have a few tips that may be if interest.

Sometimes we don't even remember what we ate, not to mention the quantity or even the taste. When it is time to eat, turn off the TV, sit down, slow down, breath, and use temperance in all things. Mindfully savoring two or three bites is more satisfying than mindlessly gobbling down the entire serving and wondering where it went. When we savor our food and eat mindfully, we eat much less and enjoy it far more. The brain lags behind the stomach in that there is a delay between the intake of food and the brain receiving the chemical signal that it is full and that we need to stop eating. It does not get a 'full' signal until there is a change in body chemistry and that takes time. The 'full feeling' is supposed to tell us when we have had enough to eat, but if we eat too fast and in large bits, we can eat way past our calorie needs before the brain realizes it. Chewing and eating more slowly in a mindful manner gives the brain time to get the message in a timelier fashion resulting in a more satisfied feeling. Mindlessly scarfing down whatever is in fount of us while watching TV or on the run is a recipe for indigestion, gastrointestinal disorders, hypertension, and obesity.

People sometimes unknowingly get an overabundance of calories by drinking them so it is always a good idea to read labels or stick to water and green or white tea flavored only with fruit if anything at all. Eating mindfully and drinking a glass or two of water before meals will trigger the 'full feeling' sooner and help balance weight. Our cells and vital organs crave water to keep them running smoothly and sipping water during the day can help keep skin healthy, bowels moving regularly, and muscles energized. And avoid drinking alcohol in any form to unwind. Alcohol is for social lubrication and then only in conscious moderation. To unwind, we substitute alcohol with herbal tea, warm milk or some other beverage without sugar or caffeine. A simple breathing exercise, a soothing non-alcoholic beverage, good music, yoga, and/or meditation will be just as effective, is more satisfying, and avoids the toxic aftershock of alcohol.

When we are watching TV for information or entertainment, we avoid watching violence and negativity, mute the commercials, and use the time to practice breathing. It is the advertiser's job to make us want their product. Most commercials contain subliminal or subconscious suggestions that are designed to make us think we need their product, especially pharmaceuticals and fast food. Food commercials are designed to make us want to eat their food and pharmaceutical companies try to make us own "your" disease and believe that we simply must have the product. Muting TV commercials and using the time to do something mindful or just observe our breath brings the mind back to the present and balance. Now is good. It provides an opportunity to think and ask, "Is there something else I could be doing that would be more fulfilling?"

Before a meal gets out of control and we start eating mindlessly, we Stop, Smile, and Breathe (DSCR) with gratitude. It is not a sudden attack of stress yet but if we do not get mindless, unconscious eating under control it will be a stress problem later. Some people find that doing the (5-7-9) Breath or going for a mindful walk using the walking meditation chant is even more helpful. If after doing the (5-7-9) Breath, and perhaps the walking meditation chant, one still feels that they cannot live without eating more food, then go ahead and eat something healthy in a mindful manner. At least the decision to eat more is a conscious one and not a primitive unconscious impulse.

6.4.3 Exercise

Exercise programs tend to be just as controversial as diets because there is such a huge market, and all the self-appointed experts have to find a way to be unique, but exercise can also be simple. The average person just needs to do a few basic stretches every day, choose a few simple aerobic moves that maintain or improve flexibility and strength, and find an enjoyable activity. It is important to make them fun and do them at least four or five times a week. Remember that there's a difference between good health and maximum performance.

Enjoy a swim, walk briskly, ride a bicycle, do aerobics, play tennis, play basketball, or other fun activity. Doing stressful exercise has no positive impact on longevity and, in fact, it has a negative impact because it increases the probability of injury. As many former athletes have discovered, when a vigorous exercise program is abruptly stopped without changing eating habits, it results in atrophy and fat buildup. An overzealous exercise program is often worse than no plan at all. It is easy to overdo it, injure oneself or become discouraged because it is difficult, painful, or shows little immediate results. Unless one is training for a physical event, a simple program that is enjoyable is the best. Doing something that is fun and enjoyable is more likely to become a healthy habit than a difficult, painful exercise program. It is best to have an exercise program that can be done in some form at any age, and when we cultivate gratitude for our mind/body, it will do pretty much everything we require.

The terms "lose weight" or "weight loss" imply that we have lost something, and the Subconscious usually wants to find things that we have lost, like our wallet, purse, or keys, so we prefer to use terms like "weight management," "weight reduction," or "balance" instead. Another word that we usually avoid is "exercise." For many people it has a "no pain, no gain" connotation and that is NOT what we need for Perfect Health, Happiness, Vitality, Longevity, and Harmony. We prefer the word "activity." It is about halfway between an Olympic athlete and couch potato, or maximum performance and atrophy, and is geared toward balance and whatever is most conducive to longevity. Professional athletes have no better chance of living past the age of 100 than couch potatoes. It is usually safest in the middle, no matter what the subject. Few people who live beyond the age of 100 have ever been famous athletes, bodybuilders, extreme health nut, or come from a long line of 100-year-old relatives. They are, however, almost always Grateful, Patient, Kind and adaptable.

Moderate activity releases endorphins which foster a feeling of well-being. In a study carried out by Duke University in North Carolina, it was found that moderate activity is a more effective treatment for depression than antidepressants. In addition, there are fewer relapses and a higher recovery rate. A trimmer, healthier body also develops self-esteem and confidence. For the most part, we rely on the image of a happy, healthy, calm mind at peace to guide our decisions regarding weight. We see an image of a strong, lean, clean, healing machine that glows but a few easy-to-follow tips will augment that tactic.

Remember the magic of incremental steps discussed in Part I. Start by doing small things like taking the stairs or walking to the store down the street, instead of taking the car. Taking a walk in natural surroundings has a soothing effect on the mind, and it has been shown that brisk walking for 30 minutes a day (3-4 times a week) energizes the immune system, cuts the risk of diabetes dramatically, and is easier on the joints than jogging. Make special efforts to experience the joys and beauties of nature. Use as many senses as possible to notice things. Anyone who has ever walked through a pine tree forest knows the awesome spiritual power inherent in the great outdoors. Some people prefer aerobic exercise such as dancing, swimming, or cycling and those who prefer the company of others can sign up for a calming yoga class or Tai Chi. Both yoga and Tai Chi improve lower back and abdominal muscles which gives a feeling of balance and control. The movements require control of both mind and body, and the physical sense translates into emotional balance.

Tai Chi was invented by a Taoist monk in the 13th century and has gained thousands of admirers in the West who practice this gentle exercise to reduce stress, improve health, balance the emotions, and extend youth. The technique consists of slow and continuous bodily movements done preferably in open spaces since it is based on the Taoist philosophy of being in harmony with nature and going with the universal flow. In China, Tai Chi is practiced outdoors during sunrise or sunset and is believed to strengthen the weak, raise the sick, invigorate the debilitated, and encourage the timid. Every part of the body is used, and there are no negative side effects.

How we think or perceive our mind/body may be the single biggest factor in whether we can successfully reach and maintain a healthy weight, according to a new study in the journal Health Education and Behavior. Those of us who think their weight is predetermined by genetics are far more likely to fall into behaviors that encourage weight gain. Researchers say that those who believe the power to perfect weight lies within are the ones who get in shape. The fact is, our weight is determined in large part by the action of our genes, but how those genes behave is determined primarily by our perceptions and lifestyle choices. People are not born to be fat or born to be thin. When a member of a culture genetically prone to being thin is suddenly transplanted into a culture of people who are generally overweight, the transplanted person often accepts the perceptions and habits of the new culture and begins to gain weight.

A study of just under nine thousand men and women found that those who believe that weight is outside of their control have less healthy BMIs, make poorer food choices, avoid activity, and report lower levels of personal well-being than those who do not. They engage in more behaviors that are rewarding in the short term, rather than healthful behaviors with more long-term benefits for weight management. The researchers found that as people get older, the belief that weight is determined by inherited genes is associated with less healthy eating behavior, less activity, and eating more frozen meals, restaurant meals, and ready-to-eat foods. For example, as people age, they are less likely to examine food nutrition labels and to make fruits and vegetables available at home. Practicing Medimaginosis helps us maintain focus and sustain a healthy mind/body image.

6.5 **(5-7-9) Integration**

We have found that experienced practitioners of Medimaginosis can combine their twice daily (5-7-9) Breath with a simple Tia Chi move and manifest a short affirmation at the same time. Unlike multitasking, it combines conscious mindful awareness (monitoring the count) with subconscious physical movements (steps 5 thru 8) and mind/body/soul BEING, or literally becoming one of the Principles of Harmony (Grateful, Patient, Kind, etc.) arranged in a pyramid to make it easier to follow. It requires a high degree of awareness, control, and focus, but takes less than 3 minutes and has many benefits.

We do a warm-up by relaxing with the (DSCR) Breath followed by a recitation of the affirmation pyramid in a single out-breath while executing a simple, graceful body move. After the warm-up, the main event starts at the "at rest" position 4, moves to three other positions and returns to the "at rest" position 8. Position 4 and 8 are the same. We raise the arms in a circular motion to the fully extended horizontal position 5 expanding the lungs as we breathe IN for a count of five, HOLD the breath for a count of seven while moving the arms up as high as we can reach, continuing the circle to position 6. As the hands cross paths, bring them straight down the center of the body (as shown in position 7) to facilitate intercostal contraction as we breathe OUT to a count of nine. The object is to draw IN good things (the affirmation) with the breath, HOLD it there allowing it to become a part of our BEING while breaking up and replacing negative energy, and then draw it down through the body permeating every cell with the OUT breath. It is helpful to make a copy of the following two figure, enlarge them, and tape them to a wall just above eye level so that they can be used to focus on each individual step, or affirmation, one at a time. Both figures are also in the Appendix section of Part VII.

(5-7-9) Position Chart

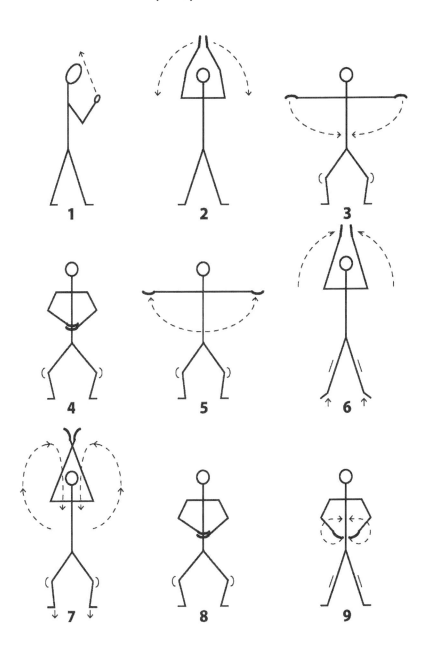

DSCR

1) Grateful

2)   Patient

3)   Kind

4)   Happy

5)   Healthy

6)   Calm Mind at Peace

7) Balance & Harmony w/t Universe

8) Evolve Perfect Health, Happiness, Vitality, Longevity, and Harmony

For those who are unable to physically complete the exercise as shown in the figure, the word is "Adapt." The moves can be done from a chair or even lying down with personal modifications.

Steps 1 thru 4 are done consciously; then the Conscious mind moves to the task of monitoring the count, and the Subconscious mind takes over the task of executing physical moves of step 5 thru 8 automatically, as it would walking or riding a bicycle. While the Conscious mind is monitoring the count and mindfully coordinating the IN – HOLD – OUT breath, the Subconscious mind is running the preprogrammed movements and visually observing the printed word in the pyramid (affirmation). Seeing the word triggers subconscious feelings and images that it sends to the Unconscious mind-of-the-body for manifestation. We literally begin to BECOME the affirmation. After the Conscious mind has finished the count (5-7-9 eight times) it takes back control of the body movement and does step 9, consciously finishing the exercise in the same Gasho or prayer position with which it began. To train the Subconscious to take over steps 5 thru 8, we need to practice it a few times until it can be done without conscious supervision.

(5-7-9) Integration:

1. As a warm-up we begin with the Gasho or prayer position, standing straight, head slightly bowed with hands together and feet shoulder width apart. We honor in reverence, the incomprehensible power of the undefinable Source of all things, relax, breathe, and think Deeper, Slower, Calmer, Regular. Then take a deep breath IN and read the entire affirmation pyramid out loud with the exhale while moving through positions 1 thru 4. At position 1, we keep our hands together and slowly raise them above the head as high as possible to position 2. At the top of the circle, with arms straight, separate the hands and bring them down to the horizontal position 3 with palms down and knees beginning to bend. Continue the wide circle bringing the hands down to the lower abdomen or the "at rest" position 4 with knees slightly bent as if to brace for an oncoming basketball. At the "at rest" position we have fully exhaled and are out of breath because we have just completed the verbal recitation of all 8 items on the affirmation pyramid. Hands are at the lower abdomen with palms facing up. The fingers of the right hand rest in the palm of the left hand with thumb tips touching, knees slightly bent, and feet flat on the floor.

2. After the warm-up, focus the eyes on the first affirmation (Grateful), allow the Subconscious to take over the physical movements and turn Conscious awareness to the (5-7-9) count and the breath. From the "at rest" position 4, breathe IN for a slow count of FIVE while moving the arms up and out to the side in a wide circular motion. The palms slowly turn up until the hands are as far apart as possible, knees begin to straighten, and weight begins to shift slightly forward. As shown in position 5, the arms open as the chest and lungs expand and fill to capacity drawing in the positive energy of the affirmation. Underneath all this, the Unconscious mind-of-the body is manifesting the image created by the Subconscious as it observes the printed word in the pyramid taped to the wall.

3. To the count of SEVEN, we consciously HOLD the breath as the arms subconsciously (or automatically like riding a bicycle) continue the circle from position 5 to position 6. The legs straighten and the body weight shifts slightly to the toes as if to reach as high as possible. The advanced student will feel the positive energy as it dissolves, breaks up, and replaces negative energy. At the top (in a smooth continuous motion) our hands begin to cross paths.

4. To the count of NINE, we slowly breathe OUT as our weight shifts from the toes to the whole foot, and knees begin to bend again as shown in position 7. It's like we are letting the air out of a balloon, slow and easy, relaxing more and more with each out-breath. Our hands move straight down the center of the body to the lower abdomen where the hands will pass through the "at rest" position 8. A smooth continuous movement many not always allow the thumb tips to touch or brush each other as they pass into the next repetition, but ideally they will. The advanced students will feel the positive energy permeating every single cell as it is drawn down through the body from the top of the head to the shoulders, chest, abdomen, and right down to the toes, with a slight smile.

5. Repeat position 5 through 7 for each of the eight affirmations in the pyramid and then at the bottom of the last affirmation, we shift our conscious attention from the breath and the count back to the mind/body and position 9. As if to start another repetition, we mindfully breathe IN and smoothly begin the circle outward but make only a half circle, straighten the legs, and bring the hands into the beginning Gasho or prayer position. With the out-breath we repeat the words, "thank you" three times and feel a

deep, sincere gratitude for all that we have and the peace of the present moment.

6. This is a good time to state one's worthy purpose, mission statement, (8th Affirmation), and/or begin a 10-20 minute meditation because the mind/body is more receptive than usual.

* Note that this is an <u>advanced</u> exercise and is not easy for the beginner. Even if one has learned to execute the moves subconsciously (without conscious attention), maintaining conscious focus on the count and feeling the unconscious manifestation of the affirmation is quite difficult. It develops <u>control</u> and is the mark of a Master.

6.6 **Summary**

Our quest for harmony began with an in-depth study of epigenetics, psychoneuroimmunology, stress management, meditation, guided imagery, religion, spirituality, the physics of chi, and Dr. Herbert Bensons "Faith Factor." The thirty-year project involved hundreds of books, experts, courses and seminars, three trips to the Orient, and thousands of research and study hours.

The *Imagine Harmony* project explores the reality of adversity, its cause and cure, Medimaginosis, how it works, and redefines POSSIBLE. We discussed the relationship between science and spirituality, how they actually support one another, and how both are used to begin our evolution from stress to gratitude, perfect health, happiness, vitality, longevity, and harmony. An introduction to Stress Management provided insight, perspective, and a simple exercise that works.

We explained the importance of perception plasticity, the ability to accept and adapt to circumstances, breath control and how it leads to conscious control of the mind/body and eventually gene function. We discussed Dr. Bensons Relaxation Response, breath awareness, and practiced the three basic breathing skills that form the foundation for the <u>Three Imperative Breathing Techniques</u> used to facilitate conscious access to the Subconscious Control Room of the Unconscious Mind-of-the-body. We learned to develop conscious control and how to expand it into areas previously ignored. With a background knowledge of the power we have in our breath, we learned how simple meditation can focus and enhance that power.

In Part III, we learned that perceptions and attitudes determine the direction and quality of our lives and that it is possible to control and direct them. We explored the powerful connection between thought, feeling, emotion, and behavior, established that we are not victims of our circumstances, anger, or fear and are not controlled by the past or uncertain future unless we allow it. We learned the art of non-reaction, non-resistance, non-judgment, non-attachment, how to develop conscious awareness, the five steps to gratitude, and how to find a "Worthy Purpose" in life. We learned to tap into the motivating power of spirituality and seven basic principles that form the foundation of all major religions.

We showed how the mind, body, and soul work together and how they handle thoughts and use wisdom. We examined discoveries made in the field of psychoneuroimmunology and epigenetics that support our contention that human beings can consciously control their gene function if they choose to, and looked into the attempts by the outside world to control our thoughts, feelings, spending habits, and life itself. We explained how dangerous it is to allow the outside world to control our lives, how the paradigms are changing for the better, and that we can get where we need to go from where we are. We discussed conscious awareness and that being alive is being in the present moment where life is, and although adversity happens, stress is optional. We can evolve from stress to gratitude. Then we discussed the healing power of the four classifications of meditation, how they work, the secret to controlling tension and pain, the art of letting go, and how to choose and use a mantra.

We learned to practice and use Concentration meditation to develop mental discipline, the ability to focus, and gain control of the mind. We learned to practice and use Mindfulness meditation without judgment or attachment to develop conscious awareness, deep relaxation, and the ability to let it go. Then we moved on to Contemplation meditation where we learned to solve problems and turn ordinary thoughts and ideas into simple, pure, natural wisdom without the fluff and attachments. Finally, the fourth classification, Creative meditation, was practiced to develop our uniquely human gift of imagination and the power of belief and wisdom. We learned to create our own affirmations based on our personal "Worthy Purpose" making it feel more real and part of our being. Then we combined them all into the practice we call Medimaginosis and examined the relationships between Interactive Imagery, affirmations, the placebo effect, how to control them, and how to deal with resistance.

We learned to travel without having to pack a bag and embarked upon 'five essential journeys' to and beyond the most beautiful place in all of creation. We went to our own Personal Place of Peace were we are always safe, happy, and well, and learned how to return to it anytime we like in a matter of seconds. We learned to relax and let go there, how to unload unwanted stress, discomfort, and pain. From there, we set out on the 2nd essential journey where we met our own Personal Mentor or inner advisor; a protective and compassionate, wise and trusted counselor, guide, coach, teacher, and healer, all in one; a kind, caring knowledgeable healer within whom we can confide because it already knows us better than we do. We learned to evaluate and turn the new insights into action and safely carry them into daily life.

The 3rd essential journey took us to a magical Place of Discovery where we learned to expand on Contemplative meditation and enhance Creative meditation using Interactive Imagery. We learned to investigate an issue, feeling, emotion, symptom, problem, thing, or question in a different way, to get closer, view it from a distance, speak to it, get familiar with it, and exchange places with it to see things from its point of view for a better perspective and understanding. The 4th essential journey was to the Subconscious Control Room of the Unconscious mind-of-the-body where we took conscious control of mind/body functions and gene expression. The most critical 5th essential journey was the deepest, most powerful journey of them all. We traveled to our inner being and met with our Soul, our personal connection to the Source of all things: our OM. We learned to use universal wisdom and belief as a power booster. Then we learned to move beyond thought with <u>action</u> to create our reality.

6.7 Action Assignment

* Experienced practitioners know that it is almost never a waste of time to go back and review the basics from time to time. Practice the <u>Bellows Breath</u> to wake up in the morning, warm up, stimulate circulation and awareness when feeling drowsy and disconnected, or when there is a need to be particularly alert. Review and master the three prerequisite breathing awareness skills, the "Observe the Natural Breath, Exhalation Focus and Squeeze, and the Diaphragmatic or Abdomen Breath." Then apply those skills to the <u>Three Imperative Breath Techniques </u>described in Part II.

* Practice the first Imperative Breath Technique, the <u>Three-Part-Breath</u>, when feeling sluggish or particularly fatigued to oxygenate and detoxify the

cells and to dramatically increase physical energy. Practice calming and grounding the mind by mindfully filling the lungs completely.

* Associate the sudden onset of stress with a Big Red Smiling Stop Sign! "Stop, Smile, Breathe, and say Thank you, Thank you, Thank you." Breathe using the second Imperative Breath Technique, the (DSCR) Deeper, Slower, Calmer, Regular Breath. In addition to stressful moments, practice the (DSCR) Breath using the "Abdominal Breathing" skill as many times a day as possible: in line at the supermarket, during commercials while watching TV, at traffic lights, and any time patience is appropriate. Place sticky notes in strategic areas as reminders to practice.

* Recognize, Neutralize, Dismiss, and Replace harmful thoughts with worthy thoughts: Gratitude, Patience, and Kindness.

* Associate the "Slow down, Simplify, and Be Grateful, Patient, and Kind" attitude and the third Imperative Breath Technique, the (5-7-9) Breath, with something done twice a day. One should never leave the house without doing the (5-7-9) Breath. It's that important.

* Remember that every problem has at least three solutions: 1) Fix it with kindness. 2) Accept, adapt perceptions, and look for opportunity. 3) Walk away or around it, let it go, let it be, and move on. Develop a mind that is open to everything and attached to nothing.

* Meditate at least once a day, every day. It needs to be done to recharge the mind. Even a few seconds is better than not doing it at all. Never will we put so little into something and receive so much in return. We take the time to eat, brush our teeth, and sleep every day. If we put meditation on the list of things we just always do every day, we are evolving.

* In addition to strategically deployed (DSCR) and (5-7-9) sticky note reminders, our students are asked to make three signs and tape them to the wall at eye level in the area normally used for meditation. The first is a two-part sign and goes in the center. The top half states the practitioners "Reason or Motivation for Daily Meditation" determined in Part II and the bottom half is a one-sentence statement of the practitioners "Worthy Purpose" determined in Part III followed by a more detailed "Mission Statement" that supports and develops the worthy purpose with secondary objectives: The Plan. The second sign is a copy of the numbered "Seven Stages of Adversity" and is taped to one side of the first. The third sign is taped to the other side and is a copy of the "Seven Principles of Harmony (I

am We Affirmations) with the addition of the practitioners (8th Affirmation) determined in Part IV. Use the signs to review these critical bits of wisdom, commit them to memory, and recite them in a Contemplation meditation.

* When jogging, walking, or waiting in line, say or think, "I am we - we are one - with all that is - Be Grateful - Patient - Kind - Happy - Healthy - Calm mind at peace - in Balance - and Harmony - with the Universe." This can also be an add-on to (DSCR) practice discussed in Part II when high stress is not an immediate factor.

* Practice all four classifications of meditation from time to time because each has its own special benefits. Practice Concentration meditation by focusing on the breath and then expand it to harmoniously include the mantra. Practice Contemplation meditation using a predetermined theme, subject, or problem and annotate any ideas, visions, or epiphanies. Practice Mindfulness meditation using the Progressive Relaxation body scan to deepen the body's memory of the deep relaxed state. Make it a point to choose a task in daily life and do it mindfully, in the present moment, using all six senses. Practice Creative meditation using the Rapid Return signal, spend some time in the Personal Place of Peace, and practice all five essential journeys from time to time to maintain familiarity, not just in times of need.

* Review and use the seven basic Medimaginosis steps following the checklist:

Meditation checklist:

Before
1) State the predetermined intention, Relax, and Breathe.
2) Scan the mind/body and release any tension into the breath.

Warm Up
3) Use the Progressive Relaxation technique and/or the (5-9-9>1) Rapid Return signal to return to the Personal Place of Peace.
4) Relax even deeper with a Mantra and breath focus.

Main Event
5) Meditate on a predetermined intention.

Cool Down
6) Return to the breath and return to the outside world slowly with the Three-Part-Breath.

After

7) Annotate insights, evaluate them consciously, and safely carry them into daily life.

* Try not to try or impatiently <u>try</u> to force change. Simply put up the three signs, <u>do</u> the meditations, adopt the techniques outlined in this book, and <u>allow</u> the mind/body to evolve from Stress to Gratitude. We go beyond thought, to action, to being. We manifest Perfect Health, Happiness, Vitality, Longevity, and Harmony with Gratitude, Patience, and Kindness and let stress, diet, activity, and everything else balance themselves.

* Review the Action Assignments at the end of each Part in this book, review the stress busters including the cloud, bubble, backpack technique, healing light, healing hands, the glove anesthesia, and read the Appendix section. Remember that our ideas, dreams, and epiphanies might remain mere fantasy if we do not take steps to make them real. Medimaginosis can direct the Unconscious mind-of-the-body to manifest psychophysiological evolution, but conscious action is required to effect the outside world.

* Experienced students who practice the "(5-7-9) Integration" exercise, make a copy of the "Principles of Harmony Affirmation Pyramid" in Appendix K, enlarge it, and tape it to the wall above the meditation area signs. This area is more conducive to emersion and integration and the placement above eye level encourages expansion on the in-breath.

6.8 **Final Note**

If it is acceptable for us to look down upon others whom we feel are inferior, less civilized, hygienically challenged, mentally aberrant or inadequate, and/or socially inept, then it is acceptable for those who think they are superior to look down on us. If it is acceptable for us to limit the right of a bum to live as he chooses, then we should be concerned that it is acceptable for others to limit our right to live as we do. And if it is acceptable to persecute others because they do not believe exactly as we do, then it is acceptable for others to persecute us for believing as we do. We are free to do as we choose as long as it does not interfere with the right of others to do as they choose.

Mahatma Gandhi taught us that we need to first BE what we want to see in others. If we want a hooligan to behave in a civilized manner toward us, we need to first behave in a civilized manner toward him. If we can show him that the world will treat him better and that life will be easier for him if he, at least, pretends to be Grateful, Patient, and Kind, he will be less threatening. And if we can teach him to adopt Gratitude, Patience, and Kindness as a way of life, all conflict will be manageable.

Human beings are at the beginning of the next and higher level of evolution: the emergent multi-human super-organism known as Humanity. We need to evolve into a cohesive, synergistic, multicultural whole wherein self-interest is compatible with universal well-being. Human Evolution will depend on the progression of accumulated awareness, synergy, and harmony.

If we can only teach one thing, it would be that an attitude of Gratitude, Patience, and Kindness is the key to happiness, harmony, and the next level of evolution. Please, please use it.

THE ~~END~~

BEGINNING

PART VII

Appendix

and

Glossary

Gratitude is an attitude and a powerful antidote to virtually all stress, unhappiness, and frustration.
Dr. Richard Carlson

APPENDIX A
Longevity
by Dale R. Duvall

Regardless of earthly treasures, your mind and body are your most precious possessions, and their health is your most valuable asset. Treat them with care. Act Now like you will need them for a hundred more years, creating a mind and body for longevity, over maximum performance.

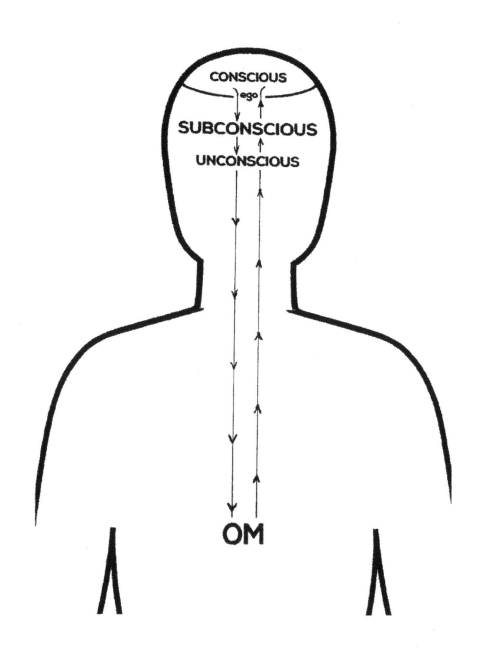

APPENDIX C
Stop, Slow down, Key 2 Happiness

Smile

Breathe
IN-Deeper
OUT-Slower
IN-Calmer
OUT-Regular

Thank you, Thank you, Thank you

Simplify
and be
Grateful, Patient, and Kind

(5-7-9) Breath

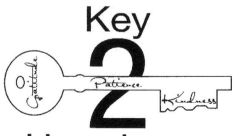

APPENDIX D
Seven Stages of Adversity
And the Key to Happiness: Gratitude, Patience, and Kindness
by
Dale R. Duvall

There is no evil greater than anger and no virtue greater than Patience. But Patience takes practice, so we are grateful for every opportunity to practice. When someone harms, frustrates, annoys, rejects, or embarrasses us, we Stop, Smile, Breathe, and say, "Thank you, thank you, thank you" as a sincere expression of Gratitude for the opportunity to practice Patience, Kindness, and our right to choose the thoughts upon which to focus. We recognize, neutralize, dismiss, and replace anger, fear, guilt, worry, sadness, shame, and other harmful thoughts with Gratitude, Patience, and Kindness, knowing that something good will come of this. We are Grateful that it was not worse and feel Compassion for those who are worse off. We understand the powerful connection between thought, feeling, and behavior, and that we can choose our feelings, and thus our behavior, by choosing to focus on more appropriate thoughts. It is impossible to feel sad without spending time with sad thoughts, or angry without dwelling on angry thoughts. We feel Gratitude and Compassion for our tormentors because they have been valuable teachers and are afflicted with the disease of anger, harming themselves most of all. We accept the situation for what it is and adapt to the present moment with Patient positive thoughts, wisdom, and curiosity. We ask if the problem can be resolved, and look for opportunity. Then, with a calm, peaceful mind, we allow our own natural wisdom to determine the best course of action. We remain balanced and centered, happy and at peace, with a sincere intent to promote harmony and the understanding that everything is and was as it should be.
Harmony is the ultimate objective of all pursuits.

1) Situation or event.

2) Stop, Smile, Breathe, and say, "Thank you, thank you, thank you" as a sincere expression of Gratitude for the opportunity to <u>practice</u> Patience, Kindness, and our right to choose the thoughts upon which to focus.

3) Recognize, neutralize, dismiss, and replace harmful thoughts with Gratitude, Patience, and Kindness, knowing that something good will come of this. Be Grateful that it was not worse and feel Compassion for those who are worse off.

4) Accept and adapt to the present moment with Patient positive thought, wisdom, and curiosity.

5) Ask if the problem can be resolved, and look for opportunity.

6) With a calm, peaceful mind, we allow our own natural wisdom to determine the best course of action.

7) Remain balanced and centered, happy and at peace, with a sincere intent to promote Harmony.

Harmony is the real goal - Life is fun

APPENDIX E
Like a Fertile Garden
by Dale R. Duvall

Like a fertile garden, the subtle (or Subconscious) mind will return, in abundance, whatever we plant. If we plant kindness, it will return kindness. If we plant hostility, it will return hostility. If we choose to plant corn in our garden, water and care for it, it will return hundreds of corn kernels for every one that we plant. If we choose to plant nightshade, it will return poison in just as wonderful abundance. It is impersonal. It does not care what we plant. It will return an abundance of what we plant, but it will not judge what we plant. Judgment is a function of Ego and the Conscious mind, not the subtle or Subconscious mind. Things are always popping up from the subtle mind, some good and some not so good, and it is the job of the Conscious mind to observe and weed the garden by identifying and discarding harmful thoughts while allowing worthy thoughts to grow and flourish.

Tend your wonderful garden. Tell your subtle mind what you want it to do. Plant good seeds, worthy goals, and ideals. Then nurture them, care for them, and observe what pops up. Pull out the weeds and let the seeds of your goals grow. You need to be diligent, or the weeds will take over and kill your seeds. Simply observe and choose your thoughts. Recognize, neutralize, dismiss, and replace harmful thoughts with worthy thoughts, Gratitude, Patience, and Kindness.

APPENDIX F
I am WE
by
Dale R. Duvall

I cannot exist without my body or my mind or my soul, just as water cannot exist without the elements of oxygen or hydrogen. And as water is not oxygen and it is not hydrogen, I am not my body, I am not my thoughts, and I am not an invisible soul. Body is only a vessel, thoughts are only tools that I can choose to use or dismiss, and soul is only my incorporeal life force connection to the source of all creation.
I am we.

We are the body, the Conscious mind, the Subconscious (or subtle) mind, and a very subtle light that was before the body exIsted and will be after it dies. (Some call it the soul, the spirit, or life force energy) The body provides a physical being and represents us to others. The mind holds only one thought at a time but jumps around like a wild monkey from one picture to another to another providing us with an endless stream of thoughts, ideas, and past experiences wrapped in the emotion of the time. It can be guided by the Conscious mind as a gardener tends a fertile garden, or it can be allowed to run wild indiscriminately reacting to egotistical whims. And soul is our life force energy, a timeless connection to all that is, providing the true self, the observer, the interpreter, and the witness beyond the self-image. We are one cohesive, synergistic unit greater than the sum of the parts.
I am we.

We are awareness, consciousness, wisdom and loving-kindness in a form that thinks. We are a piece of the source of all things, and all things are of the source. It is like we are all holding hands as universal chi. We acknowledge our ego, but identify with and speak from our true self, the light within, the soul, the spirit, the wisdom and loving-kindness that is of the source of all things, to which we are all connected.
I am we.

As two fingers of the same hand are separate, they are of the hand, which is of the body, which is of the source of all things, of which we are all a part, uniting us all as one. We are like a single cell in the body of the Universe, nourished by the same life force energy source, separated only by an invisible ego.
I am we.

Our essence is a field of awareness that is consciousness and universal intelligence that conceives, manifests, and governs the body and mind. The essential we is inseparable from our source, and all that is.
I am...We

APPENDIX G
PRINCIPLES OF HARMONY

1) Be one with all that is, with reverence, love, and kindness.

2) Be aware in the present moment, accepting and adapting with wisdom and curiosity.

3) Recognize, neutralize, dismiss, and replace anger, fear, guilt, worry and other harmful thoughts with gratitude, patience, and kindness, the wonder of life and the beauty of the gift of breath.

4) Be a happy, healthy, calm mind at peace, in balance and harmony with the Universe.

5) Be free of the past with acceptance and forgiveness, as only change is permanent.

6) Pursue life diligently with integrity, purpose, sincerity, and joy.

7) Understand that harmony is the real goal, the ultimate objective of all pursuits. Imagine harmony, be harmony, live harmony.

I am we.
We are one with all that is.
Harmony is an attitude at the deepest level.
Therefore,
I am Harmony at the deepest level.

Principles of Harmony
(I am We Affirmations)

1) We are one with all that is, with reverence, love, and kindness.

2) We are aware in the present moment, accepting and adapting with wisdom and curiosity.

3) We recognize, neutralize, dismiss, and replace harmful thoughts with gratitude, patience, and kindness, the wonder of life and the beauty of the gift of breath.

4) We are a happy, healthy, calm mind at peace, in balance and harmony with the Universe.

5) We are free of the past with acceptance and forgiveness, as only change is permanent.

6) We pursue life diligently with integrity, purpose, sincerity, and joy.

7) We understand that harmony is the real goal, the ultimate objective of all pursuits. We imagine harmony, we are harmony, we live harmony.

8) My 8th Affirmation

Now

by

Dale R. Duvall

Now is good.
Now has no room for past or future, guilt or worry.
Past no longer exists except in memory.
Future does not exist except in imagination.
Past and future have no reality of their own.
Only Now exists, only Now is real.
Now is good.
Look around you.
Now we are safe.
Now we are warm.
Now we are free of the past with acceptance and
forgiveness.
Now is good.
Now we are grateful, patient, and kind.
Now we are a calm mind at peace,
in balance and harmony with the Universe.
Now is real life,
a fun adventure of curiosity and wonder.
Now is a friend.
Now is all that IS, and a wonderful place to BE.
If we do not accept what IS,
we are accepting what is not.
Now is good.

APPENDIX I
It's Your Choice
by Dale R. Duvall

We cannot always control events, but we can choose our thoughts. It's not the event or situation that makes us feel good or bad; it is the <u>thoughts</u> we choose to focus on that create our moods or feelings. Choose your thoughts and you will choose your feelings and thus, your behavior. THOUGHT creates feeling, FEELING creates behavior, and your BEHAVIOR creates your life.

If you want to be happy, then BE HAPPY. If you want to feel good, then FEEL GOOD. It's your choice. Simply choose the appropriate thoughts. If you think good thoughts, you feel good. If you think bad thoughts, you feel bad. If you think about nothing, you feel nothing. You are only one thought away from a good feeling. Ice Cream! The smile of a happy grateful child; Chocolate; A playful puppy or a white fluffy kitten playing with a ball of yarn; A beautiful flower, fragrance or melody.

We can choose to be miserable, or we can choose to be happy. When harmful thoughts pop up, we STOP, SMILE, and BREATHE. We say, "Thank you, thank you, thank you" as a sincere expression of gratitude for the opportunity to practice patience, kindness, and our right to choose the thoughts upon which to focus. We recognize harmful thoughts for what they are and neutralize them by understanding that they may have been appropriate at one time but NOT NOW. Then we replace those nasty thoughts with worthy thoughts: Gratitude, Patience, and Kindness.

I have been searching for paradise and happiness all my life, from beautiful beaches and mountain highlands to remote Pacific islands, and from the pampered life of affluence to abject poverty. Well...I found it!! It's here! It's all around me! Wherever I go, there it is. Paradise is where we make it. Where one person sees a dirty window, another might see a beautiful landscape. Look beyond adversity and see the innocents. Recognize, neutralize, dismiss and replace harmful thoughts, and nurture good thoughts.

We choose what we see and what we feel...by choosing our thoughts.

APPENDIX J
Gems of Wisdom

Of all the laws, rules and regulations of mankind, we only need one:

Be kind.

All the others are just elaborations in varying degrees of complexity.

* Where there is life, there is hope.

* Existence is a universal symphony, and the essence of all things is an incomprehensible, possibly infinite, dynamic, vibrating energy.

* Do something nice for someone and tell no one about it. It is better to know we are kinder than we say we are than to say we are kinder than we know we are.

* There are grateful people, and there are depressed people, but there are no truly grateful, depressed people.

* Life is not an emergency or a race to death, it is a fun adventure experienced in the present moment, the Now, with curiosity and wonder.

* We need to learn from the past and plan for the future, but live in the present; remember in the present, plan in the present, BE in the present.

* It is better to be KIND and happy than to be RIGHT and miserable.

* We are a drop in the ocean and an ocean within the drop.

* All things are possible when the soul is willing to believe we can. It may require some adaptation, but all things are possible.

* Every moment is fragile, think with care.

* If one can find nothing nice to say, say nothing at all.

* Conscious evolution is more a matter of choice than chance.

* If you search the Universe, you will find no one more deserving of love and affection than yourself.

Today is going to be a happy day,
because I am going to make it a happy day.
I will make myself happy.
I will make others happy.
When I see this again, I will still have a smile on my face.

Kind loving people - see a kind, loving world.
Angry, hostile people - see an angry, hostile world.
Our world - is our mirror.

DSCR

1) Grateful

2) Patient

3) Kind

4) Happy

5) Healthy

6) Calm Mind at Peace

7) Balance & Harmony w/t Universe

8) Evolve Perfect Health, Happiness, Vitality, Longevity, and Harmony

APPENDIX L
(5-7-9) Position Chart

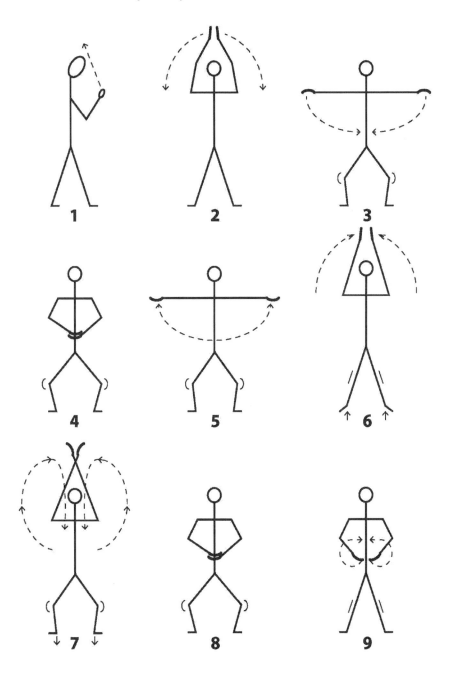

APPENDIX M
MEDI - IMAGI - NOSIS

MEDI

FOCUS

Meditation: directed concentration of focused attention.
Learn to relax and practice focusing the
mind on a predetermined object or mantra
such as the breath, or body sensations.
Feel the flow…letting go of any trying.

IMAGI

VISUALIZE INTENT

Imagine, visualize or sense the predetermined objective or goal.
See it on the screen of the third eye like a movie,
already attained and complete in every detail.
Feel it using all senses.

NOSIS

BELIEVE

The Greek word meaning "to know" or believe.
Relax deep into the Om; deep into the low
alpha or high theta mind state. Create the
physiological and psychological change needed
to remain in harmony with the vision. It is real now.

APPENDIX N
Mean Nasty People
by Dale R. Duvall

Mean Nasty People Suck	*Of all the laws, rules, and regulations of mankind, we only need one:*
	- - - - - -
	Be kind.

When someone is mean of rude to us, we just smile and show them our laminated bookmark. It makes no judgment of the person, it just states a fact and leaves it up to the reader to decide whether they qualify or not.

Copy the figure, cut it out, fold it in half, and laminate.

APPENDIX O
Metta meditation

May I be safe
May I be happy
May I be healthy
May I be content
May I love myself completely
And with great kindness
Just as I am now
No matter what happens

May you be safe
May you be happy
May you be healthy
May you be content
May you love yourself completely
And with great kindness
Just as you are now
No matter what happens

May all beings be safe
May all beings be happy
May all beings be healthy
May all beings be content
May all beings love themselves completely
And with great kindness
Just as they are now
No matter what happens

GLOSSARY

Attachment is a bond that involves a desire for regular contact and the experience of distress during separation.

Attitude is our position or bearing as indicating action, feeling, or mood; a complex mental state involving beliefs, emotions, values and opinions that affect the expression of thought.

Autonomic nervous system (ANS or involuntary nervous system) is a control system that acts largely unconsciously and regulates heart rate, digestion, respiratory rate, pupillary response, urination, and sexual arousal. For our purposes, the ANS is divided into two major subsystems, the sympathetic nervous system (SNS) which is associated with the "defense mode" and the fight-or-flight response, and the parasympathetic nervous system (PSN) which is associated with the a "evolve, renew, and repair mode" and the relaxation response. Although they work together, they have opposite actions where one activates a physiological response, the other inhibits it. A third subsystem governs the function of the gastrointestinal system but works in concert with the SNS and PNS and will be addressed through them.

Awareness means that one is fully present, and that whatever is happening at the moment is happening with complete consciousness. Conscious awareness is the state or ability to perceive, to feel, or to be conscious of events objects or sensory patterns. It refers to our individual awareness of our unique thoughts, memories, feelings, sensations, and environment.

Bellows Breath is a yoga exercise often called the Stimulating Breath because it stimulates circulation and awareness. It is a series of quick breaths through the nose not unlike the rapid pumping of a bellows.

Breathe into: To breathe into a part of the body is to focus on it and imagine the breath moving from the nose, into the lungs where it mixes with the nutrient rich blood and flows to that predetermined part of the body. We can imagine the breath being absorbed into and loosening muscles and joints, allowing them to relax and separate, creating space for the oxygen and nutrient rich blood to flow into and around them. Imagine the cells loosening and expanding like tiny sponges hungrily soaking up the oxygen and nutrients, repairing, healing, and rebuilding. Feel the warmth of new energy returning and restoring perfect function as it nourishes the predetermined body part and expels any tension that might still be there with the out-breath. Expel it all the way up the body and out with the breath.

Chi (or Qi) is the life force energy that is the difference between life and death. It is "energy flow" or the "force" that moves life energy creating growth and is the central underlying principle in traditional Chinese medicine. A mountain has a spirit or energy, but the only chi it has is in the trees, grass, and other living things that make it their home. Chi is referred to as ki in Japanese, prana in Hindu, mana in Hawaiian, pneuma in ancient Greece, and vital energy in Western philosophy. Soul is the True Self. Spirit is that part of Soul that is its energy and is directly connected to the Source of all things. Chi is that part of Sprit that is the life <u>force</u> and flows through the body at varying speeds and intensity. OM is the center and essence of them all.

Compassion is a deep awareness of suffering with the desire to alleviate it: a deep bond between one's self and all creatures.

Conscious mind or self-aware mind, as opposed to the Subconscious and Unconscious part of the brain, is the integrator that makes us human. It is like the captain in the wheelhouse of a huge ocean liner that hosts, feeds, and fills to the needs of thousands of passengers. The captain is not the source of power for the boat and cannot be involved in the details of every operation but is the one controlling the speed, holding or changing the course, and directing the mission. It has been estimated that the Conscious mind is associated with about 12% of the brain and can process approximately 40 nerve impulses per second while the Subconscious process over 40 <u>million</u> impulses per second. In comparison, the Conscious mind is slow, has a short attention span, and cannot be everywhere, so it needs the automatic reactions of the Subconscious, especially in emergency situations where quick action is required. It allows Subconscious programs to control most of our life experience but monitors and observes them so it can step in and stop, alter, or replace harmful, inappropriate, defective or wrong reactions with more appropriate responses. The Conscious mind knows that feelings are not facts, analyzes the past, imagines the future, expresses free will, and is aware of itself and the present. It is the evolved integration of the human Conscious mind that provides us with logic, reason, willpower, language, decision-making, and superior judgment.

Consciousness is the quality, state or condition of being awake and aware of self and environment. It is a sense of one's personal or collective identity, including the attitudes, beliefs, and sensitivities.

Contentment in its fullest sense, is a state of inner awareness that enables a person to maintain inner calmness. Contentment is evidence of happiness, and discontentment is evidence of misery.

Control Room: see Subconscious mind.

Cosmos is often used interchangeably with 'universe' but usually refers to an ordered, harmonious, and possibly infinite, Multiverse that includes the Universe we currently know exists for sure.

Dantian is loosely translated as "energy center" and is an important focal point for meditative and exercise techniques such as chi gong and martial arts.

DSCR is an acronym for the Deeper, Slower, Calmer, Regular breath.

Ego has one foot in the Conscious mind and one foot in the Subconscious mind and stands at the gate between the two functions filtering and allowing only that information it feels is appropriate to pass. It filters sensory information from the Subconscious going to the Conscious as well as all imagined instructions and goals formed in the Conscious going to the Subconscious. The Ego tries to protect the Subconscious from non-conforming beliefs and thoughts from the Conscious mind and the outside world allowing only those instructions that it deems safe and appropriate to pass through the gate and on to the Subconscious for action in the Control Room. Ego is not evil or even bad, just wrong a lot and although it is a tiny part of whole, Ego thinks that IT alone represents "I" and believes it must fight for itself in the world. Ego is an expression of separateness and is ultimately unaware and unconscious of its own true nature. The Ego is often associated with compulsive thinking in order to be assured of its future existence, automatically reacting from past programming rather than responding from wisdom.

Emotion is a natural intuitive or instinctive feeling or state of mind deriving from one's thoughts, circumstances, mood, or relationships often accompanied by physiological changes.

Epigenetics is a field of science that involves the study of changes in gene expression and how cells adjust their biology to the environment, emotional as well as physical. Epigenetic modifications do not involve a change in the DNA sequence of an organism's genome rather they involve factors that prevent or allow access of specific DNA sequences that govern timing and to what degree genes are expressed.

Failure is falling short of expectations and can be characterized by the people who look where they have fallen and not where they have slipped. It is the state or condition of not meeting a desirable or intended objective, and may be viewed as the opposite of success.

Fair is a subjective judgment that reflects a person's perceptions, beliefs, expectations, needs, and wants.

Fear is an unpleasant emotion induced by a threat perceived by living entities. Fear may occur in response to a specific stimulus happening in the present, recalled from the past or to a future imagined situation which is perceived as risk to health or life, status, power, security, or control. The fear response arises from the perception of danger leading to the fight-or-flight response or, in extreme cases of fear, can be a freeze response or paralysis.

Forgive is to cease to blame or hold resentment against someone or something; to let go. Forgiveness is not excusing, justifying, condoning, pardoning, nor forgetting a transgression. Instead, it is a sincere intention to replace negative emotions such as avoidance of the transgressor, revenge, resentment, hate, and anger with positive emotions such as compassion, empathy, and even gratitude. In many cases our tormentors have been valuable teachers and are inflicted with the disease of anger, harming themselves most of all. Studies have shown that an inability to forgive has been associated with anxiety and depression while forgiveness has been associated with improving mental health, lower blood cholesterol, less back pain, and spiritual well-being.

Goals and objectives focus on a stated outcome in the future while intentions focus on the present and provide the guiding light to living mindfully moment-to-moment. They are all intermediate steps toward the ultimate goal of harmony.

God: The Great Spirit, Allah, Yahweh, or Jehovah is a term used by many to represent their deity; the eternal, the infinite, the incomprehensible Source of all things. God is the name some have given to the Source that formed the billions of galaxies scattered across the Universe, each with billions of stars, and the Source that formed (and is in) the smallest subatomic particles which cannot be seen even with our most powerful microscopes; a dynamic vibrating energy that cannot be created or destroyed. Some have given this Source a name and a face, reducing an unfathomable entity to a mental idol that they can believe in and worship; often a vision or image similar to that of the perceiver.

Gratitude is the quality of being thankful and showing appreciation. It is a feeling, attitude, or mindful acknowledgment of a benefit that one has received or will receive and is regarded as a virtue that shapes not only emotions and thoughts but actions and deeds as well. Gratitude is not the same as indebtedness. While both emotions occur following help, indebtedness occurs when a person perceives that they are under an obligation to make some repayment of compensation for the aid. The emotions lead to different actions; indebtedness can motivate the recipient of the aid to avoid the person who has helped them, whereas gratitude can motivate the recipient to seek out their benefactor and to improve their relationship with them.

Happiness is a state of mind. It is a mental state of well-being characterized by positive emotions ranging from contentment to intense pleasure. Happiness is a choice, not a condition.

Harmony is the pleasing or congruent arrangement of all parts and has been associated with nirvana, paradise, utopia, and Heaven. It is the embodiment of bliss, happiness, love, respect, peace, and joy. It is the elegant resolution of discord, conflict, and resistance in all forms. It is the ultimate objective of all pursuits. Harmony is sweet freedom to fly in any direction, totally unobstructed by anything, propelled by inspiration and chi.

Heart: Not to be confused with the organ that pumps blood throughout the body, Heart is the Sprit within the human Soul.

Homeostasis is simply the natural, innate, stable state of equilibrium: in balance and harmony with the universe.

Hyperventilation syndrome is also known as over breathing. Breathing too frequently causes this phenomenon. Although it feels like a lack of oxygen, this is not the case at all. This over-breathing causes the body to lose considerable carbon dioxide. This loss of carbon dioxide triggers symptoms such as gasping, trembling, choking and the feeling of being smothered. Regrettably, over breathing often perpetuates more over breathing, lowering carbon dioxide levels more, and thus become a nasty sequence. Hyperventilation syndrome is common in 10% of the population. Fortunately, slow, deep breathing readily alleviates it. The deliberate, even, deep breaths help to transition the person to a preferable diaphragmatic breathing pattern. People often do not realize when they are hyperventilating because they are usually more focused on the anxiety-provoking situation or thought causing the rapid breathing.

Hypnosis is an altered state of consciousness which results in an increased receptiveness and response to suggestion. It can be triggered naturally from environmental stimuli as well as purposefully from an operator, often referred to as a hypnotist. While associated with relaxation, hypnosis is actually an escape from an overload of message units, resulting in relaxation. Both a hypnosis session and a meditation session might lead to a relaxing guided visualization, but hypnosis often uses trance techniques that overload, disorganize, and trigger the fight/flight mechanism as defined by Dr. John Kappas who, in 1973, defined the profession of hypnotherapy in the Federal Dictionary of Occupational Titles. The meditator enters the same state using stillness of mind and relaxation.

Iatrogenic disease is disease or illness caused by medical errors or reactions to drugs and medical treatment. It was found to be one of the leading causes of death in the U.S. in a ten-year study of government statistics.

Inflexible Perceptions are the root of all human suffering, stress, and illness by creating resistance and the inability or unwillingness to adapt. All things change, and when we try to form a perception or belief that does not change, stress is inevitable. The most troubling of these perceptions are 1) distorted or obsolete beliefs and attitudes 2) negative thought and expectation 3) attachment and inflexible desire 4) preoccupation with the past or future.

Intuition is simply one's own natural wisdom and is often referred to as our sixth sense. It is immediate cognition, or the ability to understand something immediately, without the need for logical, conscious reasoning or rational processes. Intuition is defined as "power of knowing without recourse to reason" and is perceived by inner seeing, inner listening, and inner feeling.

Joy is an intense happiness of mind, body, and spirit, in the absence of desire and attachment.

Judgment is the act or process of forming an opinion, estimate, notion, or conclusion, as from circumstances presented to the mind. Its use is often ambiguous in that it can refer to exercising a proper preference or sitting in improper judgment of circumstances or other people and even condemning them.

Kindness is the practice, quality or act of being good, pleasant, friendly, generous, and warm-hearted in nature. It is showing concern for others, compassion or understanding, acceptance, forgiveness, respect. Simply, it is facilitating the comfort of others.

Love is a sincere desire for the happiness of another, attention without judgment, giving without expectation. Love is a cultivated skill, a deep ineffable feeling of affection and solicitude, representing kindness, compassion, and a profound oneness.

Loving-kindness is called *maîtri* in Sanskrit, which is often translated as "unconditional compassion."

Medimaginosis is an omni-denominational meditation/imagery/wisdom driven wellness practice that directs the mind, body, and soul to manifest harmony and to evolve as one cohesive, synergistic unit with perfect health, happiness, vitality, and longevity. Medimaginosis is made up of three syllables: Medi – for meditation, directed concentration, and focused attention: Imagi – for imagine, visualize, pretend, and immerse or assimilate: And Nosis – for knowledge, belief, and wisdom. It is the power source that supplies the energy to act on imagined concepts. The practice is based on the results of scientific research and the documented physiological responses to over two thousand years of meditative practice. It begins with the familiar relaxation and attitude awareness that has been promulgated for decades but seldom executed effectively, and gradually evolves into conscious control of gene expression.

Meditation is directed concentration of focused attention in order to increase awareness, reduce stress, promote relaxation, and enhance personal growth. Basic meditation is simply a matter of quieting the mind/body with focused attention, preferably on the breath, while more advanced techniques are used to target specific therapeutic needs. Both a hypnosis session and a meditation session might lead to a relaxing guided visualization, but hypnosis often uses trance techniques that overload, disorganize, and trigger the fight/flight mechanism as defined by Dr. John

Kappas who, in 1973, defined the profession of hypnotherapy in the Federal Dictionary of Occupational Titles. The meditator can enter the same state using stillness of mind and relaxation.

Metaphysics is "meta" meaning beyond and "physics" meaning nature or beyond nature. It is the study of universal existence and its nature. It is the branch of philosophy that examines the nature of reality, including the relationship between mind and matter, substance and attribute, fact and value. Metaphysics looks at this subject logically without involving emotions or faith. It is more scientific in its approach than spirituality.

Mind/Body and Mind/Body/Soul: The term Mind/Body refers to the concept that the mind and the body are one. Mind/Body/Soul adds the vital element of Spirit, Chi or life force energy, and represents the whole living person. They are in constant communication with each other and cannot function separately. It is like trying to separate the left side of the heart from the right side and expecting it to work properly.

Mindfulness is simply the state of conscious awareness in the present moment where life happens. Mindfulness is paying attention on purpose and a state of mind that brings one's complete attention to the present experience on a moment-to-moment basis. Mindfulness meditation is a directed concentration of focused attention on the state of conscious awareness in the present moment where life happens. It is a kind of non-judgmental, present-centered awareness in which each thought, feeling, or sensation that arises in the field of attention is acknowledged and accepted as it is.

OM is that very subtle energy or light at the center of the Soul that was before the body existed and will be after it dies. It radiates in all directions, exists in every living cell, and is the difference between life and death. OM has been called the Soul, Spirit, and the Heart (not to be confused with the organ that pumps blood throughout the body) and is centered slightly below the physical heart and just above the solar plexus at the middle dantian. OM is an extension of the Source of all things and is one's personal connection to a vast, possibly infinite, repository of wisdom made up of incomprehensible, dynamic, constantly changing forms of vibrating energy. OM is that part of us that is infinite, eternal, and directly connected to all that is, making us a part of one big harmonious symphony. It is the stillness underneath the mental noise, the love and joy underneath the emotional pain and stress, and our direct line of communication to what some call

God, The Great Spirit, Allah, Yahweh, or Jehovah. Soul is the True Self. Spirit is that part of Soul that is its energy and is directly connected to the Source of all things. Chi is that part of Sprit that is the life <u>force</u> and flows through the body at varying speeds and intensity. OM is the center and essence of them all.

Parasympathetic nervous system (PNS) is that part of the autonomic nervous system (ANS) that controls the relaxation response or "evolve, renew, and repair mode" as opposed to the sympathetic nervous system (SNS) that elicits the fight-or-flight response or "defense mode." The parasympathetic nervous system activates tranquil functions, such as cellular repair, growth, and the immune functions. It tends to act in opposition to the sympathetic nervous system by slowing down the heartbeat and elicits the relaxation response. Negative energy and blockages begin to soften, and the path to the Control Room becomes clearer and easier to navigate. The sympathetic system speeds up functions while the parasympathetic returns us to normal.

Patience is the ability to control one's emotions even when being criticized or attacked and refers to the character trait of being steadfast. It often involves trust, reflects the state of one's mind/body, and is a mental skill that one will never forget. Dr. Jon Kabat-Zinn has said that patience is a form of wisdom because it demonstrates an understanding and acceptance of the fact that sometimes things need to unfold in their own time. Some things just should not be rushed.

Peace is a state of harmony characterized by the lack of violent conflict. Commonly understood as the absence of hostility, peace also suggests the existence of healthy or newly healed relationships both interpersonal and international, prosperity in matters of social or economic welfare, the establishment of equality, and a working political order that serves the true interests of all. In international relations, peacetime is not only the absence of war or conflict but also the presence of cultural and economic understanding.

Perception is what we interpret from our six senses, touch, smell, sight, hearing, taste, and intuition or wisdom. It comes from the Latin word 'perceptio' which means receiving, collecting, and the action of taking possession with the mind or senses. Perception is the process of attaining awareness, interpreting, or understanding sensory information. It is our way of regarding, the way that we notice, interpret, think about or understand something using our senses that leads to belief when confirmed. See also "Inflexible Perception."

Perspective has a Latin root meaning "look through" and all the meanings of perspective have something to do with looking. Perspective is an evaluation or analysis of something as "seen through" one's perception or belief system. It is the way we see something in relation to its surroundings or other relevant information. Perspective is a point of view or a sense of proportion as seen by the eyes or a mental view through the mind's eye filtered or biased by one's established beliefs or perception. Things are often not as they first appear, and everyone has a different perspective of everything because everyone has a different perception of everything.

Perspective vs. Perception: Perception refers to an interpretation or belief system that an individual forms through sensory awareness, and perspective refers to one's point of view as seen through their perception or belief system. It is the perception of our reality that governs our perspective toward our life. Perspectives come from our perceptions. What we see (perspective) depends on our beliefs (perception). If one's perceptions have led to the belief that toys corrupt children's minds, then from their perspective a toy shop is an evil place.

Plasticity of Perception is the ability to adapt to changes, to be aware, flexible, accept and adapt to circumstances. It involves relaxing, letting go of, and replacing rigid inappropriate perceptions. It allows the wisdom of the OM, creativity, and adaptability into our circumstances and events and is key to facilitating our evolution from stress to gratitude, perfect health, happiness, vitality, longevity, and harmony.

Psychoneuroimmunology (PNI) is the investigation (ology) of the interaction between the mind (psycho), the brain and nervous system (neuro), and the body's biochemical resistance to disease and abnormal cell development (immun). It might also be called psycho_endo_neuroimmunology because it also includes the study of the (endocrine system) or hormonal system and integrates several other disciplines including genetics, pharmacology, and molecular biology.

Purpose is the reason for which something is done or created or for which something exists, and a "worthy purpose" is our reason to live. Human beings are goal oriented organisms and need a worthy purpose to provide direction, clarity, and motivation. People who have a clear purpose in life deal more effectively with stress and see achievement as well as setbacks as a stepping stone toward their ultimate objective. Having a one-sentence purpose statement can focus the mind and gives us the power to think and act more intelligently.

Relaxation Response is a term popularized by Dr. Herbert Benson, a cardiologist and Professor of Medicine at Harvard Medical School, and counters the fight-or-flight response which is a term coined in the 1920's by another Harvard Medical School professor, psychologist Dr. Walter Cannon. The relaxation response is a physiologic response that enables the parasympathetic nervous system. It is a facilitated healing state that heals from the inside out and can be defined as our personal ability to make our body release chemicals and brain signals that make our muscles and organs slow down and increase blood flow to the brain: physically relaxed and mentally alert.

Religion can be an external manifestation of spiritual experience or an organized social entity in which individuals share some basic beliefs and practices. One can be spiritual without being religious or religious without being spiritual.

Sleep is a natural state of the mind/body characterized by relaxation of voluntary muscles and reduced consciousness and sensory activity. It is as important as healthy food and activity, but it is sometimes elusive to people who think about stressful moments over and over again or worry about things over which they have no control.

Soul is the True Self as opposed to the perceived self or Ego and is the incorporeal component in living things that continues after death. The problem we face is that there is no clear or unique definition of Soul and Spirit but we will use the word Soul to represent the True Self. Spirit is that part of Soul that is its energy and is directly connected to the Source of all things. Chi is that part of Sprit that is the life <u>force</u> and flows through the body at varying speeds and intensity. OM is the center and essence of them all.

Source of all things: (see God) The Source of all things, is just that. It has been given many names and undergone countless attempts at definition, but none are adequate.

Spirit has been described as that part of the Soul that emanates from a point of very subtle spiritual light which does not disintegrate in death as opposed to the subtle or Subconscious mind which disintegrates in death and the Conscious mind which does not exist when one is sleeping and does not exist in death. Spirit means breath, energy, life, or essence, comes from the same root word as inspire, and is the opposite of expire or death. It is used to describe the animating force that gives the mind/body life, energy, and power. It is the Soul that comprises who we are, but it is our Spirit that provides the energy. Spirit is also used to describe the power and majesty of nature such as rivers and mountains, but the only chi they have is in the trees, grass, and other living things that make it their home. Soul is the True Self. Spirit is that part of Soul that is its energy and is directly connected to the Source of all things. Chi is that part of Sprit that is the life force and flows through the body at varying speeds and intensity. OM is the center and essence of them all.

Spirituality is a person's orientation toward or experiences with the transcendent existential features of life such as meaning, direction, purpose, and connectedness with something greater. It supplies the catalyst to become greater than the sum of the parts. Spirituality differs from religion in that religion is linked to formal institutions, whereas spirituality does not depend on collective or institutional context. Spirituality is the feelings, thoughts, beliefs, experience, and behaviors that often arise from the search for a divine being, higher power, or ultimate reality, as perceived by the individual. One can be spiritual without being religious or religious without being spiritual.

Stress is any change that requires adaptation. It is any action or situation that upsets the body's equilibrium. Stress occurs when an event is perceived to challenge one's resources or capacity to respond. Acute stress is short-term, sudden onset stress that results from a fire alarm, almost being hit by a car, a job interview, or being pulled over by a police officer and it is completely normal. Chronic stress is a dangerous psychophysiological response to cumulative stressors. It is the result of repeated exposure (over a long period of time) to events or situations over which one seems to have little or no control. Examples include constant marital conflict, financial pressure, abusive or uncooperative co-workers, and having to endure a job that one hates.

Subconscious mind receives all physical and sensory information and stores it with all past input. It stores everything and can add to or alter memories but (barring physical damage) they will remain until death. Everything we have ever seen, heard, or experienced (including TV shows and scary movies) is sitting somewhere in our Subconscious, affecting our current thoughts, decisions, and actions. Communication through words, thoughts, and images are interpreted on a deeper level than most people realize, both the positive and negative. The Subconscious mind contains the Control Room of the Unconscious mind-of-the-body and operates like a huge impersonal computer. It is our "autopilot", our habits, and all that we do automatically. It acts without conscious thought and runs our lives most of the time. The Subconscious mind, Control Room, and the Unconscious mind-of-the-body are associated with the neural activity of approximately 82% of the brain, can organize choices and decisions, and are much faster but lack the free will and intentions of the Conscious mind.

Success is the progressive realization of a worthy intent, ideal, or goal. It's more about the journey and less about the destination. It is not about being at the top of one's field and making a lot of money unless it is something that the person enjoys doing and is truly happy doing it. A success is the entrepreneur who starts his own company because that was his dream; a well-defined intent that is powered by belief. A success is the school teacher who is teaching because that is what he or she wants to do, and a success is the wife and mother who loves what she is doing and does a good job of it. A success is anyone who is realizing a worthy predetermined ideal, because that is what he or she decided to do, deliberately.

Sympathetic nervous system (SNS) is that part of the autonomic nervous system that prepares us for the fight-or-flight response or "defense mode." It is involved in the stimulation of the body for action, such as increasing the heart rate, increasing the release of sugar from the liver into the blood, and numerous other responses that serve to fight off or retreat from danger. The sympathetic nervous system is the mind/body's way of dealing with perceived threats, whether real or imagined, and it is absolutely necessary for survival but over stimulation of the sympathetic nervous system is a major cause of chronic illness.

True self is our natural state unaffected by Ego and is also referred to as Soul, Spirit, OM, or Light within.

Trust is a firm reliance on the integrity, ability, or character of a person or thing.

Unconscious mind is the mind-of-the-body and is like a vast computer coordinating and controlling thousands of operations and functions at the same time. This awesome capacity is blind and exists in a dark closet with only the Subconscious to guide it and tell it what the environment is like and what needs to be done. It accepts instructions from the Subconscious Control Room and acts on them without question. Conscious concepts need to pass through the ego gate guarded by the Ego, be accepted by the Subconscious and then, if conditions are right in the Control Room, they pass on to the Unconscious mind where they will manifest as psychophysiological adaptations.

Universe: The word 'universe' is often used interchangeably with 'cosmos' and can refer to a Multiverse that is potentially infinite or to just the known part of the cosmos in which we live.

Wisdom is often referred to as intuition or our sixth sense and unlike ordinary thoughts or knowledge, wisdom is a silent voice that exists only when the mind is calm. Natural wisdom is a deep understanding and realization of people, things, events or situations, resulting in the ability to choose, act, or inspire optimum results with a minimum of time, energy, or thought, but is limited to the human brain. Universal wisdom is the infinite repository of all knowledge everywhere. It is only accessible through the OM or Soul which is our direct connection to the Source of all things.

The difference between a smart person and a wise one is that the smart person can find a way out of a difficulty that a wise person will not get into in the first place.

All things are possible when the Soul is willing to believe we can.
It may require some adaptation, but all things are possible.